Drafting Business Leases

Drafting Business Leases

Fifth Edition

Kim Lewison QC

LAW & TAX

© Pearson Professional Ltd 1996

Kim Lewison has asserted his right under the Copyright, Designs and Patents Act 1988 to be identified as the author of this work

ISBN 07520 0243 0

Published by
FT Law & Tax
21–27 Lamb's Conduit Street
London WC1N 3NJ

A Division of Pearson Professional Limited

Associated offices
Australia, Belgium, Canada, Hong Kong, India, Japan, Luxembourg, Singapore, Spain, USA

All rights reserved. No part of this publication may be reproduced, stored in a retrieval system, or transmitted, in any form or by any means, electronic, mechanical, photocopying, recording or otherwise, without the prior written permission of the publishers.

No responsibility for loss occasioned to any person acting or refraining from action as a result of the material in this publication can be accepted by the authors or publishers.

A CIP catalogue record for this book is available from the British Library.

Printed in Great Britain by Bell and Bain of Glasgow

Contents

List of Examples ix
Preface xiii
Table of Cases xv
Table of Statutes xxxi
Table of Statutory Instruments xxxiv

1 The Interpretation of Leases 1
  1 Intention of the Parties 1
  2 Ordinary and Technical Words 3
  3 Lease Construed as a Whole 3
  4 Clear Words 4
  5 Construction against Grantor 5
  6 Implied Terms 5
  7 Principles of Construction 7
  8 Uncertainty 9
  9 Prima Facie Assumptions 10
  10 Statutory Rules of Construction 10
  11 Date for Applying Rules of Construction 11
  12 Making it Work 12
  13 Practicalities 12

2 Description of Property 15
  1 The Use of Plans 15
  2 Forms of Plan 16
  3 Boundaries 17
  4 Party Structures 21
  5 Appurtenances and Curtilage 23
  6 Access 24
  7 Car Parking 29
  8 Advertisements, Signs and Nameplates 30

	9 Sanitary Facilities	32
	10 Telecommunications	33
	11 Exceptions and Reservations	33
	12 Perpetuity	36
	13 Fixtures	37
	14 Renewal Leases	38
3	**Landlord and Tenant (Covenants) Act 1995**	41
	1 The Running of Covenants	41
	2 Release of Covenants on Assignment	42
	3 Authorised Guarantee Agreements	43
	4 Joint and Several Liability	43
	5 Overriding Leases	43
	6 Variations	44
	7 Fixed Charges	44
	8 Anti-Avoidance	46
4	**The Term of the Lease**	47
	1 Practical Problems	47
	2 Tenancy at Will	50
	3 Term Certain	51
	4 Commencement of the Term	54
	5 Break-Clauses	56
	6 Options to Renew	62
	7 Renewal Leases	68
5	**Rent and Rent Review**	71
	1 The Initial Rent and Rent-Free Periods	71
	2 Deductions from Rent	73
	3 Rent Review	74
	4 Index-Linked Rents	74
	5 Turnover Rents	77
	6 Rent Geared to Subrents	83
	7 Rent Geared to Head Rent	92
	8 Periodic Review to Market Rent	93
	9 Time Limits in Rent Review Procedure	95
	10 Review Procedure	101
	11 Valuation Formula	109
	12 Review of Reviews	141
	13 Interim Provisions and Interest	142
	14 Subleases	147
	15 Renewal Leases	147

6	**Insurance and Service Charges**	149
	1 Insurance	149
	2 Service Charges	163
7	**Repairs and Improvements**	184
	1 Repairs	184
	2 Alterations and Improvements	201
8	**Use of the Demised Property**	212
	1 Warranties as to Fitness for Use	212
	2 Town and Country Planning Act 1990	213
	3 Absolute and Qualified Restrictions on Use	215
	4 Negative and Positive Obligations	217
	5 Defining the Permitted Use	220
	6 Widening a Prohibition	223
	7 Restrictions on Competition	223
	8 Covenants Ancillary to Use	225
	9 Modification of Use Covenants	230
	10 Renewal Leases	230
9	**Assignment and Subletting**	231
	1 Not to Assign	231
	2 Not to Underlet	232
	3 Not to Part with Possession	234
	4 Wider Forms of Covenant	234
	5 Absolute Prohibitions on Alienation	235
	6 Specified Circumstances in which the Landlord May Withhold Consent or Impose Conditions	238
	7 Qualified Covenants Against Alienation	243
	8 Building Leases	248
	9 Requirement to Surrender Before Assigning or Subletting	249
	10 Fines and Premiums	251
	11 Costs	252
10	**Statutory Protection**	254
	1 Part II of the Landlord and Tenant Act 1954	254
	2 Tenancy	254
	3 Identity of the Tenant	257
	4 Nature of the Property	259
	5 Use of the Demised Property	259
	6 Excluding the Right to Compensation	260
	7 Property Where Subletting is Envisaged	261
	8 Residential Accommodation	262

viii   DRAFTING BUSINESS LEASES

11 The Liability of Sureties   264
  1 Co-extensiveness   264
  2 Termination of the Tenancy   264
  3 Discharge of the Surety   265
  4 Disclaimer   268
  5 Protecting the Surety   269
  6 Authorised Guarantee Agreements   271
  7 Change of Landlord   273
  8 Renewal Leases   273

Forms

Form 1	Standard Form of Lease for Letting of Shop in Parade	275
Form 2	Lease of Shop in Shopping Centre	279
Form 3	Underlease of Motor Showroom	288
Form 4	Lease of Secondary Shop with Upper Part	290
Form 5	Quarterly Tenancy of Lockable Stall in a Market or Store	292
Form 6	Underlease of Office Accommodation above a Shop	294
Form 7	Lease of Office Block: Rent Geared to Sublettings	298
Form 8	Lease of Suite of Offices	301
Form 9	Lease of Industrial Property on Industrial Estate	304
Form 10	Underlease of Part of Building Let as Clothing Factory	307
Form 11	Tenancy Agreement of Start Up Workshop	310
Form 12	Lease of Hotel: Rent Based on Turnover	312
Form 13	Lease of Licensed Squash Club	317
Form 14	Agreement for Lease of Land to be Used as Car Park Pending Redevelopment	322
Form 15	Renewal of Lease by Reference to Expired Lease	324
Form 16	Licence to Share Professional Offices	326

Index   329

List of Examples

Chapter 1: Interpretation of Leases
　1:1　Definitions clause for business lease　13

Chapter 2: Description of Property
　2:1　Parcels clause of office suite　20
　2:2　Parcels clause of open land　21
　2:3　Parcels clause of building excluding airspace　21
　2:4　Parcels clause with details of boundaries　21
　2:5　Declaration as to party structures　23
　2:6　Right of way: unlimited times and vehicles　26
　2:7　Right of way: limited times and vehicles; right to load, etc　26
　2:8　Right of way: right to load etc in loading bay　26
　2:9　Right of way: limited times　27
　2:10　Right to use passenger lift　29
　2:11　Right to use passenger and goods lift　29
　2:12　Composite rights of parking　30
　2:13　Right to display advertisement permitted by regulations　31
　2:14　Right to display advertisement in prescribed form　31
　2:15　Easement to use sanitary facilities　33
　2:16　Exceptions and reservations　36
　2:17　Definition of service pipes　36
　2:18　Covenant to yield up tenant's fixtures　38
　2:19　Covenant to remove tenant's fixtures if required　38
　2:20　Covenant by tenant to inquire about removal of fixtures　38

Chapter 3: Landlord and Tenant (Covenants) Act 1996
　3:1　Limitation on landlord's liability　42
　3:2　Statement contained in overriding lease　44
　3:3　Restriction on landlord's ability to sue original tenant　45

Chapter 4: The Term of the Lease
　4:1　Definition clause making tenant liable for rent during holding over period　49
　4:2　Clause making the tenant liable to pay rent and interim rent　50
　4:3　Informal tenancy at will　50
　4:4　Landlord's power to break　60
　4:5　Tenant's power to break on refusal of planning permission　61

x DRAFTING BUSINESS LEASES

4:6	Tenant's right to break preventing exercise of rights under Landlord and Tenant Act	62
4:7	Tenant's conditional right to break	62
4:8	Tenant's conditional right to break (alternative form)	62
4:9	Option to renew	67
4:10	Option to renew contracted out tenancy	67
4:11	Clause negativing perpetual renewal	68

Chapter 5: Rent and Rent Review

5:1	Clause preventing landlord from charging VAT	72
5:2	Clause preventing landlord from waiving exemption from VAT	73
5:3	Covenant to pay rent	73
5:4	Index-linked rent: upwards only from initial rent	77
5:5	Turnover rent	80
5:6	Turnover rent for theatre or cinema based on box office receipts	82
5:7	Rent geared to subrents receivable	89
5:8	Side by side rent sharing	90
5:9	Definition of rent linked to head rent	93
5:10	Alternative definition	93
5:11	Tenant's power to make time of the essence	101
5:12	Rent review machinery; notice, counternotice reference to arbitration	108
5:13	Rent review machinery; no notice; determination by expert	108
5:14	Landlord's option to select method of resolving disputes	108
5:15	Disputes procedure for inclusion in an underlease	109
5:16	Either party to initiate the procedure	109
5:17	Clause permitting reliance on other awards	109
5:18	Rent review clause requiring valuation of a notional building	114
5:19	Assumptions about the physical condition of the property	115
5:20	Disregard of improvements	128
5:21	Extension of disregard to improvements under previous lease	128
5:22	Valuation formula for occupational lease	133
5:23	Alternative valuation formula	133
5:24	Valuation formula: short form	134
5:25	Valuation formula: disregard of review clause and no disregard of tenant's improvements (for use in a building lease)	134
5:26	Review to modern ground rent	135
5:27	Valuation formula with built-in rent-free period	138
5:28	Assumption that tenant has had access for fitting out	138
5:29	Assumption about VAT	139
5:30	Alternative assumption about VAT	139
5:31	Clause admitting accounts	141
5:32	Alternative clause admitting accounts	141
5:33	Review of review periods	141
5:34	Definition of rate of interest	143
5:35	Alternative definition of rate of interest	144
5:36	Payment on account pending rent review	144
5:37	Review to market rent: upwards only	144
5:38	Alternative form of review to market rent: upwards only	145

LIST OF EXAMPLES

Chapter 6: Insurance and Service Charges

6:1	Tenant's covenant to insure and reinstate	157
6:2	Landlord's covenant to insure and reinstate	158
6:3	Proviso for protection of landlord	158
6:4	Alternative covenant by landlord to insure and either reinstate or provide modern equivalent	158
6:5	Landlord to insure in unspecified amount: reinstatement or modern equivalent: demised property forming part of larger building	159
6:6	Proviso for abatement of rent	161
6:7	Tenant's break clause on total loss	162
6:8	Tenant's covenant not to cause increase in premium	162
6:9	Tenant's covenant to pay service charge: limited payment in advance	180
6:10	Service charge—provision for reserve and payment in advance	181
6:11	Trust of reserve fund	183
6:12	Landlord's power to replace plant	183

Chapter 7: Repairs and Improvements

7:1	Exemption of liability	189
7:2	Definition of structure	192
7:3	Definition of interior of the demised property	193
7:4	Tenant's covenants to repair and decorate	198
7:5	Landlord's restricted power to enter to repair	199
7:6	Tenant's covenant to repair and rebuild: insured risks excepted	199
7:7	Tenant's covenant to repair interior	199
7:8	Tenant's covenant to decorate	199
7:9	Tenant's covenant to decorate linked to rent review dates	200
7:10	Tenant's covenant to inspect	200
7:11	Landlord's covenant to repair exterior and to decorate	200
7:12	Tenant's covenant to repair (fire damage excepted)	200
7:13	Tenant's covenant to carry out work required by statute etc	200
7:14	Tenant's covenant against alterations	209
7:15	Tenant's covenant against structural alterations; qualified covenant against non-structural alterations	209
7:16	Tenant's covenant relating to statutes	210
7:17	Proviso limiting tenant's liability	210
7:18	Alternative proviso limiting tenant's liability	210
7:19	Tenant's covenant to carry out improvements	210
7:20	Tenant's covenant to yield up in a fit state	210
7:21	Covenant by tenant to give security for compliance with conditions	211

Chapter 8: Use of the Demised Property

8:1	Tenant's covenant relating to planning and development	214
8:2	Hybrid use covenant	217
8:3	Hybrid use covenant	217
8:4	Positive covenant: business use only	219
8:5	Tenant's proviso to keep open covenant	220
8:6	Positive covenant: mixed use	220
8:7	Covenant by landlord	224

8:8	Covenant by tenant	225
8:9	Covenants ancillary to use: short form	228
8:10	Covenants ancillary to use: long form	228
8:11	Covenant not to pollute	229
8:12	Covenant relating to licence	229

Chapter 9: Assignment and Subletting

9:1	Absolute prohibition on alienation of part; qualified as to whole	240
9:2	Absolute prohibition subject to exceptions	240
9:3	Absolute conditions for alienation	241
9:4	Circumstances in which the landlord may withhold consent to assignment: objective criteria	241
9:5	Circumstances in which the landlord may withhold consent to an assignment: subjective criteria	242
9:6	Conditions which the landlord may impose on assignment	242
9:7	Proviso permitting group company sharing	243
9:8	Provisions regulating group company sharing	243
9:9	Tenant's qualified covenants against alienation	246
9:10	Restrictions on alienation in building lease	249
9:11	Requirement to offer to surrender	251
9:12	Simple exclusion of s 144	252
9:13	Exclusion of s 144 where amount of permitted premium is defined	252
9:14	Costs	252
9:15	Costs: fuller version	252

Chapter 10: Statutory Protection

10:1	Exclusion of 1954 Act	256
10:2	Statement of purpose of tenancy	257
10:3	Exclusion of right to compensation	261

Chapter 11: The Liability of Sureties

11:1	Basic covenant by surety	265
11:2	Proviso limiting discharge of surety	267
11:3	Surety deemed to be principal debtor	267
11:4	Surety to be bound by variations	268
11:5	Covenant by surety to take a lease on disclaimer	269
11:6	Surety's right to require assignment	271
11:7	Authorised guarantee agreement	272
11:8	Requirement to provide sureties	274
11:9	Alternative form of surety covenant including obligation to take lease on disclaimer	274

Preface

The last edition of this book was published in 1993, when the property recession was still in full flow. In the intervening years, the most important single development in the law affecting business leases has been the passing of the Landlord and Tenant (Covenants) Act 1995. The 1995 Act was the culmination of a long campaign to remove the contractual liability of original tenants following assignment. The implications of the Act for the commercial property world have still to be worked out, but this edition of this book offers some preliminary thoughts on how the Act will affect lease drafting.

The world of rent review has continued to develop, and I have taken account of those cases, notably the 'headline rent' cases, which affect lease drafting.

As in previous editions, I have tried to incorporate new material which is relevant for the purposes of understanding the general legal background to the drafting and negotiating of business leases, concentrating on those developments which give rise to drafting points.

I am grateful to all those who have commented on previous editions of this book, but naturally I bear responsibility for any errors which remain.

The law is, in general, stated as at 1 January 1996, although I have managed a few additions at proof stage.

Kim Lewison QC
Falcon Chambers
Falcon Court
London EC4Y 1AA

Table of Cases

Abrahams v MacFisheries Ltd [1925] 2 KB 18; [1925] All ER 194 234
Accuba Ltd v Allied Shoe Repairs Ltd [1975] 3 All ER 782; [1975] 1 WLR 1559; (1975) 119 SJ 775 142
Adams v Green (1978) 247 EG 49, CA 69
Addiscombe Garden Estates Ltd v Crabbe [1958] 1 QB 513; [1957] 3 WLR 980; [1957] 3 All ER 563, CA 255
Adelphi (Estates) Ltd v Christie (1984) 269 EG 221, CA 3, 12
Adler v Upper Grosvenor Street Investment Ltd [1957] 1 All ER 229; [1957] 1 WLR 227; (1957) 101 SJ 132 250
Agavil Investments Ltd v Corner (1975) unreported, 3 October 171
Air India v Balabel [1993] 2 EGLR 66; [1993] 30 EG 90; (1993) *The Times*, 16 April 246
Al Saloom v Shirley James Travel Services Ltd (1981) 42 P&CR 181; (1981) 125 SJ 397, CA 99
Aldin v Latimer Clark Muirhead & Co [1894] 2 Ch 437; (1894) LJ Ch 601; (1894) 42 WR 553 35
Aldwych Club Ltd v Copthall Property Co Ltd (1962) 185 EG 219 .... 121, 230
Allnatt London Properties Ltd v Newton [1984] 1 All ER 423; (1983) 45 P&CR 94; (1983) 265 EG 601, CA; *affg* [1981] 2 All ER 290; (1980) 41 P&CR 11; (1980) 257 EG 174 250
Altmann v Boatman (1963) 186 EG 109, CA; *revsg* (1962) 184 EG 653; [1962] CLY 1732 26
Alton House Holdings Ltd v Calflane (Management) Ltd [1987] 2 EGLR 52; (1988) 20 HLR 129; (1987) 283 EG 844 168
Amalgamated Estates Ltd v Joystretch Manufacturing Ltd (1980) 257 EG 489, CA 102
Amarjee v Barrowfen Properties [1993] 2 EGLR 133; [1993] 30 EG 98 148
Amax International Ltd v Custodian Holdings Ltd [1986] 2 EGLR 111; (1986) 279 EG 279 .... 5, 129
Amherst v Walker (James) Goldsmith & Silversmith Ltd (1980) 254 EG 123, CA 7
Amherst v Walker (James) Goldsmith & Silversmith Ltd [1983] 2 All ER 1067; [1983] Ch 305; [1983] 3 WLR 334, CA 97
Amika Motors Ltd v Colebrook Holdings Ltd (1981) 259 EG 243, CA 68, 69
Anstruther-Gough-Calthorpe v McOscar [1924] 1 KB 716; [1923] All ER 198; (1923) 13 LT 691 .... 12, 187
Antaios Compania Naviera SA v Salen Rederierna AB ('The Antaios') [1985] AC 191; [1984] 3 WLR 592; [1984] 3 All ER 229 12
Arenson v Casson Beckman Rutley & Co [1977] AC 405 106
Arnold v National Westminster Bank plc [1991] 2 WLR 1177; [1991] 2 AC 93; [1991] 3 All ER 41, HL 129
Art & Sound v West End Litho [1992] 1 EGLR 138; (1991) 64 P&CR 28; [1992] 14 EG 110 96
Ashburn Anstalt v Arnold [1988] Ch 1, CA 3

TABLE OF CASES

Associated Dairies Ltd v Pierce (1983) 265 EG 127, CA; *affg* (1981) 259 EG 562; (1982) 43 P&CR 208, DC 265
Avon County Council v Alliance Property Co Ltd (1981) 258 EG 1181 132
Ayling v Wade [1961] 2 QB 228; [1961] 2 WLR 873; [1961] 2 All ER 899 185
Bagettes Ltd v GP Estates Co Ltd [1956] Ch 290; [1956] 2 WLR 773; [1956] 1 All ER 729, CA 261
Bailey (CH) Ltd v Memorial Enterprises Ltd [1974] 1 All ER 1003; [1974] 1 WLR 728; (1973) 27 P&CR 188, CA 142
Bairstow Eves (Securities) Ltd v Ripley (1992) 65 P&CR 220; [1992] 32 EG 52; [1992] EGCS 83, CA 64
Balfour v Kensington Gardens Mansions Ltd (1932) 49 TLR 29; (1932) 76 SJ 816 244
Bandar Property Holdings Ltd v Darwen (JS) (Successors) Ltd [1968] 2 All ER 305; 19 P&CR 785 .... 6, 152, 173
Barclays Bank Ltd v Ascott [1961] 1 All ER 782; [1961] 1 WLR 717; (1961) 105 SJ 323 .... 265, 273
Barclays Bank plc v Daejan Investments (Grove Hall) [1995] 18 EG 117 215
Barnes v City of London Real Property Co [1918] 2 Ch 18 .... 167, 170, 171
Barrett v Lounova (1982) Ltd [1989] 1 All ER 351; (1988) 20 HLR 584; [1988] 36 EG 184, CA 191
Barrett Estate Services v David Greig (Retail) [1991] 2 EGLR 123; [1991] 36 EG 155 98
Barton v Reed [1932] 1 Ch 362; [1931] All ER 425 223
Barton (WJ) Ltd v Long Acre Securities Ltd [1982] 1 All ER 465; [1982] 1 WLR 398; (1982) 263 EG 877, CA 140
Basildon Development Corporation v Mactro Ltd [1986] 1 EGLR 137; (1985) 278 EG 406, CA 2, 221
Basingstoke and Deane Borough Council v Host Group [1988] 1 WLR 348; [1988] 1 All ER 824; (1987) 284 EG 1587, CA 7, 93, 118
Bass Holdings Ltd v Morton Music Ltd [1987] 2 All ER 1001; [1988] Ch 493; [1987] 3 WLR 543 64
Bassett v Whiteley (1983) 45 P&CR 87, CA 65
Bates (Thomas) & Son Ltd v Wyndham's (Lingerie) Ltd [1981] 1 All ER 1077; [1981] 1 WLR 505; (1980) 257 EG 381, CA 110, 124
Beacon Carpets Ltd v Kirby [1984] 2 All ER 726; [1985] QB 755; [1984] 3 WLR 489, CA 154
Beaumont Property Trust v Tai (1983) 265 EG 872 .... 55, 95
Bedford v University College Medical School (1974) CLY 2063 205
Beech v Bloomfield (1953) CLY 1988; [1953] CPL 672, Cty Ct 258
Beesly v Hallwood Estates Ltd [1961] Ch 105; [1961] 2 WLR 36; [1961] 1 All ER 90, CA .. 66
Bell v Franks (Alfred) & Bartlett Co Ltd [1980] 1 All ER 356; [1980] 1 WLR 340; (1979) 39 P&CR 591, CA 30, 260
Bernstein of Leigh (Baron) v Skyviews & General Ltd [1978] QB 479; [1977] 2 All ER 902; (1977) 241 EG 917 19
Berry (Frederick) Ltd v Royal Bank of Scotland [1949] 1 KB 619; [1949] LJR 913; [1949] 1 All ER 706 31
Berton v Alliance Economic Investment Co Ltd [1922] 1 KB 742; (1922) 91 LJ KB 748; (1922) 127 LT 422 223
Betty's Cafés Ltd v Phillips Furnishing Stores Ltd [1957] 1 Ch 67; [1956] 3 WLR 1134; [1957] 1 All ER 1, CA 68
Bickenhall Engineering Co v Grandmet Restaurants [1995] 1 EGLR 110 98
Bickmore v Dimmer [1903] 1 Ch 158 .... 3, 201
Bisney v Swanston (1972) 225 EG 2299, CA 2
Blumenthal v Gallery Five Ltd (1971) 220 EG 33 .... 74, 75
Blythewood Plant Hire v Spiers (In Receivership) [1992] 48 EG 117 148
Bocardo SA v S & M Hotels Ltd [1980] 1 WLR 17; [1979] 3 All ER 737; (1979) P&CR 287, CA 250
Boots the Chemist v Pinkland [1992] 28 EG 118 .... 148, 218, 230
Borman v Griffith [1930] 1 Ch 493; (1930) LJ Ch 295 24
Borthwick-Norton v Collier [1950] 2 KB 594; [1950] 2 All ER 204; (1950) 1 P&CR 147, CA 213

TABLE OF CASES xvii

Boswell v Crucible Steel Co [1925] 1 KB 119 192
Bovis Group Pension Fund Ltd v GC Flooring & Furnishing Ltd (1984) 269 EG 1252, CA;
 affg (1983) 266 EG 1005; (1983) 133 New LJ 203 .... 113, 131
Bowes, *Re* [1896] 1 Ch 507 177
Bracey v Read [1963] Ch 88; [1962] 3 WLR 1194; [1962] 3 All ER 472 259
Bracknell Development Corporation v Greenlees Lennards Ltd (1981) 260 EG 500 66
Braddon Towers Ltd v International Stores Ltd [1987] 1 EGLR 209 218
Bradley v Chorley Borough Council [1985] 2 EGLR 49; (1985) 83 LGR 623; (1985) 275
 EG 801, CA 34
Bradley (C) & Sons Ltd v Telefusion Ltd (1981) 259 EG 337 96
Bradshaw v Pawley [1980] 1 WLR 10; [1979] 3 All ER 273; (1979) 40 P&CR 496 55
Brett v Brett Essex Golf Club Ltd [1986] 1 EGLR 154; (1986) 52 P&CR 330; (1986) 278
 EG 1476, CA 11, 125, 130
Brew Brothers Ltd v Snax (Ross) Ltd [1970] 1 QB 612; [1969] 3 WLR 657; [1970] 1 All
 ER 587, CA 187
Brewers Co v Viewplan [1989] 2 EGLR 133; [1989] 45 EG 153 .... 11, 222
British Airways v Heathrow Airport [1992] 1 EGLR 141; [1992] 19 EG 157; [1991] NPC
 127 93
British Anzani (Felixstowe) v International Marine Management (UK) [1980] QB 637;
 [1979] 3 WLR 451; [1979] 2 All ER 1063 73
British Gas Corporation v Universities Superannuation Scheme Ltd [1986] 1 WLR 398;
 (1986) 130 SJ 264; [1986] 1 All ER 978 129
British Home Stores Ltd v Ranbrook Properties Ltd [1988] 1 EGLR 121; [1988] 16 EG
 80 129
British Railways Board v Elgar House Ltd (1969) 209 EG 1313 87
British Telecommunications v Sun Life Assurance Society [1995] 4 All ER 44 194
Broadgate Square v Lehman Brothers [1995] 1 EGLR 97 137
Brown v Gould [1972] Ch 53; [1971] 3 WLR 334; [1971] 2 All ER 1505 .... 9, 66
Brown v Liverpool Corporation [1969] 3 All ER 1345, CA 192
Buffalo Enterprises v Golden Wonder [1991] 1 EGLR 141; [1991] 24 EG 171 .... 122, 128
Burfort Financial Investments Ltd v Chotard (1976) 239 EG 891 .... 6, 225
Burnett (Marjorie) Ltd v Barclay (1980) 258 EG 642; (1980) 125 SJ 199 65
C & A Pensions Trustees Ltd v British Vita Investments Ltd (1984) 272 EG 63 .... 120, 217
Cadogan (Earl) v Guinness [1936] Ch 515; [1936] 2 All ER 29 55
Caerphilly Concrete Products Ltd v Owen [1972] 1 WLR 372; *sub nom* Hopkin's Lease, *Re*
 [1972] 1 All ER 248; (1971) 23 P&CR 15, CA 65
Cairnplace Ltd v CBL (Property Investment) Co Ltd [1984] 1 All ER 315; [1984] 1 WLR
 696; (1984) 47 P&CR 531, CA 265, 273
Calabar (Woolwich) Ltd v Tesco Stores Ltd (1977) 245 EG 479, CA 3
Calthorpe v McOscar. *See* Anstruther etc
Camden Theatre Ltd v London Scottish Properties Ltd (1984) unreported 156
Campbell v Edwards [1976] 1 All ER 785; [1976] 1 WLR 403; (1975) 119 SJ 845, CA 106
Campden Hill Towers Ltd v Gardner [1977] 1 All ER 739; [1977] QB 823; [1977] 2 WLR
 159, CA 192
Cannock v Jones (1849) 3 Exch 233 196
Capital & Counties Freehold Equity Trust Ltd v BL plc [1987] 2 EGLR 49; (1987) 283 EG
 563 169
Cardiothoracic Institute v Shrewdcrest Ltd [1986] 1 WLR 368; [1986] 3 All ER 633;
 [1986] EGLR 57 256
Cardshops Ltd v Davies [1971] 2 All ER 721; [1971] 1 WLR 591; (1971) 22 P&CR
 499, CA 250
Cave v Horsell [1912] 3 KB 533; (1912) 81 LJ KB 981 227
CBS (United Kingdom) Ltd v London Scottish Properties Ltd (1985) 275 EG 718; [1985]
 2 EGLR 125 69
Central Estates v Secretary of State for the Environment [1995] EGCS 110 .... 60, 100
Cerium Investments v Evans (1991) 62 P&CR 203; [1991] 20 EG 189; (1991) 135
 SJ (LB) 217, CA 9, 264
Chandris v Isbrandtsen-Moller Co [1951] 1 KB 240; [1950] 2 All ER 618; (1951) 94 SJ
 534, CA 8

TABLE OF CASES

Chapman v Freeman [1978] 3 All ER 878; [1978] 1 WLR 1298; (1978) 36 P&CR 323, CA 263
Chapman v Mason (1910) 103 LT 390 162
Chatterton v Terrell [1923] AC 578, HL 233
Chelsea Cloisters Ltd (In Liquidation), Re (1980) 41 P&CR 98, CA 168, 178
Cheryl Investments Ltd v Saldanha; Royal Life Society v Page [1979] 1 All ER 5; [1978] 1 WLR 1329; (1978) 37 P&CR 349, CA 262
CIN Properties Ltd v Barclays Bank plc [1986] 1 EGLR 59; (1985) 277 EG 973, CA 166, 179
City and Westminster Properties (1934) Ltd v Mudd [1959] Ch 129; [1958] 3 WLR 312; [1958] 2 All ER 733 2
City of London Corporation v Fell [1994] 1 AC 458; [1993] 3 WLR 1164; [1993] 4 All ER 968, HL 49, 61
City Offices v Allianz Cornhill International Insurance Co [1993] 11 EG 129; [1992] NPC 151 137
Clapman v Edwards [1938] 2 All ER 507 30
Clarke v Findon Developments Ltd (1984) 270 EG 426 .... 121, 136
Clements (Charles) (London) Ltd v Rank City Wall Ltd (1978) 246 EG 739 .... 121, 230
Cleveland Shoe Co Ltd v Murray's Book Sales (King's Cross) Ltd (1973) 229 EG 1465, CA; revsg (1973) 227 EG 987 .... 153, 160
Clore v Theatrical Properties Ltd [1936] 3 All ER 483 255
Coates v Diment [1951] 1 All ER 890 .... 8, 59
Cockburn v Smith [1924] 2 KB 119; [1924] All ER 59; (1924) 68 SJ 631 18
Combe v Greene (1843) 11 M & W 480 196
Comber v Fleet Electrics Ltd [1955] 2 All ER 161; [1955] 1 WLR 566; (1955) 99 SJ 337 .. 252
Commission for the New Towns v R Levy & Co [1990] 2 EGLR 121; [1990] 28 EG 119 102
Compton Group Ltd v Estates Gazette Ltd (1978) 36 P&CR 148; (1977) 244 EG 799, CA 110, 131
Concorde Graphics Ltd v Andromeda Investments SA (1982) 265 EG 386 .... 164, 179
Connaught Restaurants Ltd v Indoor Leisure Ltd [1994] 1 WLR 501; [1993] 46 EG 184; [1993] EGCS 143, CA 4, 73
Cook v Shoesmith [1951] 1 KB 752; [1951] 1 TLR 194, CA 233
Co-operative Insurance Society v Argyll Stores (Holdings) [1996] 09 EG 128; (1995) The Times, 29 December, CA 218
Co-operative Wholesale Society Ltd v National Westminster Bank plc [1995] 1 EGLR 97, CA 4, 136
Cornwall Coast Country Club Ltd v Cardgrange Ltd [1987] 1 EGLR 146; (1987) 282 EG 1664 .... 123, 140, 147
Coronation Street Industrial Properties v Ingall Industries [1989] 1 WLR 304; [1989] 1 All ER 979; [1989] 24 EG 125, HL 268
Corson v Rhuddlan Borough Council [1990] 1 EGLR 255; (1990) 59 P&CR 185, CA 9, 65
Costain Property Developments Ltd v Finlay & Co Ltd [1989] 1 EGLR 237; (1989) 57 P&CR 345, DC 218
County Personnel (Employment Agency) Ltd v Alan R Pulver & Co [1987] 1 All ER 289; [1987] 1 WLR 916; [1986] 2 EGLR 246, CA 92
Coventry City Council v J Hepworth & Sons Ltd (1983) 265 EG 608; (1983) 46 P&CR 170, CA 100
Coventry City Council v IRC [1979] Ch 142; [1978] 2 WLR 857; [1978] 1 All ER 1107 71
Cramas Properties Ltd v Connaught Fur Trimmings Ltd [1965] 2 All ER 382; [1965] 1 WLR 892; (1965) 109 SJ 414, HL 222
Credit Suisse v Beegas Nominees [1994] 4 All ER 803; [1993] EGCS 157; (1993) The Independent, 15 September 188, 190
Creer v P & O Lines of Australia Pty Ltd (1971) 125 CLR 84; (1971) 45 ALJR 697 250
Cressey v Jacobs (1977) unreported 269
Crossley v Lee [1908] 1 KB 86 37
Cuff v Stone (J & F) Property Co Ltd [1979] AC 87; [1978] 3 WLR 256 (N); [1978] 2 All ER 833 110
Cumshaw v Bowen [1987] 1 EGLR 30; (1987) 281 EG 68 75

TABLE OF CASES   xix

D & F Estates Ltd v Church Commissioners for England [1988] 2 All ER 992; [1988] 3
 WLR 368; (1988) 132 SJ 1092, HL 189
Daejan Investments Ltd v Cornwall Coast Country Club (1984) 49 P&CR 157; [1985] 1
 EGLR 77; (1985) 273 EG 1122 .... 111, 147
Davey v Harrow Corporation [1958] 1 QB 60; [1957] 2 WLR 941; [1957] 2 All ER 305 16
Davies v Yadegar [1990] 1 EGLR 71; (1990) 22 HLR 232; [1990] 09 EG 67, CA 20
Davstone (Holdings) Ltd v Al-Rifai (1976) 32 P&CR 18 102
De Meza v Ve-Ri-Best Manufacturing Co Ltd (1952) 160 EG 364; [1952] CPL 733, CA 28
Dean and Chapter of Chichester Cathedral v Lennards Ltd (1977) 35 P&CR 309; (1977)
 244 EG 807; (1977) 121 SJ 694, CA 101
Deanplan v Mahmoud [1992] 3 WLR 467; [1993] Ch 151; [1992] 3 All ER 945 43
Demetriou v Poolaction [1991] 1 EGLR 100; (1990) 63 P&CR 536; [1991] 25 EG 113,
 CA 191
Denley's Trust Deed, Re [1969] 1 Ch 373; [1968] 3 WLR 457; [1968] 3 All ER 65 177
Dennis & Robinson Ltd v Kiossos Establishment [1987] 1 EGLR 133; (1987) 54 P&CR
 282; (1987) 282 EG 857, CA 112
Deutsche Genossenschaft Bank v Burnhope [1995] 4 All ER 717 10
Dickinson v St Aubyn [1944] KB 454 .... 60, 198
Dikstein v Kanevsky [1947] VLR 216 28
Doe d Baker v Jones (1848) 2 Car & Kir 743 196
Doe d Pitt v Hogg (1824) 4 D & R KB 226; (1824) 1 Car & P 160 231
Drebbond Ltd v Horsham District Council (1978) 246 EG 1013; (1978) 37 P&CR 237,
 DC 98
Dresden Estates Ltd v Collinson [1987] 1 EGLR 45; (1988) 55 P&CR 47; (1987) 281 EG
 1321, CA 255
Drive Yourself Hire Co (London) Ltd v Strutt [1954] 1 QB 250; [1953] 3 WLR 1111; [1953]
 2 All ER 1475, CA 233
D'Silva v Lister House Development Ltd [1971] Ch 17; [1970] 2 WLR 563; [1970] 1 All
 ER 858 260
Duke of Westminster v Guild [1985] QB 688; [1984] 3 All ER 144; [1984] 3 WLR 630,
 CA 6, 32, 167
Dunn v Blackdown Properties Ltd [1961] Ch 433; [1961] 2 WLR 618; [1961] 2 All ER
 62 .... 35, 36
Dyer v Dorset County Council [1989] QB 346; [1989] RVR 41, CA 23
East v Pantiles (Plant Hire) Ltd (1982) 263 EG 61, CA 56
Eastern Counties Building Society v Russell [1947] 2 All ER 734, CA; affg [1947] 1 All ER
 500 5
Eastwood v Ashton [1915] AC 900 16
Edmonton Corporation v WM Knowles & Son (1962) 60 LGR 124 167
Edwards (JH) & Sons Ltd v Central London Commercial Estates Ltd (1984) 271 EG 697,
 CA 69
Electricity Supply Nominees Ltd v FM Insurance Co Ltd [1986] 1 EGLR 143; (1986) 278
 EG 523 129
Electricity Supply Nominees Ltd v London Clubs Ltd (1988) 34 EG 71 140
Elite Investments Ltd v TI Bainbridge Silencers Ltd (No 2) [1986] 2 EGLR 43; (1987) 283
 EG 747 187
Embassy Court Residents' Association v Lipman (1984) 271 EG 545, CA 169
English Exporters (London) Ltd v Eldonwall Ltd [1973] 1 All ER 726; [1973] Ch 415;
 [1973] 2 WLR 435 111
Enlayde Ltd v Roberts [1917] 1 Ch 109; (1917) LJ Ch 149; (1917) 61 SJ 86 3
Equity and Law Life Assurance Society plc v Bodfield Ltd [1987] 1 EGLR 124; (1987)
 P&CR 290; (1987) 281 EG 1448, CA 129
Esselte v Pearl Assurance [1995] 37 EG 173 218
Essexcrest Ltd v Evenlex Ltd [1988] 1 EGLR 69; (1988) 55 P&CR 279; [1988] 01 EG
 56, CA 256
Esso Petroleum Co Ltd v Anthony Gibbs Financial Services Ltd (1983) 267 EG 351, CA;
 (1982) 263 EG 661 101
Esso Petroleum Co Ltd v Mardon [1976] QB 801; [1976] 2 WLR 583; [1976] 2 All ER 5,
 CA 212

TABLE OF CASES

Essoldo (Bingo) Ltd's Underlease, Re (1971) 23 P&CR 1; (1971) 115 SJ 967 103
Estates Projects Ltd v Greenwich London Borough Council (1979) 251 EG 581 127
Euston Centre Properties Ltd v Wilson (H & J) Ltd (1982) 262 EG 1079 126
Evans (FR) (Leeds) Ltd v English Electric Co Ltd (1977) 36 P&CR 185; (1977) 245 EG 657 112
Facchini v Bryson [1952] 1 TLR 1386; (1952) 96 SJ 395, CA 255
Factory Holdings Group Ltd v Leboff International Ltd [1987] 1 EGLR 135; (1987) 282 EG 1005 104
Family Housing Association v Jones [1990] 1 WLR 779; [1990] 1 All ER 385; [1990] 22 EG 118, CA 2
Farimani v Gates (1984) 271 EG 887; (1984) 128 SJ 615; (1984) 81 LS Gaz 1999, CA 156
Fawke v Viscount Chelsea [1979] 3 All ER 568; [1980] QB 441; [1979] 3 WLR 508, CA . 121
Featherstone v Staples (1984) 273 EG 193; (1985) 129 SJ 66; (1984) P&CR 273 258
Fernandez v Walding [1968] 2 QB 606; [1968] 2 WLR 583; [1968] 1 All ER 994, CA 39
Field v Barkworth [1986] 1 EGLR 46; [1986] 1 All ER 362; (1985) P&CR 182................. 233
Finchbourne Ltd v Rodrigues [1976] 3 All ER 581, CA 170, 173, 179
First Leisure Trading v Dorita Properties [1991] 1 EGLR 133; [1991] 23 EG 116 .... 111, 123
Fisher v Winch [1939] 1 KB 666 .... 16, 17
Follett (Charles) Ltd v Cabtell Investments Co Ltd [1986] 2 EGLR 76; (1988) 55 P&CR 36; (1987) 283 EG 195, CA 94, 147
Forte & Co Ltd v General Accident Life Assurance Ltd [1986] 2 EGLR 115; (1987) 54 P&CR 9; (1986) 279 EG 1227 .... 119, 131, 216
Fourboys v Newport Borough Council [1994] 1 EGLR 138 148
Francis v Cowcliffe Ltd (1976) 33 P&CR 368; (1976) 239 EG 977, DC 28, 167
Fraser Pipestock v Gloucester City Council [1995] 36 EG 141 87
Freehold & Leasehold Shop Properties Ltd v Friends Provident Life Office (1984) 271 EG 451, CA 87
Freeman and Taylor's Contract, Re (1907) 97 LT 39 16
Friends Provident Life Office v British Railways Board [1995] EGCS 140 44
Frish v Barclays Bank Ltd [1955] 2 QB 541; [1955] 3 WLR 439; [1955] 3 All ER 185, CA 258
Frobisher (Second Investments) Ltd v Kiloran Trust Co Ltd [1980] 1 All ER 488; [1980] 1 WLR 425; (1979) 40 P&CR 442 .... 143, 165, 168
Galashiels Gas Co Ltd v O'Donnell [1949] AC 275; [1949] LJR 540; [1949] 1 All ER 319 27
Gardner v Blaxill [1960] 2 All ER 457; [1960] 1 WLR 752; (1960) 104 SJ 585 64
General Accident Fire & Life Assurance Corporation plc v Electronic Data Processing Co plc [1987] 1 EGLR 113; (1987) 53 P&CR 189; (1987) 281 EG 65 129
Gentle v Faulkner [1900] 2 QB 267, CA 231, 232
Giles v County Building Constructors (Hertford) Ltd (1971) 22 P&CR 978 17
Gleniffer Finance Corporation Ltd v Bamar Wood & Products Ltd [1978] 2 Lloyd's Rep 49; (1978) 37 P&CR 208; (1978) 122 SJ 110 152
Glofield Properties v Morley (No 2) [1989] 2 EGLR 118; [1988] 33 EG 59 95
Godbold v Martin (The Newsagents) Ltd (1983) 268 EG 1202 126
Goh Eng Wah v Yap Phooi Yin [1988] 2 EGLR 148; [1988] 32 EG 55, PC 124
Gold v Brighton Corporation [1956] 3 All ER 442; [1956] 1 WLR 1291; (1956) 100 SJ 749, CA 230
Goldberg v Edwards [1950] Ch 247; (1950) 94 SJ 128, CA 40
Goldfoot v Welch [1914] 1 Ch 213; (1914) 83 LJ Ch 360; (1914) 109 LT 820 18
Good's Lease, Re, Good v Trustee of the Property of W, A Bankrupt, and W [1954] 1 All ER 275; [1954] 1 WLR 309; (1954) 98 SJ 111 233
Gooderham and Worts Ltd v Canadian Broadcasting Corporation [1947] AC 66 190
Gordon v Selico Co Ltd [1986] 1 EGLR 71; (1986) 18 HLR 219; (1986) 278 EG 53, CA 166, 168
Granada Theatres Ltd v Freehold Investment (Leytonstone) Ltd [1958] 2 All ER 551; [1958] 1 WLR 845; (1958) 102 SJ 563 191
Graysim Holdings v P & O Properties [1994] 4 All ER 831; [1993] 05 EG 141; [1992] EGCS 108 262
Graystone Property Investments Ltd v Margulies (1984) 269 EG 538; (1984) 47 P&CR 472,

TABLE OF CASES xxi

CA; *affg* (1983) 133 New LJ 894 18
GREA Real Property Investments Ltd v Williams (1979) 250 EG 651 127
Greater London Properties Ltd's Leases, *Re*, Taylor Brothers (Grocers) v Covent Garden
  Properties Co [1959] 1 All ER 728; [1959] 1 WLR 503; (1959) 103 SJ 351 245
Greene v Church Commissioners for England [1974] Ch 467; [1974] 3 WLR 349; [1974] 3
  All ER 609, CA 250
Greenhaven Securities Ltd v Compton (1985) 275 EG 628; [1985] 2 EGLR 117 98
Grigsby v Melville [1974] 1 WLR 80; (1974) 117 SJ 632; [1973] 3 All ER 455, CA 19
Groveside Properties Ltd v Westminster Medical School (1983) 267 EG 593; (1984) 47
  P&CR 507, CA 263
Guardian Assurance Co Ltd v Gants Hill Holdings Ltd (1983) 267 EG 678 215
Guys 'n' Dolls v Sade Brothers Catering (1984) 269 EG 129, CA; *revsg* (1982) 263 EG
  979 .... 122, 128
Hafton Properties v Camp; Camp v Silchester Court (Croydon) Management Co [1994] 1
  EGLR 67; [1994] 03 EG 129; [1993] EGCS 101 191
Hagee (London) Ltd v Co-operative Insurance Society [1992] 1 EGLR 57; (1991) 63
  P&CR 362; [1992] 07 EG 122 .... 201, 202
Hagee (London) Ltd v Erikson (AB) and Larson [1976] QB 209; [1975] 3 WLR 272;
  [1975] 3 All ER 234, CA 50, 255
Haines v Florensa [1990] 1 EGLR 73; [1990] 09 EG 70; (1990) 59 P&CR 200, CA 20
Hambros Bank Executor & Trustee Co Ltd v Superdrug Stores Ltd [1985] 1 EGLR 99; (1985)
  274 EG 590 .... 125, 130
Hamish Cathie Travel England Ltd v Insight International Tours Ltd [1986] 1 EGLR 244 . 127
Hansford v Jago [1921] 1 Ch 322 23
Harben Style v Rhodes Trust [1995] 1 EGLR 118 104
Harmsworth Pension Funds Trustees v Charringtons Industrial Holdings Ltd (1985) 49
  P&CR 297; (1985) 274 EG 588; [1985] 1 EGLR 97 .... 8, 121
Harris v Black (1983) 266 EG 628; (1983) 46 P&CR 366, CA 258
Hatfield v Moss [1988] 2 EGLR 58; [1988] 40 EG 112, CA 18
Havenridge Ltd v Boston Dyers Ltd [1993] 2 EGLR 73; [1994] NPC 39; [1994] EGCS
  53 153
Hayns v Secretary of State for the Environment (1977) 36 P&CR 317; [1977] JPL 663;
  [1978] 245 EG 53 25
Heard v Stuart (1907) 24 TLR 104 .... 201, 234
Heath v Drown [1973] AC 498; [1972] 2 WLR 1306; [1972] 2 All ER 561 34
Henderson v Arthur [1907] 1 KB 10 2
Henry Smith's Charity Trustees v Wagle [1989] 1 EGLR 124; [1989] 2 WLR 669; (1989)
  133 SJ 484, CA 263
Henry Sotheran v Norwich Union Life Insurance Society [1992] 31 EG 70; [1992] 2
  EGLR 9 107
Herbert Duncan v Cluttons. *See* London City Corporation v Fell etc
Heywood v Mallalieu (1883) 25 ChD 357 32
Hill v Harris [1965] 2 QB 601; [1965] 2 WLR 1331; [1965] 2 All ER 358, CA 212
Hill (William) (Southern) v Cabras [1987] 1 EGLR 37; (1987) 54 P&CR 42; (1987) 281 EG
  309, CA 31
Hilton v Smith (James) & Sons (Norwood) Ltd (1979) 257 EG 1063, CA 25
Hindcastle v Barbara Attenborough Associates [1996] 1 All ER 737 268
Holiday Fellowship Ltd v Hereford (unreported); *appvd* [1959] 1 All ER 433, CA 192
Holland v Hodgson (1872) LR 7 CP 328 37
Hollies Stores Ltd v Timmis [1921] 2 Ch 202 265
Holme v Brunskill (1877) 3 QBD 495; (1877) 47 LJ QB 610; (1877) 38 LT 838 .... 44, 266
Holt & Co v Collyer (1881) 16 ChD 719; (1881) 50 LJ Ch 311; (1881) 44 LT 214 3
Hope Brothers Ltd v Cowan [1913] 2 Ch 312; (1913) 82 LJ Ch 439; (1913) 108 LT 945 18
Hopgood v Brown [1955] 1 WLR 213; (1955) 99 SJ 168; [1955] 1 All ER 550, CA 15
Horner v Franklin [1905] 1 KB 479 205
Horsey Estate Ltd v Steiger [1899] 2 QB 79, CA 231
Howard de Walden Estates v Pasta Place [1995] 1 EGLR 79 266
Hupfield v Bourne (1974) 28 P&CR 77 170
Hyams v Titan Properties Ltd (1972) 24 P&CR 359; (1972) 116 SJ 884, CA 180

TABLE OF CASES

Ideal Film Renting Co Ltd v Neilson [1921] 1 Ch 575; (1921) 90 LJ Ch 429; (1921) 124 LT 749 245
IRC v Southend-on-Sea Estates Co Ltd [1915] AC 428 59
Ipswich Town Football Club v Ipswich Borough Council [1988] 1 EGLR 146; [1988] 32 EG 49 124
Jacob Isbicki & Co Ltd v Goulding & Bird Ltd [1989] 1 EGLR 236 174
Jacobs v Chaudhuri [1968] 2 QB 470; [1968] 2 WLR 1098; [1968] 2 All ER 124, CA 258, 259
James v British Crafts Centre [1987] 1 EGLR 139; (1988) 55 P&CR 56; (1987) 282 EG 1251, CA 120, 122
Janes (Gowns) Ltd v Harlow Development Corporation (1979) 253 EG 799 148
Jeffries v O'Neill (1984) 269 EG 131; [1983] 46 P&CR 376 .... 12, 112
Jenkins v Price [1907] 2 Ch 229; [1908] 1 Ch 10; (1908) 76 LJ Ch 507 251
Jervis v Harris [1996] 2 WLR 220; [1995] EGCS 177 195
Johnson v Jones (1839) 9 Ad & El 809 73
Johnson v Moreton [1980] AC 37; [1978] 3 WLR 538; [1978] 3 All ER 37, HL 246
Johnston & Sons Ltd v Holland [1988] 1 EGLR 264, CA 35
Jones v Christy (1963) 107 SJ 374, CA 259
Jones v Morris (1849) 3 Exch 742 73
Joseph v Joseph [1967] Ch 78; [1966] 3 WLR 631; [1966] 3 All ER 486, CA 251
Joseph v London City Council [1914] 111 LT 276 201
JT Sydenham v Enichers Elastomers [1989] 1 EGLR 257 219
Junction Estates Ltd v Cope (1974) 27 P&CR 482 .... 61, 265
Keith Bayley Rogers & Co v Cubes Ltd (1975) 31 P&CR 412 58
Kelsen v Imperial Tobacco Co (of Great Britain and Ireland) Ltd [1957] 2 QB 334; [1957] 2 WLR 1007; [1957] 2 All ER 343 19
Kenilworth Industrial Sites Ltd v Little (EC) & Co Ltd [1975] 1 All ER 53; [1975] 1 WLR 143; (1974) 29 P&CR 141, CA 142
Killick v Second Covent Garden Property Co Ltd [1973] 2 All ER 337; [1973] 1 WLR 658; (1973) 25 P&CR 332, CA 5
King, Re, Robinson v Gray [1963] 1 All ER 781; [1963] Ch 459; [1963] 2 WLR 629, CA; revsg [1962] 2 All ER 66; [1962] 1 WLR 632; (1962) 106 SJ 509 154
King's Motors (Oxford) v Lax [1970] 1 WLR 426; [1969] 3 All ER 665; (1970) 114 SJ 168 .... 9, 65
Kirkwood v Johnson (1979) 38 P&CR 392; (1979) 250 EG 239, CA 39, 70
Kitney v Greater London Properties Ltd (1984) 272 EG 786 64
Knight, Re, ex parte Voisey (1882) 21 ChD 442 164
Lace v Chantler [1944] KB 368; [1944] 1 All ER 305; (1944) 113 LJ KB 282 9
Ladbroke Group plc v Bristol City Council [1988] 1 EGLR 126; [1988] 23 EG 125, CA 2
Ladyman v Wirral Estates Ltd [1968] 2 All ER 197; (1968) 19 P&CR 781 56
Lam Kee Ying Sdn Bhd v Lam Shes Tong (Trading as Lian Joo Co [1975] AC 247; [1974] 3 WLR 784; [1974] 3 All ER 137, PC 234
Lambert v FW Woolworth & Co Ltd (No 2) [1938] Ch 883; [1938] 2 All ER 664, CA 202
Lambourn v McLellan [1903] 2 Ch 268; (1903) 72 LJ Ch 617; (1903) 88 LT 748 8
Land and Premises at Liss, Hants, Re [1971] Ch 986; [1971] 3 WLR 77; [1971] 3 All ER 380 .... 51, 256
Land Reclamation Co Ltd v Basildon District Council; Pitsea Access Road, Basildon [1979] 2 All ER 993; [1979] 1 WLR 767; (1979) 123 SJ 302 259
Land Securities v Westminster City Council [1993] 1 WLR 286; [1993] 4 All ER 124; (1992) 65 P&CR 387 105
Lang v House (1961) 178 EG 801 17
Langham House Developments Ltd v Brompton Securities Ltd (1980) 256 EG 719 132
Langton v Henson (1905) 92 LT 805 232
Laura Investments v Havering London Borough Council [1992] 1 EGLR 155; [1992] 24 EG 136; [1992] EGCS 57 .... 10, 124
Laura Investments v Havering London Borough Council (No 2) [1993] 08 EG 120; [1992] NPC 117 132
Laurence v Lexcourt Holdings Ltd [1978] 2 All ER 810; [1978] 1 WLR 1128; (1977) 122 SJ 681 212

TABLE OF CASES
xxiii

Law Land Co Ltd v Consumers' Association Ltd (1980) 255 EG 617, CA 12, 112, 120
Laybourn v Gridley [1892] 2 Ch 53 19
Lear v Blizzard [1983] 3 All ER 662; (1983) 268 EG 1115; (1983) 133 New LJ 893 110
Leathwoods Ltd v Total Oil (Great Britain) Ltd [1985] 2 EGLR 237; (1985) 51 P&CR 20;
  (1984) 270 EG 1083 34
Lee-Parker v Izzet [1971] 1 WLR 1688; [1971] 3 All ER 1099; *sub nom* Lee-Parker v Izzet
  (Hassan) (1971) 22 P&CR 1098 73
Legal & General Assurance (Pension Management) Ltd v Cheshire County Council
  (1983) 265 EG 781; (1983) 46 P&CR 160 100
Leppard v Excess Insurance Co Ltd [1979] 2 All ER 668; [1979] 1 WLR 512; (1979)
  122 SJ 182, CA 194
Leschallas v Woolf [1908] 1 Ch 641; (1908) 77 LJ Ch 345; (1908) 98 LT 558 38
Leslie & Godwin Investments v Prudential Assurance Co [1987] 2 EGLR 95; (1987) 283
  EG 1565 180
Levermore v Jobey [1956] 1 WLR 697; [1956] 2 All ER 362; (1956) 100 SJ 432, CA 2, 12
Lewis v Barnet (1982) 264 EG 1079 98
Lewis (A) & Co (Westminster) Ltd v Bell Property Trust Ltd [1940] Ch 345 224
Linden v DHSS [1986] 1 WLR 164; (1986) 130 SJ 128; [1986] 1 All ER 691 263
Lipinski's Will Trusts, *Re* [1977] 1 All ER 33; [1976] Ch 235; [1976] 3 WLR 522 177
Lister Locks Ltd v TEI Pension Trust Ltd (1981) 264 EG 827 128
Little v Courage (1994) 70 P&CR 469 64
Liverpool City Council v Irwin [1977] AC 239; (1976) 238 EG 879; (1984) 13 HLR 38,
  HL 27, 28
Lloyds Bank v Bowker Orford [1992] 31 EG 68; [1992] 2 EGLR 44 .... 171, 172
London and Blenheim Estates v Ladbroke Retail Parks [1992] 1 WLR 1278; [1993] 1
  All ER 307 .... 29, 37
London and Leeds Estates v Paribas (1993) 66 P&CR 218; [1993] 30 EG 89; [1993] EGCS
  71, CA 114
London and Manchester Assurance Co Ltd v Dunn & Co (GA) (1983) 265 EG 39, CA; *affg*
  (1982) 262 EG 143 142
London and Provincial Millinery Stores Ltd v Barclays Bank Ltd [1962] 1 WLR 510; (1962)
  106 SJ 220; [1962] 2 All ER 163, CA 68
London and Suburban Land and Building Co (Holdings) v Carey (1991) 62 P&CR 481 25
London City Corporation v Fell; Herbert Duncan v Cluttons (A Firm); *sub nom* City of
  London Corporation v Fell [1992] 3 All ER 224; (1991) 63 P&CR 135; [1992] 1 EGLR
  101 49
London City Council v Hutter [1925] Ch 626; (1925) 95 LJ Ch 1; (1925) 134 LT 56 202
London Regional Transport v Wimpey Group Construction [1986] 2 EGLR 41; (1987)
  P&CR 356; (1986) 280 EG 898 76
London Scottish Properties Ltd v Mehmet (1970) 214 EG 837 225
Long (Nevill) & Co (Boards) Ltd v Firmenich & Co (1983) 268 EG 572; (1984) 47 P&CR
  59, CA 236
Lorien Textiles (UK) v SI Pension Trustees Ltd (1981) 259 EG 771 92
Lurcott v Wakely & Wheeler [1911] 1 KB 905; [1911–13] All ER 41; (1911) 80 LJ KB
  713 .... 185, 187, 207
Lynnthorpe Enterprises v Sidney Smith (Chelsea) [1990] 2 EGLR 131; [1990] 40 EG 130,
  CA; *affg* [1990] 08 EG 93 .... 116, 118
McDougall v Easington District Council [1989] 1 EGLR 93; (1989) 21 HLR 310; (1989)
  58 P&CR 201, CA 188
McGreal v Wake (1984) 269 EG 1254; (1984) 128 SJ 116; (1984) 81 LS Gaz 739, CA . 34, 194
McIlraith v Grady [1968] 1 QB 468; [1967] 3 WLR 1331; [1967] 3 All ER 625, CA 25
Mackusick v Carmichael [1917] 2 KB 581; (1917) 87 LJ KB 65; (1917) 117 LT 372 233
Mammoth Greetings Cards v Agra [1990] 2 EGLR 124; [1990] 29 EG 45 98
Mancetter Developments Ltd v Garmanson and Givertz [1986] QB 1212; [1986] WLR 871;
  [1986] 1 All ER 449, CA 37
Manchester Bonded Warehouse Co Ltd v Carr (1880) 5 CPD 507; [1874–80] All ER 563 . 186
Manchester City Council v National Car Parks Ltd (1981) 262 EG 1297 255
Manor House Drive Ltd v Shahbazian (1965) 195 EG 283; (1965) 109 SJ 666, CA 173
Marks v Warren [1979] 1 All ER 29; (1978) 37 P&CR 275; (1978) 248 EG 503 231

TABLE OF CASES

Marsh [1991] 42 EG 94 72
Matthews v Smallwood [1910] 1 Ch 777; (1910) 79 LJ Ch 322; (1910) 102 LT 228 4
Matthey v Curling [1922] 2 AC 180; (1922) 91 LJ KB 593; (1922) 127 LT 247 194
Mecca Leisure Ltd v Renown Investments (Holdings) Ltd (1984) 271 EG 989; (1985) 49 P&CR 12, CA 99, 102
Meggeson v Groves [1917] 1 Ch 158; (1917) 86 LJ Ch 145; (1917) 115 LT 683 55
Mercury Communications v Director-General of Telecommunications [1996] 1 WLR 48 .... 106, 169, 179
Methuen-Campbell v Walters [1979] QB 525; [1979] 2 WLR 113; [1979] 1 All ER 606, CA 23, 24
Metrolands Investments Ltd v JH Dewhurst Ltd [1986] 3 All ER 659; (1986) 52 P&CR 232; [1986] 1 EGLR 125, CA 100
Miller v Emcer Products Ltd [1956] Ch 304; [1956] 2 WLR 267; [1956] 1 All ER 237, CA 6, 32
Millett (R & A) (Shops) Ltd v Legal and General Assurance Society Ltd [1985] 1 EGLR 103; (1984) 274 EG 1242 .... 57, 129
Millett (R & A) (Shops) Ltd v Leon Allan International Fashions Ltd [1989] 1 EGLR 138; [1989] 18 EG 107, CA 92
Mills v Cannon Brewery Co Ltd [1920] 2 Ch 38; (1920) 89 LJ Ch 354; (1920) 123 LT 324 245
Milmo v Carreras [1946] KB 306; [1946] 1 All ER 288 49
Mirabeau v Scheckman (1959) 174 EG 39 259
Moat v Martin [1950] 1 KB 175; (1950) 93 SJ 677; [1949] 2 All ER 646, CA 245
Monro v Lord Burghclere [1918] 1 KB 291; (1918) 87 LJ KB 366; (1918) 118 LT 343 205
Montross Associated Investments v Moussaieff [1990] 2 EGLR 61; [1990] 45 EG 109; (1990) 61 P&CR 437, DC 219
Moody v Steggles (1879) 12 ChD 261 31
Moorcroft Estates Ltd v Doxford (1979) 254 EG 871 175
Moss v Mobil Oil Co Ltd [1988] 1 EGLR 71; [1988] 06 EG 109, CA 59
Mullaney v Maybourne Grange (Croydon) Management Co Ltd [1986] 1 EGLR 70; (1985) 277 EG 1350 .... 173, 188
Multiservice Bookbinding Ltd v Marden [1979] Ch 84; [1978] 2 WLR 535; [1978] 2 All ER 489 76
Multon v Cordell [1986] 1 EGLR 44; (1985) 277 EG 189 63
Mumford Hotels Ltd v Wheler [1963] 2 All ER 250; [1964] Ch 117; [1963] 3 WLR 735 .... 152, 153
Narcissi v Wolfe [1960] Ch 10; [1959] 3 WLR 431; [1959] 3 All ER 71 261
National Car Parks v Paternoster Consortium [1990] 1 EGLR 99; [1990] 15 EG 53 69
National Westminster Bank Ltd v BSC Footwear Ltd (1980) 257 EG 277; (1981) 42 P&CR 90, CA 66
Naylor v Uttoxeter Urban District Council (1974) 231 EG 619 77
Never-Stop Railway (Wenbley) Ltd v British Empire Exhibition (1924) Inc [1926] 1 Ch 877 38
New Pinehurst Residents Association (Cambridge) Ltd v Silow [1988] 1 EGLR 227 179
New Zealand Government Property Corporation v HM & S Ltd [1982] 1 All ER 624; [1982] QB 1145; [1982] 2 WLR 837, CA 37, 113, 125
Newman v Dorrington Developments Ltd [1975] 3 All ER 928; [1975] 1 WLR 1642; (1975) 31 P&CR 26 110
Newman v Jones (1982) unreported 29
Nicholas v Kinsey [1994] 2 WLR 622; [1994] 16 EG 145; [1994] EGCS 9 256
99 Bishopsgate Ltd v Prudential Assurance Co Ltd (1985) 273 EG 984, CA; *affg* (1984) 270 EG 950; (1984) 134 New LJ 813 132
Northways Flats Management Co (Camden) v Wimpey Pension Trustees [1992] 2 EGLR 42; [1992] 31 EG 65; [1992] EGCS 63, CA 166, 179
Norton v Deane (Charles) Productions Ltd (1969) 214 EG 559 227
Norwich Union Life Insurance Society v British Railways Board [1987] 2 EGLR 137; (1987) 283 EG 846 190
Norwich Union Life Insurance Society v British Telecommunications [1995] EGCS 148 122

TABLE OF CASES

Norwich Union Life Insurance Society v Trustee Savings Bank Central Board [1986] 1 EGLR 136; (1985) 278 EG 162 115
O'Brien v Robinson [1973] AC 912; [1973] 2 WLR 393; [1973] 1 All ER 583, HL 194
O'Callaghan v Elliot [1966] 1 QB 601; [1965] 3 WLR 746; [1965] 3 All ER 111, CA 260
O'Cedar v Slough Trading Co Ltd [1927] 2 KB 123; (1927) 96 LJ KB 709; (1927) 137 LT 208 162
O'May v City of London Real Property Co Ltd [1982] 1 All ER 660; [1983] 2 AC 726; [1982] 2 WLR 407, HL 147, 179, 180
Orchid Lodge (UK) v Extel Computing [1991] 2 EGLR 116; [1991] 32 EG 57; [1991] EGCS 21, CA 113, 120, 122, 131
Orlik (G) (Meat Products) Ltd v Hastings and Thanet Building Society (1974) 29 P&CR 126; (1974) 118 SJ 811, CA 39
Oscroft v Benabo [1967] 2 All ER 548; [1967] 1 WLR 1087; (1967) 111 SJ 520, CA 131
Overcom Properties v Stockleigh Hall Residents Management (1989) 58 P&CR 1; [1989] 14 EG 78 35
Owen v Gadd [1956] 2 QB 99; [1956] 2 WLR 945; [1956] 2 All ER 28, CA 35
Owens v Thomas Scott & Sons (Bakers) Ltd [1939] 3 All ER 663 23
Oxford Shipping Co Ltd v Nippon Yusen Kaisha ('The Eastern Saga') [1984] 3 All ER 835; [1984] 2 Lloyd's Rep 373 108
P & A Swift Investments v Combined English Stores Group plc [1988] 2 All ER 885; [1988] 3 WLR 313; [1988] 43 EG 73, HL 273
Page v Mallow Investments Ltd (1974) 29 P&CR 168; (1974) 119 SJ 48 55
Palmer v Weaver (1952) 159 EG 141, Cty Ct 258
Panavia Air Cargo v Southend-on-Sea Borough Council [1988] 1 EGLR 124; [1988] 22 EG 82; (1988) 56 P&CR 365, CA 96
Panther Shop Investments Ltd v Keith Pople Ltd [1987] 1 EGLR 131; (1987) 282 EG 594 125
Parkinson v Barclays Bank Ltd [1951] 1 KB 368; (1951) 94 SJ 724; [1950] 2 All ER 936, CA 59
Parkside Knightbridge v German Food Centre [1990] 2 EGLR 265 95
Parkus v Greenwood [1950] Ch 644; (1950) 66 TLR (Pt 1) 496; *sub nom* Re Greenwood's Agreement [1950] 1 All ER 436, CA 65
Patel (Bhanubhai) v Peel Investments (South) [1992] 30 EG 88; [1991] NPC 82 103
Patoner v Lowe [1985] 2 EGLR 155; (1985) 275 EG 540 222
Pearl Assurance plc v Shaw (1984) 274 EG 490; [1985] 1 EGLR 92 .... 118, 215
Pegler v Graven [1952] 2 QB 693; [1952] 1 All ER 685, CA 258
Pembery v Lamdin [1940] 2 All ER 434 .... 188, 192
Phelps v City of London Corporation [1916] 2 Ch 255; (1916) 85 LJ Ch 535; (1916) 114 LT 1200 18
Phipps-Faire Ltd v Malbern Construction Ltd [1987] 1 EGLR 129; (1987) 282 EG 460 97
Pioneer Shipping Ltd v BTP Tioxide Ltd ('The Nema') [1982] AC 724; [1981] 3 WLR 292; [1981] 2 All ER 1030, HL 1
Piper v Muggleton [1956] 2 QB 569; [1956] 2 WLR 1093; [1956] 2 All ER 249, CA 255
Pittalis v Sherefettin [1986] QB 868; [1986] 2 WLR 1003; [1986] 2 All ER 227, CA .. 97, 103
Pivot Properties Ltd v Secretary of State for the Environment (1980) 41 P&CR 248; (1980) 256 EG 1176, CA; *affg* (1979) 39 P&CR 386 .... 2, 117
Plesser (A) & Co Ltd v Davis (1983) 267 EG 1039 265
Plinth Property Investments Ltd v Mott, Hay & Anderson (1978) 38 P&CR 361; (1978) 249 EG 1167, CA; *affg* (1977) 38 P&CR 361 .... 119, 121, 216
Plumrose Ltd v Real and Leasehold Estates Investment Society Ltd [1970] 1 WLR 52; (1970) 113 SJ 1000; [1969] 3 All ER 1441 10
Pole Properties Ltd v Feinberg (1981) 259 EG 417; (1982) 43 P&CR 121, CA 12, 171
Ponsford v HMS Aerosols Ltd [1979] AC 63; [1978] 2 All ER 837; [1978] 3 WLR 241, HL 110, 124
Pontsarn Investments v Kansallis-Osake Pankki [1992] 1 EGLR 148; [1992] 22 EG 103; [1992] NPC 56 113
Port v Griffith [1938] 1 All ER 295 223
Portavon Cinema Co Ltd v Price [1939] 4 All ER 601 155
Posner v Scott-Lewis [1986] 3 All ER 513; [1987] Ch 25; [1986] 3 WLR 531 170

TABLE OF CASES

Post Office v Aquarius Properties [1987] 1 All ER 1055; (1987) 54 P&CR 61; (1987) 281 EG 798, CA 187, 190
Postel Properties and Daichi Lire (London) v Greenwell [1992] 47 EG 106; (1992) 65 P&CR 239; [1992] EGCS 105 118
Poster v Slough Estates Ltd [1969] 1 Ch 495; [1968] 1 WLR 1515; [1968] 3 All ER 257 .. 262
Power Securities (Manchester) Ltd v Prudential Assurance Co Ltd [1987] 1 EGLR 121; (1987) 281 EG 1327 99
Prenn v Simmonds [1971] 1 WLR 1381; (1971) 115 SJ 654; [1971] 3 All ER 237, HL 1
President of India v La Pintada Compania Navigacion SA [1984] 2 All ER 773; [1985] AC 104; [1984] 3 WLR 10, HL 143
Price v Esso Petroleum Co Ltd (1980) 255 EG 243, CA 34
Property & Bloodstock Ltd v Emerton; Bush v Property & Bloodstock [1968] Ch 94; [1967] 3 WLR 973; [1967] 3 All ER 321 236
Prothero v Bell (1906) 22 TLR 370 223
Proudfoot v Hart (1890) 25 QBD 42; [1886–90] All ER 782; (1890) 6 TLR 305 .... 2, 185, 197
Prudential Assurance Co v Grand Metropolitan Estates [1993] 2 EGLR 153; [1993] 32 EG 74 124
Prudential Assurance Co v Gray [1987] 2 EGLR 134; (1987) 283 EG 648 95
Prudential Assurance Co v London Residuary Body [1992] 2 AC 386; [1992] 3 WLR 279; [1992] 3 All ER 504, HL 9
Prudential Assurance Co v 99 Bishopsgate [1992] 03 EG 120; [1992] 1 EGLR 119; [1991] EGCS 36 .... 122, 128
Prudential Assurance Co v Salisbury's Handbags [1992] 1 EGLR 153; (1992) 65 P&CR 129; [1992] 23 EG 117 117
Pugh v Smiths Industries Ltd (1982) 264 EG 823 130
Pwllbach Colliery Co Ltd v Woodman [1915] AC 634; [1914–15] All ER 124; (1915) 84 LJ KB 874 6
Quick v Taff-Ely Borough Council [1985] 3 All ER 321; [1986] QB 809; [1985] 3 WLR 981, CA 187
Railstore Ltd v Playdale Ltd (1988) 35 EG 87 131
Rapid Results College Ltd v Angell [1986] 1 EGLR 53; (1986) 277 EG 856, CA; *affg* [1985] 2 EGLR 66 .... 169, 173
Ravenseft Properties Ltd v Davstone (Holdings) Ltd [1979] 1 All ER 929; [1980] QB 12; [1979] 2 WLR 898, DC 188, 207
Ravenseft Properties Ltd v Director-General of Fair Trading [1977] 1 All ER 47; *sub nom* Revenseft Properties' Application [1978] QB 52; [1977] 2 WLR 432 224
Ravenseft Properties Ltd v Park [1988] 2 EGLR 164; [1988] 50 EG 52, DC 124
Reardon Smith Line Ltd v Hansen-Tangen; Hansen-Tangen v Sanko Steamship Co ('The Diana Prosperity') [1976] 1 WLR 989; [1976] 3 All ER 750; [1976] 2 Lloyd's Rep 621, HL 1
Regional Properties Ltd v City of London Real Property Co Ltd; Sedgwick Forbes Bland Payne Group v Regional Properties Ltd (1980) 257 EG 64 .... 34, 195
Regis Property Co Ltd v Dudley [1959] AC 370; [1958] 3 WLR 647; [1958] 3 All ER 491, HL 193
Regis Property Co Ltd v Redman [1956] 2 QB 612; [1956] 3 WLR 95; [1956] 2 All ER 335, CA 32, 171
Rene Claro (Haute Coiffure) Ltd v Hallé Concerts Society [1969] 2 All ER 842; [1969] 1 WLR 909; (1969) 20 P&CR 378, CA 58
Reohorn v Barry Corporation [1956] 2 All ER 742; [1956] 1 WLR 845; (1956) 100 SJ 509, CA 68
Reston v Hudson [1990] 2 EGLR 51; [1990] 37 EG 86 .... 20, 186
Retail Parks Investments v Royal Bank of Scotland (1995) *The Times*, 18 July 218
Richards v De Freitas (1974) 29 P&CR 1 266
Ridgeons Bulk v Commissioners of Customs & Excise [1994] STC 427; *discussed* [1992] 37 EG 97 .... 71, 72, 206
Ritz Hotel (London) Ltd v Ritz Casino Ltd [1989] 2 EGLR 135; [1989] 46 EG 95 116
Ropemaker Properties v Noonhaven [1989] 2 EGLR 50; [1989] 34 EG 40 222
Ross Auto Wash Ltd v Herbert (1978) 250 EG 971 255
Rossi v Hestdrive Ltd [1985] 1 EGLR 50 222

TABLE OF CASES xxvii

Rother v Colchester Corporation [1969] 2 All ER 600; [1969] 1 WLR 720; *sub nom* Rother v Colchester Borough Council (1969) 113 SJ 243 224
Rothschild v Moser [1986] NPC 46 34
Rowlands (Mark) Ltd v Berni Inns Ltd [1986] Ch 211; [1985] QB 211; [1985] 3 WLR 964 157
Royal Bank of Scotland v Jennings [1995] 35 EG 140 104
Royal Exchange Assurance v Bryant Samuel Properties (Coventry) [1985] 1 EGLR 84; (1985) 272 EG 132 .... 111, 112
Rushmoor Borough Council v Goacher [1985] 2 EGLR 140; (1986) 52 P&CR 255; (1985) 276 EG 304 131
Russell v Laimond Properties (1984) 269 EG 946 167
Russell (Nevile) v Commissioners of Customs & Excise [1987] VATTR 194 72
Safeway Food Stores Ltd v Banderway Ltd (1983) 267 EG 850 130
St Edmundsbury & Ipswich Diocesan Board of Finance v Clark (No 2) [1975] 1 All ER 772; [1975] 1 WLR 468; (1974) 29 P&CR 336, CA 5, 25, 33
St Marylebone Property Co Ltd v Tesco Stores Ltd [1988] 2 EGLR 40; [1988] 27 EG 72 .... 11, 221
Saner v Bilton (1878) 7 ChD 815 34
Saunders v Vautier (1841) 4 Beav 115 178
Savill Brothers Ltd v Bethell [1902] 2 Ch 523 5
Scarfe v Adams [1981] 1 All ER 843; (1980) 125 SJ 32, CA 15
Scholl Mfg Co Ltd v Clifton (Slim-Line) Ltd [1967] Ch 41; [1966] 3 WLR 575; [1966] 3 All ER 16, CA 50, 58, 256
Scottish & Newcastle Breweries plc v Sir Richard Sutton's Settled Estates [1985] 2 EGLR 130; (1985) 276 EG 77 .... 123, 125, 126, 132
Secretary of State for the Environment v Reed International [1994] 1 EGLR 22; [1994] 06 EG 137 111
Securicor Ltd v Postel Properties Ltd [1985] 1 EGLR 102; (1985) 274 EG 730 130
Sella House v Mears [1989] 1 EGLR 65; [1989] 12 EG 67; (1989) 21 HLR 147, CA 174
Selous Street Properties Ltd v Oronel Fabrics Ltd (1984) 270 EG 643, 743; (1984) 134 New LJ 886 .... 266, 268
Sergeant v Nash Field & Co [1903] 2 KB 304 233
Sheerness Steel Co v Medway Ports Authority [1992] 12 EG 138; [1992] 1 EGLR 133; [1991] EGCS 121, CA 118, 124
Shell-Mex and BP Ltd v Manchester Garages Ltd [1971] 1 All ER 841; [1971] 1 WLR 612; (1971) 115 SJ 111, CA 254, 255
Shirlcar Properties Ltd v Heinitz (1983) 268 EG 362, CA 101
SI Pension Trustees v Ministerio de Marina de la Republica Peruana [1988] 1 EGLR 119; [1988] 13 EG 48 120
Simons v Associated Furnishers Ltd [1931] 1 Ch 379 65
Sinclair-Lockhart's Trustees v Central Land Board (1950) 1 P&CR 195; (1950) SLT 283 ... 23
Singh (Gian) & Co v Nahar [1965] 1 All ER 768; [1965] 1 WLR 412; (1965) 109 SJ 74, PC 232
Sirros v Moore [1975] QB 118; [1974] 3 WLR 459; [1974] 3 All ER 776, CA 105
6th Centre v Guildville; Jeanmamod-Karim v Same [1989] 1 EGLR 260 131
Skelton (William) & Son v Harrison & Pinder Ltd [1975] QB 361; [1975] 2 WLR 238; [1975] 1 All ER 182 49
Skilleter v Charles [1992] 1 EGLR 73; [1992] 13 EG 113, CA 170
Skillion v Keltec Industrial Research [1992] 1 EGLR 123; [1992] 05 EG 162 .... 5, 8
Sleafer v Lambeth Borough Council [1960] 1 QB 43; [1959] 3 WLR 485; [1959] 3 All ER 378, CA 191
Smedley v Chumley and Hawke Ltd (1981) 44 P&CR 50; (1981) 125 SJ 33; (1982) 261 EG 775, CA 185, 188
Smith v Wilson (1832) 3 B & Ad 728 3
Smith's (Henry) Charity Trustees v AWADA Trading & Promotion Services Ltd. *See* Trustees of Smith's (Henry) Charity v AWADA Trading & Promotion Services
Smith's Lease, *Re*, Smith v Richards [1951] 1 TLR 254; [1951] 1 All ER 346; [1951] WN 51 .... 238, 244, 250
Sotheby v Grundy [1947] 2 All ER 761 188

TABLE OF CASES

South Tottenham Land Securities Ltd v R & A Millett (Shops) Ltd [1984] 1 All ER 614; [1984] 1 WLR 710; (1984) 48 P&CR 159, CA 143
Southport Old Links Ltd v Naylor [1985] 1 EGLR 66; (1985) 273 EG 767 59
Spark's Lease, Re [1905] 1 Ch 456; (1905) 74 LJ Ch 318; (1905) 92 LT 537 244
Sparrow and James' Contract, Re [1910] 2 Ch 60 16
Spiro v Glencrown Properties [1991] 2 WLR 931; [1991] Ch 537; [1991] 1 All ER 600 .. 64, 251
Staffordshire Area Health Authority v South Staffordshire Waterworks Co [1978] 3 All ER 769; [1978] 1 WLR 1387; (1978) 122 SJ 331, CA 76
Staines Warehousing Co Ltd v Montagu Executor & Trustee Co Ltd [1987] 2 EGLR 130; (1987) 54 P&CR 302; (1987) 283 EG 458, CA 104
Stapleton Enterprises of Man Ltd v Bramer Machine Shop Ltd [1978] 1 WWR 29 235
Stent v Monmouth District Council [1987] 1 EGLR 59; (1987) 54 P&CR 193; (1987) 282 EG 705, CA 188
Stephens v Junior Army and Navy Stores [1914] 2 Ch 516; (1914) 84 LJ Ch 56; (1914) 111 LT 1055 .... 7, 197
Sterling Land Office Developments Ltd v Lloyds Bank plc (1984) 271 EG 894 . 111, 118, 120
Straudley Investments Ltd v Barpress Ltd [1987] 1 EGLR 69; (1987) 282 EG 1124, CA 19
Street v Mountford [1985] AC 809; [1985] 2 All ER 289; [1985] 2 WLR 877, HL . 2, 232, 255
Stuart v Diplock (1889) 43 ChD 343 224
Sturge v Hackett [1962] 3 All ER 166; [1962] 1 WLR 1257; (1962) 106 SJ 568, CA 18, 19
Stylo Shoes Ltd v Manchester Royal Exchange Ltd (1967) 204 EG 803 148
Sudbrook Trading Estate Ltd v Eggleton [1983] AC 444; [1982] 3 All ER 1; [1982] 3 WLR 315, HL 66, 104
Sun Alliance & London Assurance Co Ltd v British Railways Board [1989] 2 EGLR 237 .. 174
Sweet & Maxwell Ltd v Universal News Service Ltd [1964] 2 QB 699; [1964] 3 WLR 356; [1964] 3 All ER 30, CA 231
Sykes v Land (1984) 271 EG 1264, CA 258
Taylor v British Legal Life Assurance Co [1925] Ch 395 35
Taylor Woodrow Property Co Ltd v Lonrho Textiles Ltd (1985) 275 EG 632; (1986) 52 P&CR 28; [1985] 2 EGLR 120 99
Tea Trade Properties v CIN Properties [1990] 1 EGLR 155; [1990] 22 EG 67 .... 217, 219
Teasdale v Walker [1958] 3 All ER 307; [1958] 1 WLR 1076; (1958) 102 SJ 757, CA 257
Tennant Radiant Heat Ltd v Warrington Development Corporation [1988] 1 EGLR 41; [1988] 11 EG 71; (1988) 4 Const LJ 321, CA 19, 167, 191
Texaco Antilles Ltd v Kernochan (Dorothy) [1973] AC 609; [1973] 2 WLR 381; [1973] 2 All ER 118, PC 11
Thompson v Hickman [1907] 1 Ch 550 18
Tod-Heatly v Benham (1888) 40 ChD 80; (1888) 58 LJ Ch 83; (1888) 60 LT 241 227
Toplis v Green [1992] EGCS 20, CA 17
Tottenham Hotspur Football & Athletic Co Ltd v Princegrove Publishers Ltd [1974] 1 All ER 17 256
Touche Ross & Co v Secretary of State for the Environment (1983) 265 EG 982; (1983) 46 P&CR 187, CA 98
Toyota (GB) Ltd v Legal & General Assurance (Pensions Management) Ltd [1989] 2 EGLR 123; [1989] 42 EG 104; (1990) 59 P&CR 435, CA 117
Trailfinders Ltd v Razuki (1988) 30 EG 59 35
Transworld Land Co v J Sainsbury [1990] 2 EGLR 255 .... 79, 218
Tredegar (Viscount) v Harwood [1929] AC 72; (1929) 97 LJ Ch 392 152
Trelcar v Bigge (1874) LR 9 Exch 151; (1874) 43 LJ Ex 95 246
Treseder-Griffin v Co-operative Insurance Society Ltd [1956] 2 QB 127; [1956] 2 WLR 866; [1956] 2 All ER 33 76
Trim v Sturminster RDC [1938] 2 KB 508 23
Trollope & Colls Ltd v North West Metropolitan Regional Hospital Board [1973] 1 WLR 601; (1973) 117 SJ 355; [1973] 2 All ER 260, HL 6
Troop v Gibson [1986] 1 EGLR 1, CA 233
Truckell v Stock [1957] 1 All ER 74; [1957] 1 WLR 161; (1957) 101 SJ 108, CA 19
Trust House Forte Albany Hotels Ltd v Daejan Investments Ltd (1980) 256 EG 915 .... 6, 112, 143
Trustees of Smith's (Henry) Charity v AWADA Trading & Promotion Services (1984) 269 EG 729; (1984) 47 P&CR 607; (1984) 269 EG 729, CA. 98, 142

TABLE OF CASES

Tucker v Granada Motorway Services Ltd [1977] 3 All ER 865; [1977] 1 WLR 1411; (1977) 121 SJ 664 77
Tulapam Properties Ltd v De Almeida (1981) 260 EG 919 235
Tunstall v Steigmann [1962] 2 QB 593; [1962] 2 WLR 1045; [1962] 2 All ER 417, CA 258
Twyman v Charrington [1994] 1 EGLR 243 173
UBH (Mechanical Services) Ltd v Standard Life Assurance Co (1986) *The Times*, 13 November 167, 172
United Scientific Holdings Ltd v Burnley Borough Council; Cheapside Land Development Co v Messels Service Co [1978] AC 904; [1977] 2 All ER 62; [1977] 2 WLR 806, HL 9, 10, 60, 96, 104, 143
Upjohn v Hitchens [1918] 2 KB 48; (1918) 87 LJ KB 1205; (1918) 119 LT 108 151
Upsons Ltd v Robins (E) Ltd [1956] 1 QB 131; [1955] 3 WLR 584; [1955] 3 All ER 348, CA 68
Urban Small Space v Burford Investment Co [1990] 2 EGLR 120; [1990] 28 EG 116 140
Vaux Group v Lilley [1991] 1 EGLR 60; [1991] 04 EG 136; (1990) 61 P&CR 446 ... 244, 249
Visionhire v Britel Fund Trustees [1992] 1 EGLR 128 97
VT Engineering Ltd v Richard Barland & Co Ltd (1968) 19 P&CR 890; (1968) 207 EG 347 .... 25, 234
Vural v Security Archives (1990) 60 P&CR 258 .... 154, 156
Waite v Jennings [1906] 2 KB 11, CA 252
Walker Property Investments (Brighton) Ltd v Walker (1947) 177 LT 204, CA 2
Wallington v Townsend [1939] Ch 588; [1939] 2 All ER 235 16
Walmsley and Shaw's Contract, *Re* [1917] 1 Ch 93 .... 8, 23
Walsh v Lonsdale (1882) 21 ChD 9; (1882) 52 LJ Ch 2; (1882) 46 LT 858 164
Walter v Selfe (1851) 4 De G & Sm 315; (1851) 20 LJ Ch 433 227
Wandsworth London Borough Council v Attwell [1996] 01 EG 100 64
Wang v Wei (1975) 119 SJ 492; (1975) *The Times*, 5 July 257
Webb v Bevis (Frank) Ltd [1940] 1 All ER 247 37
Webb v Nightingale (1957) 169 EG 330 15
Webb's Lease, *Re*, Sandom v Webb [1951] Ch 808; (1951) 95 SJ 367; *sub nom Re* Webb, Sandom v Webb [1951] 2 All ER 131 .... 18, 31, 36
Weinbergs Weatherproofs Ltd v Radcliffe Paper Mill Co Ltd [1958] Ch 437; [1958] 2 WLR 1; *sub nom Re* Bleachers' Association's Leases, Weinbergs Weatherproofs v Radcliffe Paper Mill Co [1957] 3 All ER 663 58
Weller v Akehurst [1981] 3 All ER 411; (1981) 42 P&CR 320; (1980) 257 EG 1259 96
West Central Investments Ltd v Borovik (1976) 241 EG 609 10
West Country Cleaners (Falmouth) Ltd v Saly [1966] 3 All ER 210; [1966] 1 WLR 1485; (1966) 119 EG 563, CA 60, 64
West Horndon Industrial Park v Phoenix Timber Group [1995] 1 EGLR 77 266
Westminster City Council v Haymarket Publishing Ltd [1980] 1 All ER 289; [1980] 1 WLR 683; (1979) 40 P&CR 130 219
Westminster (Duke) v Guild. *See* Duke of Westminster v Guild
Wheeler v Mercer [1957] AC 416; [1956] 3 WLR 841; [1956] 3 All ER 631, HL 255
Whelton Sinclair (A Firm) v Hyland [1992] 2 EGLR 158; [1992] 41 EG 112, CA 56
White v Harrow (1902) 86 LT 4; (1902) 18 TLR 228 .... 4, 227
Wig Creations Ltd v Colour Film Services Ltd (1969) 113 SJ 688; (1969) 20 P&CR 870, CA 68
Wiggington & Milner v Winster Engineering [1978] 1 WLR 1462; (1978) 122 SJ 826; [1978] 3 All ER 436, CA 16
William Hill (Southern) Ltd v Cabras Ltd. *See* Hill (William) (Southern) v Cabras
Willmott v London Road Car Co Ltd [1910] 2 Ch 525; (1910) 80 LJ Ch 1; (1910) 103 LT 447 245
Wilson v Whateley (1860) 1 J & H 436 8
Windvale Ltd v Darlington Insulation Co Ltd (1983) *The Times*, 22 December 105
Wingfield (LR) v Clapton Construction & Investment Co Ltd (1967) 201 EG 769 56
Wong v Beaumont Property Trust Ltd [1965] 1 QB 173; [1964] 2 WLR 1325; [1964] 2 All ER 119, CA 6
Woodhouse & Co Ltd v Kirkland (Derby) Ltd [1970] 2 All ER 587; [1970] 1 WLR 1185 ... 26
Woodhouse (Edwin) Trustee Co Ltd v Sheffield Brick Co plc (1983) 270 EG 548 100

TABLE OF CASES

Woollerton & Wilson Ltd v Costain (Richard) Ltd [1970] 1 WLR 411; (1970) 114 SJ 170 .. 20
Woolworth (FW) & Co Ltd v Lambert [1937] Ch 37 4
Wrenbridge Ltd v Harries (Southern Properties) Ltd (1981) 260 EG 1195 103
Wright v Dean [1948] Ch 686; (1948) 92 SJ 393; [1948] 2 All ER 415 67
Wright v Macadam [1949] 2 KB 744; (1949) 93 SJ 646; [1949] 2 All ER 565, CA 40
Wyndham Investments v Motorway Tyres and Accessories [1991] 2 EGLR 114; [1991] 30 EG 65; [1991] EGCS 9, CA 75
Yarmarine (IW), *Re* [1992] BCLC 276; [1992] BCC 28 268
Yorkbrook Investments Ltd v Batten [1985] 2 EGLR 100; (1986) 52 P&CR 51; (1985) 276 EG 493, CA 166, 167
Young v Dalgety plc [1987] 1 EGLR 116; (1986) 130 SJ 985; (1987) 281 EG 427, CA 37, 113
Zetland (Marquess) v Driver [1939] Ch 1; [1938] 2 All ER 158; (1938) 107 LJ Ch 316, CA 227

Table of Statutes

Arbitration Act 1950 105
    s 18(3) 105
    s 27 .... 97, 103, 105
Building Act 1984 204
    s 102 204
Capital Allowances Act 1990
    ss 4, 6, 7, 15 219
Civil Evidence Act 1995 105
Coast Protection Act 1949—
    s 10 73
Companies Act 1985—
    s 736 243
Defective Premises Act 1972
    s 4(4) 195
Disability Discrimination Act 1995 204
    s 16 204
    s 22 237
    s 27 204
Environment Act 1995 211
    s 57 208
Environmental Protection Act 1990 211
    s 35(3) 208
       (4) 204
    s 61 208
    Pt IIA 208
    s 78G 204
Factories Act 1961—
    s 7(1) 32
    s 22(2) 28
    s 28(1) 27, 28
    s 122 32
    s 176(1) 27, 28
Finance Act 1931—
    s 28 53
Fire Precautions Act 1971 .... 204, 207
Fires Prevention (Metropolis) Act 1774—
    s 83 .... 154, 155
General Rate Act 1967—
    s 17A 219
Health and Safety at Work etc Act
    1974 204

Highways Act 1980—
    s 212 73
Housing Act 1988 .... 235, 263
    Sched 1, para 4 218
Income and Corporation Taxes Act 1988
    s 34 206
    s 38 54
    s 349 73
Inheritance Tax Act 1984—
    Chap III 178
Insolvency Act 1986—
    ss 178–182, 315–321 268
Land Registration Act 1925—
    s 8 53
    s 70(1)(*g*) 66
    s 123 54
Landlord and Tenant Act 1927 203
    Pt I (ss 1–17) 202, 206
    s 2(1)(*b*) 206
    s 3(1), (4) 203
    s 16 151
    s 18 196
    s 19 41
       (1) 238, 244
        (*b*) 54, 88
       (1A) 238, 239, 241, 242
       (1C) 239
       (2) 202, 248, 249
       (3) 215
    s 23 63
    s 25 260
Landlord and Tenant Act 1954 ..... 49–51, 58,
    59, 62, 69, 70, 85, 91, 117, 121, 205, 206,
    230, 236, 249, 250, 256, 258–263, 273
    Pt II (ss 23–46) ... 38, 49, 50, 52, 57, 218,
                     232, 250, 254, 255
    s 23(1) 254, 257
       (3) 39
       (4) 259
    s 24 .... 58, 63, 67, 248, 256, 257, 265
       (1) 262

TABLE OF STATUTES

Landlord and Tenant Act 1954—*Contd*
s 24(2) 61
s 24A 49, 50, 94, 121, 248, 256, 257
s 25 .... 48, 49, 52, 57, 58, 61, 67,
248, 256, 257, 262
s 26 .... 58, 61, 67, 248, 256, 257
   (1) 52
   (4) 58, 61
ss 27, 28 .... 67, 248, 256, 257
s 30(1)(*e*) 260
   (*f*) 59, 260
   (*g*) 59, 68, 260
s 31A 39, 59
s 32 262
   (1A) 39
   (2) 39, 262
   (3) 39
s 33 68
s 34 .... 11, 67, 81, 125, 130, 147, 206
   (1) 148
     (*a*), (*b*) 89, 134
     (*c*) 134
   (2) 130, 206
   (3) 66, 147
s 35 .... 179, 230, 265
s 37 .... 52, 53, 57, 261
   (2), (3) 53
s 38(1) 251
   (2), (3) 53, 261
   (4) 51, 256
s 41 .... 232, 258
s 41A 259
s 42 .... 243, 258
s 43(1)(*a*), (*b*) 260
   (2) 257
   (3) 52, 256
     (*a*), (*b*) 256
s 69(1) 61, 232
Landlord and Tenant Act 1987
   s 42 168
Landlord and Tenant Act 1988 .... 236, 245
   s 1(1) 236
     (3)–(5) 246
   s 4 246
Landlord and Tenant (Covenants) Act
   1995 .... 41, 46, 48, 49, 67, 89, 116,
238, 244, 248, 264, 270–272, 274
   s 1 44
   s 2 42
   s 3 42
     (5) 224
   s 5 42
   ss 6–8, 11 43
   s 13(1), (2) 43
   s 16 .... 43, 239, 271
     (2) 13
     (3)(*b*) 43
     (4) 271
     (5) 271, 272

Landlord and Tenant (Covenants) Act
   1995—*contd*
   s 17 43
     (2)–(4), (6) 45
   s 18 .... 44, 202, 216
     (2), (4) 267
   s 19 .... 44, 270
   s 20 44
   s 24(2) 240, 264
   s 25 .... 44, 46, 224
   s 28(1) 42
Landlord and Tenant (Licensed Premises)
   Act 1990 260
Law of Property Act 1922—
   s 145 65
   Sched 15 65
Law of Property Act 1925—
   s 38 22
   s 41 10
   s 44 212
   s 54 52
   ss 58, 61 10
   s 62 .... 24, 39, 40
     (4) 40
   s 84 230
     (12) 54
   s 86(1) 233
   s 87(1) 233
   s 140 267
   s 144 .... 85, 251, 252
   s 146 .... 164, 252, 267
   s 147 197
   s 196 63
     (5) 64
   s 205(1)(xxvii) 51
Law of Property Act 1969 130
Law of Property (Miscellaneous Provisions)
   Act 1989—
   s 2 .... 52, 64, 251
Leasehold Property (Repairs) Act 1938 .. 195
   s 7 53
Local Government (Miscellaneous Provisions) Act 1973—
   s 33 73
London Building Act 1930—
   s 5 22
London Building Acts (Amendment) Act
   1939—
   s 4 22
   Pt VI (ss 44–59) 22
   s 44 22
Offices, Shops and Railway Premises Act
   1963—
   s 9(1) 32
   s 16 27
   s 42(6) 32
   s 43(4) 32
Perpetuities and Accumulations Act 1964—
   s 1 .... 37, 177

Race Relations Act 1976—
  s 24 237
Rent Act 1977 263
Restrictive Trade Practices Act 1956 224
Sex Discrimination Act 1975—
  s 31 237
Sexual Offences Act 1956—
  s 35(2) 225
  Sched 1 225
Stamp Act 1891—
  Sched 1 .... 53, 54
Sunday Trading Act 1994 219
Supply of Goods and Services Act 1982—
  ss 13, 15 173
Taxation of Chargeable Gains Act 1992—
  s 154(7) 54
  Sched 8, para 1 54
Telecommunications Act 1984—
  s 96 .... 33, 204

Telecommunications Act 1984—*contd*
  Sched 2 33
Town and Country Planning Act 1990 ... 131,
                                        211, 213, 215, 216
  s 72(1)(*b*) 213
  s 106 213
  s 168 52
  s 172(4) 213
  s 179(1) 213
  s 191(2) 214
  s 192 214
  s 336(1) 213
Value Added Tax Act 1994
  s 89(2) 72
  s 96(1) 54
Water Industry Act 1991 211
Water Resources Act 1991 .... 208, 211

Table of Statutory Instruments

Collection and Disposal of Waste Regulations 1988 (SI No 819)—
  reg 9 208
  Sched 6, para 14 208
Controlled Waste Regulations 1992 (SI No 588)—
  reg 9 208
Land Registration Rules 1925 (SI No 1093)—
  r 54 15
Offices, Shops and Railway Premises (Hoists and Lifts) Regulations 1968 (SI No 849) 28
  reg 6(1) 28
Rating Surcharge (Suspension) Order 1980 (SI No 2015) 219
Supply of Beer (Tied Estate) Order 1989 (SI No 2390) 226
  arts 5, 6 226
Town and Country Planning (Control of Advertisements) Regulations (SI No 666) 31
Town and Country Planning (Use Classes) Order 1972 (SI No 1385) 11
Town and Country Planning (Use Classes) Order 1987 (SI No 764) 11, 221
  Class B1, B2, B8 135
Workplace (Health, Safety and Welfare) Regulations 1992 (SI No 3004)—
  regs 17, 18 27
  reg 20 32

EC Legislation

EC Treaty (25 March 1957)—
  art 85 226
Commission Reg 1984/83—
  recital (13) 226

1

The Interpretation of Leases

A lease of business property is a commercial contract. It must, therefore, be drafted and perused against the background of the principles developed by the courts for construing commercial contracts. The most important of these principles are briefly set out below. A fuller treatment of the principles applicable to the interpretation of contracts may be found in *The Interpretation of Contracts* (Sweet and Maxwell, 1989) by the author.

1 Intention of the Parties

The object sought to be achieved in construing any commercial contract is to ascertain what the mutual intentions of the parties were as to the legal obligations each assumed by the contractual words in which they chose to express them (*Pioneer Shipping Ltd v BTP Tioxide Ltd* [1982] AC 724). When one speaks of the intention of the parties to the contract one is speaking objectively—the parties cannot themselves give direct evidence of what their intention was. What must be ascertained is the intention that a reasonable person would have had if placed in the situation of the parties. What the court must do is place itself in thought in the same factual matrix as that of the parties (*Reardon Smith Line Ltd v Hansen-Tangen* [1976] 1 WLR 989).

Thus, in construing a written agreement the court is entitled to take account of surrounding circumstances (with reference to which the words of the agreement were used) and the object appearing from those circumstances that the person had in view; but the court may not look at the prior negotiations of the parties as an aid to construction of the written contract resulting from those negotiations (*Prenn v Simmonds* [1971] 1 WLR 1381).

For example, the standard of repair required by a covenant to keep property in repair will be determined by reference to the age, character and locality of the demised property at the time of the demise (*Proudfoot v Hart* (1890) 25 QBD 42). So also the size of the property may be relevant to the interpretation of the use covenant (*Basildon Development Corporation v Mactro Ltd* [1986] 1 EGLR 137 *per* O'Connor LJ), as is its physical layout (*Levermore v Jobey* [1956] 1 WLR 697). Equally, in construing a rent review clause, the court has been aided by a consideration of valuation methods which the parties must have envisaged would be applied at the review date (*Pivot Properties v Secretary of State for the Environment* (1980) 41 P&CR 248). Where the extent of the demise is ambiguous or lacks definition, oral evidence will be admitted to identify it (*Bisney v Swanston* (1972) 225 EG 229). An ambiguity in an executed lease may be resolved by a consideration of an agreement for lease, and a draft annexed to it, pursuant to which the lease was granted (*Ladbroke Group plc v Bristol City Council* [1988] 1 EGLR 126).

In general, however, the intention of the parties is to be ascertained from the words of the lease itself and oral evidence will not be admitted to vary or contradict the written document. Thus, where a covenant in a lease provided for the payment of rent in advance, the tenant was not entitled to prove an antecedent oral agreement under which he was to pay by way of bill of exchange maturing some time after tender (*Henderson v Arthur* [1907] 1 KB 10). There are some exceptions to the rigours of this rule: an oral agreement was allowed to be proved where it formed one comprehensive contract with the written lease (*Walker Property Investments (Brighton) Ltd v Walker* (1947) 177 LT 204); and a tenant in breach of the user covenant in his written lease was allowed to prove an antecedent oral collateral contract permitting the breach complained of (*City and Westminster Properties (1934) Ltd v Mudd* [1959] Ch 129).

Nevertheless, the aim of the draftsman must always be to ensure that the lease as executed represents the full intention of the parties. The parties cannot, however, by an express statement of intention alter the legal consequences of their bargain. Thus an express term that a transaction is not intended to be a lease but is intended to be a licence will not be given effect (*Street v Mountford* [1985] AC 809). Similarly, where a clause in a written agreement states that exclusive possession is not granted to the occupier, the clause will not be taken into account in deciding whether a licence or a tenancy is created (*Family Housing Association v Jones* [1990] 1 WLR 779).

2 Ordinary and Technical Words

Where there is nothing to show that the parties have used language in any other than its strict and ordinary sense, and where the words interpreted in that sense are sensible with reference to extrinsic circumstances, it is an inflexible rule of construction that the words shall be interpreted in that strict and primary sense even though they may be capable of some popular or secondary interpretation and even though the most conclusive evidence of the intention to use them in such popular sense is tendered (*Enlayde Ltd v Roberts* [1917] 1 Ch 109: obligation to reinstate property destroyed by fire included an obligation to reinstate where the destruction was caused by incendiary bombs). If the parties wish to give an ordinary word some special meaning, an express definition clause should be included. Where a definition in a lease states that a defined term 'includes' a particular meaning, the term may also be construed in its ordinary sense, even if that sense is not within the definition (*Adelphi (Estates) v Christie* (1984) 269 EG 221).

Technical words will be construed in a technical sense. Many words and phrases commonly found in leases are terms of art—for example, 'the usual quarter days'. These will be given the meaning they bear among lawyers. In some cases evidence may be admitted to show that a word is used in a technical or local meaning. An odd example of the rule is provided by an old case in which it was proved that 1,000 rabbits meant 1,200 rabbits (*Smith v Wilson* (1832) 3 B & Ad 728). A more modern example is 'prime position' as applied to a shop (*Ashburn Anstalt v Arnold* [1989] Ch 1). Even the meaning of a word such as 'supermarket' may be proved by oral evidence (*Calabar (Woolwich) Ltd v Tesco Stores Ltd* (1977) 245 EG 479). Where a word used in a lease has multiple meanings, one of which is its ordinary meaning and the other of which is some technical meaning, there must be some objective evidence that the parties intended the technical meaning to be adopted, otherwise the word will be construed in its ordinary sense (*Holt & Co v Collyer* (1881) 16 ChD 719).

3 Lease Construed as a Whole

The court must take into consideration the whole of the lease and the purposes for which it was granted, and then see what is the proper construction of a particular covenant (*Bickmore v Dimmer* [1903] 1 Ch 158). The draftsman must, therefore, express himself consistently throughout the lease, for a word used in one part of the lease will probably be construed as having the same meaning if used in another part of the same document. Thus, where the draftsman used the phrase 'adjoining premises' in one part of the lease and the phrase 'adjoining or neighbouring premises' in another part of it, it was held that the former phrase only applied to property that came into physical contact with the demised property because the words 'or neighbouring' must have added something to the word 'adjoining' (*White v Harrow* (1902) 86 LT 4). The danger of inconsistency is most pronounced where the draftsman takes parts of his draft from different precedents.

Where there is an apparent inconsistency, the court will do its best to resolve it. Thus where there was a covenant against alterations without the landlord's consent, and an absolute covenant against the making of waste, spoil or destruction, the covenant against waste was interpreted as not applying to anything covered by the qualified covenant against alterations (*FW Woolworth v Lambert* [1937] Ch 37).

If there is an inconsistency between lease and counterpart *prima facie* the lease prevails. However, where there is an ambiguity on the face of the lease it is permissible to look at the counterpart to explain it. Thus, a proviso for re-entry on breach of the 'covenant' contained in the lease was construed as extending to all covenants in the lease (*Matthews v Smallwood* [1910] 1 Ch 777).

4 CLEAR WORDS

In some cases, the court applies a particularly exacting standard to the interpretation of a clause. Instead of simply interpreting the clause it requires clear words to be used before it will interpret a clause as having a particular effect. Thus where a lease required the tenant to pay rent 'without deduction', it was held that clear words were necessary in order to exclude the tenant's remedy of equitable set-off, and that the words 'without deduction' were not clear enough (*Connaught Restaurants Ltd v Indoor Leisure Ltd* [1994] 1 WLR 501). Similarly, where landlords sought to argue that various forms of rent review clause entitled them to receive a 'headline rent' on review it was held that only the most unambiguous of clauses would be interpreted as having that effect (*Co-operative Wholesale Society Ltd v National Westminster Bank plc* [1995] 1 EGLR 97). It is by no means clear in what circumstances this principle will apply, but it seems to emerge whenever the court would otherwise be forced to an interpretation which it considers is unfair.

5 Construction against Grantor

It is a well-known maxim of construction that in case of ambiguity a contract is construed *contra proferentem*. In the case of a lease this will usually mean that the ambiguity will be construed against the landlord (*Killick v Second Covent Garden Property Co Ltd* [1973] 2 All ER 337, although in *Amax International Ltd v Custodian Holdings Ltd* [1986] 2 EGLR 111, Hoffmann J suggested that, technically, the tenant might be the *proferens*). The landlord is usually the party who settles the form of the lease (albeit it may be amended many times before execution) and most of the covenants are inserted for his protection. He will, therefore, usually be the *proferens*. But this does not mean that a dispute about the interpretation of the lease must be decided against the landlord if it possibly can be. Thus where the issue is the width of the use covenant, the application of the *contra proferentem* rule points towards greater freedom of use on the part of the tenant rather than narrower, even if the tenant is arguing for a narrower use so as to secure a benefit on rent review (*Skillion v Keltec Industrial Research* [1992] 1 EGLR 123). However, some parts of the lease will be construed against the tenant, since by a legal fiction he may be treated as a grantor. This is seen at its most capricious in the case of exceptions and reservations. It is a settled rule of construction that where there is a grant and an exception out of it the exception is taken as inserted for the benefit of the grantor and is to be construed in favour of the grantee (*Savill Brothers Ltd v Bethell* [1902] 2 Ch 523). In the case of an exception the grantor will be the landlord and the grantee will be the tenant. However, where the lease contains a reservation in favour of the landlord it is construed as if the right reserved had been granted to the landlord by the tenant. Any ambiguity will be construed against the tenant (*St Edmundsbury & Ipswich Diocesan Board of Finance v Clark (No 2)* [1975] 1 All ER 772).

A covenant by a surety will be construed strictly against the principal creditor (*Eastern Counties Building Society v Russell* [1947] 2 All ER 724).

6 Implied Terms

Certain terms will be implied in a lease by operation of law, although many such terms may be excluded by agreement. Thus, the use of the word 'demise' will give rise to two implied covenants on the part of the landlord: namely, that he is entitled to grant some term in the demised property and that the tenant shall have quiet enjoyment of the demised property. However, there is no room for the implication of the covenant in a demise if the landlord enters into an express covenant for quiet enjoyment (and gives no covenant for title). The reason for this is that an express covenant as to one branch of the covenant implied by the word 'demise' excludes the other branch on the principle that *expressio unius est exclusio alterius* (the expression of one thing is the exclusion of another) (*Miller v Emcer Products Ltd* [1956] Ch 304). The court is, however, reluctant to find implied terms in commercial contracts especially where there is a formal document which, on the face of it, represents the apparently complete bargain between the parties (*Westminster (Duke) v Guild* [1985] QB 688). An unexpressed term can be implied if and only if the court finds that the parties must have intended that term to form part of their contract: it is not enough for the court to find that such a term would have been adopted by the parties as reasonable men if it had been suggested to them. It must have been a term that went without saying, a term necessary to give business efficacy to the contract, a term that, although tacit, formed part of the contract the parties made for themselves (*Trollope & Colls Ltd v North West Metropolitan Regional Hospital Board* [1973] 1 WLR 601). Thus, the court has refused to imply a term that a landlord entitled to recover the cost of insurance from his tenant is obliged to choose the cheapest method of insuring (*Bandar Property Holdings Ltd v Darwen (JS) (Successors) Ltd* [1968] 2 All ER 305) or that the tenant is under an obligation not to use the demised property for an immoral purpose (*Burfort Financial Investments Ltd v Chotard* (1976) 239 EG 891) or that the landlord is entitled to interest on a retrospective increase in rent (*Trust House Forte Albany Hotels Ltd v Daejan Investments Ltd* (1980) 256 EG 915).

However, the court will readily imply the grant of such easements as may be necessary to give effect to the common intention of the parties with reference to the manner and purposes for which the demised property is to be used. It is essential for this purpose that the parties intend that the demised property should be used in some definite and particular manner. It is not enough that the property should be intended to be used in a manner that may or may not involve this definite and particular manner (*Pwllbach Colliery Co Ltd v Woodman* [1915] AC 634). Thus, where a tenant covenanted to use a basement as a restaurant, not to cause any nuisance, to control and eliminate all smells and to comply with Food Hygiene Regulations, he was entitled to an easement to erect a ventilation duct on his landlord's wall (*Wong v Beaumont Property Trust Ltd* [1965] 1 QB 173).

Certain other terms are implied into leases by virtue of statute and these are dealt with in their respective contexts. In some cases a term implied by statute may not be excluded by agreement.

7 Principles of Construction

(a) Expressio unius est exclusio alterius

This principle of construction has already been touched on. Its basic principle is: where one specific thing is mentioned but another is not, that other thing is taken to have been deliberately not mentioned. Where, for example, a tenant covenants 'to keep in repair the demised property and the windows, window frames, boilers and air-conditioning plant' it might be successfully argued on his behalf that he is not liable to repair the doors because they were not mentioned in the catalogue. Thus, the draftsman should be especially careful before embarking on a long list of matters that fall within a particular covenant. However, this principle is of little weight where it produces an unfair and unreasonable result (*Basingstoke and Deane BC v Host Group* [1988] 1 WLR 348).

Similarly, where an agreement specifies the time for doing three things (eg, taking procedural steps towards a rent review) and two of the three are stated to have a time limit which is of the essence of the contract and the other one does not, then it follows that, in all probability, where it is not stated to be of the essence, it is not intended to be of the essence. If the parties, when they wish something to be made of the essence, say so in terms, then obviously it is of the essence if they do say so, and the probability is, that where they do not say so, it is not intended to be of the essence (*Amherst v Walker (James) Goldsmith & Silversmith Ltd* (1980) 254 EG 123).

(b) Express terms negative implied terms

An express term in a lease generally excludes the possibility of the implication of a term dealing with the same subject matter as the implied term. Thus, where a lease contained a covenant to build certain buildings by a specified date and an obligation to keep them in repair, it was held that once the tenant had failed to build the buildings on time, no further covenant to build could be implied from the covenant to repair (*Stephens v Junior Army and Navy Stores* [1914] 2 Ch 516).

(c) Eiusdem generis

The *eiusdem generis* rule is an important principle of construction. If one can find that the things described by particular words have some common characteristic one ought to limit the general words that follow them to things of that genus (*Lambourn v McLellan* [1903] 2 Ch 268). Thus, where there was a contract for the sale of land and 'buildings material etc' it was held that the word 'etc' referred to 'material' and did not embrace a right of way (*Re Walmsley and Shaw's Contract* [1917] 1 Ch 93). Similarly, a power entitling a landlord to re-enter for 'building sites or planting or other purposes' did not entitle him to re-enter in order to build a sports stadium (*Coates v Diment* [1951] 1 All ER 890).

The rule usually applies where a genus can be found. For example, where a tenant covenanted to yield up certain articles together with 'all doors, wainscots, shelves, presses, dressers, drawers, locks, keys, bolts, bars, staples, hinges, hearths, chimney pieces, mantelpieces, chimney-jambs, floor-pans, slabs, covings, window-shutters, partitions, sinks, water-closets, cisterns, pumps, and rails and water-tanks and other additions, improvements, fixtures and things' it was held that there was no discernible genus which restricted the general words (*Wilson v Whateley* (1860) 1 J & H 436). It is, therefore, possible by sheer verbosity to defeat the operation of the rule; but this is hardly a method to be recommended. However, the absence of a genus does not of itself preclude the operation of the rule: it is an indication that the parties did not intend the general words to be restricted (*Chandris v Isbrandtsen-Moller* [1951] 1 KB 240; *Skillion v Keltec Industrial Research* [1992] 1 EGLR 123). One method of avoiding the operation of the rule is to reverse the order of the two parts of the clause so that the general words are placed first and the list of specific items are prefaced by a phrase like 'for example', or 'without prejudice to the generality of the foregoing', or 'such as'.

(d) Party not to take advantage of his own wrong

A lease will be construed so far as possible so as not to permit a party to it to take advantage of his own wrong. Thus the tenant will not be permitted to rely on his own breach of his repairing obligations in order to depress the rent payable on review (*Harmsworth Pension Funds Trustees v Charringtons Industrial Holdings* (1985) 49 P&CR 297), and a surety who had guaranteed the obligations of a tenant was not allowed to rely on the tenant's failure to register an assignment with the landlord in order to escape liability under his surety covenant (*Cerium Investments v Evans* (1991) 62 P&CR 203).

8 UNCERTAINTY

The court is always reluctant to find a provision void for uncertainty, particularly where the provision is contained in a commercial agreement. 'No doubt there may be cases in which the draftsman's ineptitude will succeed in defeating the court's efforts to find a meaning for the provision in question; but only if the court is driven to it will it find a provision is void for uncertainty' (*Brown v Gould* [1972] Ch 53 *per* Megarry J). A provision will be void for uncertainty where there is real conceptual uncertainty—or example an option to renew 'at a rent to be agreed' where there was no indication of how the rent was to be agreed, not on what basis, not what was to happen if the parties failed to agree (*King's Motors (Oxford) v Lax* [1970] 1 WLR 426). But even in such a case, the court may be able to give contractual effect to the stipulation by implying a term to the effect that the rent must be a reasonable rent (*Corson v Rhuddlan Borough Council* [1990] 1 EGLR 255).

Where the difficulty is one of applying the provision rather than a conceptual uncertainty the court will not hold it to be void (*Brown v Gould*); and a provision in a lease will not be uncertain if it can be made certain. Thus, a lease which contains a rent review clause will not be uncertain merely because the amount of the rent is not known at the date of the lease. To attract the remedy of distress, however, the rent must be certain at the time it falls due (*United Scientific Holdings Ltd v Burnley BC* [1978] AC 904).

The principle is different in relation to the term for which a lease is granted. A term created by a lease must be expressed either with certainty and specifically or by reference to something that can at the time the lease takes effect be looked to as a certain ascertainment of what the term is meant to be (*Lace v Chantler* [1944] KB 368: lease 'for the duration of the war' was void for uncertainty). Thus a tenancy granted until the land was required for road widening was void for uncertainty (*Prudential Assurance Co v London Residuary Body* [1992] 2 AC 386). If the draftsman wishes to create a lease for a period that cannot be made certain at the time of the demise the only way is to express it as being granted for a fixed term subject to a power to break at the expiry of the period.

9 Prima Facie Assumptions

Sometimes the court lays down a *prima facie* assumption applicable to a certain kind of provision (eg the rule that time is not of the essence of a rent review timetable). These rules are very important, because they bring consistency to the interpretation of leases and enable parties buying and selling leases and reversions to obtain more reliable advice on what their rights and liabilities are likely to be. Thus the court will not fritter away the *prima facie* assumption on small differences in drafting (*Laura Investments v Havering LBC* [1992] 1 EGLR 155).

10 Statutory Rules of Construction

In a number of cases statute has intervened. Thus, in all leases granted after 1925 unless the context otherwise requires:
    (1) 'month' means calendar month;
    (2) 'person' includes a corporation;
    (3) the singular includes the plural and *vice versa*;
    (4) the masculine includes the feminine and *vice versa* (Law of Property Act 1925, s 61).

Many leases repeat these definitions although it is unnecessary to do so. Where a definition is qualified by a phrase like 'unless the context otherwise requires', the context may displace the defined term (for an example in an insurance policy, see *Deutsche Genossenschaft Bank v Burnhope* [1995] 4 All ER 717).

Similarly, an instrument that is expressed to be 'supplemental' to a previous instrument is construed as if the supplemental instrument contained a full recital of the previous instrument (Law of Property Act 1925, s 58). In construing the supplemental instrument the whole of the previous instrument may be looked at (*Plumrose Ltd v Real and Leasehold Estates Investment Society Ltd* [1970] 1 WLR 52).

Stipulations in a contract, as to time or otherwise, which according to rules of equity are not deemed to be of the essence of the contract, are construed at law in accordance with the same rules (Law of Property Act 1925, s 41). After a flurry of litigation it is now settled that stipulations as to time in a rent review clause are *prima facie* not of the essence (*United Scientific Holdings Ltd v Burnley BC* [1978] AC 904); nor is an obligation to prepare service charge accounts (*West Central Investments Ltd v Borovik* (1977) 241 EG 609). However, it is not certain how far this rule of construction extends. Would it, for example, apply to a covenant to redecorate the demised property in the seventh year of the term? It is suggested that if the timetable is important (as for example, a development timetable in a building lease) the draftsman should provide expressly that time is to be of the essence.

Sometimes a lease incorporates parts of a statute by reference (eg the 'disregards' in s 34 of the Landlord and Tenant Act 1954). It is important for the draftsman to make clear whether amendments to the statute are also incorporated (cf *Brett v Brett Essex Golf Club Ltd* [1986] 1 EGLR 154). Moreover, part of a statute incorporated by reference will be construed in accordance with the ordinary canons of construction as applied to the lease, not necessarily in accordance with the way the statute itself is construed (*ibid*).

Where a lease defines something by reference to a statute or statutory instruments (eg the Town and Country Planning (Use Classes) Order), a change in the statute or statutory instrument will not alter the terms of the lease (*Brewers Co v Viewplan* [1989] 2 EGLR 133).

11 Date for Applying Rules of Construction

Prima facie the rules of construction must be applied as at the date of execution of the lease: thus a word will be interpreted in the sense it bore at the time (*Texaco Antilles Ltd v Kernochan* [1973] AC 609: the phrase 'public garage' was given the meaning it bore in 1933 and not the one it bore at the date of the litigation; *St Marylebone Property Co Ltd v Tesco Stores Ltd* [1988] 2 EGLR 40 construing the word 'grocer'). The same principle probably applies where the lease refers to an Act of Parliament or statutory instruments by name. Thus, where the user covenant permits the tenant to use the demised property for any purpose falling within a class of the Town and Country Planning (Use Classes) Order 1972 (SI No 1385) the covenant will be construed as referring to the use class as it existed at the date of the demise. Thus a covenant in that form will not allow the tenant to take advantage of the much greater flexibility of use permitted by the Town and Country Planning (Use Classes) Order 1987 (SI No 764) (*Brewers Co v Viewplan* above). The same would be the case if the 1987 Order were to be amended. In order to avoid this result the draftsman should define a reference to an Act of Parliament etc as including a reference to that Act etc as amended or re-enacted from time to time.

Equally, the standard of repair demanded by a covenant to keep the demised property in repair will be determined by reference to the age, character and locality of the property at the date of the demise. If the locality deteriorates during the term the standard of repair required will not (*Anstruther-Gough-Calthorpe v McOscar* [1924] 1 KB 716).

12 MAKING IT WORK

All the above rules of construction will yield to the overriding importance of making the lease work. If detailed semantic and syntactical analysis of words in a commercial contract is going to lead to a conclusion that flouts business common sense, it must be made to yield to business common sense (*The Antaios* [1985] AC 191). Thus the court has modified a use covenant in a lease for the purposes of a rent review (*The Law Land Company Ltd v Consumers' Association Ltd* (1980) 255 EG 617, in which Brightman LJ recognised that some modification had to be made to the strict wording of the rent review clause if it was to work. He justified that approach on the basis that 'the lease is a commercial document and we have to find a commercial solution to the problem posed'). Similarly, the court has implied the grant of a right of way, solely for the purpose of a rent review, in order that the rent review clause should have a practical effect (*Jefferies v O'Neill* (1983) 269 EG 131) and has enlarged a definition of 'lessor' in a lease in order to give effect to a general scheme for the maintenance of a building and the recovery of a service charge (*Adelphi (Estates) Ltd v Christie* (1984) 269 EG 221). The development of this approach to commercial documents is in its infancy, but it may well lead to greater judicial activity in shaping the mutual obligations of the parties. At its most extreme, it may result in the court rewriting the terms of a lease in order to do what is fair and reasonable between the parties in circumstances which they did not foresee at the date of the lease (*Pole Properties Ltd v Feinberg* (1981) 259 EG 417).

13 PRACTICALITIES

'A lease is not intended to be either a mental exercise or an essay in literature; it is a practical document dealing with a practical situation' (*Levermore v Jobey* [1956] 2 All ER 362 *per* Dankwerts LJ at 370). For this reason, in drafting a lease the draftsman should constantly have in mind the nature of the demised property. A long lease of a large property acquired for investment may well require far different treatment

THE INTERPRETATION OF LEASES

from a lease of second rate property let to a small businessman at a rack rent. Many of the burdensome covenants inserted in the former kind of lease will be wholly inappropriate to the latter. Although the draftsman may never see the lease again once it has been executed, others will have to live with it and try to manage the property according to its terms. An over-sophisticated document may make that task far more difficult than it need be.

This approach is reflected in the forms in the Appendix. Although some of them have been drafted in an 'institutional' style, others have been deliberately kept simple. The simpler forms are designed for less prestigious or valuable property. The essential point is that the draftsman always has the choice.

Example 1:1 Definitions clause for business lease

(1) The following definitions apply:

'Act' means an Act of Parliament whenever passed and a reference to a specific Act includes any legislation amending or replacing it or made under it

'Approved' means approved in writing by the Landlord

'Authorised guarantee agreement' means an agreement authorised by section 16(2) of the Landlord and Tenant (Covenants) Act 1995

'Consent' means the Landlord's written consent

'Insured Risks' means the risks covered by the policy of insurance arranged by the Landlord to include (subject to cover being available on reasonable terms) loss or damage by fire storm tempest flood earthquake aircraft and articles dropped from them riot or civil commotion malicious damage impact bursting and overflowing of pipes tanks and other apparatus and any other risks insured against by the Landlord

'Landlord' includes the successors in title of the original landlord and where there is a superior landlord includes him as well

'Last Year' means the period of twelve months ending on the Termination of the Term

'Legislation' means any regulation or directive of the European Union, any Act and any subordinate legislation made under or by virtue of them

'Notice' means written notice

'President' means the President for the time being of the Royal Institution of Chartered Surveyors or a person acting on his behalf

'Tenant' includes the successors in title of the original tenant

'Term' includes both the term expressly granted by this Lease and also any statutory continuation of it

'Termination of the Term' includes termination by effluxion of time, notice, forfeiture, surrender, disclaimer or any other means

(2) Where a party consists of two or more persons the obligations

of that party are joint and several

(3) Any covenant by the tenant not to do something includes a covenant not to permit or suffer that thing to be done

(4) All payments to be made by the tenant are exclusive of value added tax

2
Description of Property

1 The Use of Plans

Where the demised property is clearly bounded there is no need for a plan to be included in the lease. In other cases a plan is desirable, provided that the plan is drawn on sufficiently large a scale not to be merely confusing. If the lease is to be registered at HM Land Registry and the demised property is part only of a building, then unless the land can be accurately identified on the General Map a plan must be provided (Land Registration Rules 1925, r 54).

In every case the draftsman should consider whether the plan is to prevail over the verbal description or *vice versa*. On this decision will depend the phrase by which the plan is referred to in the parcels clause itself. If the plan is small scale or consists of an extract of the Ordnance Survey map it is suggested that the verbal description should prevail. In the former case the plan is unlikely to provide sufficient information to enable the boundaries to be accurately ascertained, while in the latter case the plan will reflect features on the ground rather than boundaries between different owners. It is absolutely essential that each parcel should be described with such particularity and precision that there is no room for doubt about the boundaries of each, and for such purposes if a plan is intended to control the description of part only of a building, an Ordnance map on a scale of 1:2500 is worse than useless (*Scarfe v Adams* [1981] 1 All ER 843).

The following phrases will prevent the plan from prevailing over the verbal description:
 'for the purpose of identification only'
 'for the purpose of facilitating identification only'
 'only for the purposes of identification'
(*Hopgood v Brown* [1955] 1 WLR 213; *Webb v Nightingale* (1957) 169

EG 330). On the other hand the following phrases will prevent the verbal description from prevailing over the plan:
'more particularly delineated'
'more particularly described'
'more precisely delineated'
(*Eastwood v Ashton* [1915] AC 900; *Wallington v Townsend* [1939] Ch 588).

A middle course may be achieved by the phrase: 'for the purpose of delineation only', which has been held to mean that the plan must not be taken to be drawn to scale but the lines are correct diagrammatically (*Re Freeman and Taylor's Contract* (1907) 97 LT 39).

Where the plan is subordinate to the verbal description it may be referred to in order to elucidate boundaries, so long as it does not conflict with anything explicit in the verbal description (*Wiggington & Milner v Winster Engineering* [1978] 1 WLR 1462).

2 Forms of Plan

There is no implied warranty that a plan used in a lease is accurate (*Re Sparrow and James' Contract* [1910] 2 Ch 60). Nevertheless, an inaccurate plan that prevails over the verbal description may have the same effect as a verbal misdescription. The landlord may also owe the tenant a duty of care as regards the preparation of accurate plans (see Tromans, *Commercial Leases* (Sweet & Maxwell, 1987) p 18). Accordingly, the draftsman should so far as possible ensure that the plan is accurate.

The lease plan is often based on an extract from the Ordnance map. The Ordnance map may well show the boundary of the parcel as the centre line of any boundary feature, irrespective of its legal ownership (see *Fisher v Winch* [1939] 1 KB 666). Judicial notice is taken of this practice (*Davey v Harrow Corporation* [1958] 1 QB 60). Accordingly, where the parcels are described simply by references to the Ordnance map (either by specifying the numbers of the enclosures or by a plan that prevails over a verbal description) the parcels will be taken to be those shown on the Ordnance map (*Fisher v Winch* above). The tenant may, therefore, find that his demise does not include the whole of a boundary feature, contrary to the intention of the parties. This problem can usually be resolved by the standard preliminary inquiries. Where the Ordnance map is used as the basis of the lease plan the draftsman should ensure that the edition he has used is clearly specified in the lease. A problem that arises from time to time is that a new edition of the Ordnance map is published with altered enclosured numbers and often altered enclosures.

A plan usually shows the boundaries of the property in question at ground level (or floor level). Where the demised property is an entire building with curtilage this will usually be sufficient. Where the property is part only of a building the draftsman should also consider whether some further visual description is necessary. Although the use of vertical elevations or sectional drawings is rare in leases there is no reason why they should not be used; and where the property overhangs or interlocks with another property they may be the only practical or readily comprehensible way of describing it. The same problem may also arise where the demised property is to include some projection. Developments in modern technology may make it possible for three dimensional models of the property to be stored on computer.

When construing a plan an objective approach must be assumed, namely that a plan is addressed to a lay reader and is to be construed by the ordinary reasonable observer. It must not be construed in isolation, but in context, including replies to inquiries before contract and the surrounding circumstances. The question is: what would the reasonable layman think he was buying? (*Toplis v Green* [1992] EGCS 20)

3 BOUNDARIES

(a) Hedges and ditches

Prima facie the boundary runs along the edge of the ditch away from the hedge. The rationale behind this presumption is that the ditch digger is assumed to have dug the ditch at the extremity of his own land and then to have thrown the spoil onto his own land to make a bank on which the hedge is planted (*Fisher v Winch* [1939] 1 KB 666).

(b) Roads

Prima facie a lease of land adjoining a road operates to pass one half in width of the road, even where the road is a private one (*Lang v House* (1961) 178 EG 801). The presumption probably only operates where the conveyancing history of the land is unknown, and may not operate at all where the land in question is part of a building estate (*Giles v County Building Constructors (Hertford) Ltd* (1971) 22 P&CR 978). In any event the presumption is rebuttable and will be fairly easily rebutted where a developer needs to retain ownership of the road in order to build it or to dedicate it as a public highway. There is no similar presumption in relation to land bounded by a railway (*Thompson v Hickman* [1907] 1 Ch 550).

(c) External wall

In the case of a demise of one floor of a building, or of a room on any floor that is bounded or enclosed on one or more sides by an outside wall, unless the outside wall is excepted or reserved, or there is some context which leads to the contrary conclusion, *prima facie* the premises demised comprise both sides of the outside wall (*Hope Brothers Ltd v Cowan* [1913] 2 Ch 312 *per* Joyce J; *Goldfoot v Welch* [1914] 1 Ch 213; *Sturge v Hackett* [1962] 3 All ER 166). If such walls are not excepted, the landlord may, for example, be restrained from maintaining an advertisement on the walls enclosing the demise (*Re Webb's Lease* [1951] Ch 808).

(d) Horizontal divisions

There are no clear presumptions relating to horizontal divisions between individually let parts of buildings. It is, however, established that the demise of one floor of a building extends at least as far as the underside of the joists supporting the floor above it (*Sturge v Hackett* above). The ordinary expectation is that the tenant will be entitled to occupy all that space between the floor of his demise and the underside of the floor above, unless there are cogent reasons to assume otherwise (*Graystone Property Investments Ltd v Margulies* (1983) 269 EG 538). So the demise of a flat or a particular floor of a building will include a roof space accessible only from that flat where there is no reservation to the landlord of any rights relating to the roof space (*Hatfield v Moss* [1988] 2 EGLR 58). However, a demise of a 'suite of rooms' on the top floor of a building will not include the common roof (*Cockburn v Smith* [1924] 2 KB 119). Equally, it has been said that half the ceiling structure and half the floor structure is included in a lease of the space between them (*Phelps v City of London Corporation* [1916] 2 Ch 255). The position is different where the demise is freestanding or is a building in a terrace. In such a case the roof and the airspace above it will normally be included in the demise (*Straudley Investments Ltd v Barpress Ltd* [1987] 1 EGLR 69; *Tennant Radiant Heat Ltd v Warrington Development Corporation* [1988] 1 EGLR 41). If the precise boundaries of the demised property are of importance (as where the tenant covenants to keep 'the demised property' in repair) the draftsman should make express provision for horizontal divisions. Where the property is air-conditioned, consideration should be given to the question whether the air-conditioning units should be included or excluded from the demise. Many landlords prefer to retain air-handling units within their control, so that the air-conditioning system may be dealt with as an integrated whole.

(e) Projections

Prima facie an external feature (whether ornamental or not) fixed to an external wall enclosing the demise will itself be part of the demised property (*Sturge v Hackett* above). Likewise, where the footings on eaves of a building project beyond the edge of an external wall they will be included in the demised property, although the column of air between them will not (*Truckell v Stock* [1957] 1 All ER 74).

(f) Airspace and underground

It is a fundamental proposition that in the absence of indications to the contrary a conveyance of land includes not only everything on the surface but everything beneath it down to the centre of the earth and the space directly above (*Grigsby v Melville* [1974] 1 WLR 80). Thus, a conveyance of land may include a cellar below ground level that can only be reached from an adjoining shop (*ibid*). Similarly, part of a room that projected above ground level into the property conveyed has been held to pass in the conveyance (*Laybourn v Gridley* [1892] 2 Ch 53).

Nowadays different considerations affect airspace. It appears that the rights of an owner of land in the airspace above his land extend only to such height as is necessary for the ordinary use and enjoyment of the land and any structure upon it (*Bernstein of Leigh (Baron) v Skyviews & General Ltd* [1978] QB 479). Nevertheless, in the absence of a reservation the landlord may find that he is unable to display advertisements on his adjoining property or that he is unable to redevelop adjoining property economically if those activities would involve a trespass to his tenant's airspace (*Kelsen v Imperial Tobacco Co Ltd* [1957] 2 QB 334;

Woollerton & Wilson Ltd v Costain (Richard) Ltd [1970] 1 WLR 411).

A lease of the top floor of a building which includes the roof may well carry with it the airspace over the building, thereby entitling the tenant to enlarge the premises into the airspace (*Davies v Yadegar* [1990] 1 EGLR 71; *Haines v Florensa* [1990] 1 EGLR 73).

Where the demise includes the whole of a building (or the top floor) the draftsman may therefore wish to consider whether the airspace above the building should be excluded from the demise. The advantage of so doing, from the landlord's point of view, is that the tenant will not be entitled to raise the height of the building (eg by adding additional floors) without committing a trespass. Accordingly, if the question should later arise, the landlord will be free to demand a premium or an increased rent as the price of a demise of the airspace. But if the airspace is excluded from the demise, the tenant's adviser should ensure that the tenant obtains a right to enter the airspace for the purpose of performing his covenants.

(g) Fences

In the case of wooden fences it is likely to be inferred that in the absence of freeboard the owner of land will use his land to the fullest extent; and the fence will be deemed to belong to the person on whose side the rails and posts are placed, the palings being placed on his neighbour's side (4 *Halsbury's Laws of England* (4th edn) para 849).

(h) Windows

The lease should make clear whether windows are included in or excluded from the demise, especially where the responsibility for repair is divided between landlord and tenant (*Reston v Hudson* [1990] 2 EGLR 51). The draftsman should consider not only window glass, but also window frames, window sills, mastic joints, soffits. If the building is constructed with glazed curtain walling, care must be taken over the precise words used.

Example 2:1 Parcels clause of office suite

ALL THAT suite of rooms on the [   ] floor of the building known as [   ] (excluding the outer faces of the walls enclosing the said building and its roof and roof structure but including the structure supporting the floor of the said rooms) and for the purpose of identification only edged in red on the attached plan

Example 2:2 Parcels clause of open land

ALL THAT parcel of land in [   ] and numbered [   ] on the Ordnance Map ([   ] edition) for the said district a copy of which is attached hereto (including the entirety of the hedge and ditch on the western boundary of enclosure number [   ] but excluding the entirety of the hedges and ditches on the northern boundaries of the said enclosures and the entirety of the road on the southern boundaries thereof)

Example 2:3 Parcels clause of building excluding airspace

ALL THAT building known as [   ] shown edged red on the attached plan but excluding the airspace lying above the existing roof of that building together with a right for the tenant with or without workmen to enter that airspace for the sole purpose of inspecting the building or carrying out any works for which the tenant is liable under this lease

Example 2:4 Parcels clause with details of boundaries

ALL THAT the [   ] floor of the building known as [   ] ('the property') including:

(1) all non-loadbearing walls situated wholly within the red edging on the attached plan

(2) one half (severed vertically) of all non-loadbearing walls separating the property from any other part of the building

(3) all plaster or other decorative finish applied to any wall bounding the property and not included in paragraph (1) or (2) above or applied to any column or loadbearing wall within the property

(4) the whole of all doors door frames windows window frames (including mastic joints or seals) bounding the property

(5) all ceilings bounding the property and any void between any suspended ceiling and the structural slab above

(6) all floor finishes and floor screeds including raised floors and floor jacks supporting such floors

(7) all light fittings and air-conditioning units incorporated in any ceiling but not any other part of the air-conditioning system

4 PARTY STRUCTURES

Where the landlord retains no property adjoining the demised property, the question of party structures will rarely arise as between him and his tenant. In such cases the best course is for the lease to remain silent, leaving problems to be resolved as and when they arise.

Where the landlord retains adjoining property, or where he lets a building in separate parts, party structures must be considered.

(a) Inner London

Party structures in the Inner London boroughs are regulated by Part VI of the London Building Acts (Amendment) Act 1939. The Act applies to party walls and party fence walls (defined in s 44 and s 4 of the Act) separating lands or buildings belonging to different owners. For this purpose the owner will include any person in occupation other than as a tenant from year to year or for any less term or as tenant at will (London Building Act 1930, s 5). The Act provides a comprehensive code regulating the repair, demolition and rebuilding of party walls. Accordingly, where each adjoining tenant is an 'owner' within the meaning of the Act there is no need for the landlord to allocate responsibility for party walls. The Act does not apply to all party floors but only to a floor partition which separates buildings or parts of buildings approached solely by separate staircases or entrances from without (London Building Acts (Amendment) Act 1939, s 4). Thus, where parts of a building are separated by a party floor, the draftsman should define the boundaries between each part and allocate responsibility for repairs. It is suggested that either each adjoining tenant should be responsible for carrying out repairs to half the structure or the landlord should be responsible for carrying out all the repairs, subject to reimbursement of the cost of so doing.

(b) Other areas

In other areas party structures are regulated by the common law and by the Law of Property Act 1925, s 38. Where the landlord is able to choose how to divide ownership and responsibility for a party structure it is suggested that the structure be divided between adjoining owners and that each owner have an easement of support over the other's half. If the lease contains a comprehensive service charge the landlord should undertake responsibility for repair of party structures; if it does not, each adjoining tenant should be liable to carry out repairs and to pay a fair proportion of the cost of repairs carried out by the other. The tenant's liability to carry out repairs will be covered by a covenant to keep 'the demised property' in repair; but a covenant to pay a fair proportion of the cost of repairing party structures not included in the demise must be separately imposed.

Example 2:5 Declaration as to party structures

It is hereby agreed that:
(1) one half in thickness of every internal wall floor and ceiling separating the demised property from any adjoining property is included in this demise
(2) each such structure is a party structure
(3) the tenant shall maintain each of them as such and shall be liable to pay a fair proportion of the cost of repairing or maintaining any such structure which shall have been incurred by any adjoining occupier or tenant or by the landlord such proportion to be determined (in default of agreement) by an arbitrator appointed by the President for the time being of the Royal Institution of Chartered Surveyors

5 Appurtenances and Curtilage

Property is often demised together with the 'appurtenances' or the 'curtilage' belonging to it. Each of these expressions deserves consideration.

Strictly, land cannot be appurtenant to other land. Thus, a lease of a shop 'with appurtenances thereto' was held not to pass the forecourt immediately in front of the shop (*Owens v Thomas Scott & Sons (Bakers) Ltd* [1939] 3 All ER 663). However, appurtenances will include incorporeal hereditaments such as rights of way (*Hansford v Jago* [1921] 1 Ch 322) and in the case of a demise of a house they will also include an orchard, yard, garden or curtilage (*Trim v Sturminster RDC* [1938] 2 KB 508) but not a paddock (*Methuen-Campbell v Walters* [1979] QB 525). What is included in the appurtenances of property is a question of fact. It is doubtful whether a right of way over other land belonging to the landlord can ever be an appurtenance, strictly so called (*Re Walmsley and Shaw's Contract* [1917] 1 Ch 93).

A curtilage is a small and necessary area of land about a building (*Dyer v Dorset CC* [1989] QB 346). The curtilage of a building will include the ground that is used for the comfortable enjoyment of that building even though it has not been marked off or enclosed in any way (*Sinclair-Lockhart's Trustees v Central Land Board* (1950) 1 P&CR 195). However, it is not sufficient to constitute two pieces of land parts of one and the same curtilage that they should have been conveyed or demised together, for a single conveyance or lease can comprise more than one parcel of land, neither of which need be in any sense an appurtenance of the other or within the curtilage of the other; nor is it sufficient that they have been occupied together; nor is the test whether the enjoyment of one is advantageous or convenient or necessary for the full enjoyment of the other. For one corporeal hereditament to fall within the curtilage of another the former must be so intimately associated with the latter as to lead to the conclusion that the former in truth forms part and parcel of the latter (*Methuen-Campbell v Walters* above).

General words will be implied in all leases (other than an agreement for lease for a term exceeding three years (*Borman v Griffith* [1930] 1 Ch 493)) unless a contrary intention appears in the lease. By the Law of Property Act 1925, s 62, a lease of land with buildings thereon will include all outhouses, cellars, areas, courtyards, sewers, drains, ways, passages and other rights appertaining or reputed to appertain to the property or at the time of the conveyance occupied or enjoyed therewith.

Where a building is demised together with its curtilage, or where the draftsman chooses not to exclude the operation of s 62, consideration should be given to the taking of special covenants from the tenant. For example, it will be of importance to some tenants (particularly greengrocers and other shopkeepers) to know whether they are entitled to trade from a forecourt. This should be dealt with expressly in the lease. Equally, the landlord may wish to ensure that a yard adjoining a building does not become obstructed by trade empties or unrestricted car parking. Failure to deal with these matters on the grant of the lease often leads to complaints from adjoining tenants and sometimes to an action against the landlord for derogation from his grant.

If the draftsman wishes to ensure that the tenant only acquires easements expressly granted to him, s 62 should be expressly excluded.

6 ACCESS

(a) Roads

If access is gained by a road that serves only the demised property, the draftsman should include the road in the demise. The landlord will have no need to retain day-to-day control over it and any necessary restrictions can be imposed by covenant. In this way the tenant will also be under an obligation to keep the road in repair if he covenants to keep 'the demised property' in repair.

If other properties in the landlord's ownership are also served by the road it may be more convenient for him to retain it. Although no tenant will be directly responsible for the repair and maintenance of the road the landlord may recover his outlay by way of a suitably drawn service charge. In such a case the tenant's adviser should insist on an express covenant by the landlord to keep the road in repair and the grant of an express easement to the tenant to use the road.

Where the landlord retains a roadway he may be under a positive duty to the tenant to prevent obstruction of it (*Hilton v Smith (James) & Sons (Norwood) Ltd* (1979) 257 EG 1063).

The mode of use of the road should be clearly defined, although some restriction on user may be implicit in the physical nature of the road itself (*St Edmundsbury & Ipswich Diocesan Board of Finance v Clark (No 2)* [1975] 1 WLR 468). If the right of way is in terms a right to use it with vehicles it will be difficult, in the absence of express words, to show that it is restricted to a particular type or size of vehicle (*ibid*). In many cases, therefore, the draftsmen should take express instructions on the capacity of the road.

The grant of a right of way over a road will include the following ancillary rights:

(1) the right to stop for such time as is necessary to load and unload vehicles (*McIlraith v Grady* [1968] 1 QB 468) but only where there is no other convenient place to stop (*London and Suburban Land v Carey* (1991) 62 P&CR 480); and

(2) the right to a sufficiency of vertical space immediately above the road for the purpose of loading and unloading (*VT Engineering Ltd v Barland (Richard) & Co Ltd* (1968) 19 P&CR 890).

It will not, however, include:

(a) any lateral space outside the limits of the road (*VT Engineering Ltd v Barland (Richard) & Co Ltd* above); or

(b) a right to visibility splays beyond the edges of the road (*Hayns v Secretary of State* (1977) 36 P&CR 317).

These implied ancillary rights may be excluded by agreement; but the tenant's adviser should not agree to their exclusion unless the tenant has access to delimited loading bays and an express right to load and unload. Special restrictions on loading and unloading may be imposed. It will usually be desirable for the landlord to have power to make regulations about traffic management. This is normally done by imposing upon the tenant a covenant to comply with regulations made from time by the landlord. The tenant's adviser should seek to restrict the power to the making of reasonable regulations.

If the draftsman wishes to restrict the identity of the persons whom the tenant may authorise to use the road (eg staff but not customers) this must be done expressly (see *Woodhouse & Co Ltd v Kirkland (Derby) Ltd* [1970] 2 All ER 587).

Example 2:6 Right of way: unlimited times and vehicles

The right in common with the landlord and all others having the like right to pass and repass (but not to park or except in emergency to stop) with or without vehicles at all times and for all purposes connected with the use of the demised property (but not otherwise) over the road coloured [　] on the attached plan

Example 2:7 Right of way: limited times and vehicles; right to load, etc

The right in common with the landlord and all others having the like right to pass and repass on foot and with vehicles not exceeding [　] feet in length or [　] tonnes (unladen weight) at any time between 6 am on Monday and 8 pm on Friday in each week (except public holidays) for all purposes connected with the use of the demised property (but not otherwise) over the road coloured [　] on the attached plan and to park any such vehicle for such period as may be reasonable for the purpose only of loading or unloading it

Example 2:8 Right of way: right to load etc in loading bay

The right at all times with or without vehicles to pass and repass over the road leading from [　] to the demised property (but not to halt or park any vehicle thereon except in case of emergency) for all purposes connected with the use of the demised property and the right for the same purposes to use the loading bay coloured [　] on the attached plan for loading and unloading any such vehicle

(b) Stairs and passages

In a lease of property on an upper floor of a building there will be implied an easement of necessity to use a staircase that is its sole means of access (*Altmann v Boatman* (1963) 186 EG 109). The tenant will also have implied rights to use any passages or corridors that are necessary means of access. Nevertheless, it is good practice to grant the tenant express rights of access over the common parts of the building. The landlord may seek to restrict access over common parts to specified parts of the day, or to 'normal working hours'. In the case of a self-contained building this should not be accepted by the tenant. But in the case of a single floor of an office building or a unit in a covered shopping centre, the landlord may have a legitimate concern to avoid the necessity of providing services (eg heating, lighting, hot water, security) for one tenant only. The tenant's adviser has two approaches. If the additional expenditure would be recoverable by the landlord through the service charge, he may reasonably point out that the landlord will not suffer any actual loss. Consequently, the landlord has no financial interest in preventing the tenant from using the building round the clock, and may have a financial interest in permitting him to do so, since the rent may be enhanced on review. If, however, the expenditure is not so recoverable, the tenant may have to agree either to forego such services out of hours or to pay the costs of them. In any case, however, the landlord should insist that the tenant either pays for the costs of security, or indemnifies the landlord against third party claims arising out of the use of the building out of hours. It should also be noted that a covenant limiting hours of access may not limit hours of use of the demised property, provided that the tenant arrives before permitted hours cease and leaves after they recommence.

The tenant's adviser should ensure that the landlord undertakes responsibility for the repair, maintenance and cleaning of the common parts. In the absence of express provision certain duties are imposed on the landlord at common law and by statute. At common law the landlord will be liable to take reasonable care to keep in repair any essential means of access retained in his possession. Similarly, if the access is useless without artificial lighting he will be liable to take reasonable care to maintain adequate lighting (*Liverpool City Council v Irwin* [1977] AC 239). In the case of buildings let in separate parts for use as factories, more onerous duties are imposed on the landlord. He will in such cases be under an absolute duty to keep floors, stairs, passages and gangways maintained in an efficient state and in good repair (Factories Act 1961, s 28(1), s 176(1); *Galashiels Gas Co Ltd v O'Donnell* [1949] AC 275). A corresponding duty is imposed in the case of lettings of offices and shops (Offices, Shops and Railway Premises Act 1963, s 16). Similar duties are imposed on employers (Workplace (Health, Safety and Welfare) Regulations 1992 (SI No 3004) regs 17 and 18).

Example 2:9 Right of way: limited times

The right in common with the landlord and all others having the like right at all times between 8.30 am and 6.30 pm on weekdays and between 8.30 am and 1.30 pm on Saturdays (but not on public holidays) to pass and repass on foot only through the main entrance to the building of which the demised property forms part and over the stairs and corridors leading therefrom to the demised property

(c) Lifts

A right to use a lift may be implied in the case of a letting on, say, the tenth floor of a block (*Liverpool City Council v Irwin* [1977] AC 239) or where it would be inconvenient and uneconomic for the tenant to use the stairs (*Dikstein v Kanevsky* [1947] VLR 216). A right to use a lift is in the nature of an easement.

Where property is demised together with the use of the lift the landlord will be under a duty to provide a working lift (*De Meza v Ve-Ri-Best Manufacturing Co Ltd* (1952) 160 EG 364). Equally, where the lift is an essential means of access he will be under a duty to take reasonable care to keep it in working order (*Liverpool City Council v Irwin* above). Such an obligation may be enforced against the landlord by way of specific performance (*Francis v Cowcliffe Ltd* (1976) 33 P&CR 368).

In the case of a building let in separate parts for use as factories, the landlord will be under an absolute duty to keep lifts in an efficient state and in good repair (Factories Act 1961, s 22(1), s 176(1)). A corresponding duty is imposed on him in the case of lettings of offices and shops (Offices, Shops and Railway Premises (Hoists and Lifts) Regulations 1968 (SI No 849)). In addition, the landlord must ensure that every hoist or lift is thoroughly examined by a competent person at least once in every six months (Factories Act 1961, s 22(2); Offices, Shops and Railway Premises (Hoists and Lifts) Regulations 1968, reg 6(1)). This will usually be done by the landlord entering into a long-term maintenance contract with a specialist. In such cases the draftsman should provide for the costs of periodic maintenance and inspection to be recoverable from the tenants, for they may not always fall within a provision to pay the cost of repairs.

In most cases the tenant should not be permitted to load the lift to an unlimited extent. This may be achieved either by way of limitation in the grant of the right itself or by way of separate covenant. It may also be necessary to specify in the lease the lifts that are passenger lifts and those that are goods lifts.

Example 2:10 Right to use passenger lift

The right at all times in connection with the use of the demised property (but not otherwise) to use the lifts in the building for the carriage of passengers only and their hand luggage provided that the landlord shall not be liable for any loss or damage caused by a temporary failure of the lifts

Example 2:11 Right to use passenger and goods lift

The right in common with the landlord and all others having the like right during normal office hours to use:
    (1) the lift marked [   ] on the attached plan for the carriage of passengers only and their hand luggage
    (2) the lift marked [   ] on the attached plan for the carriage of goods provided that the lift shall not be loaded in excess of the permitted weight displayed therein

7 CAR PARKING

Where there is car parking space attached to the building or development in question, the draftsman has two basic methods of dealing with it. On the one hand, he may include individual parking spaces within each demise; on the other, he may grant each tenant a general right to park cars, either limited to a specified number of cars *per* tenant or on a daily 'first come first served' basis. The grant of a right to park in a defined area takes effect as a legal easement (*Newman v Jones* (1982) unreported; *London and Blenheim Estates v Ladbroke Retail Parks* [1992] 1 WLR 1278). It is suggested that the best solution is to combine both methods.

The inclusion of specified car parking spaces within each demise has the advantage that each tenant knows precisely how many cars he (or his staff or visitors) may park, and where. However, it has the disadvantage that there is no flexibility in available space. Thus, if a tenant's business expands or becomes more labour intensive unauthorised encroachments may be made into the parking spaces of other tenants, or there may be parking on access and service roads. It is by no means unusual for an aggrieved tenant to sue the landlord for derogation from his grant.

The grant of a right, but not the exclusive right, to park cars has the advantage of flexibility. However, the very fact that the right to park is not exclusive means that one tenant may appropriate more than his fair share of parking spaces. If the landlord attempts to take counter measures (eg by erecting lockable posts in some spaces and issuing keys to some of the tenants and not others) he may face an action for interfering with the other tenants' easements.

Accordingly, the draftsman should attempt to combine both methods. He should include in each demise a small number of spaces the availability of which the tenant can be sure. In addition, the tenant should be granted a right to park in a delineated area, subject to the availability of space from time to time. It may also be desirable to set aside a small area for short-term parking and the use of that area may be restricted to the tenants' visitors. If this is done the tenants and their staff should be expressly prohibited from using the visitors' car park and time limits on parking there should be imposed.

The right to park is often limited to 'private' motor vehicles. A 'private' motor vehicle is one which is used for personal or domestic purposes: not for business purposes (*Bell v Franks (Alfred) & Bartlett Co Ltd* [1980] 1 All ER 356). It is suggested, therefore, that if the tenant wishes to park vehicles actively used for business purposes, the word 'private' should be deleted from the draft lease.

Example 2:12 Composite rights of parking

Together with:
(1) the parking spaces numbered [   ] and marked on the attached plan
(2) the right in common with the landlord and all others having the like right to park private motor vehicles belonging to the tenant and the tenant's staff (subject to the availability of space from time to time) in the area designed 'Staff Car Park' on the attached plan
(3) the right for the tenant's visitors in common with the visitors of other tenants in the building to park private motor vehicles for temporary periods not exceeding one hour in any period of twenty-four hours (subject to the availability of space from time to time) in the area designated 'Visitors' Car Park' on the attached plan

8 ADVERTISEMENTS, SIGNS AND NAMEPLATES

In the absence of agreement to the contrary the tenant will be entitled to exhibit advertisements, signs and nameplates in any part of the property included in the demise. The nature of the advertisements is not restricted to purposes connected with the tenant's business (*Clapman v Edwards* [1938] 2 All ER 507). Conversely, the landlord will not be entitled to maintain an advertisement on any part of the demised property, even if the advertisement was in position at the beginning of the tenancy (*Re Webb's Lease* [1952] Ch 808).

These rights concern only the property actually demised; not the common parts. If a tenant takes only an upper floor of a building and has no more than a right to use the entrance hall for the purposes of approaching the property demised he must stipulate for the right to put a nameplate outside the property (other than that part demised to him) if he desires this convenience (*Berry (Frederick) Ltd v Royal Bank of Scotland* [1949] 1 KB 619 *per* Lord Goddard CJ at 621). If such a right is granted to the tenant it will take effect as a legal easement (*Moody v Steggles* (1879) 12 ChD 261; *William Hill (Southern) Ltd v Cabras Ltd* [1987] 1 EGLR 37).

The draftsman should either designate in the lease the place where the advertisement may be maintained, or grant the tenant a right to maintain an advertisement in such place as may be designated from time to time by the landlord or his surveyor. The form of the advertisement may either be left to the discretion of the landlord (or his surveyors) or be dealt with in the lease. If the draftsman chooses the latter course it is suggested that the tenant be permitted to display any advertisement permitted by the Town and Country Planning (Control of Advertisements) Regulations 1992 (SI No 666).

If further restrictions on displaying advertisements are to be imposed, the tenant's adviser should ensure that the tenant still has sufficient ability to carry on his business efficiently (eg by exhibiting advertisements as part of a window display).

Example 2:13 Right to display advertisement permitted by regulations

The right to display in and on the demised property any advertisement permitted to be displayed without the express consent of the local planning authority by virtue of the Town and Country Planning (Control of Advertisements) Regulations 1992 or any modification or replacement thereof

Example 2:14 Right to display advertisement in prescribed form

The right to display on the front door of the demised property a name plate not exceeding [   ] in area and advertising the business carried on in the demised property and to display the name or style of that business on the name board situated in the entrance hall of the building of which the demised property forms part with letters provided by the landlord

9 SANITARY FACILITIES

Where the demised property consists of part only of a building the draftsman may either include sanitary facilities in each demise or he may grant each tenant a right to use communal facilities. The right to use a lavatory will take effect as a legal easement (*Miller v Emcer Products Ltd* [1956] Ch 304) as will a right to use a washroom (*Heywood v Mallalieu* (1883) 25 ChD 357); but a right to a supply of hot water is a matter of personal contract rather than an easement (*Regis Property Co Ltd v Redman* [1956] 2 QB 612).

Sanitary facilities may be included in a demise where the building is amply provided with them or where the position of the lavatories and washrooms is such that access cannot be directly obtained from the common parts. In all other cases it is advisable to grant tenants easements to use the facilities in common with the other tenants in the building. The principal reason for so doing is the effect of statutory duties imposed on the landlord in respect of the provision of sanitary facilities in a multi-occupied building.

Where part of a building is let off as a separate factory the landlord will be responsible for providing and maintaining in efficient working order and good repair sufficient and suitable sanitary conveniences for the persons employed in the factory (Factories Act 1961, s 7(1), s 122). A corresponding duty is imposed on him in respect of lettings of offices and shops (Offices, Shops and Railway Premises Act 1963, ss 9(1), 42(6), 43(4)).

The number of conveniences required to be provided varies according to the number of persons employed in the building (Workplace (Health, Safety and Welfare) Regulations 1992 (SI No 3004) reg 20). The draftsman should, therefore, consider whether to impose on the tenant a limit to the number of persons who may be employed in the demised property in order to avoid overloading the available facilities.

In the absence of an express obligation, the landlord will have no duty to keep in repair any pipe or drain through which the tenant discharges soil or water, even if the pipe or drain is retained in the possession of the landlord (*Westminster (Duke) v Guild* [1984] 3 All ER 144). However, the tenant has the implied right to enter the landlord's land in order to carry out any necessary works of repair (*ibid*). This situation is unlikely to be satisfactory to either party especially if the pipe is shared or runs under a shared access. Accordingly, provision should be made for the expenses of cleaning and maintaining the sanitary facilities. This may be done by including such expenses among the items for which the landlord is entitled to recover a service charge.

Example 2:15 Easement to use sanitary facilities

> The right in common with the other tenants of the building to use the ladies' lavatories and washrooms on the [   ] floor of the building and the gentlemen's lavatories and washrooms on the [   ] floor of the building

10 TELECOMMUNICATIONS

The tenant must consider whether the needs of his business require the grant of rights to maintain telecommunication apparatus on the building (eg satellite dishes). If so, this should be covered by the grant of an express right. Although provision is made for the acquisition of such rights under the Telecommunications Code (Telecommunications Act 1984, Sched 2), it is unwise merely to rely on the statutory machinery. A covenant prohibiting alterations has effect in relation to the installation and running of telecommunication systems as if it were a covenant not to alter without the landlord's consent such consent not to be unreasonably withheld (Telecommunications Act 1984, s 96). Reasonableness is determined having regard to the principle that no person should unreasonably be denied access to a telecommunication system (*ibid*).

11 EXCEPTIONS AND RESERVATIONS

Although used almost interchangeably the words 'exception' and 'reservation' are, strictly, different mechanisms. An exception is always of part of the thing granted, and only a thing that exists can be excepted; a reservation is of a thing not in existence, but newly created or reserved out of land (12 *Halsbury's Laws of England* (4th edn) para 1529). Thus, the retention of an exterior wall will be an exception, but the retention of a right to enter the demised property will be a reservation. The practical significance of this distinction is that in cases of ambiguity an exception will be construed against the landlord, while a reservation will be construed against the tenant (*St Edmundsbury & Ipswich Diocesan Board of Finance v Clark (No 2)* [1975] 1 All ER 772).

(a) Right to enter

Where the landlord has undertaken obligations to repair or decorate the demised property, he has an implied right to enter the demised property for that purpose (*Saner v Bilton* (1878) 7 ChD 815). In the exercise of that right the landlord may exclude the tenant from occupation, but only for a reasonable time, and only if to do so is essential for the execution of the work (*McGreal v Wake* (1984) 269 EG 1254). But where the landlord has no such obligations, then in the absence of an express right he is not entitled to enter the demised property in order to carry out repairs even where the tenant has failed to repair and is in breach of covenant (*Regional Properties Ltd v City of London Real Property Co Ltd* (1980) 257 EG 64). Accordingly, the draftsman should reserve to the landlord a right to enter the demised property for the purposes of inspecting the state of repair and making good defects if the tenant fails to do so. Where the demised property is part only of a building the right should extend to entering the demised property for the purpose of repairing other parts of the building not included in the demise. A right of entry to repair will not entitle the landlord to enter to carry out improvements (*Rothschild v Moser* [1986] NPC 46). The draftsman should therefore consider whether the landlord should have the right to enter the demise for other purposes also (eg testing the property, taking samples from it or measuring it for the purpose of rent review). However, the draftsman should not draw the right too widely. If, for example, the landlord is entitled to enter the demised property in order to carry out substantial improvements or to reconstruct it the tenant may be able to defeat a claim to determine his tenancy on the ground of demolition and reconstruction (*Heath v Drown* [1973] AC 498). Thus, where a landlord was entitled to enter the demised property to carry out such improvements, additions and alterations as he considered reasonable, he was held to be entitled to demolish and reconstruct all the existing buildings comprising the demised property without putting an end to the tenancy (*Price v Esso Petroleum Co Ltd* (1980) 255 EG 243). A power to carry out improvements will not usually entitle a landlord to replace existing buildings with buildings in which the tenant cannot carry on the business permitted under the lease (*Leathwoods Ltd v Total Oil (Great Britain) Ltd* [1985] 2 EGLR 237). The landlord will have to make good damage to decorations caused by carrying out of works by him (*Bradley v Chorley BC* [1985] 2 EGLR 49). But it is good practice for the tenant's adviser to ensure that a right of entry is expressly conditional on the landlord making good any damage caused by his entry. Consideration should be given to the question whether 'damage' is to be restricted to physical damage or is to extend to loss of profits caused by disturbance of the tenant's business.

(b) Right to develop adjoining property

Where the landlord retains adjoining property, a right to develop it should be reserved. If it is not, the landlord will be unable to deal with the property if to do so would interfere materially with the demised property (*Aldin v Latimer Clark Muirhead & Co* [1894] 2 Ch 437). Even the erection of temporary scaffolding may amount to a breach of covenant for quiet enjoyment (*Owen v Gadd* [1956] 2 QB 99). These restrictions originate in the doctrine of non-derogation from grant, and such restrictions will apply equally to land acquired by the landlord after the date of the lease (*Johnston & Sons Ltd v Holland* [1988] 1 EGLR 264). Where such a right is reserved, it will give the landlord power to interfere with easements granted to the tenant, provided that the interference stops short of total extinguishment (*Overcom Properties v Stockleigh Hall Residents Management* (1989) 58 P&CR 1). The tenant's adviser should, therefore ensure that such a power is kept as narrow as possible.

(c) Right to use services

Prima facie a reservation of a right to the free passage of water, gas and electricity through the demised property will be constructed as a right to use the existing system and will not entitle the landlord to introduce any new wires or pipes (*Taylor v British Legal Life Assurance Co* [1925] Ch 395). If the landlord wishes to have the right to introduce new wires and pipes it must be expressly reserved, but such a right will not be exercisable outside the perpetuity period (*Dunn v Blackdown Properties Ltd* [1961] Ch 433). It should be made clear that the right is to extend to wires of a novel kind, eg computer cables (*Trailfinders Ltd v Razuki* (1988) 30 EG 59).

The landlord may also wish to reserve the right to divert services along different routes. But in such a case, the tenant's adviser should seek to ensure that a supply is maintained to the demised property at all times, and that any new route will not involve the tenant in extra expense.

(d) Other rights

Where the tenant has been granted rights (eg a right of support) the landlord will be entitled to rights that are in their nature reciprocal to the rights he has granted, or is taken to have granted, to the tenant (*Re Webb's Lease* [1952] Ch 808). Nevertheless, it is good practice to reserve such rights expressly.

Example 2:16 Exceptions and reservations

Excepting and reserving to the landlord:
(1) Easement rights and privileges over the demised property corresponding to those expressly granted to the tenant over the other parts of the building
(2) The right to build on develop deal with use any adjoining or neighbouring property retained by the landlord in such manner as he thinks fit even though the amenity of the demised property or the access of light or air to it may be lessened and without making any compensation to the tenant
(3) The right at reasonable times and on reasonable notice (except in emergency) to enter the demised property for the purposes of:
   (a) inspecting its condition and state of repair
   (b) carrying out any works (whether of repair or otherwise) for which the landlord or the tenant is liable under this lease
   (c) carrying out any works (whether of repair or otherwise) to any property adjoining the demised property or to any party structure sewer drain or other thing used by the tenant in common with others
   (d) measuring testing or valuing the demised property (including the right to take samples of materials and to open up parts of the demised property which would otherwise be inaccessible)
but making good any damage caused by such an entry
(4) The right for the landlord and the other tenants of the building to pass through the demised property in case of fire or other emergency

Example 2:17 Definition of service pipes

'Service pipe' means any pipe drain sewer flue duct gutter wire cable optic fibre conduit channel or other means of passage or transmission of water soil gas air smoke electricity light information or other matter and all ancillary equipment or structures

12 PERPETUITY

Prima facie the rules against perpetuities applies to the grant of easements over things not in existence at the date of the lease. This will apply, for example to the grant of a right to introduce future installations into the property (eg pipes or cables) (*Dunn v Blackdown Properties Ltd* [1961]

Ch 433) or to park on land which the landlord does not own at the date of the lease (see *London & Blenheim Estates v Ladbroke Retail Parks* [1992] 1 WLR 1278). However, a perpetuity period not exceeding eighty years may be specified in the lease (Perpetuities and Accumulations Act 1964, s 1); and where the grant of future rights is contemplated, this should be done.

13 Fixtures

The general maxim of the law is that what is annexed to the land becomes part of the land. Whether annexation is sufficient depends on the circumstances of each case, and mainly on two circumstances, as indicating intention, namely the degree of annexation and the object of the annexation (*Holland v Hodgson* (1872) LR 7 CP 328 *per* Blackburn J). If an object is annexed to land in order to enjoy it as a chattel (eg a carpet nailed to the floor) it will not become a fixture but will remain a chattel. It will not therefore form part of the demised property and obligations relating to the demised property will not apply to it.

Where an article has become a fixture it is treated as part of the demise during the term. Accordingly, the landlord may not distrain upon it (*Crossley v Lee* [1908] 1 KB 86). But at the expiry of the term the tenant has the right to remove those fixtures which are tenant's fixtures. Tenant's fixtures are those fixtures which the tenant fixes into the property for the purposes of his trade, but which do not become part of the structure itself (*New Zealand Government Property Corporation v HM & S Ltd* [1982] 1 All ER 624). The essential qualities of a tenant's fixture are that it may be removed without causing irreparable damage to the building and that it may be set up and used again in another building or place (*Webb v Bevis (Frank) Ltd* [1940] 1 All ER 247; *Young v Dalgety plc* [1987] 1 EGLR 116). Accordingly, fixtures such as office partitioning which cannot be removed without destroying the partitions will be a landlord's fixture rather than a tenant's fixture.

The tenant may exercise his right to remove tenant's fixtures so long as he is in possession as a tenant, whether under the original contract of tenancy or a new tenancy or by holding over (*New Zealand Government Property Corporation v HM & S Ltd* above). Where the right is exercised, the tenant must make good damage caused by the removal of the fixtures (*Mancetter Developments Ltd v Garmanson* [1986] QB 1212). However, it is important to remember that the tenant has a right and not a duty to remove tenant's fixtures, unless the fixtures were affixed in breach of covenant (*Never-Stop Railway (Wembley) Ltd v British Empire Exhibition (1924) Inc* [1926] 1 Ch 877). But if the tenant chooses to leave fixtures, they must be left in repair. Accordingly, when damages for dilapidations at the end of the term come to be assessed, the tenant is entitled to have the damages assessed according to the cheaper option of stripping out the fixtures or leaving them in repair. This position may be altered by agreement. Thus, a tenant may contract to yield up the demised property including tenant's fixtures (*Leschallas v Woolf* [1908] 1 Ch 641). Conversely the tenant may contract to remove fixtures either unconditionally, or conditionally upon being requested to do so by the landlord. In a case where substantial fitting-out work is in contemplation it is suggested that the draftsman should give the landlord the right to require the removal of fixtures. Where the landlord has such a right, it is often overlooked in practice, and the landlord does not make a requirement until it is too late. Accordingly, the draftsman should consider imposing on the tenant an obligation to ask the landlord, say six months before the expiry of the term which (if any) fixtures the landlord requires him to remove.

Example 2:18 Covenant to yield up tenant's fixtures

at the expiry or sooner determination of the tenancy to yield up the demised property including all tenant's fixtures in good repair and clean and tidy

Example 2:19 Covenant to remove tenant's fixtures if required

if so required by the landlord by written notice given not later than three months before the term date to remove (or pay for the removal of) all fixtures affixed to the demised property by the tenant or such of them as may be specified in the notice

Example 2:20 Covenant by tenant to inquire about removal of fixtures

not later than six months before the expiry of the term to inquire in writing of the landlord which (if any) tenant's fixtures the landlord requires the tenant to remove on the termination of the term

14 RENEWAL LEASES

(a) Extent of the demise

Although the tenant is entitled to the protection of Part II of the Landlord and Tenant Act 1954 in respect of the whole of the property comprised in his tenancy, he is only entitled to be granted a new tenancy of his holding. The tenant's holding is that part of the property occupied by him (whether or not for business purposes) or by an employee of his employed in the business giving rise to protection (s 23(3)). If there is no agreement as to the extent of the holding, it is designated by the court by reference to the circumstances existing at the date of the order (s 32(2)).

The court cannot normally order the grant of a new tenancy of part only of the holding (*Fernandez v Walding* [1968] 2 QB 606). However, where the landlord opposes the grant of a new tenancy on redevelopment grounds, the tenant may be entitled to a new tenancy of an economically separable part of the holding if the landlord's redevelopment would not be impeded (s 31A; s 32(1A)).

Equally, the court cannot normally order the grant of a new tenancy of more than the holding. But the landlord has an absolute right to require the tenant to take a new tenancy of the whole of the property comprised in the current tenancy even though the tenant does not occupy the whole of it (s 32(2)).

(b) Ancillary rights

Where the current tenancy includes rights enjoyed by the tenant in connection with the holding, those rights are included in the new tenancy unless the landlord and tenant agree or the court determines otherwise (s 32(3)). However, the court cannot create new rights over the landlord's land and cannot elevate informal personal privileges into property rights (*Orlik (G) (Meat Products) Ltd v Hastings and Thanet BS* (1974) 29 P&CR 126). In addition the rights must still be subsisting at the date of the court's order (*Kirkwood v Johnson* (1979) 38 P&CR 392).

(c) Law of Property Act 1925, s 62

By the Law of Property Act 1925, s 62 a lease of land will include all liberties, privileges, easements, rights, and advantages whatsoever appertaining or reputed to appertain to the land or any part thereof at the date of the lease, demised, occupied, or enjoyed with or reputed or known as part or parcel of or appurtenant to the land or any part thereof. Where the tenant is already in occupation at the date of execution of the lease, s 62 may convert mere personal licences into legal rights, provided that they are rights known to the law (*Wright v Macadam* [1949] 2 KB 744; *Goldberg v Edwards* [1950] Ch 247). Section 62 may be excluded by the terms of the lease (s 62(4)). The draftsman should give consideration to doing so in all renewal leases (see Form 15 below) but if this is done, the tenant's adviser must ensure that all necessary ancillary rights are expressly granted by the lease.

(d) Alterations carried out under previous lease

In many cases, the tenant renewing his lease will have carried out alterations to the property during the term of the expired lease. He may have undertaken obligations to reinstate. The draftsman should ensure that those reinstatement obligations are carried forward into the new lease, so that the tenant remains under an obligation to reinstate when the new lease comes to an end.

The tenant's adviser should ensure that the rental value of any alterations carried out under the expired lease is ignored in assessing the rent payable on any rent review under the new lease.

3

Landlord and Tenant (Covenants) Act 1995

On 1 January 1996 the Landlord and Tenant (Covenants) Act 1995 came into force. It has made the most radical changes to the law of landlord and tenant for many years. Many of those changes do not have direct impact on the practice of drafting business leases, and where there is direct impact, the relevant provisions are considered later in this book. However, every draftsman should be aware of the overall structure of the Act. Many of the main changes in the law apply only to new tenancies. A new tenancy is one which is granted on or after 1 January 1996. However, a tenancy granted on or after that date will not be a new tenancy if it is granted pursuant to:
- (1) an agreement for lease made before that date;
- (2) an option granted before that date (irrespective of the date when the option is exercised); or
- (3) a court order (eg for the grant of a new tenancy) made before that date.

The main changes which apply only to new tenancies are:
- (a) the new rules for the running of covenants;
- (b) the abolition of privity of contract, and associated changes;
- (c) the amendment of s 19 of the Landlord and Tenant Act 1927;
- (d) the ability of the landlord to seek a release from privity of contract on assignment of the reversion.

1 THE RUNNING OF COVENANTS

The Act has abolished the traditional distinction between covenants which run with the land and covenants which do not (Landlord and

Tenant (Covenants) Act 1995, s 2). All covenants now run with the land. The exceptions to this principle are:

(1) a covenant does not bind an assignee if it did not bind the assignor immediately before the assignment (personal waivers and releases being disregarded for this purpose); and

(2) a covenant will not bind an assignee if it is expressed to be personal to the assignor

(Landlord and Tenant (Covenants) Act 1995, s 3).

Thus where, for example, the tenant is a government department, and the lease contains a covenant by the tenant to insure, but it is subject to a proviso that for as long as the tenant is a government department it may carry its own insurance, the proviso would be a personal waiver or release, so that an assignee would be bound by the covenant to insure. And where, for example, the original tenant is given the personal right to use the property for some special purpose, that right will not pass to an assignee on assignment. It seems highly unlikely that these changes will affect traditional drafting practices.

It is specifically provided that where a covenant is expressed (in whatever terms) to be personal to any person the Act does not make that covenant enforceable against any other person. It is considered that this will continue to permit a covenant to be drafted so that it ceases to bind a person after he has parted with his interest in the property. This form of drafting is normally found in the case of landlord's covenants.

Example 3:1 Limitation on landlord's liability

> The Landlord covenants with the Tenant (but not so as to impose any liability on the Landlord after it has parted with its reversion) as follows:

2 Release of Covenants on Assignment

If the tenant assigns the premises demised to him, he is released from the tenant covenants of the tenancy, and ceases to be entitled to the benefits of the landlord covenants (Landlord and Tenant (Covenants) Act 1995, s 5). The tenant covenants of the tenancy will include not only covenants contained in the lease, but also any covenant contained in a collateral agreement (eg a side letter or licence granted during the tenancy) (s 28(1)). Where the assignment is of part only, the release extends only to the extent that the covenants fall to be complied with in relation to the part assigned.

The automatic release does not apply on an excluded assignment. An excluded assignment is one which is in breach of a covenant of the tenancy, or an assignment which takes place by operation of law (s 11). However, the automatic release will apply to the next assignment which is not itself an excluded assignment (*ibid*).

If the landlord assigns his reversion, he is not automatically released. However, he has the right to apply to be released, either by agreement with the tenant or if the county court declares that it reasonable for him to be released (ss 6–8).

3 Authorised Guarantee Agreements

Although the tenant is automatically released from liability under his covenants on assignment, he may be required to guarantee the obligations of the immediate assignee. This is done by an authorised guarantee agreement. The agreement must comply with the formal requirements of s 16 of the Act. In addition, the tenant may only be required to enter into such an agreement where he is required to do so as a condition (lawfully imposed) of consent to the assignment (s 16(3)(b)). The circumstances in which such a condition may be imposed are discussed in Chapter 9 below.

4 Joint and Several Liability

Where two or more persons are bound by the same covenant in consequence of the Act, they are jointly and severally liable (s 13(1)). Moreover, where two or more persons are jointly and severally liable by virtue of the Act, a release of one of them will not release the others (s 13(2)). This reverses the general law under which the release of one contracting party releases the others (*Deanplan v Mahmoud* [1992] 3 WLR 467). However, the statutory provision applies only to persons bound by virtue of the Act, and so will not apply to persons who are bound independently of the Act (eg two original tenants who are bound jointly and severally solely by contract).

5 Overriding Leases

Where a former tenant or guarantor makes full payment of any sum which he has been required to pay under s 17 of the Act (ie a payment of a fixed charge which was the primary liability of the tenant in possession) he is entitled to claim an overriding lease of the property (Landlord and Tenant (Covenants) Act 1995, s 19). The overriding lease will be granted for a term of three days longer than the unexpired residue of the lease, and (subject to any agreed modifications) will be on the same terms as the underlying lease, barring personal obligations and spent obligations (*ibid*). An overriding lease must state:

(1) that it is a lease granted under s 19, and

(2) whether or not it is a new tenancy for the purposes of s 1

(s 20). An overriding lease will be a new tenancy if (and only if) the underlying lease is a new tenancy (*ibid*).

Example 3.2 Statement contained in overriding lease

This lease:

(1) is a lease granted under section 19 of the Landlord and Tenant (Covenants) Act 1995; and

(2) is [not] a new tenancy for the purposes of section 1 of that Act

6 VARIATIONS

A subsequent variation of a lease will not bind a former tenant or guarantor if at the time when the variation was made the landlord had the absolute right to refuse to allow it, or would have had that right but for a previous variation (Landlord and Tenant (Covenants) Act 1995, s 18). At common law, an original tenant is not bound by a variation of the lease (*Friends Provident Life Office v British Railways Board* [1995] EGCS 140), and unless the contract otherwise provides, a guarantor would be wholly discharged by such a variation (*Holme v Brunskill* (1877) 3 QBD 495). At common law, the parties may agree what they please, but the parties cannot contract out of the Act (s 25). It appears therefore that even if the former tenant or guarantor expressly consents to the variation, he will not be bound by it. However, the Act does not appear to prevent a person from entering into a fresh guarantee of the lease as varied, although it is arguable that a fresh guarantee would be struck down by the extremely wide anti-avoidance provisions contained in s 25 (see '8 Anti-avoidance' below).

7 FIXED CHARGES

The Act limits the liability of former tenants and guarantors in respect of fixed charges. This limitation applies to all leases, not merely new

tenancies. A fixed charge is
(1) rent;
(2) any service charge;
(3) any amount payable under a tenant covenant of the tenancy providing for the payment of a liquidated sum in the event of a failure to comply with any such covenant

(Landlord and Tenant (Covenants) Act 1995, s 17(6)).

Where the landlord wishes to recover a fixed charge from a former tenant or a guarantor, he must serve a notice within the period of six months from the date when the charge became due. The notice must be in the prescribed form, and must inform the recipient:
(1) that the charge is now due; and
(2) that the landlord intends to recover from the recipient such amount as is specified in the notice and (where payable) interest calculated on the basis specified in the notice

(s 17(2), (3)). If no such notice is served in time, the former tenant or guarantor is not liable for the fixed charge. Where the amount of the fixed charge has not been finally determined (eg there is a pending rent review, or service charge accounts have not been finalised) the notice may inform the recipient of the possibility that liability may be determined subsequently. In such a case, the landlord may recover the amount finally determined, if he serves a further notice within three months of the final determination (s 17(4)).

These provisions apply only to fixed charges (as defined). They will not apply to claims for unliquidated damages (eg damages for dilapidations). The tenant may seek to extend protection against liability under all covenants. It is unlikely that, except in a strong tenants' market, the landlord will agree to forego all claims against the tenant. A possible compromise is that the landlord must first have attempted to pursue others who may be jointly and severally liable with the tenant.

Example 3:3 Restriction on landlord's ability to sue original tenant

(1) At any time after the lawful assignment of this lease by [*name of original tenant*] the landlord shall not be entitled to enforce against him (either as former tenant or as guarantor under an authorised guarantee agreement) the tenant's obligations under this lease unless the landlord has first
(a) recovered judgment against all other persons against whom the landlord is or has become entitled to enforce those obligations either as principal or surety and
(b) attempted to levy execution upon such judgment

(2) upon payment by [*name of original tenant*] of any sum due under such judgment the landlord shall assign to him the benefit of it

(3) 'authorised guarantee agreement' has the same meaning as in the Landlord and Tenant (Covenants) Act 1995

8 ANTI-AVOIDANCE

Section 25 of the Act contains stringent anti-avoidance provisions. Any agreement relating to a tenancy is void to the extent that:

(1) it would otherwise have effect to exclude, modify or otherwise frustrate the operation of any provision of the Act, or

(2) it provides for:
  (a) the termination or surrender of the tenancy, or
  (b) the imposition on the tenant of any penalty, disability or liability,

  in the event of the operation of any of the provisions of the Act, or

(3) it provides for any of the matters referred to in (2)(a) or (b) and does so (whether expressly or otherwise) in connection with, or in consequence of, the operation of any provision of the Act.

However, a covenant against assignment does not fall foul of these provisions merely because it prohibits assignment, and an authorised guarantee agreement similarly does not fall foul of them.

4

The Term of the Lease

1 Practical Problems

The length of the term that the landlord is prepared to grant, and the tenant to take, is usually outside the draftsman's province. It is almost always determined by commercial considerations. The draftsman should, nevertheless, be aware of some of the practical problems that arise in connection with the choice of tenancy to be granted and in appropriate cases should draw them to the attention of his client.

The norm for the duration of commercial leases has for many years been twenty-five years. This has been prompted by investment considerations. The landlord requires security of income for a long period, and this is specially desirable where the landlord is an investing institution which pays out pensions or insurance policies, because a period of twenty-five years' secure income facilitates the actuarial calculations necessary in order to determine the level of payments which the landlord can make. Since such institutions are the heaviest investors in commercial property, their requirements have driven the market, so that even landlords who are not institutions require an 'institutionally acceptable' investment. In addition, income security for a long period decreases the risks associated with the investment. This in turn diminishes the yield (or rate of return) required by an investor. Since the capital value of an investment is determined by a multiple of the rent, and the multiplier (or years' purchase) is the reciprocal of the yield, the lower the yield, the higher the capital value of the investment.

However, in the recession of the early 1990s, landlords became less able to impose these requirements on tenants who were unwilling to enter into such a long-term contractual commitment. Although the basic pattern of a twenty-five-year lease remained largely intact, tenants were able to secure the right to terminate the lease before its expiry. In addition, the pace of development in technology meant that office buildings had a shorter economic life, so that landlords recognised the need to refurbish at intervals more frequent than twenty-five years. Now that the Landlord and Tenant (Covenants) Act 1995 has abolished privity of contract of the original tenant after assignment, it remains to be seen whether the twenty-five-year lease will retain its investment attractions, or, conversely, whether a twenty-five-year term will become more attractive to tenants.

Where the landlord has redevelopment plans for the property in question, the term of the lease should be short enough for him to be able to recover possession in time to redevelop. This is of great importance in practice because planning permissions are invariably granted subject to a condition that the permitted development is begun within a stipulated time. It is often forgotten that the service of a notice determining the tenant's tenancy under the Landlord and Tenant Act 1954, s 25, is only the first step in the process of recovering possession. After the service of the notice the tenant is entitled to apply to the court for a new tenancy. The application will take several months (or longer) to come on for hearing. Even if the application is dismissed, the tenant's tenancy will continue for a further three months plus time for appeal, which is currently four weeks. Moreover, except by consent, the court cannot make an order for possession against the tenant in the application; so that if the tenant refuses to leave at the expiry date of his tenancy, the landlord will be compelled to take fresh proceedings against him. It is, therefore, quite possible that the tenant is still in occupation of the demised property two or more years after his tenancy was expressed to expire.

Where the landlord is the owner of other property adjoining the demised property, or where the demised property is part only of a building, the date on which the tenancy is expressed to expire may be of importance. On the one hand, if the landlord has redevelopment plans or if a higher rent could be achieved on a reletting of a greater part of the building, it will be in the landlord's interest to ensure that all tenancies are expressed to expire on the same date. On the other hand, if the landlord is likely to relet the demised property at the end of the tenancy without incorporating it into any greater unit it may be prudent to spread the termination dates so as to prevent a cash flow crisis, which might be occasioned by too many voids at the same time.

Where the landlord is himself a leaseholder, the draftsman should have in mind the length of the landlord's own lease. If he grants a sublease for a term longer than the term of his own lease, the grant may take effect as an assignment of that lease (contrast *Milmo v Carreras* [1946] KB 306 and *Skelton (William) & Son v Harrison & Pinder Ltd* [1975] QB 361). If he retains a short but more than nominal reversion he may find that at the expiry of the sublease he is unable to relet the property. Or, if his reversion is less than fourteen months longer than the sublease, on the expiry of the sublease he will not be the competent landlord for the purposes of Part II of the Landlord and Tenant Act 1954 if his own landlord is prompt in serving a s 25 notice. In that case he will not be able to increase the rent payable under the subtenancy or to oppose the grant of a new tenancy to the subtenant should he wish to do so (see 'Business Tenancies—Traps for the Unwary' (1978) LSG 371).

The tenant's adviser should have in mind and advise the tenant about the obligations assumed by an original tenant. Significant changes have been made by the Landlord and Tenant (Covenants) Act 1995, which are discussed in Chapter 3. However, the tenant should be advised that he will assume liability for performance of covenants during the period of his own tenure, that he may be required to guarantee performance of covenants by his assignee. In addition to the statutory mechanism for the protection of tenants, the tenant's adviser should also consider:

(1) regular tenant's break-clauses throughout the term;
(2) the reservation of a right of re-entry on assignment.

In view of the fact that a tenant may be required to guarantee the payment of rent by his immediate assignee, who may hold over under the Landlord and Tenant Act 1954, it is considered that it is still in the landlord's interest to define the term so that it includes statutory continuation, and to include an express contractual liability to pay any interim rent which may become payable under s 24A of that Act. In the absence of express provisions to this effect liability under an authorised guarantee agreement will not extend to these payments (*City of London Corporation v Fell* [1994] 1 AC 458). If, however, there is an express contractual liability to pay rent during a continuation period and to pay interim rent, it is considered that liability under an authorised guarantee agreement will extend to these amounts (*Herbert Duncan v Cluttons* [1992] 1 EGLR 101).

Example 4:1 Definition clause making tenant liable for rent during holding over period

'the term' includes not only the term expressed to be granted by this lease but also any period after the date on which the term is expressed to expire during which the tenancy continues under the Landlord and Tenant Act 1954

Example 4:2 Clause making the tenant liable to pay rent and interim rent

> promptly to pay the rent reserved by this lease without any deduction or set-off and any rent substituted for it either as a result of a rent review under this lease or the agreement or determination of a rent payable by virtue of section 24A of the Landlord and Tenant Act 1954

2 TENANCY AT WILL

Part II of the Landlord and Tenant Act 1954 does not apply to tenancies at will (*Hagee (London) Ltd v Erikson (AB) and Larson* [1976] QB 209). The essence of such a tenancy is that either party may determine it at will. Accordingly, it may at first sight seem advantageous to a landlord to grant such a tenancy. However, the court will look very carefully at any agreement that is alleged to be a tenancy at will, particularly if the circumstances are not the classic circumstances of holding over or holding pending negotiation. Only a genuine tenancy at will will escape the provisions of the 1954 Act. A tenancy that is something else—that is to say, either periodic or for a term certain but described as a tenancy at will—will inevitably be caught (*ibid per* Scarman LJ at 217).

Features that will tend towards a tenancy at will are:
(1) the absence of a right of re-entry;
(2) the absence of onerous repairing covenants;
(3) the absence of a prohibition against assignment;
(4) the absence of any specified period of notice;
(5) a rent payable on demand.

Since machinery now exists that permits a term certain to be contracted out of the 1954 Act's security of tenure, it is unwise except in special circumstances, for a landlord to take a risk of granting a tenancy at will. It is safer to grant a tenancy for a term certain, subject to a break-clause, that is contracted out of the 1954 Act (*Scholl Mfg Co Ltd v Clifton (Slim-Line) Ltd* [1967] Ch 41 at 51). Equally, from the tenant's point of view the interest granted him under a tenancy at will is so precarious that he would almost always be better off with a fixed term to which the 1954 Act did not apply.

Example 4:3 Informal tenancy at will

> Dear Sirs,
>
> Our clients [*name*] are prepared to permit you to occupy [*parcels*] from [*date*] on the following terms:

(1) You will have exclusive possession of the premises as tenant at will only.

(2) Throughout your occupation you will pay rent calculated at the rate of £[   ] per annum payable on demand in advance (but periodic demands shall not convert this tenancy into a periodic tenancy).

(3) A proportionate part of any advance payment will be refunded to you if this tenancy is determined before the expiry of the period which such payment is intended to cover.

(4) You may use the premises for the sole purpose of [   ].

(5) You will keep the premises clean and tidy and will leave them in no worse condition than that in which they are at the date of this letter and free from rubbish.

(6) You may not do or permit to be done in the premises anything which may invalidate or increase the premium payable for any policy of insurance maintained by our clients and you will comply with all requirements and recommendations of our clients' insurers.

(7) You may not allow any other person to occupy the whole or any part of the premises.

If you agree to the above terms, please sign the enclosed copy of this letter and return it to us.

Yours etc

3 TERM CERTAIN

The term certain, or fixed term tenancy, is the most common form of business letting. It is only one species of the term of years absolute (defined in the Law of Property Act 1925, s 205(1)(xxvii)). Its main characteristic is that it can be predicated with certainty before the commencement of the term that it will come to an end (subject to any right of re-entry or option to determine) on a known date. Thus, a tenancy for a term of 'seven years and thereafter from year to year' is not a term certain because the tenancy will not come to an end until notice is served.

From the landlord's point of view one principal advantage of the term of years certain is that it can be contracted out of the security of tenure that would otherwise be provided by the Landlord and Tenant Act 1954. This may be done with the consent of the tenant and the leave of the court (Landlord and Tenant Act 1954, s 38(4)). A term certain of less than one year may also be contracted out (*Re Land and Premises at Liss, Hants* [1971] Ch 986). From the tenant's point of view, he has assured security for the term of the lease, subject to compliance with his obligations and continuing solvency.

A miscellaneous series of incidents attach to various lengths of term.

For convenience the most important of them are set out below.

Term	Characteristic
Six months	Part II of the Landlord and Tenant Act 1954 does not apply to a tenancy for a term of years certain not exceeding six months unless: (1) it contains provision for renewing the term or extending it beyond six months from its beginning; or (2) the tenant has been in occupation for a period which, together with any period during which any predecessor in his business was in occupation, exceeds twelve months (Landlord and Tenant Act 1954, s 43(3)).
One year	A tenant may only serve a request for a new tenancy under the Landlord and Tenant Act 1954, s 26, if his tenancy was granted for a term of years certain exceeding one year or for a term of years certain and thereafter from year to year (Landlord and Tenant Act 1954, s 26(1)). He may, however, serve a counter-notice in response to a landlord's notice under s 25 of that Act irrespective of the length of his tenancy.
Three years	A lease taking effect in possession for a term not exceeding three years at a rack rent need not be made by deed and may be made orally (Law of Property Act 1925, s 54; Law of Property (Miscellaneous Provisions) Act 1989, s 2). A tenancy granted for a term of years certain of which not less than three years remain unexpired is an owner's interest for the purpose of serving blight notices (Town and Country Planning Act 1990, s 168).
Five years	The tenant's right to compensation under the Landlord and Tenant Act 1954, s 37, may be excluded or modified by agreement unless: (1) during the whole of the five years immediately preceding the date on which the tenant, under a tenancy to which the Act applies is to quit the holding, premises being or comprised in the holding have been occupied for the purposes of a

THE TERM OF THE LEASE

business carried on by the occupier or for those and other purposes; and

(2) if, during those five years, there was a change in the occupier of the premises, the new occupier was a successor to the business carried on by the old occupier (Landlord and Tenant Act 1954, s 38(2), (3)). Note that the crucial date is the date on which the occupier quits, not the date on which the lease is expressed to expire.

Seven years — The Leasehold Property (Repairs) Act 1938 does not apply to a tenancy granted for a term of years certain of less than seven years (Leasehold Property (Repairs) Act 1938, s 7). A lease for a term of less than seven years need not be produced to the Commissioners of Inland Revenue (Finance Act 1931, s 28). Stamp duty is charged at the lowest rate for a term not exceeding seven years (Stamp Act 1891, Sched 1, as amended).

Fourteen years — The tenant will be entitled (in certain circumstances) to compensation under the Landlord and Tenant Act 1954, s 37, equal to the production of the appropriate multiplier and twice the rateable value of the holding if:

(1) during the whole of the fourteen years immediately preceding the termination of his tenancy, premises being or comprised in the holding have been occupied for the purposes of a business carried on by the occupier or for those and other purposes; and

(2) if during those fourteen years, there was a change in the occupier of the premises, the new occupier was the successor to the business carried on by the old occupier (Landlord and Tenant Act 1954, s 37(2), (3)). In all other cases the amount of the compensation will be equal to the product of the appropriate multiplier and the rateable value of the holding.

Twenty-one years — A lease for a term of years less than twenty-one is not registrable at HM Land Registry (Land Registration Act 1925, s 8). A lease for a term certain exceeding twenty-one years is a major interest for

	the purposes of VAT (Value Added Tax Act 1994, s 96(1)).
Thirty-five years	Stamp duty is charged at a lower rate if the term does not exceed thirty-five years (Stamp Act 1891, Sched 1 as amended).
Forty years	Where a term of more than forty years is created the tenant may, after the expiry of twenty-five years of the term, apply to the court for the discharge of any restriction affecting the user of the demised property (Law of Property Act 1925, s 84(12)). In a compulsory registration area a lease granted for a term of forty years or more must be registered at HM Land Registry (Land Registration Act 1925, s 123). A building lease for a term of more than forty years, where the lessor is not a public body, is freely assignable even if it contains a qualified covenant against alienation (Landlord and Tenant Act 1927, s 19(1)(b)).
Fifty years	A lease for a term of more than fifty years is a long lease for the purposes of income and corporation taxes. There is a series of complex rules for determining the true length of a lease (Income and Corporation Taxes Act 1988, s 38). A lease will usually be a wasting asset for the purposes of capital gains tax when its duration does not exceed fifty years (Taxation of Chargeable Gains Act 1992, Sched 8, para 1).
Sixty years	A lease for a term not exceeding sixty years is a depreciating asset for the purposes of roll-over relief (Taxation of Chargeable Gains Act 1992, s 154(7)).

4 COMMENCEMENT OF THE TERM

The date on which the term is to begin should always be clearly expressed in the lease. It is normal for a fixed term tenancy to begin on one of the usual quarter days (25 March, 24 June, 29 September and 25 December). This practice is convenient both for the purposes of managing the property (since most managing agents, or their computers, send out rent demands by reference to quarter days) and for the purpose of calculating the rent (since broken periods can often be avoided). If the rent is payable monthly it is usually best that the tenancy should begin on the first of the month.

If possible the term should be expressed as a whole number of years. This will ease the calculation of important dates during the term (for example rent review dates or years in which the tenant is liable to paint). If the tenant is let into possession or the lease is completed at a time that makes this inconvenient, the commencement date should be back-dated to a convenient date. For the purposes of calculation the term will then run from the date on which it is expressed to begin, although the tenant's interest will not vest until the date on which the lease is actually executed (*Cadogan (Earl) v Guinness* [1936] Ch 515).

Where a lease creates a term of years which is expressed to run from some date earlier than that of the execution of the lease, the term created will be a term which begins on the date the lease is executed, and not the earlier date. No act or omission before the date on which the lease is executed will normally constitute a breach of the obligations of the lease. These principles do not prevent the parties from defining the expiration of the term by reference to a date before that of execution of the lease, or from making contractual provisions which take effect by reference to such a date, as by defining the period for the operation of a break-clause or an increase of rent. There is nothing in these principles to prevent the lease from creating obligations in respect of any period before the execution of the lease. Whether in fact any such obligations have been created depends on the construction of the lease; and there is nothing which requires the lease to be constructed in such a way as to avoid, if possible, the creation of such obligations (*Bradshaw v Pawley* [1980] 1 WLR 10, where liability for rent was held to be retrospective). Normally, rent review dates and dates for the exercise of options will be calculated from the date on which the term is expressed to begin, rather than the date of execution of the lease (*Beaumont Property Trust v Tai* (1982) 265 EG 872; *Page v Mallow Investments Ltd* (1974) 29 P&CR 168).

The term of a lease is often expressed to run 'from' a particular date. *Prima facie* the term will be treated as beginning at midnight between the named date and the day following it (*Meggeson v Groves* [1917] 1 Ch 158). Thus, a lease for seven years 'from 25 March 1970' will begin at midnight between 25 March 1970 and 26 March 1970; and it will end at the stroke of midnight at the end of 25 March 1977. However, this presumption may be easily rebutted.

The court will, for example, try to construe a lease so that all payments of rent fall due during the term and in respect of periods that fall wholly within it (*Ladyman v Wirral Estates Ltd* [1968] 2 All ER 197, *Whelton Sinclair v Hyland* [1992] 2 EGLR 158). Thus, where rent is payable quarterly in advance on the usual quarter days a term of 'seven years from 25 March' will be construed as beginning at the first moment of 25 March, so that the first payment of rent will fall due on the first day of the term and the last payment of rent would be made in respect of a complete quarter, which ends at the last moment of the term. Conversely, if the rent is payable quarterly in arrears the term will be taken to begin at the first moment of 26 March, so that the last payment of rent will fall due on the last day of the term rather than the day after its expiry by effluxion of time. The safest course for the draftsman to adopt is to express the term as 'beginning on' a particular date. If the rent is payable in advance, the date chosen should be a rent day. If the rent is payable in arrear, the date chosen should be the day after a rent day. If the term is expressed to begin in the middle of a rental period, this may distort other parts of the lease; for example, a rent review timetable (*East v Pantiles (Plant Hire) Ltd* (1981) 263 EG 61).

5 Break-Clauses

Either the landlord or the tenant may be entitled to determine a term certain at a date earlier than that on which it would otherwise expire by effluxion of time. If the landlord is to have such a power it must be expressly conferred on him; if the lease is silent as to the person by whom it is exercisable it will be exercisable by the tenant alone (*Wingfield (LR) v Clapton Construction Co Ltd* (1967) 201 EG 769).

In drafting a break-clause the draftsman should consider:
  (1) the time at which the break-clause may be exercised;
  (2) the manner in which it may be exercised;
  (3) whether the circumstances in which the break-clause may be exercised should be limited in any way;
  (4) the effect on other parts of the lease of the inclusion of a break-clause.

(a) Time of exercise

A break-clause is a species of option properly so called. Accordingly, any prescribed time limits must be strictly complied with unless there is express provision to the contrary. A break-clause may be exercisable on a specified date; for example 'at the expiry of the seventh year of the term'. This form is not to be recommended to a landlord, because if his power is restricted to a power to determine for certain specified purposes, he may lose the power altogether if he cannot establish the purpose at the crucial date. A better form is 'at any time after the expiry of the seventh year of the term'. However, from the tenant's point of view this is undesirable. Even if he is able to negotiate a minimum fixed term before the landlord's power to break can be exercised, once that period has expired a notice can come at any time. This greatly impairs proper business planning and may well paralyse investment by the tenant in the property. The tenant is better served if the landlord's power to break arises only at fixed intervals. One matter for the landlord to consider is the impact of the break-clause on rent review (see *R & A Millett (Shops) Ltd v Legal and General Assurance Society Ltd* [1985] 1 EGLR 103).

Alternatively, a break-clause may be exercisable on the happening of an uncertain event; for example, if a dangerous structure notice is served or if planning permission for a particular use is refused. If the break-clause is of this kind, the party entitled to break may equally need flexibility in his choice of time at which to exercise the power. For example, if the tenant has the right to break if the local planning authority refuses to renew a temporary planning permission he may wish to appeal against that refusal. In those circumstances he would be wise to insist that provision be made for a late exercise of the break-clause following an unsuccessful appeal.

The draftsman should also be aware of the incidence of compensation under the Landlord and Tenant Act 1954, s 37. If, for example, the landlord has the right to break at the expiry of the twelfth year of the term, rather than at the expiry of the fourteenth year of the term, the tenant's right to compensation on quitting may be halved.

(b) Manner of exercise

A break-clause is usually exercisable by notice in writing. The length of notice is a matter of negotiation between the parties. Where the tenancy in question is one to which Part II of the Landlord and Tenant Act 1954 applies, it is often convenient if the minimum period of notice is six months and the form of the notice is capable of being that prescribed for the purposes of s 25 of that Act. In that way the landlord need serve only one notice (the s 25 notice), which will be effective to bring the tenancy to an end, even if the landlord is not going to oppose any application for a new tenancy (*Scholl Mfg Co Ltd v Clifton (Slim-Line) Ltd* [1967] Ch 41; *Rene Claro (Haute Coiffure) Ltd v Halle Concerts Society* [1969] 2 All ER 842; *Keith Bayley Rogers & Co v Cubes Ltd* (1975) 31 P&CR 412). If notice is given that is sufficient to satisfy the terms of the lease but not the provisions of the 1954 Act, the effect of the notice will be to convert the tenancy from a fixed term tenancy into a tenancy continuing by virtue of s 24 of the 1954 Act (*Weinbergs Weatherproofs Ltd v Radcliffe Paper Mill Co Ltd* [1958] Ch 437). In those circumstances the landlord will have to serve a further notice under the Landlord and Tenant Act 1954, s 25. The s 25 notice may expire any time after the expiry of the break-notice. This method of operating the break-clause may be advantageous to the landlord in that he may delay the service of a section 25 notice until he is in a position to establish a ground of opposition to an application for a new tenancy.

The tenant, however, need only give such notice as satisfies the terms of the lease. Where a lease contains a tenant's break-clause, and the tenancy is protected by the Landlord and Tenant Act 1954, it is possible that instead of serving a contractual break-notice, the tenant can serve a request for a new tenancy under s 26 of the Act (*Scholl Mfg Co Ltd v Clifton (Slim-Line) Ltd* above). This would entitle the tenant to have a new tenancy at the then prevailing market rent. In a falling market the tenant can thus engineer a downwards rent review. The draftsman can prevent this risk from arising by ensuring that the tenant's break-clause must be exercised by more than twelve months' notice. Since a request for a new tenancy must specify a commencement date for the new tenancy not more than twelve months after the service of the notice, this means that at the date when the tenant must serve the break-notice he is not in a position to serve a request for a new tenancy. And once the tenant has served a break-notice, he loses the right to make a request for a new tenancy (Landlord and Tenant Act 1954, s 26(4)).

If a landlord's notice expires in the middle of a rental period, rent paid in advance may need to be apportioned and part repaid. The tenant's adviser would do well to include an express provision to that effect. However, this may be resisted by the landlord since the tenant, if he is protected by the Landlord and Tenant Act 1954, may remain in occupation of the demised property even after the expiry of a break-notice, pending an application to the court for a new tenancy.

In the case of a tenant's notice a requirement that rent be apportioned may work to the prejudice of the landlord since he will need time to arrange a reletting.

(c) Circumstances of exercise

It is rare nowadays for the landlord to have an unrestricted power to determine a lease. The usual way in which his power is circumscribed is by limiting it to a right to break for certain specified purposes. The commonest of these purposes are those of redevelopment and of occupation for the purposes of a business carried on by the landlord. It will be a condition precedent to the exercise of the break-clause that the landlord has the necessary *bona fide* intention (*IR Comrs v Southend-on-Sea Estates Co Ltd* [1915] AC 428). However, some latitude is allowed if the landlord has only one opportunity to determine the lease on a specified date. Thus, where landlords were entitled to determine a twenty-one-year lease 'at the expiration of fourteen years if they shall require the premises for the purposes of a business carried on by them' it was held to be sufficient for them to show that they would need at least part of the premises before the date on which the lease would otherwise have expired by effluxion of time (*Parkinson v Barclays Bank Ltd* [1951] 1 KB 368). On the other hand, where a landlord was entitled to determine a lease for 'building sites or planting or other purposes', he was held not to be entitled to determine it for the purpose of constructing a sports stadium (*Coates v Diment* [1951] 1 All ER 890).

The most satisfactory solution for the landlord (and probably for the tenant) is for the power to break to be modelled closely on the provisions of the Landlord and Tenant Act 1954, s 30(1)(f) or (g) and for the power to be exercisable on or after a specified date. In that way the determination of the lease and of the tenant's rights under the 1954 Act can proceed in tandem. Moreover, the weight of authority on the construction of those two subsections will enable both the landlord and the tenant to be more certain of the legal scope of the power. However, it is not advisable to incorporate the section itself. First, the section deals only with 'the holding' which may not be the whole of the demise; and secondly the impact of s 31A of the Act may need to be considered. Both these features give unnecessary complexity to the termination of the contractual relationship.

Where the tenancy is protected by the Landlord and Tenant Act 1954, a break-clause which relates to only part of the property is wholly ineffective (*Southport Old Links Ltd v Naylor and Another* [1985] 1 EGLR 66). If it is desired to resume possession of part of the property to be let to a tenant, that part should be demised by a separate lease. The two tenancies may be contained in a single document (*Moss v Mobil Oil Co Ltd* [1988] 1 EGLR 71). Alternatively, the break-clause should relate to the whole property, leaving the landlord free to oppose the grant of a new tenancy.

Conditions may also be attached to the exercise of a tenant's break-clause. The tenant's adviser should resist the exercise of the break-clause being conditional on compliance with the tenant's covenants, for strict compliance will be necessary (*West Country Cleaners (Falmouth) Ltd v Saly* [1966] 3 All ER 210); see further p 64. Alternatives which the tenant's adviser should seek are:

(1) that the tenant should have committed no 'substantial' breach of covenant which is subsisting on the termination date;
(2) that the tenant should have 'reasonably' performed his covenants; or
(3) that the tenant should have undertaken to pay the cost of remedying any breach found to exist on the termination date.

It is common, however, for the exercise of the break-clause to be conditional on payment by the tenant of a multiple of the annual rent in order to compensate the landlord for the void which will ensue.

(d) Effect of break-clause

The draftsman should be aware of two important consequences of the insertion of a break-clause. First, whether the power is exercisable by the landlord or the tenant, the effect of its exercise will be to determine the tenancy prior to the expiry of the term. Thus, any covenant that takes effect at a date calculated by reference to the expiry of the term, will be unenforceable if the power is exercised. For example, where a tenant covenanted to paint in the 'last quarter of the said term' it was held that the exercise of a break-clause relieved him from his obligation (*Dickinson v St Aubyn* [1944] KB 454). It would have been otherwise if he had covenanted to paint in the quarter 'preceding the expiry or sooner determination of the said term'.

Secondly, if the tenant is entitled to break at a specified date linked to a rent review, the effect of the break-clause may be to make time of the essence as far as the review is concerned (*United Scientific Holdings Ltd v Burnley Borough Council* [1977] 2 All ER 62 at 77, 98). This is so even where there is only one date for breaking the lease under the break-clause but many reviews. The effect of the linked break-clause is to make time of the essence in respect of each review (*Central Estates v Secretary of State for the Environment* [1995] EGCS 110). If the parties wish to link a tenant's break to a rent review, one solution would be to link it not to the review date itself, but to the date on which the new rent is agreed or otherwise determined. However, if this is done, in the tenant's interest there must be a limit on the landlord's power to operate the review retrospectively. In the normal course of events, the exercise by the tenant of a break-clause will prevent him from applying to the court for the grant of a new tenancy (Landlord and Tenant Act 1954, s 26(4); s 69(1) defining 'notice to quit': s 24(2)). However, it may be possible for a tenant to preserve his rights where the break-clause is exercised by means of a s 26 request. If this is done it is probable that this will have the effect of releasing any original tenant or surety from liability in the event that the tenant should hold over under the Landlord and Tenant Act 1954 after the expiry of the break-notice (cf *Junction Estates Ltd v Cope* (1974) 27 P&CR 482; *City of London Corporation v Fell* [1993] 2 WLR 1164).

On a commercial note, it may well be that the insertion of a landlord's break will reduce the market rent obtainable for the property, a fact which will doubtless manifest itself at the time of the first rent review after the landlord's power to break has become exercisable.

Example 4:4 Landlord's power to break

(1) The landlord shall be entitled to determine this tenancy by not less than six months' notice in writing expiring on or after [*date*] if he intends at the expiry of such notice either:
  (a) to demolish or reconstruct the demised property or a substantial part of it or to carry out substantial work of construction on the demised property or part of it or
  (b) to occupy the demised property for the purposes or partly for the purposes of a business to be carried on by him
(2) The service of a notice under section 25 of the Landlord and Tenant Act 1954 shall be sufficient notice and good service for the purposes of the preceding subclause

Example 4:5 Tenant's power to break on refusal of planning permission

The tenant shall be entitled to determine this tenancy by not less than three nor more than six months' notice in writing served not more than one month after the happening of any of the following events:
  (1) the refusal or deemed refusal by the local planning authority to renew the planning permission dated [*date*] permitting the use of the demised property for [   ]
  (2) the dismissal by the Secretary of State or an appointed person of any appeal against any such refusal
  (3) the expiry of the said planning permission

Example 4:6 Tenant's right to break preventing exercise of rights under Landlord and Tenant Act

The tenant shall be entitled to determine this tenancy on [   ] by giving not less than thirteen months' previous notice to that effect

Example 4:7 Tenant's conditional right to break

The tenant shall be entitled to determine this tenancy on [   ] if:
(1) he gives thirteen months' written notice to that effect and
(2) both at the date of the notice and at the date of its expiry there are neither any outstanding arrears of rent nor any subsisting breach of covenant by the tenant for which the landlord would be entitled to recover damages of more than a nominal amount

Example 4:8 Tenant's conditional right to break (alternative form)

The tenant shall be entitled to determine this tenancy on [   ] if:
(1) he gives thirteen months' written notice to that effect and
(2) on or before the expiry of the notice he pays to the landlord a sum equivalent to one year's rent at the rate payable at the date when the notice was given and
(3) on the expiry of the notice there are no outstanding rent arrears and no substantial breach of any of the tenant's covenants

6 OPTIONS TO RENEW

Options to renew have become less frequent in commercial leases since the passing of the Landlord and Tenant Act 1954. There is, nowadays, little reason for the tenant to seek to incorporate an option to renew in his lease unless by reason of his bargaining strength he can secure that the rent payable under the new lease will be lower than that which would be fixed by the court on an application for a new tenancy under the 1954 Act. The only circumstances in which an option to renew will be of practical value to the tenant are where the landlord might be able successfully to oppose the grant of a new tenancy. In such circumstances, however, it is unlikely that the landlord would be prepared to grant an option to renew. Alternatively, an option to renew might be granted where the tenancy has been 'contracted out' of the Landlord and Tenant Act 1954. The grant of a 'contracted out' tenancy, followed by the grant of an option to renew for a term which will not be contracted out is a useful mechanism to achieve a position where the tenant's loss of security of tenure is only temporary. In such cases the tenant's adviser should ensure that exercise of the option is not conditional on the performance by the tenant of his covenants. However, there may be cases where the landlord requires that the tenant should not acquire security of tenure. In such circumstances the draftsman should ensure that any new tenancy is also 'contracted out'. In any event, the grant of an option to renew may depress the value of the landlord's reversion and reduce the number of potential purchasers of it since the plans of a purchaser who wishes to redevelop or to occupy the property for the purposes of his own business may be frustrated by the exercise of the option.

The following matters must be dealt with in drafting an option to renew:

(1) the time at which it may be exercised;
(2) the manner in which it may be exercised;
(3) the conditions (if any) which the tenant is required to fulfil;
(4) the terms of the new lease;
(5) registration of the option.

(a) Time of exercise

It is usual to provide that the tenant must exercise the option within a few months before the expiry of the lease. Such time limits must be strictly observed unless there is express provision to the contrary. However, the draftsman should choose his words with care. For example, an option exercisable six months before the 'expiry of the tenancy' might permit the tenant to exercise the option during any continuation tenancy (under the Landlord and Tenant Act 1954, s 24); conversely, an option exercisable six months before 'the date on which the term hereby granted is expressed to expire' would not. The clause should also state the earliest date upon which the option may be exercised. If no date is specified the court would probably conclude that it was to be exercised within a reasonable period ending on the last day for exercise (*Multon v Cordell* [1986] 1 EGLR 44).

(b) Manner of exercise

An option to renew is usually exercisable by notice in writing. There is rarely any need to specify a form of notice, although it is sensible to provide for service of the notice. This is usually done by incorporating the provisions of the Law of Property Act 1925, s 196, or those of the Landlord and Tenant Act 1927, s 23. Which of the two is incorporated is largely a matter of taste. It is suggested that one or other method of service be expressly incorporated. Although the Law of Property Act

1925, s 196(5) (which incorporates the method of service therein prescribed) applies to all leases unless a contrary intention appears, it applies only in respect of notices 'required' to be served by the lease in question. It does not apply to notices 'permitted' to be served by the lease. It is probable that notices exercising options do not fall within s 196(5) (*Wandsworth LBC v Attwell* [1996] 01 EG 100).

There is no need to take any special measures in order to comply with the Law of Property (Miscellaneous) Provisions Act 1989, s 2. The service of a traditional form of notice exercising an option is sufficient to bring a binding contract into existence, provided that the original grant of the option (ie the lease) was in writing and contained all the terms of the option (*Spiro v Glencrown Properties* [1991] 2 WLR 931).

(c) Conditions precedent

If conditions precedent are prescribed the tenant must fulfil them strictly. In some cases, however, the court may be able to imply a term that even if a condition precedent is not fulfilled, it will not prevent exercise of the option (*Little v Courage* (1994) 70 P&CR 469). It is common for an option to provide that the tenant must have paid all the rent and performed all the covenants. If this form is chosen even a trivial breach of covenant will defeat the tenant's option (*West Country Cleaners (Falmouth) Ltd v Saly* [1966] 3 All ER 210; *Bairstow Eves (Securities) Ltd v Ripley* (1992) 65 P&CR 220). However, a breach for this purpose means a subsisting breach, not a 'spent' breach in respect of which the landlord no longer has a cause of action (*Bass Holdings Ltd v Morton Music Ltd* [1987] 2 All ER 1001). The strict approach was questioned but nevertheless applied in *Kitney v Greater London Properties Ltd* (1984) 272 EG 786. In almost all cases an obstructive landlord will be able to find some subsisting breach of covenant on the tenant's part and thereby defeat the option. This form may, therefore, work hardship to tenants, particularly where there is a genuine dispute as to liability. The tenant's adviser should, therefore, insist that the requirement be that the tenant shall have 'reasonably' performed his covenants. In such a case the exercise of the option will be good if the tenant has performed his covenants to the extent that a reasonably-minded tenant would have done (*Gardner v Blaxill* [1960] 2 All ER 457). The inclusion of the word 'reasonably' gives the court a discretion which will be exercised in the tenant's favour where for example he has made one or two late payments of rent, but not where he has been persistently in arrear throughout the term (*Bassett v Whiteley* (1982) 54 P&CR 87).

The draftsman should next consider whether the conditions are to be fulfilled at the time of the service of the notice or at the end of the term. If they are to be fulfilled at the time of the service of the notice then, for example, the landlord may not be able to rely on a breach of covenant to decorate 'in the last year of the term' since no breach of that covenant can be positively asserted until the expiry of the complete year. On the other hand, if the conditions are to be fulfilled at the expiry of the term, the tenant will have the opportunity to remedy any breach of covenant between the service of the notice and its expiry (*Simons v Associated Furnishers Ltd* [1931] 1 Ch 379). This latter form is fairer to both parties.

(d) Terms of the new lease

The terms of the new lease should be clearly specified in the grant of the option. Usually the terms of the new lease will be the same as the terms of the old, but there is no reason why the parties should not provide for variations in those terms. The draftsman should take care in dealing with the option to renew itself. If the option to renew is included in the terms of the new lease, the lease may be treated as a perpetually renewable lease taking effect as a term of 2,000 years (*Parkus v Greenwood* [1950] Ch 644; *Caerphilly Concrete Products Ltd v Owen* [1972] 1 WLR 372; Law of Property Act 1922, s 145 and Sched 15). However, where an option clause enabled the tenant to renew for a term of seven years, and provided that the new lease was to 'contain a like covenant for renewal for a further term of seven years on the expiration of the term thereby granted', it was held that the tenant was entitled to renew twice only (*Burnett (Marjorie) Ltd v Barclay* (1981) 258 EG 642). It is difficult to see any significant differences between that case and those in which a perpetually renewable lease has been found to have been created. Accordingly, where the draftsman wishes to create more than one right to renew, it is suggested that a perpetually renewable lease should be expressly negatived.

As far as the new rent is concerned, options fall into four categories:
(1) options to renew 'at a rent to be agreed': such options are void for uncertainty unless some provision is made for determination of the rent in default of agreement (*King's Motors (Oxford) Ltd v Lax* [1969] 3 All ER 665) or some provision is made for a minimum or a maximum rent (*Corson v*

Rhuddlan BC [1990] 1 EGLR 255);
(2) options to renew at a rent to be determined in accordance with some stated formula, without any effective machinery for working it out: if necessary the court will supply the machinery in such cases (*Brown v Gould* [1972] Ch 53);
(3) options with machinery but no detailed formula: in such cases the court is likely to imply a term that the rent is to be fair and reasonable between the landlord and the tenant and will supply machinery for its determination (*Sudbrook Trading Estate Ltd v Eggleton* [1983] AC 444);
(4) options which provide both a formula and the machinery for working it out: the draftsman should attempt to make his draft fall into this category.

If the term of the new lease is to exceed, say, five years, the draftsman should make provision for the inclusion in the new lease of machinery for reviewing the rent. In the absence of express provision to this effect, the person responsible for determining the new rent will not be able to include rent reviews, nor will he be able to fix a stepped rent (*National Westminster Bank Ltd v BSC Footwear Ltd* (1980) 257 EG 277; *Bracknell Development Corporation v Greenlees Lennards Ltd* (1982) 260 EG 500). In Example 4:9 below, the arbitrator is given the powers exercisable by the court on a renewal under the 1954 Act. Those powers contain the power to include in the new lease provision for varying the rent (Landlord and Tenant Act 1954, s 34(3)).

The drafting of a suitable formula is considered in more detail in the context of rent review.

(e) Registration

An option for renewal is registrable as a Class C(iv) land charge (*Beesly v Hallwood Estates Ltd* [1961] Ch 105). If it is not registered it will be void against a purchaser of the reversion where the land in question is unregistered land. Where the land is registered land at the time of the demise, if the tenant is in actual occupation of the property the option to renew will be an overriding interest under the Land Registration Act 1925, s 70(1)(g), and will be enforceable against such a purchaser. Nevertheless, the option can and should be protected by notice or caution on the register.

If the option is defeated against a purchaser of the reversion for want of registration, it appears that the tenant may still maintain an action against the original landlord for breach of covenant (*Wright v Dean* [1948] Ch 686), unless in the meantime the original landlord has been released from liability under the procedure laid down by the Landlord and Tenant (Covenants) Act 1995. It will, therefore, be in the landlord's interest as well as the tenant's to ensure that the option is protected by registration in the appropriate register. This may be done by including in the grant of the option a proviso that it is to be void if it is not registered as an estate contract within, say, three months from the date of the lease.

Example 4:9 Option to renew

(1) The tenant may by notice in writing served not less than six months before the date on which the term hereby granted is expressed to expire call upon the landlord for a further lease of the demised property ('the further lease') provided that up to that date he has paid the rent and reasonably performed and observed his covenants

(2) The further lease shall be for a term of ten years from the said date upon the same terms and conditions as this lease (save as to rent and as to this option for renewal) and at a rent to be agreed between the parties or in default of agreement to be determined by a single arbitrator to be appointed by the President for the time being of the Royal Institution of Chartered Surveyors

(3) In determining the rent payable under the further lease the arbitrator shall have the same powers as would be enjoyed by the court determining a rent for the demised property under section 34 of the Landlord and Tenant Act 1954 and shall disregard the same matters as are specified in that section

(4) This option shall be of no effect if the tenant fails to register it as an estate contract within three months from the date of this lease

Example 4:10 Option to renew contracted out tenancy

If:

(1) the tenant wishes to take a further tenancy of the demised property for a term of five years from the expiry date of the term hereby created and

(2) the tenant gives written notice of his desire to the landlord not more than six nor less than three months before the expiry of the term and

(3) up to the date of the notice the tenant has paid the rent and substantially performed his covenants and

(4) the tenant joins with the landlord in making an application to the court for an order authorising the exclusion of the provisions of sections 24 to 28 of the Landlord and Tenant Act 1954 in relation to the further tenancy and

(5) the court makes such an order

then the landlord shall let the demised property to the tenant for a term of five years from the expiry of the term hereby created at a rent to be agreed between the parties or in default of agreement to be determined by arbitration and otherwise upon the terms of this lease (except this option for renewal)

Example 4:11 Clause negativing perpetual renewal

Nothing in this clause shall entitle the tenant to renew the tenancy for any term expiring more than twenty years after the beginning of the term of this lease

7 RENEWAL LEASES

(a) Duration of tenancy

The duration of a new tenancy granted under the Landlord and Tenant Act 1954 is to be such term as is reasonable in all the circumstances (Landlord and Tenant Act 1954, s 33). However, unless the landlord and the tenant agree, the court cannot order the grant of a term exceeding fourteen years (*ibid*).

The following factors are among those which are taken into account:

(1) the length of the previous tenancy or tenancies (*Betty's Cafes Ltd v Phillips Furnishing Stores Ltd* [1957] 1 Ch 67 at 88);

(2) any period during which the tenant has held over pending resolution of his application (*London and Provincial Millinery Stores Ltd v Barclays Bank Ltd* [1962] 1 WLR 510);

(3) the landlord's intentions as regards his own occupation of the property (*Wig Creations Ltd v Colour Film Services Ltd* (1969) 113 SJ 688 where it was held that the new tenancy should expire shortly after the landlord would become entitled to rely upon s 30(1)(g) of the Landlord and Tenant Act 1954);

(4) the prospects of redevelopment of the property (*Reohorn v Barry Corporation* [1956] 2 All ER 742; *London and Provincial Millinery Stores Ltd v Barclays Bank Ltd* above);

(5) the balance of hardship, and the relative bargaining positions of the parties (*Upsons Ltd v Robins (E) Ltd* [1956] 1 QB 131; *Amika Motors Ltd v Colebrook Holdings Ltd* (1981) 259 EG 243);

(6) the tenant's business needs (*CBS (United Kingdom) Ltd v London Scottish Properties Ltd* (1985) 275 EG 718).

(b) Break-clauses

Where the landlord asserts that there are redevelopment prospects, the court will usually order the new tenancy to contain a break-clause enabling the landlord to terminate the lease for redevelopment. It is no part of the policy of the Landlord and Tenant Act 1954 to give security of tenure to a business tenant at the expense of preventing redevelopment (*Adams v Green* (1978) 247 EG 49).

Accordingly, where the landlord proves an intention to redevelop not immediately capable of implementation, the court will order the inclusion of a break-clause exercisable when the landlord is ready. It does not matter that the redevelopment is likely to be carried out by a purchaser from the landlord rather than the landlord himself (*Adams v Green* above); nor that the redevelopment proposals are very tentative (*Edwards (JH) & Sons Ltd v Central London Commercial Estates Ltd* (1983) 271 EG 697). The function of the court in such circumstances is to strike a reasonable balance between the conflicting considerations of not preventing redevelopment on the one hand, and giving the tenant a reasonable degree of security of tenure on the other (*ibid*). The court has two objects in mind: first to give the tenant security for as long as the holding is not required for development; secondly to ensure that when the landlord is ready to proceed with the development, the development is not held up by rights possessed by the tenant (*National Car Parks v Paternoster Consortium* [1990] 1 EGLR 99). But the court may take into account hardship to the tenant. Thus, where the tenant had been innocently misled into believing that he would obtain a long term, and had invested heavily in the property next door, whereas the landlord in fact had plans for immediate redevelopment, the Court of Appeal upheld an order for a break-clause exercisable after the first three years of the term (*Amika Motors Ltd v Colebrook Holdings Ltd* (1981) 259 EG 243).

The court will take into account the fact that the landlord must prove a statutory ground of opposition in order effectively to operate the break-clause (*Adams v Green* above) and accordingly will not attach much weight to objections which could be raised by the tenant when the landlord seeks to operate the break-clause (*Amika Motors Ltd v Colebrook Holdings Ltd* above).

In the present state of the law the landlord is in a strong position if he wishes to include a break-clause in a new lease.

Where the landlord seeks a break-clause on renewal, the tenant should press for any right to break to be mutual. If the tenant accepts that the property may be redeveloped he will probably wish to be looking for alternative accommodation sooner rather than later, and he will wish to move in and terminate his liability under his existing lease as soon as he finds it.

(c) Options

The court has no jurisdiction to order a new tenancy to contain an option entitling the tenant to purchase the landlord's reversion (*Kirkwood v Johnson* (1979) 38 P&CR 392).

It is suggested that the court would not order a new lease to contain a contractual option to renew, since the Landlord and Tenant Act 1954 itself contains the code for enabling tenants to renew their leases.

5
Rent and Rent Review

1 The Initial Rent and Rent-Free Periods

The fixing of the initial rent is obviously beyond the province of the draftsman. However, there are some drafting points which should be considered.

The first concerns stamp duty. In assessing rent for the purposes of stamp duty, the Inland Revenue applies what is called the 'contingency principle'. This means that stamp duty is assessed by reference to the highest ascertainable rent which might become payable under the lease. Thus, where a lease reserved a rent calculated by a percentage of development expenditure up to a specified limit, stamp duty was assessed on the basis that the limit would be reached (*Coventry CC v IRC* [1979] Ch 142). Had the limit not been stated, the rent would have been unascertainable, and the stamp duty would have been £2.

Where a lease reserves a fixed rent for part of the term and an unascertainable rent for the balance, it is stamped *ad valorem* on the fixed rent and £2 on the unascertainable rent. A rent will be unascertainable if it is fixed by reference to facts which cannot be known at the date of the lease, eg the market rental value at a future date. Thus if a lease provides for a rent-free period to be followed by a rent review by reference to market values at the end of the rent-free period, stamp duty will be avoided. Of course, if there is a minimum rent stated in the lease, stamp duty will be levied on that minimum, on the 'contingency principle'.

Secondly, the draftsman must now consider the potential impact of VAT. Where there is a causal link between the grant of a rent-free period and the carrying out by the tenant of work to the property, and the tenant is obliged to carry out such work (eg shopfitting), the tenant will be treated as making a supply to the landlord of an amount equivalent to the rent foregone. The tenant will be liable for the VAT (*Ridgeons Bulk v Commissioners of Customs & Excise* [1994] STC 427 discussed in [1992] 37 EG 97). In addition, where the landlord pays an inducement to the tenant in order to persuade the tenant to take up the lease, that is a payment on which the tenant must account for VAT (*Nevile Russell v Commissioners of Customs & Excise* [1987] VATTR 194).

The general principle for VAT is that consideration for a supply is inclusive of VAT unless otherwise stated. Thus, if the landlord has elected to waive the exemption from VAT in respect of a particular building, he will not be able to add VAT to the rent if it is expressed as a single figure. If the rate of VAT changes, he will be able to pass on any increase. However, if the landlord has not elected to waive the exemption from VAT, VAT will not be chargeable on the rent. If he subsequently decides to waive the exemption, he will be able to add VAT unless that is forbidden by the terms of the lease (VAT Act 1994, s 89). A term in a lease does not negative this rule unless it refers specifically to VAT or to s 89 of the Act (VAT Act 1994, s 89(2)). The exemption can only be waived on a building-by-building basis. However, it seems that although the exemption can only be waived on a building-by-building basis, if the exemption is waived for a building as a whole, but if a lease of part of the building prohibits the addition of VAT, the landlord will have to account to Customs & Excise for VAT out of the net rent. Some tenants prefer, however, to seek to obtain from the landlord a covenant not to waive the exemption. If this route is taken it will be necessary, from the tenant's point of view, for the landlord to covenant to procure a similar covenant from successors in title.

If the tenant is to covenant expressly to pay VAT on rent, the VAT should itself be reserved as rent. This is because if it is not reserved as rent, the Stamp Office take the view that the application of the 'contingency principle' means that stamp duty is payable on the full amount of VAT which may become payable over the whole term of the lease. This is much more than the duty levied on an annual rent increased by 17.5 per cent (see *Marsh* [1991] 42 EG 94). It is understood, however, that the Stamp Office will only apply this principle where the lease states that the VAT is not reserved as rent.

Example 5:1 Clause preventing landlord from charging VAT

> In the event that the landlord elects to waive any exemption from value added tax in relation to the demised property or the building of which it forms part, no value added tax shall be added to the rent reserved by this lease

Example 5:2 Clause preventing landlord from waiving exemption from VAT

(1) not to elect to waive any exemption from value added tax in relation to the demised property or the building of which it forms part

(2) on any assignment of the whole or part of the reversion expectant on this lease, or the grant of any concurrent lease of the whole or part of the property, to procure that the assignee or lessee gives a covenant in the terms of this clause

2 Deductions from Rent

There are a number of circumstances in which a tenant is entitled to withhold some or all of the rent which is otherwise payable. Some of these are laid down by statute. For example, where rent is paid to a non-resident landlord, the tenant must deduct income tax from the amount of the rent (Income and Corporation Taxes Act 1988, s 349). Other statutes enable a tenant to make deductions where he has paid the cost of certain works (Highways Act 1980, s 212; Coast Protection Act 1949, s 10; Local Government (Miscellaneous Provisions) Act 1976, s 33). In other cases the tenant has a right at common law to make deductions; for example where he pays for repairs which are the landlord's responsibility (*Lee-Parker v Izzet* [1971] 1 WLR 1688), or ground rent (*Jones v Morris* (1849) 3 Exch 742) or mortgage interest (*Johnson v Jones* (1839) 9 Ad & El 809) which is the landlord's liability. In addition, the tenant is entitled to set off against his liability to pay rent any cross-claim (whether liquidated or unliquidated) which arises out of the lease itself or the relationship of landlord and tenant (*British Anzani (Felixstowe) v International Marine Management* [1980] QB 137).

The tenant's right to deduct may be excluded by the express terms of the covenant to pay rent (except in certain cases where statute prohibits contracting out). But where the draftsman wishes to exclude the tenant's right to set off, clear words must be used (*Connaught Restaurants Ltd v Indoor Leisure Ltd* [1994] 1 WLR 501). The phrase 'without deduction' is not clear enough to exclude the right to set off. It is considered that only the use of the words 'set off' themselves will be clear enough.

Example 5:3 Covenant to pay rent

To pay the rent promptly and without deduction or set-off

3 Rent Review

In recent years it has become the practice in leases granted for more than five years or so to contain some machinery for enabling the rent to be reviewed, either continuously or at periodic intervals. The rent review clause, or the indexation of rent, is the product of the conflict between the tenant who wishes to have the maximum length of term and the landlord who wishes to have the maximum return on his investment. It is nowadays quite unrealistic for a tenant even to attempt to secure a long letting of commercial property at a fixed rack rent; and no well-advised landlord would grant such a lease. Since the value of a property investment is primarily the receipt of a secure rent, the rent review clause is the most important provision in the whole lease.

The revision of rents can be achieved in a number of ways. The most common is for the rent to be periodically revised to a figure agreed between the parties, with procedure for determination by a third party if the landlord and tenant fail to agree. This is the best method because it is most closely related to the value of the property itself. It is not, however, the only method and others are considered below.

An extended treatment of the subject may be found in Clarke and Adams, *Rent Reviews and Variable Rents*, 3rd edn (Longman, 1990).

4 Index-Linked Rents

Draftsmen have sometimes attempted to link the rent payable under a lease to movements in an official index, such as the Index of Retail Prices (as happened in *Blumenthal v Gallery Five Ltd* (1971) 220 EG 33). It is understood that such clauses are more common on the Continent. Commercially, such a rent review clause may work to the disadvantage of either party. On the one hand, if the chosen index rises faster than rents, or if rents fall, the tenant may find himself paying a rent in excess of the market rent; on the other hand, if rents rise faster than the chosen index, the landlord may find himself receiving an uneconomic return from his property. In addition, a rent which is index-linked will not reflect any change in the property itself. Thus, if a High Street is turned into a four-lane urban clearway the trading potential of a shop may be severely affected, but an index-linked rent will not be capable of reflecting that change.

The drafting of an indexation clause presents various problems. First, the parties must agree on their chosen index. Various indices now exist and it may be that the choice of index should to some extent be determined by the nature of the property. Thus, the rent of a shop might be determined by reference to the Index of Retail Prices, the rent of a warehouse by reference to the Index of Wholesale Prices, and the rent of a builder's merchant's yard by reference to an index of construction costs. The index most often used for this purpose is the General Index of Retail Prices published by the Department of Education and Employment. Some of the larger firms of surveyors produce property indices, but the statistical sample is probably too small to enable them to be reliable.

Secondly, the parties should be aware that the items taken into account in compiling the index may vary from time to time. Accordingly, the basis on which the rent is calculated may itself be changed through a change in the composition of the index. This was the problem that arose in *Blumenthal v Gallery Five Ltd* (1971) 220 EG 33 and *Cumshaw v Bowen* [1987] 1 EGLR 30. It is unusual to provide expressly for this contingency and the lease is probably best left silent on this point. A major change in the composition of the index is one of the gambles inherent in this form of rent review.

Thirdly, the base figure upon which the index is calculated may be updated. Thus, if the index starts with a base figure of 100 in, say, January 1984 and rises to 300 by September 1990, the index may be recalculated from October 1990 onwards by reference to the figure shown in the index for September 1990, which becomes the new base figure of 100. The draftsman must provide expressly for this contingency, otherwise the landlord will face a sudden drop in the rent if the base figure used for the index is recalculated. There are two principal methods of dealing with this. One is to provide that the rent shall be calculated as if the index had not been adjusted. This method works fairly well provided that the publishers of the index provide a conversion table enabling the current figures to be related to earlier figures, and usually they do so. However, it may give rise to the necessity for a fairly sophisticated mathematical calculation if a conversion table is not published. If the clause provides for the substitution of figures, it is important to ensure that all necessary mathematical information is given to enable the rent to be calculated (see *Wyndham Investments v Motorway Tyres and Accessories* [1991] 2 EGLR 114 for a case where this was not done, and the index-linked rent failed completely).

The alternative method is to provide that upon any adjustment of the base figure, the rent payable immediately before the adjustment becomes a fixed amount payable under the terms of the lease (or is substituted for a fixed amount previously reserved). The indexation process then begins again, using the new figures. The advantage of this method is that there is no need for any conversion from one set of figures to another. However, the disadvantage from the tenant's point of view is that the minimum rent payable under the lease will be increased. Accordingly, he will be unable to take the benefit of any fall in the index.

The fourth point that the draftsman must cover is the possible abandonment of the index. It may become impossible to calculate the index-linked rent. Again, there are two principal methods of dealing with this contingency. First, the draftsman may provide for the substitution of a different index to be agreed between the parties or determined by a third party in default of agreement. Alternatively, he may provide for a change in the method of rent review, and if this is done it is usual to revert to the more traditional method of periodic reviews to market rent.

A third choice is to leave the new method of rent review open for agreement at the time indexation proves to be impossible. In this way either party will be able to take advantage of any significant change in market practice during the currency of the lease.

Fifthly, the clause must be mathematically correct. Since it is often difficult to translate mathematical concepts into words (see *London Regional Transport v Wimpey Group Construction* [1986] 2 EGLR 41 for judicial commendation of algebra), the formula must be checked mathematically either with a calculator or a computer.

Allied to the indexation of rent is the reservation of rent calculated by reference to the price of some specified commodity, such as gold, or by reference to the value of the pound in relation to a foreign currency. In *Treseder-Griffin v Co-operative Insurance Society Ltd* [1956] 2 QB 127 the rent reserved was £1,900 'either in gold sterling or Bank of England notes to the equivalent value in gold sterling'. The Court of Appeal held that the rent payable was £1,900 rather than the realisable value of 1,900 gold sovereigns. The decision was based on two grounds. First, it was held by Denning LJ that a 'gold clause' in a domestic contract was void as being contrary to public policy. Secondly, it was held that on the proper construction of the lease the provisions relating to gold regulated the manner of payment rather than the amount of payment. It is suggested that the first of these reasons would no longer be valid if litigated again (see *Multiservice Bookbinding Ltd v Marden* [1979] Ch 84, where Browne-Wilkinson J upheld a mortgage under which the interest payments were linked to the value of the Swiss franc, cited with apparent approval by Lord Denning MR in *Staffordshire Area Health Authority v South Staffordshire Waterworks Co* [1978] 3 All ER 769). The second of these reasons can be overcome by careful drafting.

Example 5:4 Index-linked rent: upwards only from initial rent

YIELDING AND PAYING the annual sum of £[   ] ('the basic rent') payable quarterly in advance on the 25th of March the 24th of June the 29th of September and the 25th of December in each year and in addition such sum payable on each of the above dates in advance ('the index-linked rent') as bears the same proportion to one quarter of the basic rent as is borne by the figure shown in the General Index of Retail Prices ('the index') for the month immediately preceding the months in which payment of any particular instalment of rent is due to the figure [   ] (which is the figure shown in that index for the month of [   ]) minus one quarter of the basic rent
PROVIDED THAT

(1) if after the date of this lease the index is calculated by reference to a different base date or base figure then the index-linked rent shall be calculated as if that change had not taken place

(2) if the index ceases to be published or if for any reason it becomes impossible or impracticable to calculate the index-linked rent then either the landlord or the tenant may by notice require the rent to be thenceforth reviewed at such times and in such manner as may be agreed between them or in default of agreement be determined by a single arbitrator to be appointed by the President for the time being of the Royal Institution of Chartered Surveyors who shall have regard to market practice prevailing at the time of such notice in relation to new lettings of property of the same type as the demised property

(3) in no circumstances shall the total rent payable under this lease be less than the basic rent

5 TURNOVER RENTS

Rents linked to the tenant's turnover have been common for many years, particularly in mining leases. Recently they have been applied to other commercial lettings, notably to lettings of shops, hotels and restaurants. However, it has been judicially observed that the objection to a rent representing a percentage of the tenant's turnover is that, if the price of a commodity rises at a faster rate than the cost of living, pressure is likely to develop on dealers in that commodity to reduce their margin of profit or rate of commission (*Naylor v Uttoxeter UDC* (1974) 231 EG 619 *per* Brightman J). Accordingly, the tenant may find that the proportion of rent to profit increases. The same result may occur even if the tenant does not consciously reduce his profit margin. For example, if the government were to increase the rate of VAT gross turnover may increase (and with it the rent) while the tenant's net profit remains static. This problem arose in a rather more specialised form in *Tucker v Granada Motorway Services Ltd* [1977] 3 All ER 865. In that case the Minister of

Transport granted the tenant a lease of a motorway service area at a fixed rent and an additional variable rent. The variable rent payable each year was a percentage of the gross takings for the previous year from the petrol filling station and catering services provided and from any other business activities on the service area. The gross takings included the amount of tobacco duty concealed in the selling price of tobacco. Thus, when the Chancellor of the Exchequer increased tobacco duty, the tenant's rent increased, although its ratio of profit to turnover decreased and its actual profit on each packet of cigarettes was generally speaking not favourably affected. The tenant's business was rendered uneconomic and eventually the terms of the lease were renegotiated at a cost of £122,220 to the tenant.

In times of recession, turnover rents are more favourable to tenants because the tenant's liability to pay rent is related to his ability to pay.

The tenant's advisers should study carefully the definition of turnover upon which the rent is to be calculated. It should as far as possible be related to the actual profit made by the tenant. However, from the landlord's point of view too close a relationship between rent and profit means that his income will depend to a large extent on the efficiency with which the tenant carries on business rather than on the value of the demised property.

Further matters must be taken into account when drafting a turnover rent. Should a basic rent be reserved? This is usually done. Sometimes there is a guaranteed minimum reviewed at periodic intervals. Next, the tenant's adviser should ensure that there is a minimum turnover figure, which is not to be taken into account in assessing the rent, and possibly a maximum figure above which turnover is ignored.

Where the tenant's business includes a substantial number of transactions in which he gives credit to his customers the draftsman will have to consider whether the amount of the transaction should be brought into account at the time of the transaction or at the time of payment; whether interest payments are to be included in the calculation of turnover and whether the tenant is to have an allowance for bad debts. Conversely, where the tenant is likely to give discounts to certain customers (eg those who pay by credit card, or employees), or where he is likely to have sales or special offers, his advisers should attempt to ensure that it is the amount he receives rather than the full retail price which is to be included in the calculation of turnover.

The demised property may be part only of the premises on which the tenant carries on business and in such cases the turnover may need to be apportioned. For example, a tenant who uses the demised property for the business of a dry cleaner, may receive goods for cleaning on the property but process them elsewhere. The place at which the cleaning is actually carried out may be entirely dependent on reception centres, yet the tenant may be paying rent for it. In such circumstances if the turnover of the reception centres is not apportioned in some way, the tenant will in effect pay double rent for the place at which the cleaning is carried out.

The draftsman must provide for the landlord to have sufficient power of inspection of the tenant's books to satisfy himself that any information supplied by the tenant is correct. There should probably be a provision for independent determination (by an accountant rather than a surveyor) in case of dispute. However, the tenant should not be subjected to oppressive powers of inspection and he should resist an attempt to make him pay the costs of an inspection, although it would be fair that he should pay the costs if there is a material discrepancy between the information supplied by him and the results of an inspection. Reliance on the tenant's audited accounts for the purpose of calculating turnover may be unwise for the landlord, not because those accounts may be inaccurate but because they may not be settled until well after the end of the rental period in question. Accordingly, the tenant should be required to supply regular certificates of his turnover, and there might also be a provision for the payment of interest on rent in case of delay in supplying them.

Clearly, if the demised property ceases to be used for trading, the landlord's income will drop or possibly cease. The draftsman should, therefore, insert in the lease a positive covenant to keep the demised property open for trading during normal hours (rather than relying on a negative user covenant 'not to use the property otherwise than as ...', which would permit the tenant not to use the property at all). In this way any loss of rent may be claimed as damages for breach of covenant (see *Transworld Land Co v J Sainsbury* [1990] 2 EGLR 255 for the scope of such a claim). Nevertheless, it may be prudent to provide expressly for the payment of rent where, for example, the property remains empty while the tenant is seeking to assign his lease. This may be done by deeming a certain level of turnover during any such period or by reverting to the open market rent. If the former method is chosen, the draftsman should beware lest the deemed turnover relates to the period immediately preceding the void, since the tenant may have been running down his business in preparation for a move.

A similar problem may arise when the tenant allows someone else into occupation of part of the demised property, either as a subtenant or by way of licence or franchise agreement. The draftsman should ensure that any licence fee or subrent is taken into account in the calculation of the tenant's turnover; indeed, he may think it appropriate to cover the contingency that the tenant grants a licence of part of the demised property at less than the market rate. This may be done, for example, by providing that the turnover of the subtenant or licensee is to be taken into account in calculating the tenant's turnover. In addition to Example 5.5, Forms 12 and 13 contain examples of rents based on turnover.

Example 5:5 Turnover rent

YIELDING AND PAYING THEREFOR by equal quarterly payments in advance on the usual quarter days:
 (1) the annual sum of £ [   ] ('the basic rent') and
 (2) such sum as is calculated in accordance with the Schedule hereto ('the turnover rent')

SCHEDULE

(1) In this Schedule the following expressions have the following meanings:
  (a) 'gross turnover' means the aggregate of all sums:
    (i) received by the tenant in return for goods supplied or services rendered in the course of any trade or business carried on by him in the demised property or partly in the demised property and partly elsewhere and
    (ii) payable to the tenant by any person in consideration of the use or occupation of the whole or any part of the demised property
  (b) 'a rental year' means a period of twelve calendar months beginning on [   ]
  (c) 'net turnover' means the gross turnover less:
    (i) any sum actually paid by the tenant to HM Commissioners of Customs & Excise by way of valued added tax or other tax chargeable on the supply of goods or services
    (ii) any sum refunded by the tenant to his customers in respect of defective or unsatisfactory goods or services
    (iii) [   ] per cent of any sums received by the tenant in return for services for which orders are received at the demised property but are performed wholly elsewhere
  (d) 'qualified accountant' means a member of the Institute of Chartered Accountants in England and Wales
(2) The turnover rent for a rental year shall be:
  (a) [   ] per cent of the net turnover for the year immediately preceding that rental year exceeding £[   ] but less than £[   ] and
  (b) [   ] per cent of the net turnover for the year immediately preceding that rental year exceeding £[   ] but less than £[   ]

RENT AND RENT REVIEW

(3) Within one month after the beginning of each rental year (time being of the essence) the tenant shall deliver to the landlord a certificate signed by a qualified accountant of the tenant's gross turnover and net turnover for the year immediately preceding that rental year

(4) The tenant shall upon reasonable notice permit the landlord or his agent to inspect and take copies of the tenant's books of accounts or any other document or record which in the opinion of the landlord or such agent is relevant to the determination of the turnover rent and shall bear the costs of such inspection if there shall be any material discrepancy between the information supplied by the tenant under paragraph (3) above and the results of such inspection

(5) The turnover rent shall be determined by a qualified accountant (acting as an expert) and whose decision shall be final (except so far as concerns matters of law) to be appointed by the President for the time being of the Institute of Chartered Accountants in England and Wales:
   (a) if the tenant fails to supply a certificate in accordance with paragraph (3) above (in which case the landlord's costs of the determination and the expert's fee shall be borne by the tenant) or
   (b) if there shall be any dispute between the parties as to the calculation of the turnover rent (in which case the costs of the determination and the expert's fee shall be borne as the expert directs)

(6) Until the determination of the turnover rent for any rental year the tenant shall continue to pay rent at the rate payable immediately before the beginning of the rental year in question and upon such determination there shall be due as arrears of rent or as the case may be refunded to the tenant the difference (if any) between the rent paid by the tenant for that year and the rent which ought to have been paid by him for that year plus (if the turnover rent is determined by an expert) such amount of interest as may be directed by the expert

(7) If the turnover rent for any rental year falls below £[   ] the landlord may by notice in writing served on the tenant not more than one month after the determination of the turnover rent for that year (time not being of the essence) require that there be substituted for the basic rent and the turnover rent for that year the amount for which the demised property might reasonably be expected to be let on the open market at the beginning of the year in question for a term equal to the residue of this lease then unexpired and on the same terms as this lease (save as to rent but on the assumption that the rent may be revised every five years) there being disregarded the matters set out in section 34 of the Landlord and Tenant Act 1954 (as amended) and in default of agreement the said amount shall be determined by an independent surveyor (acting as an expert not as an arbitrator) to be appointed by the President for the time being of the Royal Institute of Chartered Surveyors whose decision shall be final and whose fee shall be borne as he directs

Example 5:6 Turnover rent for theatre or cinema based on box office receipts

(1) In this Schedule:
(a) 'box office receipts' means the gross amount of all moneys payable to the tenant or any group company on the sale of tickets for theatrical cinematic or other performances in the demised property or the right to stage productions or hold conferences or other events (whether public or private) in the demised property and any moneys payable on the sale of programmes souvenirs or similar items:
  (i) treating any sale by credit card as having been a sale in consideration of the net amount recoverable by the tenant from the credit card company
  (ii) treating any amount which the tenant is entitled to receive by way of grant gift or sponsorship as part of the box office receipts and
  (iii) deducting any value added tax payable by the tenant to HM Customs & Excise
(b) 'bar receipts' means the gross amount of all moneys payable to the tenant or any group company for the supply of food and drink in the demised property:
  (i) treating any sale by credit card as having been a sale in consideration of the net amount recoverable by the tenant from the credit card company
  (ii) allowing the tenant a reduction of 2 per cent for wastage
(2) The rent payable by the tenant shall be the aggregate of:
(a) £[   ] per annum
(b) 5 per cent of the first 60 per cent of the box office receipts for any year
(c) 10 per cent of the remainder of the box office receipts
(d) 7.5 per cent of the bar receipts payable annually in arrear on 31 December in each year
(3) The tenant shall pay on account of the rent on 1 January 1 April 1 July and 1 October:
  (a) in the first year of the term £[   ] by four equal instalments
  (b) in the second and every subsequent year of the term payments at the rate of the rent payable for the last preceding year of the term by four equal instalments and as soon as possible after the end of the second and each subsequent year the amounts payable for that year under paragraph (2) above shall be agreed or otherwise determined and all necessary adjustments (whether by way further payment by the tenant or credit given by the landlord) shall be made
(4) The tenant shall:
(a) keep full and accurate books or records of account
(b) permit the landlord (or a person nominated by the landlord) to inspect the books or records of account (but not more often than once every three months) and if so required to provide the

books or records in a readily legible form
- (5) (a) at the end of each year of the term either the landlord or the tenant may require an audit of the tenant's books and records by an independent auditor (acting as an expert) to be appointed (in default of agreement) by the President of the Institute of Chartered Accountants in England and Wales
  - (b) the auditor shall certify the amount of the box office receipts and the bar receipts for the year in question and his certificate shall be binding on the parties (except in so far as concerns matters of law)
  - (c) the auditor has power to determine how his costs and the costs of any representations to him shall be borne

6 Rent Geared to Subrents

Where the landlord lets property that the tenant will sublet, it is not uncommon for the rent due under the headlease to be geared to the rents due under subleases granted by the tenant. The rent due under the headlease will usually be a basic rent plus a percentage of the subrents. This concept is mainly found in development leases, where the parties are in economic (though not legal) partnership. The landlord puts in the land, the tenant puts in the construction costs and his development skills, and the result is an investment in which both landlord and tenant participate. The landlord will require a return on the land value; the tenant will require a return on the costs and risk of development; and both parties may wish to participate in any super profit. This kind of scheme is often known as a side by side scheme. In these cases the rental income is often divided between the landlord and the tenant in slices, each slice representing a particular return on investment by landlord and tenant respectively. If this is done, care must be taken to ensure that each slice receives its proper priority in order of payment, otherwise one party may take the lion's share of the income at the expense of the other. As with index-linked rents, any mathematical formula should be carefully checked by calculator or computer.

Where the head rent is a fraction of market rental value rather than rents receivable, slightly different problems may arise.

(a) Receipts

The principal receipt will be the rents payable under the subleases. But there may also be:

(1) receipts of mesne profits in the case of subtenants holding over;
(2) premiums paid for surrenders or lease variations;
(3) money payable under insurance policies for damage to the scheme or for loss of rent and commissions paid by the insurers to the tenant;
(4) damages for breach of covenant (eg dilapidations);
(5) interest on late rent, on reviewed rent, and on damages;
(6) grants or other public money paid for works to the scheme;
(7) compensation for compulsory acquisition.

All these ought to be considered.

(b) Deductions

If the headtenant is liable to pay the rates under the terms of some or all of the subleases, and is also liable to pay the rates under the terms of the headlease, the rates should be deducted from the gross amount of the subrents for the purposes of the rent review under the headlease. Similarly, if the headtenant collects VAT from the subtenants in respect of any services which he provides for them, the amount of such VAT should also be deducted. Where VAT is payable on the sub-rents, that should also be deducted, whether or not VAT is charged on the head rent.

Problems may also arise where the headtenant provides services to his subtenants, particularly where the subtenant's service charge is reserved as rent. It will clearly be in the interest of the headtenant if the service charge is left out of account for the purposes of the rent review under the headlease. On the other hand, if the headtenant charges a profit element or management fee to the subtenants, the landlord may argue that profit ought to be taken into account. Such a profit element may include not only a straightforward management fee but also a hidden profit, such as a discount, which may be given to the headtenant under a block policy of insurance.

The tenant may also find that in order to attract subtenants he must pay inducements, often in the form of a contribution to the subtenant's fitting-out costs. This must be deducted from the income received. There is considerable debate among valuers about the correct method of amortising such payments. Preferably the parties' surveyors should agree on an appropriate method of amortising such payments, which can then be written into the lease.

In addition the tenant may have to pay compensation to occupying subtenants for non-renewal of tenancies under the Landlord and Tenant Act 1954 and may himself have to pay damages for breach of obligation (eg an unreasonable refusal of consent to assign). He will seek to ensure that these are permitted deductions.

(c) Premiums

It may be that the headtenant will grant subleases in consideration of a premium and a low rent. The premium may be a payment in cash or a payment in kind (such as the carrying out of substantial repairs or improvements). The draftsman should cover this possibility and there are at least four methods of doing so.

First, the draftsman may provide that a specified proportion of the premium be paid by the headtenant to the landlord. If this is expressly provided for in the lease the parties will not fall foul of the Law of Property Act 1925, s 144. A payment of this kind may be capital or income (for tax purposes) in the hands of the landlord, depending on the circumstances. The draftsman should consider this question as well as whether the landlord's cash flow position would be appreciably helped by the payment of a proportion of premiums exacted by the headtenant.

Secondly, he may provide for the premium to be decapitalised, either at a fixed number of years' purchase or at the rate prevailing at the time of the subletting, with the amount thus calculated being added to the rent reserved by the sublease for the purposes of the rent review under the headlease. The tenant may well benefit from this arrangement since he will have in his hands a lump sum before he is called upon to make any payment to his own landlord.

Thirdly, he may provide that for the purposes of the rent review under the headlease, the sublet property shall be deemed to be let at a rack rent. This is probably the most satisfactory method for the landlord since the regularity of his cash flow will be maintained. However, the tenant's advisers must study closely the terms of the deemed subletting. First, is the deemed subletting to be at a fixed rent or at a rent subject to review? It is probably in the tenant's interest for a fixed rent to be assumed. However, if a review is to be assumed the tenant should ensure that the notional review coincides with the actual review under the headlease, otherwise there may be periods when the headtenant's profit rent is eroded. If there is to be a review, the rent review clause should specify whether the review is to be upwards only or simply a review to market rent.

Fourthly, the terms of the lease may prohibit letting except at a rack rent. This is the most common method of dealing with the problem. From the point of view of the landlord, the income payable by the headtenant remains secured by the income payable by the subtenants. The calculation of the head rent is also easier if there are subleases in existence. From the point of view of the tenant, he has the security of the rents payable by the subtenants, and is not called on to find income from other resources.

(d) Voids

The tenant's advisers should attempt to secure some allowance for the tenant in case of voids. This may well be resisted by the landlord on the basis that the risk of unlet property should fall on the tenant. In addition the risk of voids may already be reflected in the percentage of rent which the landlord is entitled to receive. If the landlord proves the stronger, the draftsman should make provision for the assessment of rent for empty property. This is best done by assuming a letting at a rack rent for a reasonable length of term; say, ten years. Nevertheless, the tenant should insist that he be given a reasonable rent-free period in which to find a new subtenant. If there is to be a rent review of the rent obtainable under the notional letting, the tenant should resist any suggestion that such a review should be upwards only. The purpose of a notional letting is to compensate the landlord for the share of income which he is not receiving due to the void, and if the tenant were to secure a subtenant, that subtenant would only be prepared to pay the market rent (whatever it happened to be) at the date of the letting. If the landlord is entitled to an upwards only rent review during a void period, he is over-insulated against fluctuations in the market.

Another variant is for the rent to be assessed on the assumption that the tenant continues to receive rent at the rate last payable when the void property was let. In a falling market this may mean that the tenant is required to pay rent to the landlord based on an historic rent which he could not obtain in the real world. This form of notional receipt should therefore be resisted by the tenant.

Where the head rent is based on rents received, so that the scheme is a side by side scheme, the landlord should be satisfied by a covenant by the tenant to do his best to keep the scheme fully let. Thus, the risk of voids will fall on both parties, and both will suffer the loss in the proportions in which they are entitled to participate in income.

(e) Occupation by the headtenant

The draftsman should provide expressly for the occupation of the whole or part of the demised property by the headtenant. This was forgotten by the draftsman in *British Railways Board v Elgar House Ltd* (1969) 209 EG 1313, where it was nevertheless held that for the purposes of the rent calculation parts of the demised property occupied by the headtenant should be deemed to be let at a rack rent. The court will try to prevent the tenant from cheating the landlord out of his share of the rental income (*Freehold & Leasehold Shop Properties Ltd v Friends Provident Life Office* (1984) 271 EG 451 *per* Griffiths LJ). As with the case of voids the terms of any deemed subletting should be carefully considered by the tenant's advisers.

Where, however, the rent was to be the highest of (a) a fixed sum; (b) the rent payable during the previous rent period; and (c) 8 per cent of the rents receivable by the tenant, it was held that where the tenant was in occupation, there were no rents receivable by him, and that since the parties had provided for alternative methods of calculating the rent, there was no room for supplying a different method of calculation (*Fraser Pipestock v Gloucester City Council* [1995] 36 EG 141). This problem would not, of course, have occurred if the draftsman had provided expressly for the consequences of occupation by the tenant.

If the draftsman provides for a notional lease to be valued while the tenant is in occupation, it should be made clear whether any revaluation is to be on an upwards only basis or is simply to be a revaluation to market rent. In the case of a side by side sharing, it is suggested that the review should not be upwards only because if, instead of occupying the property himself, the tenant were at any given time to sublet he would only receive the then going rate.

(f) Improvements

A rent geared to subrents is most commonly found in building leases. Accordingly, the tenant will have carried out substantial improvements, the cost of which will form a large part of the consideration given by him for the grant of the lease. His sublettings, on the other hand, will be sublettings of the improved property. It is, therefore, important that the value of those improvements be taken into account in assessing the rent of any part of the property deemed to be sublet. Accordingly, the draftsman should not provide for the usual disregard of tenant's improvements in the valuation formula. However, it should be borne in mind that the subtenants may themselves carry out improvements which, as against the tenant, are to be disregarded on rent review. Normally it is unnecessary to make special provision for this since the rent the tenant pays is linked to the rent he receives. In a special case, however, it may be appropriate to deal expressly with improvements made by subtenants.

(g) Other obligations

Since the landlord's income will usually depend on rents generated by actual lettings of the property, the landlord will require the tenant to enter into a series of obligations designed to ensure that the scheme is kept fully let at rack rents. Those obligations will include:
(1)   a covenant to try his best to keep the scheme fully let;
(2)   a covenant not to let at less than the market rent obtainable at the date of the letting;
(3)   a covenant not to grant rent-free periods or concessionary rent periods without the landlord's consent;
(4)   a covenant not to sublet except in defined subletting units;
(5)   a covenant not to waive or commute any rental payments under subleases;
(6)   a covenant not to accept any surrender of any sublease without the landlord's consent;
(7)   a covenant to enforce subtenants' covenants in subleases;
(8)   a covenant not to permit any sub-underletting of a sublet part.

All these obligations are designed to ensure that the tenant keeps up the real value of the scheme and that the landlord's income remains as high as possible.

In addition the draftsman should prohibit the assignment of the lease to a person holding an interest inferior to the lease. The object of such a provision is to prevent circumstances arising in which a sublease could be merged in the headlease. If a merger were to take place, the landlord might find that the rental being paid under a sublease would cease to be payable to the tenant with a resulting loss in rental income to the landlord. In many cases, the lease will be one to which s 19(1)(b) of the Landlord and Tenant Act 1927 applies. The draftsman must be particularly careful to ensure that any restrictions on alienation are not avoided by that subsection. Section 19(1)(b) will not, however, apply to an assignment of a tenancy which is a new tenancy for the purposes of the

RENT AND RENT REVIEW

Landlord and Tenant (Covenants) Act 1995. See Chapter 9 below.

Example 5:7 Rent geared to subrents receivable

YIELDING AND PAYING THEREFOR by equal quarterly payments in advance on 1 January 1 April 1 July and 1 October in each year [   ] per cent of the net rents which the tenant is entitled to receive for the whole or any part of the demised property and calculated in accordance with the Schedule hereto

SCHEDULE

(1) In this Schedule the following expressions have the following meanings:
- (a) 'full rack rental value' means the best rent at which the demised property (or as the case may be the part of the demised property in question) might reasonably be expected to be let in the open market by a willing landlord to a willing tenant:
  - (i) in the case of property falling within paragraph (2) below on the terms (other than as to rent or other pecuniary consideration) upon which it is actually occupied
  - (ii) in the case of property falling within paragraph (3) below on the terms (other than as to rent or other pecuniary consideration) of this lease
  - (iii) in the case of property falling within paragraph (4) below on the terms (other than as to rent or other pecuniary consideration) upon which it was last occupied

  and in any case disregarding the matters set out in paragraphs (a) and (b) of section 34(1) of the Landlord and Tenant Act 1954 (as amended) and on the assumption that the rent so determined will be revised every five years
- (b) 'qualified accountant' means a member of the Institute of Chartered Accountants in England and Wales or the Association of Certified Accountants

(2) If the tenant lets or permits to be occupied the whole or any part of the demised property in return for any pecuniary consideration other than the full rack rental value thereof as at the date of such letting or permission or in return for no pecuniary consideration then he shall be deemed for the purposes of this Schedule to be entitled to receive the full rack rental value thereof determined as at the date of such letting or permission and redetermined (upwards only) as at every fifth anniversary thereof

(3) If the tenant himself occupies the whole or any part of the demised property then he shall be deemed for the purposes of this Schedule to be entitled to receive the full rack rental value thereof determined as at the date on which he went into occupation and redetermined (upwards or downwards) as at every fifth anniversary thereof

(4) If the whole or any part of the demised property remains vacant for three months or more then at the expiry of such period of

three months the tenant shall until the same is next occupied be deemed to be entitled to receive the full rack rental value thereof determined as at the date upon which the said period expired and redetermined (upwards or downwards) as at every fifth anniversary thereof

(5) The tenant shall one month before the beginning of each quarter (time being of the essence) deliver to the landlord a certificate signed by a qualified accountant showing a true summary of:
  (a) the gross amount of all rents and licence fees which the tenant is entitled (or deemed to be entitled) to receive in respect of the demised property and each part thereof for that quarter and
  (b) the amount of any sum included in (a) above which the tenant is entitled to recover from any subtenant or occupier of the whole or any part of the demised property either by way of value added tax or by way of service charge in respect of services or works performed or to be performed

(6) Subject to paragraph (7) below the net rents shall be the difference between the two amounts shown in the said certificate

(7) The net rents shall be determined by a single arbitrator to be appointed by the President for the time being of the Royal Institution of Chartered Surveyors if:
  (a) the tenant fails to deliver a certificate in accordance with paragraph (5) above (in which case the tenant shall pay interest on the net rents at the rate of [   ] per cent from the quarter day in question until payment) or
  (b) any dispute or difference arises between the parties in connection with the calculation of the net rents (in which case the arbitrator shall determine the amount of interest if any to be paid by the tenant)

(8) The tenant shall permit the landlord or his agent to inspect and take copies of the tenant's books or accounts or any other document or record (and if necessary the tenant shall procure any computer printout) which in the opinion of the landlord or such agent is relevant to the calculation of the net rents and shall bear the costs of such inspection if there shall be any material discrepancy between the certificate delivered by the tenant under paragraph (5) above and the results of such inspection

Example 5:8 Side by side rent sharing

SCHEDULE

(1) In this Schedule:
(a) 'rental income' means the aggregate of:
  (i) any yearly or other periodical sums payable under an occupational lease including sums payable by virtue of any enactment
  (ii) any sums payable by way of interest under an occupational lease
  (iii) any sums payable by way of damages or compensation

for any breach of a tenant's obligation under an occupational lease
- (iv) any sum payable by a guarantor of a tenant's obligation under an occupational lease pursuant to his guarantee
- (v) any premium paid or other capital payment made by a tenant under an occupational lease in connection with the grant assignment variation or surrender of an occupational lease
- (vi) any sum payable under a policy of insurance in respect of loss of rent or other income

(b) 'permitted deductions' means the aggregate of:
- (i) expenses reasonably incurred by the tenant in order to comply with its obligations as landlord under an occupational lease
- (ii) legal costs incurred by the tenant in enforcing obligations under occupational leases except to the extent that the tenant recovers those costs from a party to an occupational lease
- (iii) the amount of any compensation or damages which the tenant is liable by statute or ordered to pay to any party to an occupational lease whether for non-renewal of a tenancy breach of covenant breach of obligation compensation for improvements or otherwise
- (iv) the cost of management and rent collection not exceeding [ ] per cent of rental income

(c) 'notional rental income' means the rack rental value of any lettable unit which is either unlet or vacant or occupied by the tenant or by a group company the value to be determined as at the date on which the unit in question ceased to be let or occupied or as the case may be become occupied by the tenant or a group company and redetermined every year

(d) 'lettable unit' means a part of the property which is designed constructed or adapted for letting to an occupying retail trader

(e) 'occupational lease' means a lease under which physical possession of a lettable unit was granted by the tenant

(f) 'rack rental value' of any lettable unit at any time means the rent at which that unit might reasonably be expected to be let in the open market for a term of not less than ten years with an upwards only rent review on every fifth anniversary of the beginning of the term and on such other terms as would be expected to be negotiated in the open market (including such financial inducements and concessions as are usual in the market at that time)

(g) 'group company' means a company which would be treated as a member of the same group of companies as the tenant for the purposes of the Landlord and Tenant Act 1954

(h) 'divisible income' means the difference between:
- (i) rental income plus notional rental income and

(ii) permitted deductions
but divisible income shall never be less than nil
(i) 'the first slice' means such part of divisible income as does not exceed £[   ]
(j) 'the second slice' means such part of divisible income as exceeds £[   ] but does not exceed £[   ]
(k) 'the top slice' means such part of divisible income as exceeds £[   ]
(2) The rent payable by the tenant is the aggregate of:
(a) [   ] per cent of the first slice
(b) [   ] per cent of the second slice and
(c) [   ] per cent of the top slice
to be paid by equal quarterly payments on the usual quarter days

7 Rent Geared to Head Rent

Some subleases reserve a rent which is linked to the rent payable under the headlease. The reasons which prompt such a bargain are a desire on the part of the landlord to ensure that he suffers no rental shortfall, and in some cases a desire to have a guaranteed profit rental.

If faced with such a clause, the tenant's adviser should ensure that the tenant ascertains the amount of the head rent and receives advice from a valuer as to whether it is a fair rent (see *County Personnel Ltd v Alan R Pulver & Co* [1987] 1 All ER 289). If the rent under the sublease is made to increase at the same rate as the rent under the headlease, and the rent under the headlease is less than a market rent at the date of grant of the sublease, the rent under the sublease may well exceed the true market rent after the first rent review.

The draftsman of a clause linking the subrent to the head rent must make it clear what is to happen if the head landlord does not exercise his right to a rent under the headlease, or if the headlease is surrendered. In *Lorien Textiles v SI Pension Trustees Ltd* (1981) 259 EG 771 the rent under the sublease was to be assessed 'on the basis set out' in the headlease. It was held that this merely incorporated the words of the headlease, and that the continuing existence of the headlease was not a condition precedent to the right to review the rent under the sublease. So also where a sublease provided for the rent to be a proportion of the rent 'payable' by the landlord 'in the manner fixed' under the headlease, it was held that the rent review clause in the sublease was capable of operation despite the surrender of the headlease (*R & A Millett (Shops) Ltd v Leon Allan International Fashions Ltd* [1989] 1 EGLR 138).

If the sublease merely incorporates the valuation formula and machinery contained in the headlease, the rent review clause in the sublease will be capable of operation whether or not the rent review clause is exercised in the headlease. However, the corollary is that the rent review under the headlease and the rent review under the sublease will in effect be independent valuations and consequently there is a risk that the rent payable under each will be different.

Example 5:9 Definition of rent linked to head rent

'the reviewed rent' means the highest of
(1) the rent contractually payable immediately before the relevant review date
(2) the market rent and
(3) [   ] per cent of the rent payable under the headlease (assuming if it is not the fact that the headlease is in existence on the relevant review date)

Example 5:10 Alternative definition

if at any time the rent payable under the headlease is increased the rent payable under this lease shall be increased with effect from the date as from which the rent payable under the headlease is increased so as to equal [   ] per cent of that rent

8 PERIODIC REVIEW TO MARKET RENT

The periodic review to market rent is the most common form of rent review clause found in occupational business leases. Its principal advantage is that it most accurately reflects changes in the value of the demised property rather than the business efficiency of a particular tenant or inflation generally. In most cases the clause will operate by postulating a hypothetical letting of the demised property in the open market. Under normal circumstances this is as fair a valuation method to both parties as can be achieved. However, there are cases (such as property specially built or adapted for a particular occupier) where modifications are needed.

Judicial statements abound that the purpose of a rent review clause is to ensure that the rent payable reflects changes in the value of money and the value of the property let (eg *Basingstoke and Deane BC v Host Group* [1988] 1 WLR 348; *British Airways v Heathrow Airport* [1992] 1 EGLR 141). However, there are two different perspectives from which this general purpose can be viewed. The first perspective is that the purpose of the rent review is to revalue the original bargain between the parties in the light of changes in the value of money and of the property. This perspective leads to the conclusion that in the absence of clear words to the contrary, the hypothetical letting will be on the same terms as the actual letting. But the second perspective is that the rent review clause is the landlord's price for the grant of a long term, in the absence of which he would have granted a shorter term. Thus, the purpose of a rent review clause is not to revalue the original bargain between the parties, but to give the landlord the income which he would have got, on the terms on which he would have let, if he had had the property in hand on the rent review date. This would mean that in the absence of clear words, the terms of the hypothetical letting would be dictated by the market at the review date, and not by the terms of the lease. So far, the courts have approached rent review clauses from the first perspective only. But the parties are not confined to the first perspective. Many of the failures of rent review clauses result from a failure to consider carefully the object which the clause is designed to achieve.

A well-drawn rent review clause must provide for each of the following:

(1) the review dates;
(2) the method of initiating the review;
(3) the procedure for resolving disputes;
(4) the timetable;
(5) the valuation formula.

It should also state whether time is or is not of the essence at any of the procedural stages.

The choice of review dates is one of the basic terms of the lease which will have been agreed between the parties before the matter passes into the hands of solicitors. Some landlords attempt to introduce a review date on the last or penultimate day of the term. The purpose of doing so is to attempt to obtain for the landlord a higher rent than would be awarded by the court on an application for an interim rent under s 24A of the Landlord and Tenant Act 1954. The rent awarded by the court under s 24A may be considerably tempered by judicial discretion. A discount of 10–15 per cent is not uncommon and in an extreme case the Court of Appeal refused to disturb a discount of 50 per cent (*Charles Follett Ltd v Cabtell Investments Ltd* [1987] 2 EGLR 88). The tenant will always be better off without such a review, and consequently should resist its introduction. If, however, it is agreed that there should be a review at the end of the term, the draftsman should ensure that the term of the hypothetical lease is long enough to be realistic. Clearly letting for the residue of the actual term will not produce a worthwhile rent.

There are two methods of defining the review dates. One is to specify the actual dates of review in the lease. This produces certainty, but the tenant's adviser should be careful to ensure that the hypothetical lease has proper provision for rent review. The problem does not arise where the review takes place on the assumption of a hypothetical letting for the residue of the actual term. However, where the assumption is a letting for a term expiring after the actual term on the terms of the actual lease, the hypothetical lease may have a long period without review. For example a lease provides for rent reviews at fixed dates in the years 2000, 2005 and 2010. The term of the lease is limited to expire in 2015. The review clause provides for a hypothetical lease for a term of fifteen years from the rent review date but otherwise on the terms of the actual lease. A literal interpretation of these terms would mean that on the second rent review date what was to be assumed was a lease expiring in 2020 with a rent review in 2010 only, leaving ten years without review at the end of the hypothetical lease. The effect on the final rent review would be even more drastic. The second method is to define review dates by reference to the anniversaries of the commencement of the lease. The draftsman must, however, make it clear whether the periods are to be measured from the date from which the term of the lease is computed or from the date of the lease itself. *Prima facie* a clause which specifies review date by reference to the commencement of the term requires the measurement to be taken from the date from which the term is computed, and not the date of the lease (*Beaumont Property Trust v Tai* (1982) 265 EG 872).

The valuation date will usually be the rent review date; and the court will lean in favour of a construction which produces the result that the rent is valued by reference to values prevailing at the start of the period for which it is payable (*Glofield Properties v Morley (No 2)* [1989] 2 EGLR 118). But if the clause clearly specifies another valuation date, the court will give effect to the clause (*Prudential Assurance Co v Gray* [1987] 2 EGLR 134; *Parkside Investments v German Food Centre* [1990] 2 EGLR 265).

9 Time Limits in Rent Review Procedure

(a) The presumption

Much of the early litigation about rent review clauses concentrated on the question whether limits were of the essence. That question was thought to have been partially settled by the House of Lords in *United Scientific Holdings Ltd v Burnley BC* [1978] AC 904 where it was held that *prima facie* time limits are not of the essence, with the result that if a time limit is missed the review can still take place.

However, it was said that the *prima facie* rule could be displaced:
(1) by express words;
(2) by contra-indications in the rent review clause;
(3) by the interrelationship of the rent review clause and other clauses in the lease.

(b) The presumption rebutted

(i) By express words

The parties may always provide expressly that time limits are to be of the essence. If they do so, the court will give effect to their expressed intention, even if this means overriding words in the *reddendum* (*Weller v Akehurst* [1981] 3 All ER 411). However, if the draftsman wishes to make time of the essence of some but not all of the procedural steps he should be particularly careful to make it clear which steps carry strict time limits and which do not (as the draftsman failed to do in *Bradley (C) & Sons Ltd v Telefusion Ltd* (1981) 259 EG 337 and *Art & Sound v West End Litho* [1992] 1 EGLR 138). If it is not clear that time is of the essence of a particular procedural provision, the presumption that time is not of the essence will apply (*Panavia Air Cargo Ltd v Southend-on-Sea BC* [1988] 1 EGLR 124).

Should the parties agree that time is to be of the essence? From the tenant's point of view such an agreement has much to commend it. If the review is upwards only he is highly unlikely to want to initiate the review himself, but the uncertainty of not knowing what his rent is may hamper him in conducting or investing in his business, or in disposing of his lease. If time is of the essence, the business tenant knows where he stands.

On the other hand, as Lord Salmon observed in *United Scientific Holdings Ltd v Burnley BC* [1978] AC 904:

> I would add that a well-advised landlord is hardly likely to agree to a rent revision clause which laid down that its provisions as to time were of the essence of the contract. Were he to do so, it would mean that should he take any step later than the time specified in the clause then however slight the delay and however little it affected the ten-

ant, he would lose the benefit of the clause for the next five, seven or ten years or whatever the intervals for revision might be.

By contrast, where time is not of the essence for the service of a landlord's notice calling for a rent review, mere delay by the landlord, however lengthy and even if coupled with hardship to the tenant, does not of itself destroy the contractual right which the landlord has to serve a notice. In order to show that a landlord is precluded from exercising his right to call for a rent review, the tenant must show that the lease or the rent review clause has been abrogated by mutual consent or that the landlord's conduct has been such that he is estopped from exercising his right to a rent review (*Amherst v Walker (James) Goldsmith & Silversmith Ltd* [1983] 2 All ER 1067). The practical consequences of time limits which are not of the essence of the contract are such that they are virtually meaningless. If, therefore, the parties agree that the rent review is to be initiated and conducted according to a timetable laid down in the lease, it is suggested that time should be of the essence of the timetable. If the parties do not wish to be bound by time limits there should be none in the lease.

One possible solution is for the last step in the procedure to be the subject of a strict time limit. Normally, that step is the reference of a dispute to an independent third party. If the chosen third party is an expert, the court cannot interfere with the contractual time limit. However, if the chosen third party is an arbitrator, the court can extend time if undue hardship would otherwise result (Arbitration Act 1950, s 27), even if only one party has the right to refer the matter to arbitration (*Pittalis v Sherefettin* [1986] QB 868).

The tenant's adviser should press for the tenant to have the right to serve notice on the landlord in the event of delay, calling upon the landlord either to exercise the rent review or abandon it. Such a notice may also contain a proposal by the tenant as to the amount of the rent. But it should be made clear that any time limit within which the landlord is to act is to be of the essence, otherwise the contractual notice will be ineffective except as a preliminary to the service of yet another notice making time of the essence (*Phipps-Faire Ltd v Malbern Construction Ltd* [1987] 1 EGLR 129) although this relaxed approach has not been taken in Scotland (*Visionhire v Britel Fund Trustees* [1992] 1 EGLR 128).

(ii) By contra-indications in the rent review clause

It is extremely difficult to extract any coherent principles from the decisions of the court in relation to contra-indications in the rent review clause. This only serves to emphasise the desirability of stating expressly whether time is or is not to be of the essence.

In *Drebbond Ltd v Horsham DC* (1978) 246 EG 1013 the landlord was entitled to require arbitration by notice in writing given to the tenant within three months after the review date 'but not otherwise'. The words 'but not otherwise' were held to be a sufficient contra-indication to make time of the essence. In *Touche Ross & Co v Secretary of State for the Environment* (1982) 265 EG 982 the lease provided that the question of what was a fair market rent was to be referred to an expert 'as soon as practicable and in any event not later than' three months after service of a rent review notice. It was held that time was not of the essence. Dillon LJ pointed out that small differences in language will lead in some cases to opposite conclusions. In other cases the fact that the rent was to be 'conclusively fixed' by the landlord's trigger notice if the tenant failed to give counter-notice in time was held to be a sufficient indication that time was of the essence (*Mammoth Greeting Cards v Agra* [1990] 2 EGLR 124; *Barrett Estate Services v David Greig (Retail)* [1991] 2 EGLR 123). All those cases turned on the effect of particular words in the rent review clause. In other cases, however, the court has relied more on the procedure for review laid down in the lease.

In *Lewis v Barnet* (1982) 264 EG 1079 the lease provided that in default of agreement the rent was to be determined by a surveyor appointed by the President of the RICS on the application of the landlord made not less than three months before the review date. It was further provided that if the parties had not agreed the rent six months before the review date, and the landlord had not made the application to the President, then any notice given by the landlord to trigger the review should be void and of no effect. It was held that that provision was sufficient to make time of the essence of the time limit for the landlord's application. By contrast where the lease provided for the landlord to serve a notice, for the tenant to serve a counter-notice and said that if the tenant did not serve a counter-notice, the figure in the landlord's notice would stand as the rent payable, it was held that this was insufficient to rebut the presumption that time was not of the essence (*Bickenhall Engineering Co v Grandmet Restaurants* [1995] 1 EGLR 110). In *Smith's (Henry) Charity Trustees v AWADA Trading and Promotion Services Ltd* (1983) 269 EG 729 the rent review clause prescribed an elaborate procedure of notices and counterpoints. At each stage the clause set out the consequence of failure to serve the requisite notice or counter-notice. The court held that time was of the essence of the timetable. Similarly, in *Greenhaven Securities Ltd v Compton* (1985) 275 EG 628 the review clause prescribed three alternative ways in which the rent was to be determined, two of them introduced by 'if' clauses. It was held that time was of the essence.

In *Mecca Leisure Ltd v Renown Investments (Holdings) Ltd* (1984) 271 EG 989 the court reached a different conclusion. The review clause in that case provided that the reviewed rent was to be a sum specified in a notice served by the landlord, unless the tenant served a counter-notice on the landlord within a stated period. It further provided that if the tenant failed to serve a counter-notice he should be deemed to have agreed the rent specified in the landlord's notice. The court held that the deeming provision was not sufficient to make time of the essence of the time limit for the service of the counter-notice. An attempt to reconcile the cases was made in *Taylor Woodrow Property Co Ltd v Lonrho Textiles Ltd* (1985) 275 EG 632, where it was held that a 'two-way' deeming provision (ie which applied to both landlord and tenant) made time of the essence, but a 'one-way' deeming provision (ie which applied to the tenant alone) did not.

However, it is unlikely that such a rigid distinction may be made. Where the parties have not only required a step to be taken within a specified time but have expressly provided for the consequences in case of default, this provides an indication, of greater or less strength, that time is to be of the essence, but it is not necessarily decisive. Whether it is so or not depends on all the circumstances of the case including the context and wording of the provisions, the degree of emphasis, the purpose and effect of the default clause and any other relevant consideration. In the end, the matter is one of impression (*Power Securities (Manchester) Ltd v Prudential Assurance Co Ltd* [1987] 1 EGLR 121).

As a result of these cases it is clear that relatively small differences in the drafting of a rent review clause may have great practical consequences. In all cases it is suggested that the parties must consider whether or not to have strict time limits and ensure that their intention is clearly expressed.

(iii) By the interrelationship of the rent review clause and other clauses in the lease

The classic case of the interrelationship of the rent review clause and other clauses in the lease making time of the essence is a case where the tenant has an option to determine the term by the service of a break-notice. Whether the right to review the rent and the right to determine are contained in the same subclause of the lease (*Al Saloom v Shirley*

James Travel Service Ltd (1981) 42 P&CR 181) or in different subclauses (*Legal & General Assurance (Pension Management) Ltd v Cheshire CC* (1983) 265 EG 781) makes no difference. Nor does it matter whether the tenant may give notice after the last date for service of a rent review notice (*Coventry CC v J Hepworth & Son Ltd* (1982) 265 EG 608) or at a time which coincides with time during which a landlord may serve such a notice (*Legal & General Assurance (Pension Management) Ltd v Cheshire CC*). Where there is only one break but multiple rent reviews, the existence of the break-clause will make time of the essence for all reviews, including those which are not linked with the break (*Central Estates v Secretary of State for the Environment* [1995] EGCS 110). Where, however, the tenant also had the right to initiate the rent review and the date for the tenant's notice terminating the lease was linked to a date over which the landlord had no control (the decision of the arbitrator), the link between the rent review and the break-clause was held not to make time of the essence (*Metrolands Investments Ltd v JH Dewhurst Ltd* [1986] 3 All ER 659). The essential feature to displace the presumption is a link between a rent review timetable and the timetable for the exercise of the tenant's right to determine the lease. Where there is no such interrelation, as where the landlord does not have to serve a notice in order to exercise his right to review the rent, the mere existence of a tenant's break-clause will not lead the court to impose time limits on the landlord (*Woodhouse (Edwin) Trustee Co Ltd v Sheffield Brick Co plc* (1983) 270 EG 548). The same conclusion would probably be reached if the tenant's break-notice had to be served before the last date for service of the landlord's notice calling for a rent review.

However, if the tenant has the right to determine the lease, the draftsman must be careful lest that right should have the effect of making time limits in the rent review procedure of the essence. This danger may be met in two ways. First, the draftsman may insert in the rent review clause an express provision that time is not to be of the essence. If he chooses this method, the landlord may serve a late notice, but the tenant will not be able to serve a late break-notice. Accordingly, his break-notice must be given in ignorance of what the new rent would be. Secondly, the draftsman may ensure that the two timetables are not interrelated. This may be done by conferring on the tenant a right to serve a late notice in the event that the rent has not been determined in accordance with the timetable specified in the lease. Alternatively, the draftsman may dispense with a timetable for the rent review, and dispense with the requirement for the landlord to serve a rent review notice in order to exercise the right to review the rent.

Example 5:11 Tenant's power to make time of the essence

(1) If the landlord fails to take any step in the procedure for rent review within a period of time prescribed by this lease (whether or not that step could also have been taken by the tenant) the tenant may give the landlord written notice:
  (a) referring to the step which the landlord has failed to take
  (b) requiring the landlord to take that step within such period of not less than twenty-one days as may be specified in the notice and
  (c) informing the landlord that if he fails to take that step within the period specified in the notice he will be precluded thereafter from taking it and that time is of the essence of the period so specified

(2) If the landlord fails to take the step specified in a notice under paragraph (1) within the time specified in that notice (time being of the essence) he shall thereafter be precluded from taking it

10 REVIEW PROCEDURE

(a) Initiating the review

Many rent review clauses provide for the procedure to be initiated by the service of a notice. The principal advantage of such a requirement is that it signals, in a formal way, that the procedure is under way. If the lease requires the service of a notice, informal discussions between the parties are unlikely to be held to amount to a review of the rent (*Esso Petroleum Co Ltd v Anthony Gibbs Financial Services Ltd* (1983) 267 EG 351). However, unless the rent review is to be conducted in accordance with a prescribed timetable, there is much to be said for dispensing with notices, and removing a fertile source of potential dispute.

Some review clauses require a review notice to be in a particular form (for example, proposing a new rent); others do not. Unless one of the steps in the review machinery is the service of a counter-notice by the person upon whom the review notice is served, it is better not to stipulate for a particular form of notice because the fewer the requirements that have to be complied with the less scope there is for litigation. It is however a fundamental requirement of a review notice that it leaves the recipient in no doubt that it is intended to be the formal document invoking the landlord's right to review the rent (*Schirlcar Properties Ltd v Heinitz* (1983) 268 EG 362).

If a particular form of notice is prescribed, failure to serve notice in the prescribed form will not generally invalidate the notice (*Dean and*

Chapter of Chichester Cathedral v Lennards Ltd (1977) 35 P&CR 309); although where the timetable is tight and the landlord's notice is required to state a rental figure it may be of the essence that the notice should do so (*Commission for New Towns v R Levy & Co* [1990] 2 EGLR 121). If the general presumption does not apply in the particular case, a defective notice may usually be followed by a late notice in proper form. The general presumption might not apply where a notice initiating the review is to be followed by a counter-notice objecting to the rent proposed in the initial notice. In such a case, unless the initial notice specifies the proposed rent, a counter-notice cannot be served.

(b) Counter-notices

Where the initiator of the review is required to specify the proposed new rent it is sometimes provided that the figure so specified shall be the new rent unless the other party serves a counter-notice within a given period. Usually it is the landlord who initiates the review and the tenant who is obliged to serve the counter-notice. Generally the period for serving the counter-notice will not be of the essence (*Davstone (Holdings) Ltd v Al-Rifai* (1976) 32 P&CR 18) even where the clause also provides that in the absence of a counter-notice the tenant is deemed to have agreed the rent specified in the landlord's notice (*Mecca Leisure Ltd v Renown Investments (Holdings) Ltd* (1984) 271 EG 989).

However, it is often the case that the service of a counter-notice is the only step in the review procedure of which time is expressly made of the essence. The tenant's adviser should be on his guard against such a provision since it is little more than a trap for the tenant, particularly since the figure specified by the landlord need not be a *bona fide* and genuine pre-estimate of the market rent (*Amalgamated Estates Ltd v Joystretch Manufacturing Ltd* (1980) 257 EG 489). The tenant's adviser should, therefore delete from the draft any provision making time of the essence in relation to the service of a counter-notice; or he should delete the entire requirement to serve a counter-notice. He may derive some support from the statement of Templeman LJ in *Amalgamated Estates Ltd v Joystretch Manufacturing Ltd*:

> I think it is a great pity that any landlord should require, or that any tenant should accept, a provision making time of the essence when the consequences are so onerous.

If the landlord will not accept the amendment, then the tenant's adviser should seek to ensure that any dispute about the rent is determined by arbitration rather than by an expert. A unilateral right to require a dispute about the rent to be referred to arbitration is 'an agreement to refer future disputes to arbitration' (Arbitration Act 1950, s 27; *Pittalis v Sherefettin* [1986] QB 868) and the court has power to extend the time for service of a counter-notice if undue hardship would otherwise result (*ibid*). The court tends to adopt a relatively liberal attitude towards extensions of time for commencing arbitration (*Patel v Peel Investments (South)* [1992] 30 EG 88). Accordingly, it is suggested that the tenant will be better off if the rent is to be determined by arbitration rather than by expert.

In addition, the tenant's adviser should seek to ensure that the form of trigger notice to be served by the landlord is required to contain a clear reminder to the tenant of his right to serve a counter-notice and the consequences of a failure to do so.

(c) Agreeing the new rent

There should be a period in which the parties are able to agree the amount of the new rent before the necessity for independent determination. In the normal case three months should suffice and the period should be made to run from the service of a review notice. If the landlord is not required to serve a notice in order to initiate the review, then no fixed timetable will be necessary.

The right to have an independent determination arises when negotiations between the parties have broken down; but what if the parties have never tried to agree? A phrase such as 'in default of agreement' does not imply that the parties must have tried to agree (*Re Essoldo (Bingo) Ltd's Underlease* (1971) 23 P&CR 1), and neither does the phrase 'in the event of the parties failing to reach agreement' (*Wrenbridge Ltd v Harries (Southern Properties) Ltd* (1981) 260 EG 1195). It is suggested that whichever phrase is used, the court would be reluctant to construe it as imposing on the parties a positive obligation to negotiate.

(d) Independent determination

Three questions arise in drafting a provision for determination of the new rent by an independent person. First, who is to have the power to require such determination? Secondly, should the determination be made by an expert or by an arbitrator? Thirdly, should the lease lay down any particular procedure to be followed?

Both parties should have the right to apply for the appointment of the expert or arbitrator, even if the landlord alone has the right to initiate the rent review. If the lease is silent on the point, either party may apply (*United Scientific Holdings v Burnley BC* [1978] AC 904 at 960). Where either party may apply the tenant is not entitled to serve notice making time of the essence of the landlord's right to apply: if he is prejudiced by delay his remedy is to make the application himself (*Factory Holdings Group Ltd v Leboff International Ltd* [1987] 1 EGLR 135). This minor disadvantage to the tenant does not outweigh the advantage to the tenant in being able to initiate the determination of the rent. Where the rent review clause is not upwards only, it is of particular importance that the tenant should be able to initiate the machinery for determining the rent. The draftsman should specify the person who is to nominate the expert or arbitrator. That person is frequently the President of the Royal Institution of Chartered Surveyors who has set up an efficient administrative machinery for such appointments. If the clause specifies the President as the appointor of the expert or arbitrator, it is thought that he must do so personally. Some clauses therefore provide that an appointment may be made by a duly authorised deputy, or a person acting on behalf of the President. If, for some reason, the nominated appointor cannot or will not make an appointment, the court is likely to provide alternative machinery for determining the rent (*Sudbrook Trading Estate Ltd v Eggleton* [1982] 3 All ER 1). Similarly, where one of the parties has an obligation to apply for the appointment of an arbitrator, and refuses to do so, the court may regard this as a case of the machinery having broken down, unless the rent review clause itself provides for the consequence of a failure to apply (contrast *Harben Style v Rhodes Trust* [1995] 1 EGLR 118 and *Royal Bank of Scotland v Jennings* [1995] 35 EG 140). Where a clause requires the making of an application to the President of the RICS it is sufficient for the applicant merely to send a letter making the application, even though the application will not be processed (and hence will not come to the attention of the other party) until the requisite fee is paid (*Staines Warehousing Co Ltd v Montagu Executor & Trustee Co Ltd* [1987] 2 EGLR 130). The tenant's adviser should therefore press for an obligation on the landlord to notify the tenant of any application made by him to the President. Alternatively the tenant's adviser could amend the timetable by requiring the landlord to apply to the President and pay any requisite fee within the prescribed period.

The appointor is usually required to appoint 'an independent surveyor'. This formula may be unnecessarily restrictive where the new rent is to be determined by an arbitrator (rather than an expert). For example, if the only issue between the parties is a point of construction of the lease it may be better to have a solicitor or barrister as arbitrator. This would be possible if the lease provided for the appointment of 'an independent person'. If a surveyor is specified as the arbitrator he may well in practice appoint a legal assessor to advise him on any contested point of law.

Before deciding whether to provide for determination by expert rather than by arbitration, it is essential to appreciate the differences between them. An arbitrator is a person who is appointed to resolve a formulated dispute between the parties. He will hear evidence and submissions from each party (although these may be written rather than oral) and is bound to make his decision solely on the evidence presented to him. The evidence in question must be admissible evidence, and it will not include previous awards of other arbitrators relating to comparable properties (*Land Securities v Westminster City Council* [1993] 1 WLR 286). Despite the abolition of the rule against hearsay in civil proceedings (Civil Evidence Act 1995) it is probable that previous awards remain inadmissible. He has a wide range of powers under the Arbitration Act 1950, including the power to order discovery of documents and attendance of witnesses. His award may be enforced as if it were a judgment of the court, and there is a limited right of appeal from his award to the High Court on a point of law. He also has power to make an order as to the costs of the arbitration, and any clause in the lease which provides that a particular party is to pay his own costs (or the costs of the other party) is void (Arbitration Act 1950, s 18(3); *Windvale Ltd v Darlington Insulation Co Ltd* (1983) *The Times*, 22 December). In addition, as has been noted, the court has power to extend the time within which an arbitration must be commenced (Arbitration Act 1950, s 27).

If the arbitrator dies or is unwilling or incapable of acting a new arbitrator may be appointed under the Arbitration Act 1950, and at least while he is acting within his jurisdiction an arbitrator is immune from liability for negligence (*Sirros v Moore* [1975] QB 118).

On the other hand, an expert is a person appointed to fix the new rent. He is not bound to afford the parties an opportunity to tender evidence or submissions; and, even if a right to do so is conferred upon them by the terms of the lease, it is doubtful whether the expert need pay any attention to them. He is not bound by the strict rules of evidence. He acts on his own skill and judgment in reaching his decision, and that decision will be binding on the parties even if it is wrong (*Campbell v Edwards* [1976] 1 All ER 785). At one time it was thought that an expert's award was binding even though it contained an error of law on its face. But it has now been held by the House of Lords that where parties agree to have a contractual dispute resolved by an expert, they intend him to resolve that dispute on the basis of a correct interpretation of the contract. Thus the expert's legal rulings can be reviewed by the court (*Mercury Communications v Director-General of Telecomunications* [1996] 1 WLR 48). Since there is no statutory prohibition on challenging the legal rulings of an expert, unlike the restrictions on appealing against an arbitrator's award, it may be that the parties will have greater access to the courts when the rent is to be determined by an expert than they do when it is to be determined by an arbitrator.

If the expert is negligent he may be sued by either party (*Arenson v Casson Beckman Rutley & Co* [1977] AC 405). He has no power to order discovery of documents or the attendance of witnesses or to make any order as to costs (unless such power is expressly conferred on him by the lease); and if he dies or becomes incapable or unwilling to continue, it is doubtful whether another expert could be appointed under the lease. However, the death or incapacity of experts does not seem to have presented any problem in practice, and in any event the court would not allow a rent review to be frustrated by a breakdown in the machinery.

Which method should the draftsman choose? In general terms it is suggested that determination by expert is quicker and cheaper than determination by arbitrator. On the other hand the expert will not have had the benefit of hearing the arguments, and some observers have suggested that expert valuers rarely assess rents from the tenant's point of view.

Where the demised property is of a common type both in character and size, determination by expert is likely to be the better method. Comparables will be fairly easy to find and the determination will be able to proceed quickly. In addition the costs of the determination will remain a reasonable proportion of the rental value of the property. In a time of rapidly changing markets, or where the true market is obscured by confidentiality clauses attached to the terms of transactions, some tenants fear that a concentration on comparable evidence which is capable of proper proof is in itself a distortion of the market. There is therefore a growing feeling among tenants that, since an expert is not tied to the rules of evidence, his judgment may be a more accurate reflector of the real market. Of course while this point may work in the tenant's favour in a falling market, it is just as likely to work in the landlord's favour in a rising market.

Where the demised property is unusual either in size or in character, or where it is so valuable that small points have large financial consequences, determination by arbitration may be the better method since there will be an opportunity for full argument. The draftsman should, however, consider whether the categories of admissible evidence should be extended by agreement; eg to allow the parties to rely on awards of experts and arbitrators relating to comparable properties. Arbitration is also the better method where points of law may arise or where extensive discovery might be needed. If no particular difficulties arise at the time of the rent review the costs of the arbitration need not be great since evidence and submissions can be presented informally. However, in the case of an arbitration, either party has the right to insist on an oral hearing (*Henry Sotheran v Norwich Union Life Assurance Society* [1992] 31 EG 70). In some cases it may be desirable for the choice of method of determination of the rent to remain flexible. If so the draftsman should consider giving one of the parties (usually the landlord) the right to choose whether the person to be appointed to determine the new rent should act as expert or arbitrator. Such a right should be made exercisable by notice given before the earliest date upon which an appointment may be made.

The procedure to be adopted should be left to the discretion of the person conducting the reference. In the case of an arbitrator, the court has a supervisory jurisdiction over his conduct of the reference. No such jurisdiction exists in the case of an expert. However, it is nevertheless suggested that the draftsman is unlikely to be able to provide a satisfactory procedure for future disputes without losing most of the advantages of determination by expert. For example some leases require the expert to receive submissions or evidence from the parties. Almost invariably they are written. It is suggested that it is unsatisfactory to allow the rent to be fixed in reliance on assertions made by the parties which cannot be challenged by cross-examination, and where the expert is not to be given an opportunity of seeing and evaluating the quality of the witnesses. If the parties wish to adduce evidence in support of their cases, the appropriate way of determining the rent is by arbitration. A formal hearing may be dispensed with if the parties do not wish to avail themselves of their right to have one.

In the absence of consent of all parties, or an express term in the lease, an arbitrator cannot order a dispute referred to arbitration to be heard or determined together with another dispute involving a stranger, even though the two disputes are closely related, and a consolidated hearing would be convenient (*Oxford Shipping Co Ltd v Nippon Yusen Kaisha* [1984] 3 All ER 835). Where the draftsman can anticipate this problem arising (eg where the lease in question is a sublease or is one of a parade of identical shops) he should consider enlarging the powers of the arbitrator.

Example 5:12 Rent review machinery; notice, counter-notice reference to arbitration

(1) the landlord may serve upon the tenant not earlier than one year before the review date in question a notice ('a Review Notice') calling for a review of the rent

(2) if the landlord serves a Review Notice then the rent payable with effect from the review date to which it relates shall be:
 (a) such sum as may be specified in the Review Notice or
 (b) the higher of the rent payable immediately before that review date and the Market Rent if (but only if) the tenant so elects by counter-notice in writing served on the landlord not later than two months (time being of essence) after the service of a Review Notice

(3) if the tenant serves a counter-notice the Market Rent shall be determined in default of agreement within two months after the service of the counter-notice by arbitration

Example 5:13 Rent review machinery; no notice; determination by expert

(1) if the landlord and the tenant have not agreed the Market Rent three months before the relevant review date it shall be determined by an independent surveyor acting as an expert

(2) the independent surveyor shall:
 (a) be appointed in default of agreement by the President
 (b) give the landlord and the tenant an opportunity to make representations to him and to reply to each other's representations (but shall not be bound by them)
 (c) have power to determine how the costs of the reference shall be borne
 (d) publish his decision within two months of his appointment

(3) if the independent surveyor dies delays or becomes unwilling or incapable of acting or if for any reason the President thinks fit he may discharge the independent surveyor and appoint another in his place and may repeat this procedure as often as necessary

Example 5:14 Landlord's option to select method of resolving disputes

if the landlord and the tenant have not agreed the Market Rent three months before the relevant review date it shall be determined by arbitration or (if the landlord so elects by notice in writing given not later than one month before the relevant review date time being of the essence) by an independent surveyor acting as an expert

Example 5:15 Disputes procedure for inclusion in an underlease

if the landlord and the tenant have not agreed the Market Rent three months before the relevant review date it shall be determined by:
(1) an independent surveyor acting as an expert appointed in default of agreement by the President or
(2) at the election of either party (made not later than the making of an application to the President for an appointment time being of the essence) by the person (if any) appointed to determine the rent payable under the headlease acting in the capacity in which he is appointed under it

Example 5:16 Either party to initiate the procedure

(1) either the landlord or the tenant may serve on the other of them a written notice ('a Review Notice') calling for a review of the rent
(2) a Review Notice may be served not earlier than six months before the review date to which it relates or at any time after that review date
(3) if the landlord and the tenant have not agreed the amount of the rent to be paid with effect from the review date in question by the review date itself, the question shall be determined by an independent expert
(4) in default of agreement the expert shall be appointed by the President of the Royal Institution of Chartered Surveyors (or a person acting on his behalf) on the application of either the landlord or the tenant

Example 5:17 Clause permitting reliance on other awards

In the case of any arbitration either party shall be entitled to rely on the award of an expert or arbitrator relating to a transaction alleged to be comparable as evidence of the truth of the matters stated in the award, and the arbitrator shall give the award such weight as he thinks fit

11 VALUATION FORMULA

The most important part of the rent review clause is the valuation formula since this will define the method of calculating the new rent. In recent years this part of the rent review clause has become more sophisticated; perhaps over-sophisticated. If the rent review clause proposed in any particular case is unusual then the draftsman or the tenant's adviser should seek to ensure that it is studied by the landlord's (or the tenant's) surveyor before it is finally agreed.

(a) The basic definition

Minor variations in language in the basic definition can have surprisingly different results. For example, if the new rent is to be 'a reasonable rent for the demised premises' that rent must be assessed without regard to the fact that the tenant may have spent a large amount of money in improving the property: in effect he will have to pay for his improvements twice—once when he carries them out and again on the rent review (*Ponsford v HMS Aerosols Ltd* [1979] AC 63). On the other hand, if the new rent is to be 'such rent as is reasonable in all the circumstances' or 'such rent as would be reasonable for the landlord and the tenant to agree' the tenant's expenditure would not give rise to an increase in the rent (*Bates (Thomas) & Son Ltd v Wyndham's (Lingerie) Ltd* [1981] 1 All ER 1077; *Lear v Blizzard* [1983] 3 All ER 662). Moreover, there have been widely divergent expressions of judicial opinion as to whether the expression 'a reasonable rent' permits or precludes the valuer from taking into account freak bids or rents obtainable in the open market by special circumstances (*Cuff v Stone (J & F) Property Co Ltd* [1979] AC 87 *per* Megarry J at 90; *Ponsford v HMS Aerosols Ltd* above *per* Lord Wilberforce at 74E; *per* Viscount Dilhorne at 77D; *per* Lord Salmon at 81F; *per* Lord Fraser at 83H and *per* Lord Keith at 85G). In view of the uncertainty surrounding the meaning of these phrases, it is better to avoid them.

Even the expression 'rack rent' may mean different things in different circumstances. In a lease granted at a time when there is in force some long-standing statutory control or inhibition on the right to recover rent it will mean the maximum amount recoverable under that control (*Newman v Dorrington Developments Ltd* [1975] 3 All ER 928); but in a lease granted at a time when such control was not in the contemplation of the parties it will mean the rent unrestricted by such control (*Compton Group Ltd v Estates Gazette Ltd* (1978) 36 P&CR 148). Notwithstanding the temporary control of business rents between 1972 and 1975 it is suggested that the reimposition of such control is so unlikely that it is unnecessary any longer to make express provision for it.

The time honoured formula is:

the rent at which the demised property might reasonably be expected to be let in the open market on the review date by a willing landlord to a willing tenant.

This formula operates by reference to a hypothetical letting of the demised property in the open market. It therefore requires an objective approach. Some clauses in use require the surveyor to assess the amount which in his opinion ought to be the rent for the demised property 'having regard to rental values' current at the review date. The term 'having regard' is almost of necessity bound to create difficulties. How much regard is to be had, and what weight is to be attached to the regard when it has been had? (*English Exporters (London) Ltd v Eldonwall Ltd* [1973] 1 All ER 726 at 737 *per* Megarry J.) It may also be objected that a direction to the surveyor to have regard to rental values of other property may cause difficulties if there are no real comparables, or if some other method of valuation (eg a rent based on barrelage or throughput of petrol or profits) would be appropriate. Unless there are special reasons for adopting a subjective approach it is suggested that the objective approach does better justice between the parties.

However, the courts have said that there is little difference between a variety of phrases in common use. Thus 'full' adds nothing to 'rack rent'; 'market' does not add anything to 'rack rent'; 'open' does not add anything to 'market' and the word 'highest' only adds emphasis to what would be implicit anyway (*Royal Exchange Assurance v Bryant Samuel Properties (Coventry)* [1985] 1 EGLR 84; *Sterling Land Office Developments v Lloyds Bank* (1984) 271 EG 894; *Daejan Investments v Cornwall Coast Country Club* (1985) 50 P&CR 157).

Nevertheless, tenants are rightly suspicious of clauses which require the ascertainment of the 'best' rent, since that will undoubtedly entitle the landlord to the advantage of any special purchaser. If the actual tenant is the occupier of adjacent property he may find himself in the position of a special purchaser, since there is no rule of law which excludes him from the market (*First Leisure Trading v Dorita Properties* [1991] 1 EGLR 133). The evidence may establish that in his capacity as adjoining occupier the tenant would outbid the rest of the market. If so, his overbid may be taken into account (*Secretary of State v Reed International* [1994] 1 EGLR 22). The remedy against this is to extend the scope of the disregard of the tenant's occupation to include property (other than the demised property) which is occupied by the tenant.

The reference in the basic definition to the open market predicates the existence of an open market in which the hypothetical tenant will compete, and requires that the successful competitor will be able to use the property on offer (*Law Land Company Ltd v Consumers' Association Ltd* (1980) 255 EG 617). If there are parts of the lease which are inconsistent with that basic assumption the court will modify the lease accordingly (*ibid*).

It is advisable to provide expressly for the assumption of a willing landlord and a willing tenant, since this removes the scope for arguing that the property would fail to be let at any particular review date. The general principles to be applied to the construction of such a clause were considered in *Evans (FR) (Leeds) Ltd v English Electric Co Ltd* (1978) 36 P&CR 185. The assumption of a willing landlord or a willing tenant must not, however, be used to distort the reality of the market (*Dennis & Robinson Ltd v Kiossos Establishment* [1987] 1 EGLR 133).

(b) The property to be valued

Normally the property to be valued for the purposes of the rent review will be the demised property. In the case of a large property consideration should be given to the question whether account should be taken of the potential of the property for letting in parts. Where the rent is to be reviewed to a fraction of the market rental value, and the fraction is intended to take account of the tenant's position as mesne landlord, this is particularly important (see *Royal Exchange Assurance v Bryant Samuel Properties (Coventry) Ltd* [1985] 1 EGLR 84).

The draftsman should also ensure that the property to be valued is capable of being successfully let as a separate entity with all necessary rights of access and other easements. If it is not, he should provide for the assumption of those rights in the hypothetical letting (see *Jefferies v O'Neill* (1983) 269 EG 131 where the demised property in fact had no independent access but it was held that that fact ought to be disregarded for the purposes of the rent review).

In some cases it may be necessary to provide for the valuation of property other than the demised property. For example, the demised property may be of an unusual character making the finding of comparables difficult. If the property to be valued is to be assumed to have a lawful use different from that of the actual property, it is essential that the clause makes it clear that the notional property is physically suitable for that use. In *Trust House Forte Albany Hotels Ltd v Daejan Investments Ltd* (1980) 256 EG 915 the property consisted of an hotel, but the reviewed rent was to be assessed on the basis of a hypothetical letting of parts of the ground floor only on the assumption that those areas were 'actually let or available for letting for shopping or retail purposes'. It was held that the clause required the assumption that the property could be used for the specified purpose without illegality or breach of covenant, but did not require the further assumption that the property was physically adapted or fit for the specified use. Where the lease contained an acknowledgment by the tenant that the premises were fit for use as offices, the acknowledgment did not require the assumption that the property was in a physical condition which differed from its actual condition; it merely precluded the tenant from arguing that in its actual condition the property could not be used as offices (*Orchid Lodge v Extel Computing* [1991] 2 EGLR 116). If the draftsman wants to provide for a review of the property in an improved physical condition, clear words are needed. Similarly, where a rent review clause provided for a hypothetical letting 'for office purposes' it was held that the clause required the assumption that the property could lawfully be used for that purpose (*Bovis Group Pension Fund Ltd v GC Flooring & Furnishing Ltd* (1984) 269 EG 1252).

(c) Fit for use

Although the general rule is that the property is to be valued in its actual condition at the relevant date, it is nevertheless to be assumed that the tenant has removed from the property those fixtures which he is entitled to remove (*New Zealand Government Property Corporation v HM & S Ltd* [1982] QB 1145; *Young v Dalgety plc* [1987] 1 EGLR 116). In order to avoid the potentially depreciatory effect on the rent which such an assumption might have, and in order to counter the additional argument that the hypothetical tenant would be granted a rent-free period, it is now usual to include in the rent review clause an assumption that the property is fit for immediate use and occupation. This form does not entirely overcome the difficulty, because it leads to the question: use as what? It is suggested therefore that the draftsman states expressly that the property is to be assumed to be fit for use for the purposes permitted by the lease. Some more extreme forms of lease go on to provide that the property is to be assumed to be fitted out. The phrase 'fitted out' goes beyond merely 'fit'. The latter may simply mean free from defects and ready for fitting out; the former means that all partitions, shop fittings, office furniture etc has been installed (see *Pontsarn Investments v Kansallis-Osake Pankki* [1992] 1 EGLR 148). Where a lease provided for the assumption that all tenant's works required by the hypothetical tenant had been completed, it was held that this meant that the hypothetical tenant did not want further or different work from that carried out by the actual tenant, whose improvements were in any event to be disregarded (*London & Leeds Estates v Paribas* (1993) 66 P&CR 218). One difficulty is that the draftsman has not had in his mind's eye a mental picture of the building to be valued. In addition, provisions dealing with the physical condition of the building are often scattered through the rent review clause, sometimes as assumptions and sometimes as disregards. There is much to be said for collecting these provisions together, which will help avoid the risk that one provision may be effectively cancelled out by another.

If the parties agree that the property is to be treated as having been fitted out, it is important to specify at whose expense the fitting out is assumed to have been done. In some cases the landlord will in fact have paid for the fitting out through a contribution to the tenant's initial costs. In those cases, it may be fair to assume that the hypothetical fitting out is also carried out at the expense of the landlord, at least during the life of the original actual fitting out. But where the tenant has fitted out at its own expense, it is unfair for the rent to be assessed on the basis of a fitted-out building unless that expense to the tenant is also taken into account.

In buildings finished by the developer to 'shell and core' it is customary for the tenant to specify the fitting-out works but for the landlord to contribute towards them. In such cases one solution which is frequently adopted is for the parties' surveyors to prepare a 'rent review specification' which is annexed to the lease. For the purposes of rent review, the building is assumed to be in the condition specified in the rent review specification. The rent review specification must be sufficiently detailed to enable the valuer to form a clear picture of the imaginary physical condition of the building. An alternative would be to build in an assumption that the hypothetical tenant receives a similar contribution towards fitting out from the hypothetical landlord. Provision would need to be made for index-linking the amount of the contribution. This method has the advantage that the landlord is not tied to a rent review specification formulated at the beginning of the lease, but can respond to changes in the requirements of a modern building.

Example 5:18 Rent review clause requiring valuation of a notional building

(1) The expression 'the Market Rent' means the product of:

(a) the net lettable area of the demised property (measured in accordance with any codes of practice promulgated from time to time by the Royal Institution of Chartered Surveyors) expressed in square feet and
(b) the rate per square foot at which the notional building could reasonably be expected to be let in the open market on the review date by a willing landlord to a willing tenant
(2) The notional building referred to in clause (1) above is:
(a) located in the business centre of [ ]
(b) constructed to a standard similar to the demised property
(c) [ ] square feet in area
(d) available for letting with vacant possession on the terms of this lease (subject to any necessary modifications) together with all necessary ancillary accommodation
(e) fit for immediate occupation and use for the purposes permitted by the terms of this lease

Example 5:19 Assumptions about the physical condition of the property

The Market Rent shall be assessed on the assumption that the demised property:
　(1) is in a condition consistent with performance by the tenant of his obligations under this lease
　(2) has not been altered by the tenant in such a way as to affect its rental value (unless the alterations were carried out by the tenant under an obligation to the landlord)
　(3) has had removed from it all tenant's fixtures and partitioning and that all consequential damage has been made good
　(4) has not been destroyed or damaged by any insured risk
　(5) is free from physical defects
　(6) is to be fitted out by and at the expense of the hypothetical tenant during a rent-free period of such length as is reasonably necessary for that purpose

(d) Duration of the tenancy

The next matter to be considered is the duration of the hypothetical letting. If the clause is silent, a letting for the residue of the term will be presumed (*Norwich Union Life Insurance Society v Trustee Savings Bank Central Board* [1986] 1 EGLR 136). It used to be the general rule that the longer the letting the higher the rent was likely to be. However, recent economic conditions, and a growing awareness of the onerous liabilities of an original tenant have combined to alter tenants' desires. Whether this will change in the light of the abolition of privity of contract under new tenancies by the Landlord and Tenant (Covenants) Act 1995 remains to be seen. The optimum length of term varies according to the nature of the property and its location. There are three basic possibilities in specifying the duration of the hypothetical letting. First, the clause may provide for the length of the hypothetical tenancy to be equal to the unexpired residue of the actual term on the review date. This formula may produce different results according to which review is being operated. For example, on the fourth quinquennial review under a twenty-five-year lease the rent will be assessed as if a five-year term was being granted. A five-year term, particularly of a large building, may not be attractive to potential tenants and the rent obtainable on that review may be depressed on that account. This effect may be countered by specifying a minimum length of term. For example the hypothetical tenancy may be expressed to be for 'a term equal to the unexpired residue of the term of this lease or for a term of ten years from the review date whichever is the longer'.

Secondly, the clause may provide for the term of the hypothetical tenancy to be equal to the original term of the lease. It has been suggested that such a formula is unfair to the tenant. However, since the tenant has actually had a longer lease than the unexpired residue of the term, there is no compelling reason why he should not be charged rent on that basis, especially if the fact that the tenant is in occupation is to be disregarded in so far as it would otherwise affect the rent (see *Lynnthorpe Enterprises v Sidney Smith (Chelsea)* [1990] 2 EGLR 131 *per* Staughton LJ). Before adopting this formula, the draftsman should consider the likely effect of the assumption in relation to the last review. Even in the case of a new building let for, say, twenty-five years, the landlord might have difficulty in finding a tenant to accept a full repairing lease for a further twenty-five years, if the building is twenty years old at the date when the question arises. If the draftsman wishes to adopt this formula, the words of the clause must be clear. The court will lean in favour of a construction which, wherever possible, accords with reality. Accordingly, a clause which provided for the length of the hypothetical term to be 'equivalent to the term hereby granted' was held to require the assumption of a letting for a period equal to the residue of the actual term (*The Ritz Hotel (London) Ltd v Ritz Casino Ltd* [1989] 2 EGLR 135; *Lynnthorpe Enterprises v Sidney Smith (Chelsea)* above). It is best to quantify the length of the hypothetical term to avoid ambiguity (eg 'for a term of fifteen years beginning on the relevant review date').

Thirdly, the draftsman may adopt a flexible formula. For example the hypothetical tenancy may be assumed to be granted 'for such a term as will command the best rent'. This formula has obvious attractions for the landlord. However, since it will always result in the tenant having to pay the highest rent for the property, irrespective of the actual duration of the residue of the term, it is suggested that the tenant's adviser should resist this formula. A variant of this approach is to provide for a term 'not exceeding' a particular duration. The court has held that a flexible term should be assumed where the terms of the hypothetical lease excluded the possibility of rent review. Thus, the assumed term was that which a willing landlord would have been prepared to grant under a lease with no rent review (*Prudential Assurance v Salisbury's Handbags* [1992] 1 EGLR 153).

From the tenant's point of view, a formula based on the unexpired residue of the term, perhaps with a minimum period, is the best solution. If any other formula is chosen the tenant's adviser must make sure that the hypothetical term contains rent reviews at the same frequency as those in the actual term.

In assessing the rent for the hypothetical tenancy, the valuer may take into account the hypothetical tenant's prospects of renewing the tenancy under the Landlord and Tenant Act 1954 even where the lease specified a term 'not exceeding' a stated number of years (*Pivot Properties Ltd v Secretary of State* (1980) 256 EG 1176). Occasionally clauses provide for statutory controls on rent and security of tenure to be disregarded (eg *Toyota (GB) Ltd v Legal & General (Pensions Management) Ltd* [1989] 2 EGLR 123). Such clauses would almost certainly reduce the rent which would otherwise be payable, and should be avoided.

Where the transaction takes the form of the grant of a lease and a reversionary lease (usually to save stamp duty for the tenant), the draftsman must ensure that the existence of the reversionary lease is taken into account in assessing the rent under the lease in possession. If this is not done, the tenant may receive a windfall benefit by an assumption of a short hypothetical term whereas in reality he has the benefit of the reversionary lease as well. The court will avoid this result if possible, and may be able to imply a term to the effect that the existence of the reversionary term is to be taken into account (*Toyota (GB) Ltd v Legal & General (Pensions Management)* above). But it is not safe to rely on an implication.

(e) Terms of letting

The terms of letting should be clearly stated in the clause. The court will lean against construing a rent review clause so as to make the tenant pay for something which he has not got and cannot compel the landlord to give him (*Pearl Assurance plc v Shaw* (1984) 274 EG 490). Accordingly, if no terms are stated, the presumption is that the terms are to be those of the actual lease (*Basingstoke and Deane BC v Host Group Ltd* [1988] 1 All ER 824).

This is known as the presumption in favour of reality (*Lynnthorpe Enterprises v Sidney Smith (Chelsea)* [1990] 2 EGLR 131). However, this inference may be displaced if some of the terms of the actual lease are inconsistent with the fundamental concept of review to market rent (*Sterling Land Office Developments Ltd v Lloyds Bank plc* (1984) 271 EG 894). Further modifications may be made where the terms of the actual lease are inconsistent with some assumption which must be made for the purposes of the hypothetical lease. Thus in *Sheerness Steel Co v Medway Ports Authority* [1992] 12 EG 138 property was let as a steel rolling mill. The rent review clause required the assumption that the property was let for industrial purposes and that the tenant had an obligation to build buildings corresponding to those on site at the rent review date. It was held that the use restrictions which limited use to a particular form of industrial activity (ie steel rolling) and the restrictions on alterations could not be part of the hypothetical lease because they were inconsistent with the assumption that the property would be let for industrial purposes generally, and that the incoming tenant would have to adapt the property to make it suitable for the industrial use of his choice. Similarly, where a rent review clause provided for a hypothetical letting 'for retail purposes' it was held that restrictions in the lease on the type of retail use permitted were not to be included in the hypothetical lease (*Postel Properties v Greenwell* [1992] 47 EG 106).

As a general rule the tenant's adviser should seek to ensure that the terms of the hypothetical tenancy correspond with those of the actual tenancy.

(i) Alienation

The terms of the covenant against alienation may have a significant effect on the rent obtainable on the review. If the tenant is absolutely prohibited from subletting a large building, the available market will be restricted to those tenants capable of occupying the whole, which may have the effect of reducing rental levels. Similarly, if the tenant is prohibited from sharing occupation (as well as prohibited from assigning or subletting part of the property) the restriction may well be reflected in the reviewed rent. The effect of such a restriction may be particularly marked where the demised property is a department store (where the tenant would be unable to enter into franchise agreements or licences) or a large office where the tenant would be unable to share the accommodation with a subsidiary company. Many clauses prohibit subletting at a rent less than the rent passing under the lease itself. In a falling market, such a clause may mean that the property is effectively incapable of being sublet. This in turn may have a depressing effect on rental value. The draftsman should, therefore, be careful not to impose greater restrictions on the tenant than those necessary for the protection of the landlord. Moreover, the restrictions on alienation should always be read together with the restrictions on use.

(ii) Use

The greater the restrictions on the permitted use of the demised property, the less the market rent is likely to be, until the point comes at which the permitted use of the property is so restrictive that the court is able to reject it as being inconsistent with the concept of review in the open market. Use clauses may be divided into a number of categories for this purpose.

First, there are clauses which restrict the use of the property to a particular category of use, unless the landlord's consent is obtained, such consent not to be unreasonably withheld. Such clauses are known as 'open' clauses, and form the norm for valuation purposes. Any material deviation from this type of clause is likely to have an effect on the rent.

Secondly, there are clauses which restrict the use of the property to a particular category of use unless the landlord's consent is obtained, but do not provide that the landlord's consent is not to be unreasonably withheld. In such a case the valuer may have regard to the possibility that the landlord will consent to a change of use, since the change of use will not involve a variation of the terms of the lease, but is expressly contemplated by them (*Forte & Co Ltd v General Accident Life Assurance Ltd* [1986] 2 EGLR 115).

Thirdly, there are clauses which restrict the use of the property to a particular category of use, but make no provision for any change of use. In such a case the valuer may not take into account the possibility that the covenant will be varied by agreement between the parties, or waived by the landlord (*Plinth Property Investments Ltd v Mott, Hay & Anderson* (1978) 38 P&CR 361). Even if the landlord does purport unilaterally to waive or vary the clause otherwise than at the request of the tenant, the waiver or variation is to be ignored (*C & A Pensions Trustees Ltd v British Vita Investments Ltd* (1984) 272 EG 63).

Fourthly, there are clauses which restrict the use of the property to use by a named tenant. Where that use is the only permitted use under the lease then for the purpose of the rent review the name of the hypothetical tenant will be substituted for that of the actual tenant. In *Law Land Co Ltd v Consumers' Association* (1980) 255 EG 617 the use covenant provided that the property was not without the prior written consent of the landlord to be used other than as offices of the Consumers' Association and its associated organisations. The Court of Appeal held that for the purposes of the rent review clause it was to be assumed that the property could lawfully be used as offices of the hypothetical original tenant. The court held that to conclude otherwise would frustrate the purpose of the rent review, since there would then only be one possible tenant in the market. Similarly, in *Sterling Land Office Developments Ltd v Lloyds Bank plc* (1984) 271 EG 894 the use was defined as 'not ... for any purpose other than as a branch of Lloyds Bank Ltd'. The rent review clause was silent as to the terms of the hypothetical letting. Harman J held that for the purposes of the rent review the use covenant should be read as prohibiting use for any purpose other than as premises of the hypothetical willing tenant. A similar conclusion was reached where the use was restricted to the lessees' business of mortgage finance and insurance consultants (*SI Pension Trustees v Ministerio de la Marina Peruana* [1988] 1 EGLR 119). On the other hand where there is both a restriction on use to use by a named tenant and an alternative use provided for in the lease, the reasoning of those two cases does not apply. The existence of the alternative use means that there will be hypothetical tenants in the market for that use and consequently there is no need to modify the restriction on use to the named tenant (*James v British Crafts Centre* [1987] 1 EGLR 139; *Orchid Lodge (UK) v Extel Computing* [1991] 32 EG 57).

The lesson for the draftsman is not to impose on the tenant any restrictions greater than those necessary for the protection of the landlord. Some rent review clauses meet the problem by providing for the restrictions on use to be disregarded in assessing the rent. Although this approach protects the landlord, it is clearly unfair to the tenant who is compelled to pay for something which he does not have. The tenant's adviser should therefore delete the provision. Paradoxically, however, if the draftsman tightens the use clause so that use is restricted to the named original tenant only, the use clause in the hypothetical lease will be opened up on review. But the process of opening the lease will only make the property usable by the hypothetical original tenant. For practical purposes, therefore, the hypothetical lease will be unassignable.

Once the parties have agreed upon a use covenant the court will not modify it in a new lease granted under the Landlord and Tenant Act 1954 merely to give one party a rental advantage. This applies equally to a landlord seeking to widen the use covenant (*Clements (Charles) (London) Ltd v Rank City Wall Ltd* (1978) 246 EG 739) and to a tenant seeking to narrow it (*Aldwych Club Ltd v Copthall Property Co Ltd* (1962) 185 EG 219).

(iii) Assumed compliance with terms

Many rent review clauses contain an express assumption that the tenant has complied with his covenants. It seems that such an assumption would be implied by the court even if the review clause was silent on the point (*Harmsworth Pension Funds Trustees Ltd v Charringtons Industrial Holdings Ltd* (1985) 274 EG 588). This is consistent with the general principle of law that a person is not entitled to rely upon his own wrong. How this principle applies to the landlord's covenants is less clear. In *Plinth Property Investment Co Ltd v Mott, Hay & Anderson* (1978) 38 P&CR 361 Brandon LJ said that an arbitrator directed to have regard to the provisions of the lease had to consider the rights and obligations imposed by the lease and 'to assume that the rights will be enforced and that the obligations will be performed'.

This dictum would suggest that it should be assumed that the landlord has performed his covenants also. But in *Fawke v Chelsea (Viscount)* [1979] 3 All ER 568 the Court of Appeal held that in fixing an interim rent under s 24A of the Landlord and Tenant Act 1954, the court should have regard to the actual state of repair of the property. In that case the landlord was under an obligation to repair. Thus, the application of the principle that a person cannot take advantage of his own wrong produced the converse result in the case of a landlord. It may however be questioned whether the same result would follow in a rent review case. The rent fixed by the Court of Appeal was a differential rent, in the sense that it was to increase once the property was put into repair. By contrast, a rent fixed upon review is a constant rent (*Clarke v Findon Developments Ltd* (1984) 270 EG 426). Accordingly, if the tenant was to enforce the landlord's repairing obligation against him by specific performance, he might achieve occupation of a repaired building at a rent reflecting the disrepair. The likely resolution of this conflict is that the rent should be assessed having regard both to the actual state of the building but taking into account the existence and enforceability of the landlord's covenants.

(iv) Geared rents

Leases sometimes provide for the tenant to pay a rent fixed as a percentage of market value. The percentage may be less than 100 where the tenant has carried out substantial building works as part of the consideration for the grant. Conversely, it may be greater than 100 where the landlord has carried out special works of adaptation to the building which are of benefit to the particular tenant but which would be unlikely to affect the rental value of the building in the market. In such circumstances the draftsman should provide for the hypothetical lease to contain a rent review clause to 100 per cent of rack rental value. This is best done by specifying that the terms of the hypothetical lease are to exclude the terms of the actual lease as regards the gearing. If the draftsman fails to do this, the court will usually reach the conclusion that the gearing provisions should be omitted from the hypothetical lease anyway (*Guys 'n' Dolls v Sade Brothers Catering* (1983) 269 EG 129; *Buffalo Enterprises v Golden Wonder* [1991] 1 EGLR 141; *Prudential Assurance v 99 Bishopsgate* [1992] 03 EG 120). There can be exceptions to this (*Norwich Union Life Insurance Society v British Telecomunications* [1995] EGCS 148).

(v) Personal rights

Some leases grant personal rights to the original tenant (eg the right to use the property for a particular purpose or the right to sublet or assign to a company within the same group). The approach adopted by the court is that since such rights would not be enjoyed by an assignee, they would not be enjoyed by a hypothetical tenant, and consequently rights personal to the tenant should be excluded from the hypothetical lease (*James v British Crafts Centre* [1987] 1 EGLR 139; *Orchid Lodge (UK) v Extel Computing* [1991] 2 EGLR 116). However, since the tenant enjoys these rights, the landlord may consider that he ought to pay for them. This result can be achieved by an assumption in the rent review clause that any rights or privileges personal to the person who is the actual tenant at the date of the rent review are to be assumed to be granted to the hypothetical tenant. The tenant should ensure that personal rights are not to be assumed to be granted to the hypothetical tenant after they have lapsed in reality.

(f) Disregards

(i) Tenant's occupation

The tenant's adviser should ensure that as far as any effect on rent is concerned, the fact that the tenant has been in occupation of the demised property is disregarded. If this is not expressly provided, the new rent may be fixed taking into account that the tenant might pay more for the property simply in order to avoid having to move. The disregard does not of itself require vacant possession to be assumed (*Scottish & Newcastle Breweries plc v Sir Richard Sutton's Settled Estates* [1985] 2 EGLR 130 at 136E), nor does it exclude from consideration all evidence derived from the tenant's occupation. Such evidence is excluded only to the extent that it affects rent (*Cornwall Coast Country Club Ltd v Cardgrange Ltd* [1987] 1 EGLR 146 at 151E). Thus far, the disregard of the tenant's occupation is a standard term in rent review clauses. However, the tenant's adviser should consider whether it goes far enough to protect the tenant. In particular, it may be advisable to disregard the occupation of the tenant's subtenants and licensees, and it may also be desirable to disregard the tenant's occupation of other property (eg an adjoining building, or another unit in the same shopping centre, or a piece of land used as a car park). If this is not done then the fact that the tenant occupies adjoining property may be taken into account in fixing the rent (*First Leisure Trading v Dorita Properties* [1991] 1 EGLR 133).

(ii) Goodwill

Equally, the tenant's adviser should ensure that goodwill is disregarded in assessing the new rent, otherwise a tenant who is efficient in running his business will be charged extra on account of his efficiency. It is well known, however, that some property is valued by the profits method; that is, by ascertaining what average annual profit is likely to be made by a competent trader before deduction of rent, and then by apportioning that profit between the landlord and the tenant. If a profits method is likely, consideration should be given to deleting or modifying this disregard. For example in the case of a letting of a public house, it may be appropriate to disregard the effect on rent of goodwill to the extent that it exceeds the goodwill likely to have been generated by a tenant of average competence. Further drafting problems raised by this valuation method are discussed below. Where the lease requires the disregard of the effect on rent of the tenant's occupation it will usually follow as a matter of necessary implication that his goodwill must also be disregarded (*Prudential Assurance Co v Grand Metropolitan Estates* [1993] 2 EGLR 153).

(iii) Improvements

Unless the lease provides to the contrary, the new rent will be determined for the demised property as it stands on the review date irrespective of the identity of the person who paid for improvements (*Ponsford v HMS Aerosols* [1978] 2 All ER 837) except where the formula describing the rent allows the personal circumstances of the parties to be taken into account (as in *Bates (Thomas) & Son Ltd v Wyndham's (Lingerie) Ltd* [1981] 1 All ER 1077). This has been said to be an important *prima facie* assumption, which is not to be frittered away on minor differences in drafting (*Laura Investment Co v Havering London Borough Council* [1992] 1 EGLR 155). Sometimes, however, it has been possible to discern a clear distinction between part of the demised property (eg the site on which it was constructed) and structures erected on the site, such that only the site is to be valued for the purposes of the rent review (*Ipswich Town Football Club v Ipswich Borough Council* [1988] 1 EGLR 146). But such cases are rare (see *Goh Eng Wah v Yap Phooi Yin* [1988] 2 EGLR 148; *Ravenseft Properties v Park* [1988] 2 EGLR 164; *Laura Investment Co v Havering London Borough Council* above and *Sheerness Steel v Medway Ports Authority* [1992] 1 EGLR 133, in all of which tenants' improvements were included in the valuation). In the normal case of property taken at a rack rent the tenant's adviser should ensure that the tenant is not required to pay rent for his own improvements. Where, however, part of the consideration for the grant of the lease is the carrying out of improvements, it is fair that the landlord should receive the benefit of those works on review. So also where the tenant is recompensed for the carrying out of works by paying a proportion of the rack rental value of the property, or a proportion of rents received or receivable for the property, it is fair for the property to be valued as it stands on the rent review date. But there is one important qualification. The tenant's adviser should ensure that improvements carried out by any subtenants should be disregarded on the review. If this is not done, then the tenant may find himself in a position of rental shortfall, since he may have to pay rent for the improvements carried out by his subtenants, while being unable to recover that rent from the subtenants themselves.

If improvements are to be disregarded, the first question is to determine what improvements are. An improvement, for this purpose, is something which alters the structure of the demised property or which amounts to a landlord's fixture (*New Zealand Government Property Corporation v HM & S Ltd* [1982] QB 1145). There is no connotation of objective amelioration of the property in the word 'improvement'. What is an improvement is to be judged from the point of view of the tenant, and therefore it is quite possible that an 'improvement' may diminish the market rental value of the property.

The second question to ask is: improvements to what? Most clauses are either silent on the point, or require the disregard of improvements to the demised property. If the clause is silent on the point, it is likely that the word will be construed as meaning improvements to the demised property (cf *Brett v Brett Essex Golf Club* [1986] 1 EGLR 154 at 158H). It follows that the starting point is the property in the condition in which it was when demised. This means that work carried out by a tenant under a previous tenancy will not fall within the scope of the disregard, because it will ordinarily have become part of the property itself and therefore would form part of the demise (*Panther Shop Investments Ltd v Keith Pople Ltd* [1987] 1 EGLR 131). This is a particularly important point for the tenant's adviser in the case of a renewal lease. In the case of a new letting where the tenant has been let in to carry out fitting-out work a short time before the grant of the lease itself, the court may by a purposive construction conclude that work carried out in anticipation of the grant of the lease falls within the scope of the disregard (*Hambros Bank Executor & Trustee Co Ltd v Superdrug Stores Ltd* [1985] 1 EGLR 99). But in the case of a renewal lease there is far less scope for such a robust conclusion, and the tenant's adviser must ensure that the lease makes it clear that improvements carried out during a previous tenancy are to be disregarded. Even in the case of a new letting the point may be of significance, for it has been held that a modification to the original design of a building at the request and expense of the tenant, which resulted in the building of a structure different from that contemplated by the landlord was not an improvement for this purpose (*Scottish & Newcastle Breweries plc v Sir Richard Sutton's Settled Estates* [1985] 2 EGLR 130 at 137).

The third question is how to identify the improver. If the lease names the original tenant and then defines him as the tenant it may be possible to conclude that all work carried out by that named person, whenever carried out, potentially falls within the disregard (*Hambros Bank Executor & Trustee Co Ltd v Superdrug Stores Ltd* above). But if the lease identifies the improver as being tenant at the time the work was carried out (as does s 34 of the Landlord and Tenant Act 1954), then unless the person carrying out the work had either a legal tenancy at the date the work was carried out (*Euston Centre Properties Ltd v Wilson (H & J) Ltd* (1982) 262 EG 1079) or had an enforceable agreement for a lease (*Scottish & Newcastle Breweries plc v Sir Richard Sutton's Settled Estates* above), the improvements will fall outside the scope of the disregard. In addition the tenant's adviser should ensure that improvements carried out by persons deriving title under the tenant (eg subtenants and licensees) are within the scope of the disregard. The tenant's adviser should not lose sight of the possibility that improvements may be carried out by the landlord at the expense of the tenant, for example by recovery through the service charge. Such improvements ought to be treated in the same way as improvements carried out by the tenant himself. In addition where the landlord carries out improvements under an obligation to the tenant, many tenants feel that such an improvement should be disregarded. However, an improvement which the landlord has actually funded stands on a different footing to an improvement which, although carried out by the landlord, has been funded by the tenant. The landlord should therefore not accept a disregard of improvements which he himself has funded.

It is uncommon for the tenant to be entitled to the benefit of a disregard of all improvements. The usual provision extends to improvements carried out otherwise than in pursuance of an obligation to the landlord. The tenant's adviser should ensure that if this form of disregard is adopted, the exclusion from the disregard is limited to improvements carried out in pursuance of obligations contained in the lease. Although the court will be slow to construe a licence to make alterations as being an obligation for this purpose, nevertheless it has recognised that the obligation may be contained in some contractual document other than the lease (*Godbold v Martin the Newsagents Ltd* (1983) 268 EG 1202). The tenant's adviser should also be on his guard against hidden obligations to carry out improvements (see p 207). Landlords sometimes limit the disregard to tenants' improvements carried out with the consent of the landlord. The reasoning behind this limitation is that the landlord (particularly if he is a successor in title) wishes to avoid disputes over what improvements have actually been carried out. The requirement that the consent of the landlord be obtained before the improvements can be disregarded is a strong incentive to the tenant to comply with the obligations in the lease as regards alterations, and will normally ensure that the improvements are properly documented. If they are not, then they will not be disregarded, even if the lease contains an express assumption that the tenant is to be assumed to have complied with his obligations (*Hamish Cathie Travel England Ltd v Insight International Tours Ltd* [1986] 1 EGLR 244). If such a clause is put forward the tenant's adviser should at least ensure that improvements may be disregarded if consent was not required under the terms of the lease, or, if required, was unreasonably withheld.

There is a feeling on the part of many landlords that the giving to the tenant of a rent-free period is in effect a contribution by the landlord to the tenant's initial fitting-out costs. If the draftsman's client is of this school of thought, the disregard of improvements could be limited to those carried out after the expiry of any rent-free period contained in the lease.

In addition where the parties have agreed that the property is to be valued on the basis that it has been fitted out or is fit for immediate use and occupation, a disregard of tenant's improvements may conflict with the assumption. Thus, careful consideration must be given to the question what types of improvement should fall within the disregard.

The final series of questions relates to the instruction to be given to the valuer as to the method of carrying out the disregard. In essence there are three possibilities.

(1) To disregard the improvements themselves. This requires the valuer to assume that the improvements have never been carried out. If the improvements in question are such that any incoming tenant would carry them out, then the disregard of the improvements themselves may give the tenant a greater credit than the value of the actual (secondhand) improvements at the review date. This possibility was recognised in *GREA Real Property Investments Ltd v Williams* (1979) 250 EG 651.

(2) To disregard the effect on rent of improvements. This is the formula which is most usually adopted, and which was considered in *GREA Real Property Investments Ltd v Williams* (above) and *Estates Projects Ltd v Greenwich LBC* (1979) 251 EG 581. The main disadvantage of this formula is that nobody knows what it means, and nobody knows how to disregard the effect on rent of improvements without disregarding the improvements themselves.

(3) To make a fair allowance to the tenant on account of improvements. This method avoids the conceptual difficulties inherent in the other two methods, while at the same time preventing the tenant from arguing that he should receive the equivalent of a rent-free period on each rent review. It

must of course be recognised that this method entails a subjective approach leaving much to the discretion of the valuer, but it is better to leave arguments about value to valuers than to lawyers. This approach was adopted in the standard form of rent review clause published by the Incorporated Society of Valuers and Auctioneers.

Example 5:20 Disregard of improvements

Disregarding any effect on rent of any improvement carried out:
(1) to the demised property or any part of it
(2) by the tenant or any person deriving title under the tenant or by the landlord at the expense of the tenant
(3) with the consent of the landlord where required under this lease (unless consent was unreasonably withheld)
(4) otherwise than in pursuance of an obligation to the landlord (apart from an obligation to comply with statutes)
(5) either during the term or in anticipation of its grant

Example 5:21 Extension of disregard to improvements under previous lease

Disregarding any improvements carried out to the property demised by this lease but in the state in which it was on [   ] and either carried out at any time by the tenant named as party to this lease or a person deriving title under him or carried out by the tenant under any previous lease of the property granted on or after [   ]

(iv) Unusual terms of the lease

Where the lease contains unusual terms the draftsman should consider whether they should be disregarded for the purposes of the rent review. In some cases, the court is able to imply a disregard; for example where the unusual term requires the tenant to pay a rent additional to the market rent of the property (*Lister Locks Ltd v TEI Pension Trust Ltd* (1981) 264 EG 287; *Guys 'N' Doll Ltd v Sade Brothers Catering Ltd* (1983) 269 EG 129; *Buffalo Enterprises v Golden Wonder* [1991] 1 EGLR 141) or a rent which is a proportion of market rental value (*Prudential Assurance v 99 Bishopsgate* [1992] 03 EG 120). However, in a case where the unusual term is not inconsistent with the rent review, the court would have to give it effect. The effect to be given to a term in a lease is its real effect, and not the artificial effect which it would have if repeated verbatim in the hypothetical lease. Thus, where a lease contained a break-clause operable after the twelfth year of the term on six months' notice, it was held that the rent to be paid on the rent review at the expiry of the twelfth year of the term should be assessed on the footing of a hypothetical lease terminable on six months' notice (*Millett (R & A) Shops Ltd v Legal & General Assurance Society Ltd* (1984) 274 EG 1252).

One of the terms of the lease which should always be excluded is the amount of rent payable. However, the tenant's adviser should ensure that the rent review clause itself is not excluded. A considerable amount of litigation has taken place to determine whether on its true construction a lease was or was not intended to exclude the rent review clause from the hypothetical lease. Most of this litigation was unrealistic, since it can scarcely be supposed that parties who inserted rent review clauses into their leases precisely because they could not accurately assess a proper rent for the whole term of the lease intended the rent to be assessed on review on precisely the basis that they had rejected when fixing the initial rent. Nevertheless, judges managed to arrive at the conclusion that the parties had so intended. Ultimately the court has reached the conclusion that in the absence of clear words directing the rent review clause to be disregarded, the court will give effect to the underlying purpose of a rent review clause and hold that the hypothetical lease is to contain provisions for rent review on the same terms as the actual lease (*British Gas Corporation v Universities Superannuation Scheme Ltd* [1986] 1 WLR 398). This approach has been welcomed and approved by the Court of Appeal (*Equity and Law Life Assurance Society plc v Bodfield Ltd* [1987] 1 EGLR 124), although it was stressed that no guidelines as to construction can entitle the court to construe not the clause which the parties have entered into but the different clause which they would have entered into if they or their advisers had thought more deeply about how the clause would work in practice. The tide of authority is now firmly against the conclusion that the hypothetical lease contains no rent review clause (*Electricity Supply Nominees v FM Insurance Co Ltd* [1986] 1 EGLR 143; *Amax International Ltd v Custodian Holdings Ltd* [1986] 2 EGLR 111; *British Home Stores Ltd v Ranbrook Properties Ltd* [1988] 1 EGLR 121; *Arnold v National Westminster Bank plc* [1991] 2 WLR 1177). However, there has been the occasional aberration (*General Accident Fire & Life Assurance Corporation plc v Electronic Data Processing Co plc* [1987] 1 EGLR 112), and the unusual case of *Equity & Law Life Assurance Society plc v Bodfield Ltd* [1987] 1 EGLR 124. The particular feature in that case which complicated matters was the fact that the rent review clause was to a fraction only of market rent, and the construction advanced by the tenant would have required a partial disregard of the rent review clause anyway. Where the rent review clause is to a fraction of market rent the review clause should provide specifically for the disregard of the fraction as one of the terms of the hypothetical lease. In the case of a lease containing a normal review to a rack rent, it is sufficient if the rent review clause provides for a hypothetical letting 'on the terms of this lease other than the amount of the rent'.

The tenant's adviser should nevertheless beware of words which do require the disregard of the rent review clause itself. Words which have this effect are words such as 'disregarding the provisions of this clause' (*Pugh v Smiths Industries Ltd* (1982) 264 EG 823) or 'on the terms of this lease save for this proviso' (*Safeway Food Stores Ltd v Banderway Ltd* (1983) 267 EG 850) or 'there being disregarded this clause' (*Securicor Ltd v Postel Properties Ltd* [1985] 1 EGLR 102). The particular problem usually arises where a rent review clause appropriate to a short term with only one review date has been inserted into a lease containing numerous rent reviews.

(v) Incorporation of the statutory disregards

Many leases incorporate the disregards contained in s 34 of the Landlord and Tenant Act 1954. In a simple case this is convenient shorthand, but the draftsman should be aware of some of its limitations. First, the disregards apply only to the 'holding' (ie that part of the demised property occupied by the tenant) so that if subletting is envisaged the tenant may not reap the full benefit of the disregards. Secondly, the parties should specify whether the disregards are to be incorporated in the form in which they were originally enacted or as amended by the Law of Property Act 1969 (cf *Brett v Brett Essex Golf Club Ltd* [1986] 1 EGLR 154). Thirdly, if the disregard is incorporated in its amended form, it will extend only to improvements carried out by a person who was tenant at the time when the improvement was carried out; whereas if the disregard is incorporated in its unamended form it may extend to improvements carried out by the named tenant even before he became tenant (*Hambros Bank Executor & Trustee Co Ltd v Superdrug Stores Ltd* (1985) 274 EG 590), unless the works were carried out long before the grant of the lease (*Brett v Brett Essex Golf Club Ltd* above). Fourthly, the references in s 34(2) to improvements having been carried out not less than twenty-one years before the making of the 'application for the new tenancy' is inappropriate in the context of a rent review, although the court may be able to construe them as meaning the rent review.

(g) Planning

The disregard of the effect on rent of an improvement does not require the disregard of planning permission pursuant to which it was carried out (*Railstore Ltd v Playdale Ltd* (1988) 35 EG 87), for the potential for improvement is part of the property itself. Where the use permitted under the terms of the lease is not permitted under the Town and Country Planning Act 1990, or is permitted under a planning permission personal to the tenant, special provision should be made in the rent review clause. For an example see *Bovis Group Pension Fund Ltd v GC Flooring & Furnishing Ltd* (1984) 269 EG 1252 (where an assumption that property was to be assumed to be let 'as offices' carried with it an assumption that office use was lawful). The valuer is not entitled to take into account the possibility that the tenant may commit a breach of planning control (*Compton Group Ltd v Estates Gazette Ltd* (1978) 36 P&CR 148) but the hope of obtaining planning permission may be taken into account (*Rushmoor BC v Goacher* [1985] 2 EGLR 140; *6th Centre v Guildville* [1989] 1 EGLR 260). Where there is a difficulty over planning the draftsman should provide for an assumption that the property may be lawfully used by any person for the purposes permitted by the terms of the lease.

But the fact that a use is to be treated as lawful does not mean that the property is to be treated as having been notionally adapted physically for that use (*Orchid Lodge (UK) v Extel Computing* [1991] 32 EG 57). If the draftsman intends that the property should be physically suitable for an alternative use, this must be specified clearly in the rent review clause.

(h) Vacant possession

Many review clauses require the valuer to assume vacant possession at the review date. In most cases this is not unfair to either party. However, where the property was originally let subject to existing tenancies, the tenant's adviser should seek to ensure that such tenancies are taken into account. As a general rule the valuer should take incumbrances, including tenancies, into account (*Oscroft v Benabo* [1967] 2 All ER 548). This applies especially to leases which were in existence when the lease was granted (*Forte & Co v General Accident Life Assurance* [1986] 1 EGLR 115). But subleases granted after the date of the lease may be taken into account where rent review dates in the subleases coincide with rent review dates in the head lease (*Scottish & Newcastle Breweries v Sir Richard Sutton's Settled Estates* [1985] 2 EGLR 130) or where improvements carried out by subtenants are to be disregarded in fixing the rent under the subleases but are taken into account in fixing the rent under the headlease (*Laura Investment Co v London Borough of Havering (No 2)* [1993] 08 EG 120). However, there may be indications in the lease which produce a contrary result (*Avon CC v Alliance Property Co Ltd* (1981) 258 EG 1181, where the indications were first, use of the phrase 'rack rent', secondly, the assumption that the letting was to be of the demised property as a whole and, thirdly, the lack of an express requirement to take the subtenancies into account).

There may also be cases where it is to the landlord's advantage for the property to be valued subject to such tenancies as subsist on the rent review date. Where the tenant does not intend to occupy the property, but rather to sublet it and hold it as an investment, an assumption of vacant possession may seriously reduce the rental value of the property on the rent review because the incoming tenant would face an immediate void, instead of obtaining an immediate income (see *Bishopsgate (99) Ltd v Prudential Assurance Co Ltd* (1985) 273 EG 984).

If subtenancies are to be taken into account the draftsman should ensure that the alienation provisions require the subtenancies to contain rent reviews coincident with the rent review dates in the lease. This in itself may lead to the inference that the property is to be valued subject to subsisting subtenancies (*Scottish & Newcastle Breweries plc v Sir Richard Sutton's Settled Estates* above).

(i) Statutory control of rents

Between 1972 and 1975 there was statutory control of rents payable under business tenancies. The form of control affected only the amount of rent which the landlord was entitled to receive, and did not affect the landlord's ability to call for a rent review. Some clauses provide that if at a future date there is any statutory restriction on the landlord's right to recover rent the review is to be postponed until the lifting of that restriction. That method of dealing with the problem is satisfactory only if the statutory control is temporary; if it is permanently imposed then it may be that the review can never take place. Other clauses direct the valuer to ignore the effect of any statutory control of rents. There is no legal objection to this method (*Langham House Developments Ltd v Brompton Securities Ltd* (1980) 256 EG 719) although if business rents were to be subjected to control it might be difficult to assess a new rent

RENT AND RENT REVIEW

based on a hypothesis so far removed from reality. Of course if the valuer is directed to disregard such control the rent actually recoverable after the review will still be subject to control (ie the recoverable rent will be less than the reserved rent).

Example 5:22 Valuation formula for occupational lease

'Market Rent' means the rent at which the demised property might reasonably be expected to be let as a whole in the open market with vacant possession by a willing landlord to a willing tenant without a premium for a term equal to the unexpired residue of the term at the relevant review date (or ten years if longer) upon the terms of this lease (other than the amount of the rent) and upon the assumptions that:
  (a) the tenant has complied with his covenants
  (b) the demised property is fit for immediate use for the purposes permitted by this lease and will be fitted out by and at the expense of the incoming tenant during a period when no rent is payable

and disregarding:

(1) the fact that the tenant has been in occupation of the whole or part of the demised property

(2) any goodwill attached to the demised property by reason of the carrying on there of the tenant's business

(3) any improvement carried out at the expense of the tenant or a person deriving title under him otherwise than in pursuance of an obligation imposed on him by this lease (but in case of conflict between this paragraph and assumption (b) above assumption (b) shall prevail)

(4) any restraint or restriction on the right to recover rent imposed by or by virtue of any Act of Parliament

Example 5:23 Alternative valuation formula

'Market Rent' means the rent at which the demised property might reasonably be expected to be let in the open market either as a whole or in parts without payment of a premium by a willing landlord to a willing tenant for such a term (not exceeding the length of the term originally granted) as would command the best rent with vacant possession at the beginning of the term and upon the same terms (other than the amount of the rent) as this lease and on the assumptions that:
  (a) the tenant has observed and performed all his covenants
  (b) the demised property is fit for immediate use and occupation for the use permitted by this lease
  (c) the demised property may be lawfully used by any person for that use
  (d) in case the demised property has been damaged or destroyed it has been fully reinstated

but disregarding:

(1) the fact that the tenant or his subtenants have been in occupation of the demised property

(2) any goodwill attached to the demised property by reason of the carrying on there of the business of the tenant or his subtenants or their predecessors in their respective businesses

(3) any works carried out by the tenant or his subtenants which would diminish the rental value of the demised property

(4) the effect on rent of any improvement carried out at the expense of the tenant or his subtenants (other than improvements carried out either during a rent-free period or in pursuance of an obligation imposed by this lease or an agreement to grant it) and completed not more than twenty-one years before the rent review date in question

Example 5:24 Valuation formula: short form

'Market Rent' means the rent at which having regard to the terms of the tenancy (other than the amount of the rent) the demised property might reasonably be expected to be let in the open market with vacant possession for a term equal to the term of this lease by a willing landlord to a willing tenant assuming that the tenant has complied with his covenants and disregarding those matters set out in paragraphs (a), (b) and (c) of section 34(1) of the Landlord and Tenant Act 1954 (as amended) which would be disregarded if the tenant were applying for a new tenancy of the demised property and were in occupation of the whole of it for the purposes of a business carried on by him

Example 5:25 Valuation formula: disregard of review clause and no disregard of tenant's improvements (for use in a building lease)

'Reviewed Rent' means [   ] per cent of the best rent at which the demised property might reasonably be expected to be let either as a whole or in parts in the open market by a willing landlord to a willing tenant or tenants:

(1) for such a term as would command the best rent

(2) with vacant possession at the beginning of the term

(3) upon the same terms as this lease (subject to any necessary modifications) but excluding this rent review clause and any obligation to erect buildings

(4) on the assumption that the hypothetical lease or leases contain provisions enabling the rent to be revised upon such terms as may be reasonable having regard to market practice current at the time

(5) on the assumptions that the tenant has performed all its covenants that the demised property is fit for immediate use and occupation for the purposes permitted by this lease that no work has been carried out to the demised property which would diminish its rental value and that in case the demised property has been damaged or

RENT AND RENT REVIEW

destroyed it has been fully reinstated
but disregarding:
(1) the fact that the tenant or its subtenants have been in occupation of the demised property
(2) any goodwill attached to the demised property by reason of the carrying on there of the business of the tenant its subtenants or their predecessors in their respective business
(3) any improvement carried out by a person deriving title under the tenant and holding a leasehold interest at a rack rent other than an assignee of this lease or part of it
(4) any restraint or restriction on the right to recover rent imposed by or by virtue of any Act of Parliament

Example 5:26 Review to modern ground rent

(1) With effect from each review date the rent payable shall be the higher of:
(a) the rent payable immediately before that review date and
(b) the modern ground rent
(2) The modern ground rent is the rent for which the demised property might reasonably be expected to be let in the open market on the relevant review date by a willing landlord to a willing tenant on the following assumptions:
(a) the letting is with vacant possession
(b) all buildings landlord's fixtures and fixed plant have been demolished or removed and the site has been cleared for development
(c) all obligations relating to the removal or treatment of pollution waste or noxious or hazardous substances have been complied with and no such obligations will be imposed on the willing tenant as a result of anything done or omitted to be done before the rent review date
(d) there is in force planning permission (not subject to onerous conditions) authorising the use of the demised property for any purpose within Class B1 or B2 or B8 of the Town and Country Planning (Use Classes) Order 1987 (or any amended class which includes that use) and authorising the erection of buildings suitable for those uses and having an area no less than the area of buildings then comprised in the demised property
(e) no planning permission would be granted for any other use of the demised property
(f) mains services for water gas electricity telecommunications and other usual or necessary services are laid to appropriate points on the perimeter of the demised property and the demised property has adequate provision for surface water and foul drainage
(g) the letting is for a term of 125 years from the relevant review date

(h) the terms of the letting are those of this lease except that:
   (i) there is no obligation to build
   (ii) there is no restraint on alienation except that during the last seven years of the term the tenant may not without the landlord's consent assign or sublet the whole or any part of the demised property
   (iii) the demised property may be used for any purpose falling within the use classes specified in paragraph (d) above

(j) Rent-free period

In the cases of new lettings in the open market it is conventional for the tenant to be given a period of occupation under the lease during which he pays no rent or a concessionary rent. There is no satisfactory explanation why this happens. Sometimes it is said to be in order to allow the tenant to fit out the property, but the length of the rent-free period rarely bears any discernible relationship to the time or cost of fitting out. It may be little more than a reflection of the bargaining strength of the respective parties. It is common in a disputed rent review for the tenant to seek the equivalent of a rent-free period, on the ground that had the hypothetical letting really taken place in the market, the hypothetical tenant would have been given such an inducement to take the lease. Since the reviewed rent must be a constant figure in the absence of express agreement to the contrary (*Clarke v Findon Developments Ltd* (1984) 270 EG 426) the only way to give effect to the notional rent-free period is to spread it either to the next rent review or to the end of the hypothetical term. An alternative way in which the tenant can put the case is to adjust his analysis of comparable lettings in order to reflect the rent-free period actually granted. If the rent review clause provides for the disregard of rent-free periods, either in relation to the subject property or in relation to comparables, the result will be to distort the market and to lead to a difficult valuation. In addition it may work against the landlord, since if rent-free periods are to be disregarded, the effective rent of comparable properties (where rent-free periods were in fact agreed) will be diminished. This in turn will lower the rent to be paid for the demised property. In *Co-operative Wholesale Society v National Westminster Bank* [1995] 1 EGLR 97 the Court of Appeal considered four different drafting responses to this problem. It was held that only the most unambiguous of clauses would succeed in achieving for the landlord a headline rent, although the court was more sympathetic to a clause which merely sought to neutralise the tenant's argument that the hypothetical tenant would have to incur expenses associated with moving in. One of the drafts provided for an assumption that any rent-free period had expired immediately before the review date. The court held that if the rent-free period had expired, it could have no part to play in the negotiations which took place on the review date itself. Another provided for the rent to be payable at the rate payable following the expiry of a rent-free period which might be granted on 'a new letting' of the property. The court held that this referred to a rent-free period attributable to the fact of the letting being new and was therefore to be confined to a rent-free period given for fitting-out purposes. A third provided for an assumption that no reduction or allowance was to be made on account of any rent-free period. The court held that this meant that no reduction was to be made from the rent which would have been fixed without the assumption, and that the assumption did not entitle the landlord to increase the rent to the headline rate. The fourth, and only successful clause, provided for the rent to be that which would become payable after the expiry of a rent-free period of such length as would be negotiated in the open market. The court held that since the notional rent-free period was still to come, it could play a part in the hypothetical negotiations, and since its length was governed by the open market, it could not be restricted to a rent-free period for fitting out. This form of clause was suggested in the third edition of this book. But it is vital not to combine this method with a disregard of rent-free periods otherwise the two methods will cancel each other out (*City Offices v Allianz Cornhill International Insurance Co* [1993] 11 EG 129).

The unprecedented recession of the early 1990s failed to compel landlords to lower 'headline' rents enough to reflect fully the decline in the market. Instead they bought off tenants with extended rent-free periods. This has meant that some clauses agreed in the boom of the late 1980s have been found to work unfairly against tenants. The problem is that where a clause requires the assumption of a rent-free period which would be granted in the market, there is no easy way of separating out a rent-free period granted to recognise the need to fit out the property, and a rent-free period granted as a pure inducement to keep up the level of 'headline rent' (*Broadgate Square v Lehman Brothers* [1995] 1 EGLR 97). The tenant's adviser should not accept such a clause unless the rent-free period which is to be assumed (or the absence of which is to be disregarded) is limited to a reasonable fitting-out period.

An alternative way of coping with the problem is not to refer to rent-free periods at all but to build in an assumption that the tenant has had access to the property for fitting-out purposes.

Where the rent review clause provides for the assessment of a headline rent, and the hypothetical lease is to contain a rent review clause in similar terms, the tenant may argue that the rent review clause itself is an onerous clause which justifies a discount from what would otherwise be the headline rent. Some draftsmen sidestep this argument by providing for a hypothetical lease containing a different form of rent review clause.

Example 5:27 Valuation formula with built in rent-free period

'Market Rent' means the highest rent which would become payable immediately after the expiry of a rent-free period of such length as would reasonably be required for fitting out the demised property on a letting of the demised property between a willing landlord and a willing tenant in the open market on the review date with vacant possession for a term equal to the original duration of this lease and on the same terms (save for the amount of the rent but including this rent review clause) on the assumptions that:
   (a) the tenant has complied with all his covenants
   (b) the demised property is fit for immediate occupation
but disregarding
   (1) the fact that the tenant has been in occupation of the demised property
   (2) any improvement carried out by the tenant during the term otherwise than pursuant to an obligation imposed by this lease

Example 5:28 Assumption that tenant has had access for fitting out

assuming that the hypothetical tenant has had sufficient access to the demised property before the relevant review date during a period in which he did not pay rent for the purpose of enabling him to fit out to his requirements

(k) VAT

VAT is charged on sales of new commercial buildings. Thus, an investor will have to pay more for the same building than would have been the case if VAT had not been imposed. In order to mitigate this, a landlord has the option to charge VAT on the rent payable. The option may be exercised on a building-by-building basis. If the option is exercised, the VAT payable on the rent may be retained by the landlord until he has offset the VAT payable on the construction or acquisition of the building. The option may be exercised in relation to a building whether it is a new building or not. If the tenant is a trading company with considerable output VAT, this will not matter to the tenant, since the VAT payable on the rent will be absorbed as input tax and will merely result in a smaller net payment being made to HM Customs & Excise. But if the tenant does not have sufficient output tax to absorb the VAT on rent, the result of the exercise of the option will be to add 15 per cent to the rent. This may in turn depress the rental bid of the hypothetical tenant, or at least produce a two tier market, as between those buildings where VAT is not payable (either because they are not new, or because the option has not been exercised) and those buildings where it is. The problem will arise only in the case of new buildings (ie those less than five years old) and those where the option has been exercised, and does not therefore require to be dealt with in every case. In addition in areas where there is a high concentration of occupiers who are exempt from VAT and who cannot therefore absorb VAT on rent (eg in the City of London) the exercise of the option to tax is extremely rare. Where the point does arise the problem for the draftsman is similar to that encountered over rent-free periods, and it is suggested that the response should be the same. Thus, the rent review clause should contain an assumption that the tenant will be able to absorb any VAT payable on the rent. The market rent should also be defined as being exclusive of VAT, in order to avoid any argument by the tenant that the amount determined as the market rent is inclusive of VAT.

There is a school of thought, however, which argues that the inclusion of VAT assumptions is sufficiently complex as to distort the hypothetical market and that the safest course is to leave well alone. Until the courts have considered the effect of VAT assumptions, it is impossible to predict whether these fears are unfounded. Since such clauses only began to be drafted in the late 1980s the first rent reviews are not yet due.

Example 5:29 Assumption about VAT

on the assumption that the hypothetical tenant is and tenants in the market generally are registered for the purposes of valued added tax and will be able to set off in full by way of input tax any valued added tax payable in respect of any payment of rent against the output tax payable by him or them

Example 5:30 Alternative assumption about VAT

assuming that the hypothetical tenant is a person who for the purposes of valued added tax is a taxable person who makes only taxable supplies and no exempt supplies

(l) Profits valuation

In many cases a lease of commercial property will contain a normal rent review clause requiring the ascertainment of the market rent for the property, but instead of valuing by reference to comparables, the valuers will carry out a profits valuation. A profits valuation proceeds by ascertaining what average annual profit is likely to be made by a competent trader before deduction of rent, and then apportions that profit (usually called the divisible balance) between the landlord and the tenant. A profits valuation is relatively common in the case of leisure properties (see *WJ Barton Ltd v Long Acre Securities Ltd* [1982] 1 All ER 465 for other examples). Where a profits valuation is a likely method to be employed at the rent review, several points should be considered.

First, it will clearly be desirable to know what profits the actual tenant has made. This may work to the landlord's advantage if the tenant seeks to put forward too gloomy an estimate, or to the tenant's advantage if the landlord seeks to put forward too optimistic an estimate. But in the absence of a specific clause requiring the tenant to disclose his profits, they are inadmissible in evidence (*Cornwall Coast Country Club v Cardgrange Ltd* [1987] 1 EGLR 146 at 154; *Electricity Supply Nominees Ltd v London Clubs Ltd* (1988) 34 EG 71) although they may be obtainable on discovery (*Urban Small Space v Burford Investment Co* [1990] 2 EGLR 120). However, if the lease specifically so provides, then the tenant's accounts and other records may be made available and relied on by either party (*Electricity Supply Nominees v London Clubs* above).

Secondly, if a profits valuation is carried out, particularly if it is reliant upon the tenant's actual profits, the valuer may find it difficult to disentangle that part of the profit which is attributable to the tenant's goodwill. Accordingly the draftsman should consider not including the customary disregard of tenant's goodwill. The tenant may well wish to resist this, as he will clearly be unwilling to pay rent for his own commercial success. But it is inherent in the concept of a profits valuation, that the gross profit (which necessarily comes partly from the trader's goodwill) is divided between landlord and tenant, so that the landlord does obtain a share of the tenant's goodwill. One possibility is for goodwill to be disregarded only to the extent that it exceeds the goodwill which would have been generated by a tenant of average competence.

Thirdly, it may be desirable to make special provision for the treatment of improvements. The gross profit will be ascertained from the conduct of the business as it is; that is, from improved premises. Some valuers deal with improvements in profits valuations by deducting from the gross profit an annual sum representing interest on capital employed in carrying out the improvement plus a writing down allowance. It may be desirable to provide for this (or some other method) specifically.

Example 5:31 Clause admitting accounts

> for the purpose of ascertaining the open market rent either party shall be at liberty to rely upon the actual trading history of the demised property and the tenant shall if so required by the landlord make available to the landlord such accounts and other trading records as the landlord shall reasonably require

Example 5:32 Alternative clause admitting accounts

> on the assumption that the hypothetical tenant has had access to such accounts and information as would be made available by a reasonable tenant to a purchaser of the tenant's business (in so far as conducted in the demised property) as a going concern

12 REVIEW OF REVIEWS

Where the term of the lease is exceptionally long the draftsman should consider providing for machinery whereby the intervals between review dates may be reconsidered so as to bring those intervals into line with market practice. To a limited extent such a provision is also in the tenant's interest because an unusually long period between reviews is likely to increase the rent which would otherwise be payable.

Example 5:33 Review of review periods

> (1) Subject to paragraph (2) below the landlord may from time to time serve on the tenant a notice (a 'Review Frequency Notice') requiring the substitution for the review dates of more frequent review dates
>
> (2) A Review Frequency Notice shall not be served before the expiry of the twenty-fifth year of the term nor less than twenty-five years after the service of an earlier Review Frequency Notice nor during a year ending on a review date
>
> (3) A Review Frequency Notice shall contain the landlord's proposals as to the dates to be substituted
>
> (4) In default of agreement within two months after the service of a Review Frequency Notice the question at what dates it would be reasonable for the rent to be reviewed shall be determined by an inde-

pendent surveyor acting as an expert to be appointed in default of agreement by the President

(5) The independent surveyor shall have regard to market practice current at the date of the Review Frequency Notice in relation to new lettings with vacant possession of property comparable to the demised property

(6) If the independent surveyor shall determine that it would be reasonable for the rent to be reviewed at dates more frequent than the review dates then the dates so determined shall become the review dates

13 INTERIM PROVISIONS AND INTEREST

The draftsman should provide for the making of payments on account pending the determination of the reviewed rent. This is particularly important where the review is automatic otherwise there is a danger that no rent will be payable after the review date and before the new rent is settled (*Kenilworth Industrial Sites Ltd v Little (EC) & Co Ltd* [1975] 1 All ER 53; *Accuba Ltd v Allied Shoe Repair Ltd* [1975] 3 All ER 782) although in some cases the court will be able to interpret the lease as making provision for a minimum rent (*London and Manchester Assurance Co Ltd v Dunn & Co (GA)* (1983) 265 EG 39, 131 *per* Slade LJ). The rent payable pending the determination of the new rent is usually the unreviewed rent, although there is no reason why it should not be some higher figure (eg 115 per cent of the unreviewed rent). Indeed in *Smith's (Henry) Charity Trustees v AWADA Trading and Promotion Services Ltd* (1983) 269 EG 729 the tenant was required to make payments on account at the rate demanded by the landlord in the review notice. This provision was described by Griffiths LJ as being a 'powerful pointer' to the conclusion that time was of the essence of the timetable.

Provision should be made for the payment of the difference between the payments on account and the amount of the new rent (or for refunding to the tenant any overpayment) once the new rent has been settled. The tenant should insist that any overpayment is repaid to him rather than simply credited towards payment of the next instalment of rent so that he is not required to make the landlord a free loan. If there is a requirement that interest be paid it should operate in the tenant's favour if there is any overpayment.

If the lease so provides, the reviewed rent will operate retrospectively (*Bailey (CH) Ltd v Memorial Enterprises Ltd* [1974] 1 All ER 1003). However, it is likely that it cannot be distrained for until it has been determined (*United Scientific Holdings Ltd v Burnley BC* [1977] 2 All ER 62) and it will not be in arrear until after the rent day next following the determination (*South Tottenham Land Securities Ltd v R & A Millett (Shops) Ltd* [1984] 1 All ER 614, where O'Connor LJ remarked on the desirability of dealing specifically with what is to happen where there is a delay in arriving at a new rent beyond the review date). In most review clauses the reviewed rent is back-dated to the review date itself. However, where the review may be operated long after the review date has passed the tenant may find that he has substantial arrears to pay. His advisers should, therefore, seek to limit the power to back-date any increase in the rent to, say, one year before the service of a review notice or, alternatively to insert a provision enabling such arrears to be paid in instalments rather than in one lump sum.

At common law, the landlord is not entitled to recover damages for delay if the rent is not paid on time, and the court has no power to award interest if the rent is paid before the issue of proceedings (*President of India v La Pintada Cia Navegacion SA* [1984] 2 All ER 773). Nor will the court imply a term that interest should be paid (*Trust House Forte Albany Hotels Ltd v Daejan Investments Ltd* (1980) 256 EG 915) even where the interest sought is interest upon money actually expended by the landlord (*Frobisher (Second Investments) Ltd v Kiloran Trust Co Ltd* [1980] 1 All ER 488).

Accordingly, the draftsman should provide for the payment by the tenant of interest on all overdue payments. The rate of interest should be tied to a readily ascertainable yardstick (eg base lending rate of a clearing bank) and provision should be made for substituting a different rate should the selected yardstick cease to exist.

Since the reviewed rent will not become due until the rent day following its determination (*South Tottenham Land Securities Ltd v R & A Millett (Shops) Ltd* above) special provision must be made to deal with interest following a rent review. The tenant's adviser should seek to limit the rate of interest charged. While it is reasonable for the landlord to seek interest at a high rate where the tenant has defaulted in paying money due under the lease, it is not reasonable for the same rate to be adopted where the tenant is not in default. The tenant's adviser should also ensure that interest is not payable for any greater period than would have been the case if the reviewed rent had been ascertained by the review date.

Example 5:34 Definition of rate of interest

'the Prescribed Rate' means two per cent above the base lending rate from time to time of [   ] Bank plc or (if the landlord chooses) the rate of interest which the landlord has to pay from time to time for short-term unsecured borrowing

Example 5:35 Alternative definition of rate of interest

'the Prescribed Rate' means two per cent above the base lending rate from time to time of
    (1) [   ] Bank plc or
    (2) such other member of the Committee of London Clearing Bankers as the landlord may from time to time nominate or
if that rate cannot be ascertained such comparable rate of interest as may be agreed between the landlord and the tenant and in default of agreement determined by arbitration

Example 5:36 Payment on account pending rent review

Pending the ascertainment of the rent the tenant shall continue to make payments at the rate payable immediately before the Review Date in question and upon the ascertainment of the rent the tenant shall pay to the landlord the shortfall if any together with interest at the Prescribed Rate calculated as if the rent had been ascertained at the Review Date

Example 5:37 Review to market rent: upwards only

(1) In this Schedule:
(a) 'Review Date' means the [ ] of [ ] and every [ ] anniversary of that date
(b) 'Market Rent' means the best rent at which the Property might reasonably be expected to be let on the relevant Review Date in the open market without a premium by a willing landlord to a willing tenant for such a term as would then command the best rent and upon the terms of this lease (other than the amount of the rent) upon the assumptions that:
  (a) the tenant has complied with all his covenants and
  (b) the property is fit for immediate use and occupation (any damage having been repaired or reinstated) and disregarding:
    (i) the fact that the tenant has been in occupation of the property
    (ii) any restriction imposed by this lease upon the use of the property
    (iii) any goodwill attached to the property by reason of the carrying on there of the tenant's trade or business
and making a fair allowance to the tenant on account of any improvement to the property carried out at his expense during the period of twenty-one years immediately preceding the relevant Review Date

RENT AND RENT REVIEW 145

other than an improvement carried out (a) during a rent-free period or (b) in pursuance of any obligation to the landlord

(2) From each Review Date the rent payable by the tenant shall be the rent contractually payable immediately before that Review Date or the Market Rent on that Review Date whichever is the higher

(3) The Market Rent on any Review Date shall be determined in default of agreement between the landlord and tenant by arbitration (but no arbitrator shall be appointed before the relevant Review Date)

(4) Pending the ascertainment of the Market Rent the Tenant shall continue to make payments on account at the rate of 115 per cent of the rent payable immediately before the Review Date in question and upon the ascertainment of the Market Rent the tenant shall pay to the landlord the shortfall (if any) together with interest at the rate of three per cent below the Prescribed Rate calculated as if the Market Rent had been ascertained on the Review Date

(5) The Basic Rent payable from any Review Date shall be recorded in a written memorandum as soon as it has been ascertained

(6) If at any Review Date the landlord's right to recover or increase the rent is restrained or restricted by or by virtue of any Act of Parliament the landlord may by notice in writing given to the tenant call for an additional review of the rent upon such date as may be specified in the notice and that date shall thereupon become a Review Date and this Schedule shall apply accordingly

Example 5:38 Alternative form of review to market rent: upwards only

(1) In this clause:
'Review Date' means the [   ] of [   ] in the years [   ] and any date which becomes a Review Date under subclause (7)
'Market Rent' means the highest yearly rent which would become payable after the expiry of a rent-free period of such length as is necessary to fit out the demised property on a letting of the demised property in the open market between a willing landlord and a willing tenant
    (a) for a term equal to the unexpired residue of the term or (if longer) 15 years
    (b) with vacant possession
    (c) for the use or uses permitted under this lease (taking into account all variations and licences)
    (d) on the terms of this lease
assuming
        (i) that all the covenants in this lease have been performed
        (ii) that any rights personal to the actual tenant would be granted to the hypothetical tenant
        (iii) that the demised property may be lawfully occupied for the purposes permitted by this lease
but disregarding
    (a) goodwill attached to the demised property because the tenant

has carried on business there
- (b) any effect on rent of any improvement to the demised property made:
    - (i) with the landlord's written consent
    - (ii) either without obligation by the tenant or pursuant to an obligation to comply with statutes
    - (iii) during the term or during the currency of an agreement to grant this lease
- (c) any depreciating effect of anything done by the tenant in the demised property or installed or affixed to it by him
- (d) the fact that the tenant has been in occupation of the demised property

'Surveyor' means a chartered surveyor agreed in writing by the landlord and the tenant or in default of agreement appointed by the President

'The President' means the President of the Royal Institution of Chartered Surveyors or a person acting on his behalf

(2) From each Review Date the rent shall be the higher of:
- (a) the Market Rent on that review date and
- (b) the rent contractually payable immediately before that date

(3) If the landlord and the tenant have not agreed the market rent four months before the review date in question it shall be determined by a surveyor who
- (a) shall be appointed in default of agreement by the President and
- (b) shall act as an arbitrator unless the landlord requires him to act as an expert

(4) If the surveyor acts as an expert he shall
- (a) give the landlord and the tenant an opportunity to submit written representations and cross-representations to him
- (b) disclose each party's representations and cross-representations to the other before reaching his decision

(5) If the surveyor refuses to act or is incapable of acting then the President may appoint another in his place

(6) If the rent is not ascertained by a review date:
- (a) the tenant shall continue to pay rent on account at the rate payable immediately before the review date and
- (b) seven days after the ascertainment of the rent the tenant shall pay the difference (if any) for the period from the review date to the expiry of that seven-day period between the amount paid on account and the market rent together with interest on the difference at the rate of two per cent above the prescribed rate

(7) If on any review date legislation restricts the landlord's right to recover the rent then on the lifting of the restriction the landlord may give one month's notice requiring an additional rent review on a quarter day specified in the notice and that quarter day shall become a review date

(8) Time is not of the essence

(9) The rent shall be endorsed on the lease and counterpart whenever it is reviewed

14 Subleases

Where the lease in question is a sublease, the draftsman will usually wish to make the terms of the sublease mirror the terms of the headlease. However, it is not always enough merely to repeat the words verbatim. Each review clause will have to be applied to a particular set of facts, and the interaction between the facts and the clause will produce the rent. This may be illustrated by two cases concerning the same casino. Both *Daejan Investments Ltd v Cornwall Coast Country Club* [1985] 1 EGLR 77 and *Cornwall Coast Country Club v Cardgrange Ltd* [1987] 1 EGLR 146 concerned Crockford's Casino, the rent of which fell to be reviewed on the same date both under the headlease and under the sublease. Both leases provided for the disregard of the effect on rent of improvements carried out by the tenant and both leases provided for the disregard of any additional value attributable to the existence of a gaming licence if it belonged to the tenant or an associate of the tenant. The headtenant had carried out improvements, but the subtenant held a gaming licence. The consequence was that under the headlease, what was reviewed was an unimproved building, but taking into account the existence of the gaming licence in the hands of the subtenant, while under the sublease what fell to be reviewed was the improved building but disregarding the value attributable to the gaming licence. Thus the same form of words applied to different factual situations produced very different results. This is perhaps an extreme example, but it shows that care must be taken, and that it is not enough merely to repeat the words in the headlease without thinking through the consequences of doing so.

15 Renewal Leases

On a renewal under the Landlord and Tenant Act 1954, the rent will be determined in accordance with s 34 of the Act. Under s 34(3) the court is expressly given power to determine that the terms of the new tenancy should include such provision for varying the rent as may be specified in the determination. The discretion given to the court is very wide. In the light of *O'May v City of London Real Property Co Ltd* [1982] 1 All

ER 660, it seems likely that where the current tenancy contains provisions for rent review the court would start with a preference for the form of clause contained in the current tenancy. In *Charles Follett Ltd v Cabtell Investment Co Ltd* [1986] 2 EGLR 76 the current tenancy contained an upwards only rent review clause in which time was of the essence of the timetable. That form of clause was carried into the new tenancy. It does not appear that the tenant argued for an upwards or downwards review as a matter of principle, and the judge's decision on this point was not appealed. Until recently in the only cases where the point appears to have been argued, the court has refused to order the inclusion of an upwards only review clause (*Stylo Shoes Ltd v Manchester Royal Exchange Ltd* (1967) 204 EG 803; *Janes (Gowns) Ltd v Harlow Development Corporation* (1979) 253 EG 799). However, in more recent county court cases, judges have been divided on the point (*Boots the Chemist v Pinkland* [1992] 28 EG 118; *Amarjee v Barrowfen Properties* [1993] 2 EGLR 133; *Fourboys v Newport Borough Council* [1994] 1 EGLR 138 (upwards/downwards) and *Blythewood Plant Hire v Spiers* [1992] 48 EG 117 (upwards only)). It is suggested that it would be wrong in principle for the court to order the inclusion of an upwards only review clause, since it would only be of any practical effect if it resulted in the tenant having to pay more than the market rent. Since the court is required by s 34(1) to determine the market rent and no more, an upwards only review clause would be contrary to the spirit if not to the letter of the law. Accordingly, the tenant should insist on an upwards or downwards review.

The tenant's adviser should pay particular attention to the disregard of improvements, so as to ensure that any improvements carried out under the current tenancy will be disregarded on review under the new tenancy.

6

Insurance and Service Charges

1 INSURANCE

It is usual to include in a lease a provision requiring one or other party to insure the demised property. This requirement should always be considered in conjunction with a requirement as to reinstatement of the demised property and a proviso for abatement of rent. Within the framework of the insurance covenant itself the draftsman should specify:

(1) who is to insure;
(2) the risks against which the property is to be insured;
(3) the amount of the cover;
(4) the application of insurance moneys.

(a) Who is to insure?

In many cases the draftsman will have no control over who is to insure, but if he has then the following matters should be considered.

(i) Existing obligations

One of the parties may already be under an obligation to insure the property. Usually it will be the landlord. For example, the landlord may himself be a leaseholder and under an obligation to his own landlord to insure, or he may be obliged to insure under the terms of his mortgage. The tenant is unlikely to be under an obligation to insure unless he has paid a premium for the lease, in which case he too may be so obliged by the terms of his own mortgage. If both parties are under similar obligations their respective liabilities under the lease can only be resolved by negotiation, but it is suggested that it is better for the landlord to insure in such a case.

(ii) The nature of the property

If the demised property is part only of a building that belongs to the landlord, or if it is part of a trading estate or town centre development that belongs to the landlord, it is usually better for the landlord to insure. The advantages are that only one insurance policy need be maintained for the whole property (and, therefore, any common parts will be covered) and if the landlord is his own agent there may be a discount that can be passed on to the tenants. If the landlord wishes to retain for his own benefit any discount or commission this should be expressly provided in the lease. In the absence of such provision the tenant may be entitled to require the landlord to account to him for moneys had and received. Further, the landlord will probably be in a better position to assess the amount of cover required and the tenants will not be subject to the risk that part of a building will be uninsured. The disadvantage to the tenant is that he will be unable to control either the company with which the property is insured or the amount of the cover. This may lead to difficulties with his mortgagee, particularly if the business carried on by him is such that insurance against special or unusual risks is required. In such a case the tenant should stipulate for a measure of control over the risks against which the landlord insures.

If the demised property is a self-contained building it will often be more convenient for the tenant to insure. If this is the case the landlord should retain some control over the insurance; the policy should be in joint names so that a payment by the insurers does not pass wholly into the hands of the tenant, and the landlord should also be entitled to prescribe the risks against which the property is insured and the amount of the cover. The disadvantage to the tenant of insuring is that the risk of underinsurance will fall on him, in the sense that failure adequately to insure will be a breach of the covenant to insure.

(iii) Other provisions of the lease

If there is to be a service charge in the lease it may be convenient for the landlord to insure and to recover from the tenant the appropriate premium by way of service charge. Conversely, if the tenant's use of the property is a high insurance risk it may be better for him to insure, thereby preventing problems of apportioning a premium for a policy that covers property in addition to the demised property.

Whichever party is to insure the other party should have the right to require production of the policy (and the last receipt for the premium) and also the right to require insurance against unusual risks (on payment of any increased premium thereby occasioned).

Some landlords resist this, especially where a block policy is concerned, since they regard the details of other properties as being confidential. But the tenant should persist, for he is entitled to be satisfied by proper evidence that insurance cover is in force, especially where he is paying for it. If the landlord will not produce the policy, it may be possible to authorise the tenant to correspond directly with the insurers in order to be satisfied that the policy is in force.

Where the landlord insures and the amount of the insurance premium is increased by reason of any improvement carried out by the tenant, the tenant must pay the landlord the amount of the increase, which is recoverable from him as rent (Landlord and Tenant Act 1927, s 16).

(b) Risks

It is clearly impracticable to specify every risk against which the property is to be insured, particularly in a long lease. However, the draftsman should avoid such expressions 'comprehensive risks' or 'insurable risks' since they have no clear meaning.

If the tenant is required by the lease to insure in a named insurance office, but the lease is silent as to the risks, his obligation is to effect such a policy as is the usual policy from time to time of the named company (*Upjohn v Hitchens* [1918] 2 KB 48). In most cases this will be satisfactory, but where there is a possibility that the use of the property will require cover against additional risks a power to specify such risks should be reserved. Thus, if the tenant is to insure he should be required to insure against 'loss or damage by fire and such other risks as the landlord may from time to time reasonably prescribe'. If the landlord is to insure he should be required to insure against 'loss or damage by fire and such other risks as he thinks fit and (upon payment by the tenant of any increased premium occasioned thereby) against such risks as the tenant may from time to time reasonably request'.

Some draftsmen prefer to specify a long list of risks against which the insuring party must insure. If this is done, provision must be made for the possibility that cover against some listed risks is no longer available or is only available on unreasonable terms (eg insurance of commercial buildings against terrorist activities, which might otherwise be required to be obtained under an obligation to insure against explosion and/or malicious damage). Thus the obligation to insure against listed

risks should be qualified by a proviso that:
(1) the obligation is subject to such limitations, exclusions and excesses as may be imposed by insurers; and
(2) the obligation is subject to the availability of insurance in the market on reasonable terms.

The tenant's adviser should note that if the tenant is required to insure in a named insurance office 'or in some other responsible insurance office to be approved by the landlord' the landlord has an absolute right to withhold approval of any insurance company other than that named in the lease (*Tredegar v Harwood* [1929] AC 72). Accordingly, any such draft should be amended by inserting a proviso that the landlord's approval is not to be unreasonably withheld. It is, however, unusual to find an obligation to insure in a named office.

(c) Amount of cover

Either the landlord or the tenant can be severely prejudiced if the property is underinsured. For that reason the obligation to insure should be drawn so as to specify how much cover is required. If the requirement is merely to insure 'adequately' the obligation is fulfilled if the amount of cover is such an amount as the insurance company recommends, even if that amount in fact turns out to be too little (*Mumford Hotels Ltd v Wheler* [1963] 2 All ER 250). Even a requirement that the property is to be insured to 'its full value' may not be sufficient because such an expression is capable of meaning the full market value of the property, which may be considerably less than its reinstatement cost. Accordingly, it is suggested that the obligation should be to insure the property 'for the full cost of reinstatement'. If the landlord is to insure, the choice of such an expression will permit him to insure for the full cost of reinstatement calculated on the basis that the destruction of the property may not occur until the end of the year for which the premium is current and that there may then be a substantial delay before the work of reinstatement begins. Thus, the landlord will be entitled to take inflation of building costs into account in fixing the amount of the cover (*Gleniffer Finance Corporation Ltd v Bamar Wood & Products Ltd* [1978] 2 Lloyd's Rep 49). In the absence of any provision to the contrary the landlord is under no obligation to choose the cheapest method of insuring, even where the tenant is obliged to reimburse the amount of the premium (*Bandar Property Holdings Ltd v JS Darwen (Successors) Ltd* [1968] 2 All ER 305). Where the lease required the tenant to reimburse the amount which the landlord should 'properly' pay for insuring the premises, it was held that the landlord was entitled to recover the amount he actually paid, provided that it was no more than the 'going rate' for insurance charged by the particular insurer with whom he chose to do business (*Havenridge Ltd v Boston Dyers Ltd* [1993] 2 EGLR 73). If the tenant wishes to have some control over the premium, and in particular if the tenant wishes the landlord to have an obligation to shop around, this must be expressly provided for in the lease.

In addition to basic building costs, the obligation to insure should be expressly extended to cover architects' and surveyors' fees and other professional fees. It is sometimes forgotten that the rebuilding of the property may require planning permission which will necessitate expense in legal fees. Similarly, the cover should be extended to include the cost of any work required by local or public authorities in order to secure compliance with up-to-date legislation.

It is now common for the insurance cover to include the loss of rent for a specified period (usually two or three years). The landlord should satisfy himself that the prescribed period is likely to be adequate, having regard to possible planning delays in addition to the basic contract period. The tenant for his part should not accept an obligation to pay for insurance against loss of rent unless the lease includes a proviso for the abatement of rent after damage or destruction of the demised property. No such proviso will be implied even if the tenant pays the cost of the insurance (*Cleveland Shoe Co Ltd v Murray's Book Sales (King's Cross) Ltd* (1973) 229 EG 1465). If there is no rent abatement clause, the landlord will suffer no loss of rent, and consequently insurers will not pay for loss of rent anyway.

(d) Application of insurance moneys

The application of insurance moneys should be expressly dealt with in the lease, and the draftsman should provide for the possibility that reinstatement turns out to be impossible. If the tenant pays the cost of insurance, even if the policy is in the landlord's name, it appears that he can require the landlord to lay out the insurance moneys, as far as they will go, in the reinstatement of the property (*Mumford Hotels Ltd v Wheler* [1963] 3 All ER 250); but there appears to be no such right in favour of the landlord if the tenant insures in his own name. Accordingly, if the tenant is to insure he should be expressly required to reinstate the demised property. It should be pointed out that both parties have a statutory right to require insurance moneys to be laid out in reinstatement, but the right is only effective if a request is made to the insurance company concerned before the insurance moneys are paid out and it only applies in cases of fire damage (Fires Prevention (Metropolis) Act 1774, s 83, which applies to the whole of England).

It may happen that reinstatement is impossible or that neither party wishes the building to be reinstated. The draftsman should provide for the division of the insurance moneys in such an event. In the absence of express provision the court must draw inferences from the terms of the lease and the relevant provisions of any insurance policy. In a case where the landlord covenanted to insure and reinstate, and the tenant reimbursed the insurance premium, the court was able to draw the inference that the basic right of the parties was to have the building rebuilt for their mutual benefit, and that where they treated the insurance moneys as standing in place of the building, the moneys were to be divided between them in shares proportionate to their respective interests in the building immediately before the fire (*Beacon Carpets Ltd v Kirby* [1984] 2 All ER 726). But where the tenant covenanted to keep the property in repair, to insure in the joint names of landlord and tenant, and to apply insurance moneys in reinstatement, the court drew the inference that the purpose of the insurance was to secure performance of the tenant's obligations so that the insurance moneys were held to belong to the tenant alone (*Re King* [1963] 1 All ER 781).

It is suggested that in all but the most unusual cases the fair solution is for the insurance moneys to be divided between the parties in proportion to the values of their respective interests immediately before the loss, after giving credit to the landlord for insurance in respect of loss of rent. Upon such division the lease should be brought to an end.

(e) Reinstatement

Some aspects of the covenant to reinstate have already been touched upon. Some further aspects require comment.

First, the covenant to reinstate is often limited to an obligation to lay out insurance moneys received in reinstatement. Several consequences flow from this form of obligation. There can be no breach of this obligation until insurance moneys have in fact been received (*Re King* [1962] 2 All ER 66 at 77). It is likely that the court would imply an obligation to pursue the insurance claim diligently (*Vural v Security Archives* (1989) 60 P&CR 258), but if the insurers do not pay the covenant does not bite.

Also, if the insurance moneys are insufficient to enable reinstatement to take place, neither party is liable to make up the shortfall. The insufficiency may arise because the property was underinsured (with the consequential application of average in the case of a partial loss) or because the insurers exercise the option commonly found in insurance policies to pay on the basis of market value rather than the cost of reinstatement. Additionally, the covenant should clearly provide for insurance moneys payable for loss of rent to be excluded from the obligation. It may be doubted, however, whether the parties can effectively ensure that the landlord retains the benefit of insurance moneys payable for loss of rent in view of the wide provisions of s 83 of the Fires Prevention (Metropolis) Act 1774 which gives the tenant the right to require 'the insurance money' to be laid out in reinstatement. The solution to this problem may be solved by placing the insurance at Lloyd's, rather than in an insurance office, since the 1774 Act does not apply to Lloyd's (*Portavon Cinema Co Ltd v Price* [1939] 4 All ER 601). A covenant limited to an obligation to lay out moneys received has obvious attractions to the covenantor. It ensures that he can never be out of pocket. Usually this limitation is found in landlords' covenants and rarely in tenants'. It is suggested that the tenant should not accept this form of covenant. If the landlord is entitled to fix the amount of the cover he should in principle bear the risk of underinsurance; it should not be shifted onto the tenant. Equally, if the tenant is to insure, the risk of underinsurance should be his.

Secondly, where a landlord covenants to reinstate, his obligation is often qualified by an expression such as 'unless the insurance is avoided by reason of any act or omission of the tenant'. In a case where the landlord's obligation is merely to lay out moneys received, this qualification is unnecessary. However, it should be inserted in any other case for the protection of the landlord. If the insurance is thus avoided, the tenant only has himself to blame; but equally, he should insist on being supplied with a copy of the policy and copies of all recommendations made by the landlord's insurers so that he knows what acts and omissions will avoid the policy. The tenant should, however, resist the extension of such a qualification to acts and omissions of his subtenants and licensees, as there is no reason why he should be the landlord's insurers for their behaviour. Equally, in the case of a letting of part only of a building the tenant should not accept a proviso which releases the landlord from liability to reinstate if the policy is avoided by the acts or omissions of other tenants in the building.

Thirdly, where the landlord is to reinstate, the draftsman should ensure that the tenant's repairing covenants exclude liability for repairing damage by insured risks (except where the insurance is avoided by any act or omission of the tenant). If the tenant is not himself liable to repair, but is liable to pay the cost of repair by way of service charge, his liability should exclude liability to pay for the repair of damages caused by insured risks. If this is not done a landlord who had underinsured would effectively be able to charge the tenant with any shortfall. In addition, where the tenant is under an absolute obligation to repair, insurers of the landlord's interests under an indemnity policy might be entitled to refuse to pay on the ground that the landlord had suffered no loss.

Fourthly, consideration should be given to the question whether 'reinstatement' is what the parties want. There is no satisfactory judicial definition of what is meant by reinstatement. However, it has been held at first instance that a covenant to reinstate obliges the covenantor to restore the building to the precise form in which it existed immediately before the loss, unless such restoration would be pointless (*Camden Theatre Ltd v London Scottish Properties Ltd* (1984) unreported, Nicholls J, where a landlord was liable for breach of covenant for painting in gold paint mouldings in a discotheque which had originally been covered in gold leaf). The test has also been said to be whether the restored building element produces as efficient a result as the element which was damaged or destroyed (*Vural v Security Archives* (1989) 60 P&CR 258 where a landlord was in breach by replacing a wooden factory floor with high quality linoleum). In a case where the property is not brand new, a more appropriate obligation might be for the covenantor to undertake to provide a reasonable modern equivalent. At the least, the draftsman should consider the inclusion of an express provision entitling the covenantor to build something which is not identical to that which existed before the loss. In addition, where the property is part only of a building or an estate, the draftsman should enable the landlord to carry out work in the order of his choice, and not according to the speed or tenacity with which the tenants pursue their claims.

Fifthly, consideration should be given to specifying a timetable. If none is specified, the court will imply a term to the effect that reinstatement must take place within a reasonable time (*Farimani v Gates* (1984) 271 EG 887). From the tenant's point of view it would be desirable to have an option to terminate the lease if reinstatement has not been completed within a specified time.

Finally, where the demised property forms part of a larger building or complex, the tenant's adviser should ensure that the landlord's rein-

INSURANCE AND SERVICE CHARGES

statement obligation extends to common parts (especially means of access to the demised property).

(f) Subrogation

Where an insurer pays out on a policy of insurance he is generally entitled to be subrogated to any claim that the insured has in respect of the subject matter of the claim. However, in most cases, the right of subrogation will not extend to a claim in negligence against the tenant, since the intention of the parties to the lease will be taken to require the landlord's loss to be recouped from his insurers alone (*Mark Rowlands Ltd v Berni Inns Ltd* [1986] Ch 211). Nevertheless, it may be worthwhile for the tenant's adviser to attempt to remove the right of subrogation. It is thought that this may be done in one of two ways. First, the landlord's right to sue the tenant may be removed by the insertion of a suitable exemption clause. If such a clause is inserted the insurers will have nothing to which they can be subrogated. Secondly, the landlord may covenant to procure that the tenant's interest be noted on the policy. It is thought that the noting of the tenant's interest on the policy effectively deprives the insurers of their right of subrogation. This method has been chosen in Example 6.2.

Example 6:1 Tenant's covenant to insure and reinstate

(1) To keep the demised property insured with reputable insurers approved by the landlord (such approval not to be unreasonably withheld) in the joint names of the landlord and the tenant against loss or damage by fire and such other risks as the landlord may from time to time reasonably prescribe for an amount equal to its full reinstatement cost (including all professional fees and the cost of any work which might be required by or by virtue of any Act of Parliament) and two years' loss of rent

(2) To produce to the landlord on demand the policy of insurance maintained by the tenant and the receipt for the premium payable for it

(3) If the demised property or part of it is destroyed or damaged by fire or by any other peril against the risk of which the tenant is liable to insure forthwith to reinstate the demised property or such part of it as may have been so damaged or destroyed

(4) If it is impossible or impracticable to reinstate in accordance with subclause (3) above any moneys received under the policy of insurance (except payments in respect of loss of rent which shall belong to the landlord absolutely) shall be divided between the landlord and the tenant according to the value at the date of the damage or

destruction of their respective interests in the demised property (to be determined in default of agreement by a single arbitrator to be appointed by the President for the time being of the Royal Institution of Chartered Surveyors)

Example 6:2 Landlord's covenant to insure and reinstate

(1) To keep the demised property insured against loss or damage by fire and such other risks as he thinks fit and (upon payment by the tenant of any increased premium occasioned thereby) against such risks as the tenant may from time to time reasonably request for an amount equal to its full reinstatement cost (including all professional fees and the cost of any work which might be required by or by virtue of any Act of Parliament) and two years' loss of rent

(2) To produce to the tenant on demand the policy of insurance maintained by the landlord and the receipt for the last premium payable for it and to try his best to cause the tenant's interest to be noted on any such policy

(3) If the demised property is destroyed or damaged by fire or any other peril against the risk of which the landlord has insured and the policy of insurance not being vitiated by some act or omission by the tenant or any subtenant or licensee of his forthwith to reinstate the demised property or such part of it as shall have been so destroyed or damaged

(4) If it is impossible or impracticable to reinstate in accordance with subclause (3) above any moneys received under the policy of insurance (except payments in respect of loss of rent which shall belong to the landlord absolutely) shall be divided between the landlord and the tenant according to the value at the date of the damage or destruction of their respective interests in the demised property (to be determined in default of agreement by a single arbitrator to be appointed by the President for the time being of the Royal Institution of Chartered Surveyors)

Example 6:3 Proviso for protection of landlord

PROVIDED THAT:

(1) The landlord is under no obligation to reinstate the demised property in the form in which it existed immediately before the damage or destruction in question

(2) If the damage or destruction affects other property in which the landlord has an interest the landlord is under no obligation to reinstate the demised property until that other property has been reinstated

Example 6:4 Alternative covenant by landlord to insure and either reinstate or provide modern equivalent

(1) Subject to any exclusions excesses and conditions imposed or

INSURANCE AND SERVICE CHARGES

required by insurers to keep the demised property insured against loss or damage by the insured risks:
  (a) for such sum as the landlord considers appropriate to cover the cost of reinstatement (assuming total loss) together with site clearance debris removal professional fees value added tax and two years' loss of rent
  (b) in a reputable insurance office or at Lloyd's

(2) To use reasonable efforts to negotiate a policy under which insurers have no right of subrogation against the tenant

(3) If:
  (a) the property is destroyed or damaged by any of the insured risks and
  (b) the landlord (taking all reasonable steps) obtains all necessary licences and consents

the landlord shall lay out the insurance money received by him (apart from moneys received for loss of rent) in either:
  (a) reinstating the demised property or the damaged part of it or
  (b) at his option providing a reasonable modern equivalent

(4) 'Insured risks' means those of the following risks for which cover can be obtained on reasonable terms from reputable insurers: fire storm tempest flood earthquake aircraft and articles dropped from them riot or civil commotion malicious damage impact damage explosion bursting or overflowing of pipes tanks and other apparatus subsidence or heave and such other risks as may be specified by the landlord or by the tenant

Example 6:5 Landlord to insure in unspecified amount: reinstatement or modern equivalent: demised property forming part of larger building

(1) If (and only if) the tenant pays the insurance rent to keep the building insured with reputable insurers against the insured risks in an amount decided by the landlord together with three years' loss of rent or such other period as the landlord reasonably requires

(2) To produce to the tenant on demand the policy of insurance maintained by the landlord (or in the case of a block policy extracts from it) and the receipt for the last premium payable for it

(3) If the demised property or any means of access to it is damaged or destroyed by an insured risk and the policy of insurance remains in force to lay out the insurance moneys (except loss of rent insurance) in either:
  (a) reinstating the demised property or the means of access or the damaged part of them or
  (b) at the landlord's option providing a reasonable modern equivalent

(4) If it is impracticable to reinstate or provide a modern equivalent in accordance with subclause (3) above within three years after the event giving rise to the loss then:
  (a) the landlord shall be entitled to retain the insurance moneys

for his own use and benefit and
(b) either party shall be entitled to terminate this lease by six months' written notice to that effect
(5) The insured risks are [   ]

(g) Proviso for abatement of rent

In the absence of provision to the contrary the tenant will be liable to pay the rent even if the demised property is wholly destroyed by fire; and a proviso for abatement will not be implied even if the tenant pays the cost of insuring (*Cleveland Shoe Co Ltd v Murray's Book Sales (King's Cross) Ltd* (1973) 229 EG 1465). Accordingly, the tenant should ensure that such a proviso is included in the lease, especially where the insurer is to cover the loss of rent. If loss of rent is covered by the insurance policy, but the rent does not abate, then unless the tenant is the insured or one of the insured, the insurers will not pay, because the landlord will have suffered no loss. If, however, the tenant takes out consequential loss insurance in respect of his business, then if the rent does abate, the extent of his claim on his own policy will, to that extent, be diminished.

Several points need to be considered in drafting a proviso for the abatement of rent. First, the draftsman should ensure that the rent does not abate if the insurance is vitiated by any act or omission of the tenant, otherwise the landlord will be both deprived of his income and unable to recover under his policy. Secondly, the draftsman should consider whether the rent is to abate even in the case of minor damage. For example, it might be provided that the rent shall not abate if the demised property is repaired or reinstated within, say, three months of the occurrence of the damage. Loss of access to the demised property should also be covered. Thirdly, a proviso for the abatement of rent will reduce the rent payable for the demised property while it is in operation. This may be of significance if the proviso comes into operation shortly before a rent review where the reviewed rent is to be at least the rent payable for the demised property immediately before the review date. If market rents have fallen since the date of the lease (or the last review) an upwards only review will lose its force. Similarly, if there were to be a recurrence of statutory control of rents in the same form as that prevailing between 1972 and 1975 the rent might be incapable of an increase above the abated rent. It is possible to provide contractually that the abatement of rent shall not affect the operation of a rent review. However, it is difficult to see how the draftsman can provide against the imposition of statutory control on the rent payable on a given date. It may be that by providing that the rent shall be 'suspended' rather than 'shall cease to be payable' the draftsman will be able to protect the landlord. This suggestion is entirely speculative since if statutory control is reimposed its effect will of course depend on the construction of the particular statute.

Fourthly, where the demised property is part of a larger building or complex, the loss may not have caused damage to the demised property itself, but only to common parts (eg means of access). If damage to common parts has made the demised property unusable, even though physically undamaged, the rent should abate.

Where the building has suffered a total loss, the tenant has little option but to find alternative accommodation. He will usually have to take the alternative accommodation on a lease for a normal commercial term. Once he has done so he is quite likely not to want to return to the destroyed property. In those circumstances a rent abatement clause is insufficient protection for him, because once the period of abatement comes to an end the tenant will resume liability to pay rent. The tenant's adviser should press for a tenant's break-clause in the event of a total loss. Equally, the landlord may wish to redevelop the building in the event of a total loss in which case he will wish to terminate existing leases. Even where the loss is not total, he may wish to realign services or the layout of the building, and the existence of leases may hamper that task. Accordingly, it will often be in both parties' interest that the lease should be capable of termination by either of them if there is a major loss.

Example 6:6 Proviso for abatement of rent

(1) If the demised property or any principal means of access to it is so damaged or destroyed by a peril against the risk of which the demised property is insured as to become unfit for occupation in whole or in part and the sum insured is not wholly or partly irrecoverable by reason of any act or omission of the Tenant or any subtenant or licensee of his then the rent or a fair proportion of it shall be suspended until the demised property is again fit for occupation

(2) Subclause (1) above shall not apply if the damage is repaired or reinstated within three months after the occurrence of the damage or destruction in question

(3) Any dispute as to the proportion shall be determined by a single arbitrator to be appointed by the President for the time being of the Royal Institution of Chartered Surveyors

(4) Any reviewed rent for the demised property shall be assessed

as if subclause (1) above was not in operation at the review date and as if the damage or destruction had not occurred.

Example 6:7 Tenant's break-clause on total loss

If the demised property or any principal means of access to it is so damaged or destroyed by any peril against the risk of which the demised property is insured as to become unfit for occupation and to remain unfit for occupation for more than six months the tenant shall be entitled to determine this tenancy by not less than three months' written notice given to the landlord at any time after the expiry of that period of six months

(h) Insurance and use

The tenant's use of the property may have repercussions on the amount of the premium payable for insurance. For that reason it is good practice to include in the lease a covenant on the tenant's part not to do anything that would avoid the insurance policy or increase the premium payable. In practice the problem faced by landlords is that tenants fail to comply with recommendations made by the landlords' insurers. Often the landlord does not know whether non-compliance with those recommendations will cause the insurers to come off risk. Accordingly, it is suggested that the draftsman should extend the usual form of covenant to include a positive obligation on the tenant's part to comply with all recommendations of the landlord's insurers. Such a covenant not only has the advantage that the tenant may be restrained by injunction from using the property in such a way as to cause an increased premium to be payable (*Chapman v Mason* (1910) 103 LT 390) but also, it is submitted, the tenant may be ordered to execute works recommended by the insurers.

The tenant's advisers should note that if the tenant covenants not to cause any increase in the premium the landlord will not be under a similar correlative obligation. Thus, he will be entitled to let adjoining property for a use that causes an increased premium to be payable for the demised property (*O'Cedar v Slough Trading Co Ltd* [1927] 2 KB 123).

Example 6:8 Tenant's covenant not to cause increase in premium

Not to do permit or suffer to be done in the demised property anything which may avoid any policy of insurance maintained by the landlord in respect of the demised property or increase the rate of any premium payable for it and to comply at his own expense with all recommendations of the insurers under it

(i) Insurance other than fire insurance

(i) Plate glass

Plate glass is often insured under a separate policy from the building. In most shop lettings it is more convenient for the tenant to insure against damage to plate glass. However, the draftsman should ensure that any proviso for abatement of rent does not come into operation merely because the shop window is cracked. It will usually be sufficient if the proviso does not come into operation if the demised property is reinstated within, say, three months, because in practice any shop tenant will want to repair his shop window as soon as possible.

(ii) Lifts and boilers

The insurance of lifts, boilers and other expensive plant is usually included in a regular maintenance contract. Accordingly, the person responsible for such maintenance should be made liable for their insurance. If, as is often the case, the landlord maintains and insures and recovers the cost by way of service charge, the tenant should ensure that he is not required to contribute to a sinking fund for the replacement of such plant in addition to being liable to pay for such a contract.

(iii) Public liability

Landlords often require tenants to pay the cost of insuring the landlord against public liability by reason of any defect in the demised property or, more usually, the common parts. It is questionable whether tenants ought to accept such an obligation. If the landlord is responsible for the repair of common parts he should bear the risk of defects in them causing injury to people. Conversely, it might well be in the interest of landlords to require tenants to effect public liability insurance since a tenant faced with a substantial claim for personal injuries may find it impossible to continue to pay rent.

2 SERVICE CHARGES

The purpose of a service charge is to ensure that the landlord recovers the rent payable under the lease free from the risk that he will have to spend part of it in maintaining or repairing the demised property or otherwise incurring running costs. In other words, the risk is transferred from the landlord to the tenant. The existence of a service charge can have significant effects on the capital value of the landlord's reversion. Indeed, many of the financial institutions will not buy reversions on leases that do not contain service charges. Since the norm in the market is for 'institutionally acceptable' leases, the service charge is a vital component of the lease. Accordingly, in many cases the form of the service charge is not negotiable. However, from the tenant's point of view, the service charge represents a very large part of his cost of occupation. And an onerous service charge will almost always play a part in reducing rent on review. For those reasons the draftsman should try to ensure that a service charge not only protects the landlord's interest but is also fair to the tenant.

In practice five aspects of service charges give rise to problems:
(1) the method of payment of service charges;
(2) the items that may be recovered as part of the charge;
(3) the apportionment of charges as between tenants;
(4) the provision of reserve or sinking funds;
(5) the certification of charges.

(a) Method of payment

There are two schools of thought as to whether the service charge should be reserved as rent. In practice, it usually is. Those who believe it should, do so for the following reasons:
(1) the landlord will be able to forfeit the lease for non-payment of the charge without the need to serve a s 146 notice beforehand;
(2) the landlord will be entitled to distrain for any unpaid charge, at least once it has been quantified (*Re Knight, ex parte Voisey* (1882) 21 ChD 442) and for any interim charge if that is also reserved as rent (*Walsh v Lonsdale* (1882) 21 ChD 9).

Those who prefer a covenant to pay retort that:
(1) if a s 146 notice must be served, the period for remedying the breach of covenant may be short;
(2) the landlord cannot distrain while the service charge is in dispute (*Concorde Graphics Ltd v Andromeda Investments SA* (1982) 265 EG 386);
(3) there is a theoretical liability to pay a modest amount of additional stamp duty;
(4) if the lease is forfeit for non-payment of service charge the

tenant does not have the same automatic right to relief against forfeiture as he does for non-payment of rent although in practice he is highly likely to obtain relief if he can pay the arrears.

Whether the service charge is reserved as rent or not, it is regarded by HM Customs & Excise as part of the consideration for the grant of the lease. Thus, the service charge will be treated in the same way as the rent. So if the rent carries VAT, so will the service charge; if the rent does not carry VAT nor will the service charge. But this does not apply to services to the demised property itself. Whether such services carry VAT depends on the nature of the service.

On balance it is suggested that from the landlord's point of view the service charge is better reserved as rent, mainly because of the remedy of distress for undisputed or minimum charges.

The draftsman should make it clear that the service charge is not to abate if the demised property is destroyed or damaged by an insured risk except to the extent that services are not provided to the tenant. Moreover the service charge should not be caught by the provisions for rent review inevitably found in a lease containing a service charge.

It is rare to find a service charge in a modern lease where sums are payable on demand. Although such a scheme is found in older leases, it is unsatisfactory, since it is impossible to budget for. It can only be appropriate where expenditure is likely to be extremely infrequent and to amount to no more than the cost of repairing party walls etc.

Some provision should therefore be made for payments in advance. The landlord has to fund expenses out of his own pocket before he can recover them from the tenant (often up to a year later) and in the absence of a specific provision in the lease, he will not be entitled to charge the tenants with interest on moneys expended, even if the landlord has actually had to pay it (*Frobisher (Second Investments) Ltd v Kiloran Trust Co Ltd* [1980] 1 All ER 488). It will be unacceptable for the landlord to have to wait until the end of an accounting period to recover the capital cost. Accordingly, it is suggested that the tenant should accept a provision for payment in advance.

What provision should be made for such payments? In essence there are two methods. The lease may provide for a payment on account which is fixed in the first year of the term, and thereafter is a specified percentage of the previous year's actual charge. The percentage may be less than or more than 100. This method can only work if the tenant is required to contribute towards a reserve fund to meet non-annual expenditure (for example external redecorations). In other cases this method will not work fairly to either party. In a year in which substantial non-annual expenditure is incurred the landlord will not recover enough to enable him to meet that expenditure as it falls due, while in the following year the tenant's advance payment will be far too high.

Alternatively, the lease may provide for the tenant to pay a sum fixed each year either by the landlord or his surveyor. The tenant should not accept an obligation to pay whatever the landlord asks for, since he may find himself being used as a source of free loans. He should stipulate for the advance payment to be based on a budget for the year in question, prepared by someone exercising an independent judgment. In addition a copy of the budget should be supplied to the tenant. If there is a tenants' association (as in a shopping centre) it may be appropriate to provide for major items of expenditure to be discussed with the association before inclusion in the budget. Advance payments should be payable at the same time as the rent. There will be an implied obligation on the part of the landlord to provide estimates (*Gordon v Selico Co Ltd* [1986] 1 EGLR 71). Where there is an express obligation on the landlord to obtain estimates in advance of carrying out work, the court will probably interpret this as a condition precedent to the right to a service charge for that work. This has the result that if the landlord fails to obtain estimates in advance, he cannot recover any service charge for that item even if the cost was otherwise reasonable (*CIN Properties v Barclays Bank* [1986] 1 EGLR 59; *Northways Flats Management Co (Camden) v Wimpey Pension Trustees* [1992] 2 EGLR 42). It is therefore prudent for the draftsman to provide that failure to comply with the machinery is not to make the service charge irrecoverable.

(b) Landlord's obligation

The aim of the tenant's adviser should be to ensure that the landlord enters into an obligation to provide the services for which the service charge is to be levied. Landlords sometimes attempt to make obligations to provide services conditional upon payment by the tenant of the service charge. The court will be reluctant to construe a lease as having the effect that the landlord is entitled to withhold essential services merely because the tenant is in arrear with payments (*Yorkbrook Investments Ltd v Batten* [1985] 2 EGLR 100), but careful drafting could produce a clause which stated clearly that such was the parties' intention. The tenant should not accept such a provision.

The desire of the tenant is to ensure that the landlord has an absolute obligation to provide the services. If the landlord is willing to enter into such an obligation then the services must be provided even if this would involve the landlord in substantial capital expenditure (*Yorkbrook Investments Ltd v Batten* above) and the landlord will be in breach of such an obligation even if he cannot afford the necessary expenditure (*Francis v Cowcliffe Ltd* (1976) 33 P&CR 368). The draftsman should therefore consider whether the landlord's obligation should be limited to an obligation to use 'best' or 'reasonable' endeavours to provide the services. An obligation to use 'best' endeavours may be acceptable to the tenant, although an obligation merely to use reasonable endeavours may not be. A halfway house would be an obligation to use 'all reasonable' endeavours (*UBH (Mechanical Services) Ltd v Standard Life Assurance Co* (1986) *The Times*, 13 November). A joint committee of the Law Society and the RICS recommended that the landlord should covenant 'to use all reasonable efforts' to provide the services (see *Law Society's Gazette*, 9 April 1986, p 1057).

If the obligation to provide services is expressed in absolute terms, it is usual to qualify it by exempting the landlord from liability for temporary interruptions in services for reasons beyond his control.

The mere fact that the tenant pays a service charge does not necessarily mean that the landlord is under an obligation to provide the service (*Russell v Laimond Properties* (1984) 269 EG 947).

In some cases, however, an obligation to provide services has been implied from the tenant's obligation to pay. This is easier where the tenant pays a rent quantified in advance and which is payable in any event (*Barnes v City of London Real Property Co* [1918] 2 Ch 18), although such an obligation has been implied in other cases also (*Edmonton Corporation v WM Knowles & Son* (1961) 60 LGR 124). But such an obligation will not usually be implied (*Duke of Westminster v Guild* [1984] 3 All ER 144; *Tennant Radiant Heat Ltd v Warrington Development Corporation* [1988] 1 EGLR 41).

The landlord will often seek to restrict his obligation to the provision of essential services (eg repair of the structure, exterior and common parts; provision of air-conditioning etc), while leaving himself a discretion to provide other services (eg floral arrangements or security) if he so chooses. In principle this is not objectionable provided that the list of services which the landlord is obliged to provide is extensive enough to meet the tenant's foreseeable needs. If the landlord has a discretion whether to provide services or not, the tenant's adviser should ensure that the discretion must be exercised reasonably. In addition it is desirable from the tenant's point of view to provide that the landlord must consult the tenants before instituting or discontinuing a service.

(c) Trust funds

In the hands of the landlords or their agents interim payments are part of their general funds to be applied in accordance with the contractual arrangements between them. They are not impressed by any trust, nor are they held by the landlords or their agents as stakeholders (*Frobisher (Second Investments) Ltd v Kiloran Trust Co Ltd* [1980] 1 All ER 488). If, however, the moneys are set aside in a separate bank account then a trust may be created (*Re Chelsea Cloisters Ltd (In Liquidation)* (1980) 41 P&CR 98). In relation to dwellings, however, s 42 of the Landlord and Tenant Act 1987 requires service charge contributions to be held in trust. Normally this need not concern the draftsman of a commercial lease, but in the case of a lease of a part of a mixed development or even of a lock up shop under separately let flats, the draftsman will need to consider whether the service charge should be held on trust so as to provide uniformity of management.

Some leases provide for the service charge to be paid to a maintenance company which holds the contribution upon trust to apply the funds towards certain specified purposes (eg repair, maintenance and insurance). Under this arrangement the company is only obliged to apply the money actually received, so that if a tenant defaults, the maintenance company is not liable to make good the deficit or to carry out work for which it does not have the necessary funds (*Alton House Holdings Ltd v Calflane (Management) Ltd* [1987] 2 EGLR 52). Moreover if the tenant has a complaint about the way that the money is spent, his remedy is not an action for damages for breach of covenant, but an action for the administration of the trust (*Gordon v Selico Co Ltd* [1986] 1 EGLR 71). Procedurally this is more cumbersome than an action for damages and/or specific performance of the covenant, and in any event the tenant is less well protected by a scheme which only requires expenditure of moneys received rather than one which places an absolute obligation on the landlord (or a maintenance company) to repair and carry out other works. The tenant should not be deceived by the illusion that a trust affords him protection, when in fact it operates to deprive him of common law remedies. Trusts of reserve and sinking funds are dealt with in **(f)** below.

(d) Recoverable items

Where a particular item is recoverable by way of service charge depends on the construction of the lease in question. Where parties entrust the determination to an expert, they intend the expert to apply his expertise to the contract properly interpreted, and his interpretation may be reviewed by the court (*Mercury Communications v Director-General of Telecommunications* [1996] 1 WLR 48). Where the charge is payable by reference to costs 'incurred' by the landlord, no costs will be 'incurred' until the landlord has either disbursed the costs or become immediately liable to do so (*Capital & County Freehold Equity Trust Ltd v BL plc* [1987] 2 EGLR 49). The tenant should not accept anything more favourable to the landlord. Some leases reserve to the landlord a power to alter the services provided during the term, but it is questionable how far the terms of the bargain may be altered in this way. Nevertheless, it is suggested that the draftsman would be correct in including such a power in a long lease since it may well be impossible to predict what services will be required in the later years of the term.

The draftsman's aim should be to provide the landlord with a complete indemnity against the cost of complying with his covenants. But it does not follow that where a service charge echoes the landlord's obligations the service charge will necessarily cover those obligations (*Rapid Results College Ltd v Angell* [1986] 1 EGLR 53). Thus far, a service charge is likely to be acceptable to the majority of tenants. However, some service charges seek to go further. For example, it is not uncommon to find a provision entitling the landlord to recover from the tenant the cost of collecting the rent. Rent collection is a service of dubious value to the tenant and a well-advised tenant may not accept having to pay for it. Equally, some landlords seek to include in the service charge the cost of renewing, rebuilding or even improving the demised property. Such a provision should not be accepted by the tenant.

Some items will now be considered in more detail.

(i) Management fees

Save in exceptional circumstances, the landlord will not be entitled to recover the cost of management fees unless the lease expressly so provides (*Embassy Court Residents Association v Lipman* (1984) 271 EG 545). But there can be no objection in principle to a landlord seeking to recover from the tenant the cost of employing a managing agent to organise the various services provided for the tenant under the lease, provided that the cost is reasonable. It is common practice for agents to be paid a percentage of the service charge. Tenants reasonably object that this encourages overspending. The tenant's adviser should raise this question, but should not hope for any major change. Where the landlord is entitled to recover the cost of management, he may employ his own company as managing agent, unless this is merely a sham (*Skilleter v Charles* [1992] 1 EGLR 73). But if the lease simply provides that the landlord shall be entitled to recover the cost of employing agents he will not be entitled to an allowance for himself if he does not employ any. Nor will he be able to dress himself up as his own agent (*Finchbourne Ltd v Rodrigues* [1976] 3 All ER 581). Accordingly, the draftsman should expressly provide for the landlord to be entitled to a reasonable allowance in respect of the performance of any function that could reasonably be delegated to a managing agent. It is suggested that the allowance should not exceed ten per cent of the cost of the service in question.

Some leases provide that the landlord is to be entitled to recover a proportion of his general administrative overheads. It is suggested that the tenant should not accept such a provision but should instead accept that the landlord should have remuneration for services that he in fact performs or supervises.

(ii) Staff and staff accommodation

Where a lease reserves additional rent in respect of office cleaning and the like there will be implied a correlative obligation on the landlord to provide the service for which the tenant has covenanted to pay (*Barnes v City of London Real Property Co* [1918] 2 Ch 18). Such an obligation may be specifically enforceable (*Posner v Scott-Lewis* [1986] 3 All ER 513) and the tenant may be awarded damages if it is broken and the landlord may be restrained by injunction from selling or disposing of accommodation intended to be occupied by resident staff (*Hupfield v Bourne* (1974) 28 P&CR 77). Since staff may prove difficult to obtain, the draftsman should expressly declare that the landlord is not to be liable to the tenant for failure to provide staff. In the case of lettings of office suites the desirability of providing staff has been judicially noted:

> It is far better for the tenants that there should be some central authority who should appoint a housekeeper to look after the house generally than that each of them should be left to make provision of that kind for himself. It would not be possible for any one individual, having to make arrangements of that sort, to ensure that the occupants of the other rooms would be as careful as he might be himself in the selection of a housekeeper; and when once you had five or six different sets of cleaners coming in to perform the services of clean-

ing and dusting and so on, there would be very much inferior security to the tenants that there should not be all sorts of improper people getting in to the house and perhaps making arrangements for burglary and theft, or acquiring information which it was very desirable should not go outside the particular office. (*per* Sargant J in *Barnes v City of London Real Property Co*)

The same considerations might apply to lettings of consulting rooms to doctors or dentists where a receptionist is to be employed.

If it is contemplated that the landlord will provide staff, the draftsman should ensure that the landlord is entitled to recover more than merely the wages or salary of such staff. If his entitlement is restricted to 'wages and salaries' it is arguable that it would not extend to employer's national insurance contributions or Christmas bonuses to which the employee is not strictly entitled under his service contract. Accordingly, it is suggested that the landlord should be entitled to recover 'the full cost of employing staff', an expression that would cover the above items. Although it has been held by the Court of Appeal that notional rent foregone by the landlord in respect of accommodation provided for staff is part of the 'cost' of providing services (*Agavil Investments Ltd v Corner* (unreported, 3 October 1975); *Lloyds Bank v Bowker Orford* [1992] 31 EG 68) it is nevertheless suggested that the draftsman should provide expressly for the inclusion of notional rent in the service charge.

(iii) Heating

The cost of heating the demised property is an item commonly included in a service charge. The drafting of this item requires some care. Where the tenant pays a percentage of a global sum, the item should be the cost of heating the whole building (or development) rather than the cost of heating the demised property, otherwise the tenant will not pay the proper cost of heating his own accommodation (see *Pole Properties Ltd v Feinberg* (1981) 259 EG 417). The draftsman should avoid a provision that refers to specific dates between which heating is to be maintained. If the landlord is only entitled to recover the cost of heating the premises between, say, 1 October and 1 May in each year the tenant may refuse to pay for heating the premises during a cold September. Conversely, he may complain if they are not heated during April. But if the landlord has the discretion to fix the heating season, he cannot nullify the covenant to supply heat by making an arbitrary choice of dates (*Regis Property Co v Redman* [1956] 2 QB 612).

Equally, it is unwise to specify a temperature to which the property is to be heated. Moreover, the draftsman should ensure that the landlord is not liable to the tenants for a temporary breakdown in the heating system (cf *UBH (Mechanical Services) Ltd v Standard Life Assurance Co* (1986) *The Times*, 13 November).

(iv) Plant and machinery

The most important items to be considered under this head are lifts, boilers and air-conditioning equipment. The landlord will usually arrange for these to be maintained under comprehensive maintenance contracts. Such contracts often include payments on account of the eventual cost of replacing the plant or equipment in question. The draftsman should, therefore, ensure that the whole of the cost of such a contract is recoverable from the tenant. Accordingly, the service charge should not be limited to the 'repair and maintenance' of the equipment but should extend to include all payments made under a contract for the repair and maintenance of the equipment, including any provision made thereunder for the periodic renewal of such equipment. The tenant's adviser should scrutinise a service charge provision of this nature in order to eliminate any separate requirement to contribute to a reserve fund for the renewal of the same equipment.

All items of plant have a finite life, and all of them reach the point at which it is a question of judgment whether to continue to repair them or whether the time has come to replace them. The lease should make it clear whether the landlord has power to charge for the replacement of plant and machinery either at the end of their useful life or at a time when a prudent building owner would decide to replace them. The court will not, however, be astute to read into a service a charge a limitation which prevents the landlord from recovering capital, as opposed to revenue, costs (*Lloyds Bank v Bowker Orford* [1992] 31 EG 68). In addition, the draftsman should provide for the landlord not merely to be able to replace items of plant, but to do so with a reasonable modern equivalent.

(v) Repairs

The repair and redecoration of buildings give rise to most problems in practice. Unfortunately the problems cannot usually be solved by careful drafting. Three areas of dispute are common.

First, tenants often refuse to pay the whole of a demand resulting from repairs on the ground that the repairs were badly executed. If the landlord undertakes any form of repairing obligation it is probable that he will be held to be liable to repair to a reasonable standard. A term to this effect may now be implied by the Supply of Goods and Services Act 1982, s 13.

Secondly, expenditure is challenged on the ground that it was incurred in improving the property rather than in repairing it (eg *Mullaney v Maybourne Grange (Croydon) Management Co Ltd* [1986] 1 EGLR 70). This area of dispute can be cut down by providing expressly that the landlord is to be entitled to recover the cost of improvements. However, it is unlikely that a well-advised tenant would agree to the landlord being so entitled except in very limited circumstances (such as in the case of improvements required by statute).

Thirdly, a demand may be resisted on the ground that the work in respect of which it is made could have been carried out more cheaply, or that not all the work was strictly necessary. In general neither of these grounds will defeat the landlord's claim. The landlord is under no obligation to his tenant to choose the cheapest method of performing work (*Bandar Property Holdings Ltd v JS Darwen (Successors) Ltd* [1968] 2 All ER 305); nor is he obliged to patch up the property rather than spending more money on a permanent job (*Manor House Drive Ltd v Shahbazian* (1965) 195 EG 283). However, the amount charged to the tenant must be fair and reasonable (*Finchbourne Ltd v Rodrigues* [1976] 3 All ER 581). A term to this effect may be implied by the Supply of Goods and Services Act 1982, s 15. The landlord may find difficulties arising out of an obligation to redecorate the property at fixed intervals. If, for example, he is obliged to redecorate in every fourth year but delays the work until the fifth year, he may be met with a claim for damages for breach of covenant on the basis that in a time of rapidly rising building costs the redecoration would have been cheaper had it been carried out a year earlier. The draftsman can meet this difficulty by providing that the landlord shall redecorate 'as often as in his opinion is reasonably necessary', rather than by imposing a timetable on him.

The draftsman must also ensure that the landlord is entitled to recover the cost of repairing parts of the building. Extreme care must be taken if using phrases such as things 'used in common' (*Rapid Results College Ltd v Angell* [1986] 1 EGLR 53) which may not require the tenant of the ground floor to contribute to, say, the repair of the roof. However, it has been held that where the tenant of a ground floor flat in a house was required to contribute to the cost of repair of 'mutual structures' he was liable to contribute to the cost of repairing the roof (*Twyman v Charrington* [1994] 1 EGLR 243).

(vi) Promotional expenses

Some landlords of shopping developments actively promote them by advertising and by arranging exhibitions, Christmas decorations and entertainments within the development. The expenditure involved may be modest, but in some cases it may be the most substantial item on the service charge account. If the landlord wishes to recover some or all of the expenditure from the tenants, the draftsman must provide for it expressly. There is justification for such recovery as the promotional expenditure is calculated to increase goodwill, and with it the tenant's trading profits. However, the tenant may reasonably object that the landlord also derives substantial benefits in the form of increased rental values and that he too should bear some proportion of the cost. It is particularly important for the tenants to have some form of control over the level of expenditure in this respect, which has no definite limits. The tenant's adviser may do this by limiting expenditure to, say, two per cent of the annual rent roll. In addition, expenditure on promotional activities is a prime example of an item where consultation between landlord and tenant would be of mutual benefit. Some leases therefore provide for promotional expenses not to exceed a specified limit without the consent of the tenants' or merchants' association.

(vii) Legal costs

The landlord will not be able to recover through the service charge his legal costs of suing tenants for arrears of rent or breach of covenant unless the lease expressly so provides (*Sella House v Mears* [1989] 1 EGLR 65). A general power to employ agents and professionals will not suffice (*ibid*). The clause in the service charge must be specific.

(viii) Sweeping up

No draftsman can accurately predict precisely what services will be required over the term of a long lease. Accordingly, the list of items for inclusion in the service charge should always include provision for variation in the services. Normally such provision will be construed *eiusdem generis* with the preceding items, with the result that the landlord will not be entitled to recover the cost of providing a service of a wholly different kind (*Jacob Isbicki & Co Ltd v Goulding & Bird Ltd* [1989] 1 EGLR 236). Sometimes, however, such a clause will allow the landlord to recover the cost of introducing a new facility, eg a window cleaning cradle and track (*Sun Alliance & London Assurance Co Ltd v British*

Railways Board [1989] 2 EGLR 237). Some draftsmen negative the effect of this principle of construction by drafting the sweeping up clause very widely. This should be resisted by the tenant. The clause should either be limited to additional services of the same general description as the other items, or the consent of a majority of the tenants should be required before the introduction of any service of a radically different kind.

(e) Apportionment of charges

There are four basic methods of apportioning service charges between tenants:
- (1) according to rateable value of each letting;
- (2) according to floor area of each letting;
- (3) according to anticipated use of each tenant;
- (4) by fixed proportion.

None of these methods achieves perfect equity between the tenants. Where the apportionment is by rateable value, the apportionment will vary according to the rateable value from time to time of the property in question (*Moorcroft Estates Ltd v Doxford* (1979) 254 EG 871). An apportionment by rateable value is particularly vulnerable in a development such as a town shopping centre where identical units may have different rateable values according to their trading positions. Equally, the rateable value of a particular unit may be increased if the tenant carries out substantial improvements. In either case the tenant's use of the services may not be changed, although his contribution to their cost would be.

Where the development is to include residential accommodation, an apportionment based on rateable value may well be impossible, if the residential element was constructed or redeveloped after the abolition of domestic rating.

An apportionment by floor area can often work satisfactorily where the units are unlikely to be subdivided. However, if the units may be subdivided the apportionment is likely to be distorted by the creation of access corridors, fire lobbies and other areas that make little demand on the services. In addition, the measurement of property is a fertile area for dispute.

A variant on this method, particularly prevalent in shopping areas, is the use of a weighted floor area. This method is intended to avoid discrimination against large space users (who are often also the anchor tenants and who enjoy financial privileges). Under this method, the first, say, 1,000 square feet of a unit will be counted in full, the next, say, 2,000 will be counted at eight tenths of the actual area, the next 2,500 at three quarters rate, and so on.

Where the service charge is based on a specified percentage or floor area, the joint committee of the Law Society and the RICS recommended that the lease should provide for the landlord's surveyor to be able to vary the proportions, in order to allow for changes in the lettable areas of the development and for cessation of supply of services (see *Law Society's Gazette*, 9 April 1986, p 1056). Not all tenants will find it acceptable to leave the discretion in the hands of the landlord's surveyor.

An apportionment according to anticipated use would be the fairest method of apportionment if practicable. However, the use of certain services may change dramatically on an assignment or subletting or simply by a change in the tenant's business practice. Moreover, in order to work properly, an apportionment of every item would have to be made; for example, should the ground floor tenant be required to pay for the lift, or a labour intensive business a greater proportion of the cost of cleaning the lavatories? It is suggested that the apportionment of the service charge should be by way of fixed proportions written into the lease at the beginning of the term. The principal merit of this method is that it produces certainty. However, its disadvantage is that it may result in unfairness if the use of the premises changes significantly during the term. For example, if a shop becomes a restaurant the tenant will inevitably make a greater demand on the hot water system. For that reason, the draftsman should include some machinery for reviewing the fixed proportions. This could be done either by providing for a review at stated intervals or, more satisfactorily, by providing for the proportion to be reassessed if there is a material change in circumstances.

The tenant's adviser should insist on a stipulation that the aggregate of the proportions payable by the tenants collectively should not exceed 100 per cent. If the landlord wishes to make a profit on the provision of services this should be openly and expressly stated.

In apportioning a service charge between tenants some provision should be made for a contribution by the landlord in respect of unlet parts. If the tenants are required to make fixed contributions to the cost of services the landlord will not be provided with a complete indemnity if part of the building in question is unlet. Conversely, if the tenants are required to contribute to a reserve fund the fund may be depleted if no contributions are made in respect of an unlet part. It is suggested that the risk of voids is one that should fall on the landlord rather than on the tenants; accordingly, the draftsman should provide for the landlord to make contributions to the cost of services (especially any reserve fund) in respect of unlet parts.

Sometimes a lease will provide for the tenant to pay a 'fair' or 'proper' or 'due' proportion of the relevant costs. Unless there is clear machinery for determining what is a fair, proper or due proportion of the costs, phrases such as these are likely to give rise to dispute and should be avoided.

(f) Reserve and sinking funds

The treatment of reserve and sinking funds in leases is often haphazardly dealt with. In the first place it is important to consider what the money is intended to cover. Is it to provide for the eventual replacement of expensive capital items (such as lifts) or is it to spread the load of non-annual expenditure (such as redecoration) over the period between the recurrence of such expenditure? In the case of the former, the tenant's adviser should seek to ensure that the fund is held on trust (so that it is protected from the landlord's creditors) and invested until the time comes for its expenditure. It has long been the law that a non-charitable purpose trust cannot validly be created but trusts for the improvement of a settled estate have been upheld (*Re Bowes* [1896] 1 Ch 507) as has a trust to maintain land as a sports ground (*Re Denley's Trust Deed* [1969] 1 Ch 373) and a trust for the construction and/or improvement of a building (*Re Lipinski's Will Trusts* [1977] 1 All ER 33). In each case the trust was upheld by treating it as a trust for the benefit of ascertainable beneficiaries. It is suggested that a trust of a sinking fund would be upheld if it could also be treated as being for the benefit of ascertainable beneficiaries, ie the tenants.

Where a trust for beneficiaries is created it must conform to the rule against perpetuities. It is possible to specify a perpetuity period not exceeding eighty years (Perpetuities and Accumulations Act 1964, s 1) and since few commercial leases exceed that period, a perpetuity period should be specified. The draftsman should note that the specified period may be shorter than the maximum of eighty years which might be appropriate where it is contemplated that the building will be refurbished, or an industrial estate redeveloped within that period.

It is suggested that the beneficiaries should be the persons who will be the tenants of the building (or estate) immediately before the expiry of the perpetuity period, rather than the contributors to the reserve fund or the tenants from time to time. The reason is threefold. First, if there is no vested interest the trust is closer to a purpose trust, which is the real intention of the parties. Secondly, there is no danger that the tenants at any particular time collectively decide to put an end to the trust and appropriate the trust fund (under the rule in *Saunders v Vautier* (1841) 4 Beav 115). Thirdly, it avoids the need for each assignment of a lease to contain an assignment of the tenant's interest in the trust fund. The disadvantage is that in a case where a settlement is created with no interest in possession, a periodic charge to inheritance tax may arise (Inheritance Tax Act 1984, Chapter III). However, the practical likelihood of a charge being levied is small because (a) the charge will only arise if the tenant's contributions to the fund exceeds the current exemption limit and (b) application of the principle that any addition to the fund is treated as the creation of a separate settlement means that payments can be arranged so that the funds are applied within the statutory period.

Provision should be made for the payment of any income tax which arises on interest accruing to the trust fund as well as any other tax.

At the expiry of the perpetuity period any surplus should be distributed amongst the tenants in defined shares. The most convenient shares are those specified for the payment of the service charge itself.

Finally, it is suggested that the landlord should have the statutory power to appoint a new trustee, so that in the event of a sale of the reversion the new landlord can be quickly and cheaply appointed as the new trustee.

Where the reserve is intended to defray regular non-annual items of expenditure, a simpler approach is possible. The landlord should be required to pay the fund into a separate bank account and to pass on the moneys standing to the credit of the account in the event of a sale of the reversion. In this way the tenant will have a contractual right to ensure that the fund is available for use for the intended purpose. It may be that the court would infer that even this approach involved the creation of a trust (cf *Re Chelsea Cloisters Ltd (In Liquidation)* (1980) 41 P&CR 98).

(g) Certification of charges

Every service charge should make provision for the certification of the charge and for the recovery of the cost of certification to be recoverable as part of the charge. Usually the issue of a proper certificate is a condition precedent to the tenant's liability to pay (cf *CIN Properties Ltd v Barclays Bank plc* [1986] 1 EGLR 59; *Northways Flats Management Co (Camden) v Wimpey Pension Trustees* [1992] 2 EGLR 42 (submission of estimates for approval a condition precedent)). Where the lease provides that the certifier is to act as an expert he must act impartially and hold the balance between landlord and tenant (*Concorde Graphics Ltd v Andromeda Investments SA* (1982) 265 EG 386; *New Pinehurst Residents Association (Cambridge) Ltd v Silow* [1988] 1 EGLR 227). This means that he cannot be the landlord himself (*Finchbourne Ltd v Rodrigues* [1976] 3 All ER 581) nor the landlord's managing agent where in that capacity he has been putting forward the landlord's case (*Concorde Graphics Ltd v Andromeda Investments SA* above) unless the lease expressly provides for this. In the case of a large building or development the tenant's adviser should attempt to have the service charge accounts audited by the landlord's auditors.

The certificate is often expressed to be final. It is now established that where parties to a contract entrust a function to an expert, they intend him to perform that function according to the contract as correctly interpreted, and that his interpretation is open to review by the court (*Mercury Communications v Director-General of Telecommunications* [1996] 1 WLR 48. It appears, therefore that a certificate may only be final on matters of fact. This should be expressly stated in the lease. The landlord's position is sufficiently protected if the tenant is precluded from challenging the interim payments (thus maintaining the landlord's cash flow) but is entitled to challenge items on the final annual account.

(h) Renewal leases

The terms of any new tenancy granted under the Landlord and Tenant Act 1954 are determined, in the absence of agreement, by the court. In determining those terms the court must have regard to the terms of the current tenancy and to all relevant circumstances (Landlord and Tenant Act 1954, s 35). This means that the burden of persuading the court to impose a change in the terms of the current tenancy against the will of either party rests on the party proposing the change. The change proposed must be fair and reasonable and should take into account the relatively weak bargaining position of the tenant and the general purpose of the Act, which is to protect the business interests of the tenant (*O'May v City of London Real Property Co Ltd* [1982] 1 All ER 660).

Where the current lease contains a service charge, it is likely that the court would order its retention in the terms of a new tenancy. However, where the lease does not contain a service charge, or the charge is not as comprehensive as the landlord wishes, different considerations arise. In relation to those items which can be described as day-to-day housekeeping items, inherent in the use and occupation of property (eg cleaning common parts, lighting etc) it is likely that the court would order the inclusion of a service charge. In *Hyams v Titan Properties Ltd* (1972) 24 P&CR 359 Buckley LJ said:

> It is a fairer arrangement between landlord and tenant that the tenant should pay a proportion of the costs year by year than that an arbitrary figure should be fixed at the inception of the lease to continue in force throughout the term as the amount payable in respect of services.

However, in respect of risk items, inherent in the ownership of a long-term interest in property (eg renewal of plant and repairs to the structure) the court is unlikely to impose a service charge on the tenant (*O'May v City of London Real Property Co Ltd* above). But where the service charge does not require the tenant to contribute to the capital cost of replacement of items, nor to the cost of structural repairs, it is likely that the court will order him to pay it (*Leslie & Godwin Investments v Prudential Assurance Co* [1987] 2 EGLR 95).

Example 6:9 Tenant's covenant to pay service charge: limited payment in advance

(1) To pay to the Landlord in accordance with the provisions of this clause [   ] per cent of the costs and expenses incurred or deemed to have been incurred by the Landlord in connection with the services specified in the Schedule hereto

(2) Those costs and expenses and the Tenant's percentage of them shall be certified in respect of each financial year by the Landlord's auditors (acting as experts) as soon as practicable after the end of the financial year in question and each such certificate shall be conclusive as to all matters of fact which it purports to certify

(3) The Tenant shall pay to the Landlord on account of his liability under subclause (1) above in the first year of the term the sum of £[   ] and in each year thereafter such sum as may be specified by the Landlord (but it shall not exceed eighty per cent of the amount certified as the Tenant's percentage for the preceding financial year) payable by four equal instalments in advance on the usual quarter days

(4) Within twenty-one days after the issue of a certificate under

INSURANCE AND SERVICE CHARGES

subclause (2) above the Tenant shall pay to the Landlord or as the case may be the Landlord shall pay to the Tenant the difference between the advance payments made under subclause (3) above and the amount certified as the Tenant's percentage

(5) The expression 'financial year' means a period of twelve months beginning on in each year

(6) The percentage specified in subclause (1) above may be varied by the Landlord in the event of any material change of circumstance during the term which affects the Tenant's liability under this clause

Example 6:10 Service charge— provision for reserve and payment in advance

(1) In this clause the following expressions have the following meanings:
   (a) 'financial year' means a period of twelve months ending on in each year
   (b) 'the specified percentage' means [   ] per cent
   (c) 'the service costs' means the total sum computed in accordance with subclauses (4) (5) and (6) of this clause
   (d) 'the service charge' means the specified percentage of the service costs
   (e) 'the expert' means a professionally qualified surveyor or accountant (who may be a person employed by the landlord)

(2) The tenant covenants with the landlord to pay the service charge during the term by equal payments in advance at the times at which and in the manner in which rent is payable under this lease

(3) The service costs in respect of any financial year shall be calculated not later than the beginning of the financial year in question

(4) The service costs shall consist of a total sum equal to:
   (a) the expenditure estimated by the expert as likely to be incurred by the landlord in the financial year in question in connection with the items specified in subclause (5) of this clause together with
   (b) an appropriate amount as a reserve for or towards such of the items specified in subclause (5) as likely to give rise to expenditure either after the expiry of this lease or only once during its then unexpired term or at intervals of more than one year (for example such matters as the decoration of the exterior and common parts of the building and the replacement of lifts boilers and other equipment) PROVIDED THAT where any expenditure is to be incurred on any such item in the financial year to which the estimate relates the expert shall in computing the total sum give credit for the amount then standing to the credit of the reserve in respect of the item in question

(5) The items to be included in the service costs are the following:
   (a) the costs of and incidental to the performance of the landlord's covenants in clauses [   ] to [   ] (inclusive) of this lease

(b) the costs of and incidental to the carrying out by the landlord of any work in pursuance of any requirement of any Act of Parliament or of any local or public authority

(c) the amount of any rates taxes assessments or outgoings of any nature whatsoever payable in respect of the building and paid by the landlord

(d) the full cost of employing porters cleaners and other staff of a like nature including the cost of uniforms bonuses national insurance contributions pensions and (where the landlord provides accommodation for such persons) an amount equal to the market rental value of such accommodation and any rates or council tax payable for it

(e) the cost of periodical inspection repair and maintenance of the common parts of the building and the periodical inspection repair maintenance and replacement of the lifts boilers and other plant machinery and equipment in the building

(f) the cost of preparing accounts and certificates relating to the calculation of the service costs or the service charge

(g) the cost of employing managing agents (save in relation to the collection of rent or the letting of any property) in respect of the building or if the landlord does not employ managing agents then a fee for the landlord of ten per cent of the total of the foregoing amounts

(6) As soon as practicable after the end of each financial year the expert shall determine and certify the amount by which the estimate referred to in paragraph (a) of subclause (4) of this clause exceeds or falls short of the actual expenditure incurred by the landlord in respect of the items specified in subclause (5) in the financial year in question (giving credit for any amount applied from the reserve in payment of items of expenditure incurred during that year) and shall supply the tenant with a copy of the certificate.

(7) Within twenty-one days of the receipt by the tenant of the said certificate the tenant shall pay to the landlord the specified percentage of the deficiency or as the case may be the landlord shall repay to the tenant the specified percentage of the excess

(8) During any period when any part of the building is not let upon terms that the tenant of it is liable to pay a service charge corresponding to the service charge payable under the lease the landlord shall contribute to the reserve an amount equal to the total that would have been payable by way of such contribution if such part of the building had been so let and the reserve shall be calculated accordingly

(9) If in the opinion of the expert it is equitable to do so he may increase or decrease the specified proportion

(10) Any dispute arising out of the provisions of this clause shall be referred to the decision of a single arbitrator to be appointed on the application of either party by the President for the time being of the Royal Institution of Chartered Surveyors whose decision shall be final but this subclause shall not confer upon the tenant the right to

challenge the amount of the total sum computed under subclause (4)(a) of this clause

Example 6:11 Trust of reserve fund

(1) Any reserve paid to the landlord shall be held by the landlord upon trust during the perpetuity period to apply it and any interest accruing upon it for the purposes for which it was collected and subject to that upon trust for the persons who immediately before the expiry of the perpetuity period are contributing to it in shares equal to the proportions in which they contribute to it

(2) The landlord may invest the reserve in such manner as he thinks fit but is under no obligation to do so

(3) The power of appointing a new trustee is vested in the landlord

(4) The perpetuity period is [   ] years

Example 6:12 Landlord's power to replace plant

Where under this lease:

(1) the landlord is required or entitled to keep in repair or proper working order any plant or machinery; and

(2) in the reasonable opinion of the landlord the cost of so doing would be uneconomic or imprudent when compared with the anticipated lifespan of that item of plant or machinery

the landlord may replace that item with a modern equivalent and the cost of the replacement shall be deemed to be a repair

7

Repairs and Improvements

1 Repairs

(a) The norm

The normal way of allocating responsibility for the physical condition of commercial buildings is by reference to the concept of 'repair'. From time to time suggestions have been made that this is not the appropriate concept. Thus, the Law Society's standard form of business lease requires the tenant to 'maintain' rather than to repair; and the Law Commission has suggested that responsibility should be defined by reference to keeping the property fit for use. But these suggestions have not yet been adopted in the market. Nevertheless, the 'repairing covenant' is not the only means by which one or other party to a lease may assume responsibility for its physical condition. The covenant to comply with statutes, and the covenant to pay outgoings may also impose liability to carry out work to the property.

(b) The framework

When dealing with a covenant to repair most practical problems can be addressed by answering the following questions:
- (1) What is the subject matter of the covenant?
- (2) Has the physical subject matter of the covenant deteriorated since some earlier time?
- (3) If so, what work is necessary to restore it to its undeteriorated condition?
- (4) As a matter of fact and degree can that work fairly be called work of repair?

(c) Interpretation of covenants to repair

A covenant to repair is construed with reference to the age and nature of the property in question at the beginning of the lease (*Lurcott v Wakely* [1911] 1 KB 905; *Smedley v Chumley and Hawke Ltd* (1981) 44 P&CR 50). This principle applies both to determine the standard of repair required and to restrict the nature of the work that can be required of the covenantor. Thus, where a tenant covenants to keep in repair an old building the landlord cannot require him to keep it in a condition appropriate to a new building or to modernise it (for example, by updating the electrical system or installing a damp-proof course). It follows that where the landlord is himself a tenant a repairing obligation contained in the headlease and repeated word for word in the sublease may impose on the subtenant a lighter obligation than that contained in the headlease if the grant of the headlease and the grant of the sublease are separated by a significant length of time. In such a case the draftsman can protect the landlord by inserting in the sublease a covenant 'to observe and perform the covenants in the headlease so far as they affect the demised property'. Such a covenant is more than a covenant of indemnity: it amounts to an express covenant to perform the covenants in the headlease (*Ayling v Wade* [1961] 2 QB 228).

If the demised property is out of repair at the beginning of the tenancy the covenant to repair will be construed as requiring the property to be put into repair (*Proudfoot v Hart* (1890) 25 QBD 42), although the standard of repair will depend on the age of the property. If the tenant wishes to protect himself against liability to carry out initial repairs the covenant should be amended to read 'to keep the demised property in no worse condition than that in which it was at the beginning of this lease'. In addition, a full schedule of condition should be agreed between the parties and annexed to the lease. The schedule should take the form of a full structural survey, with photographs, otherwise it will not be of much practical use at the end of the lease. In some cases a video film with commentary may be useful.

(d) Subject matter of the covenant

Close attention should be paid to the subject matter of the covenant. It is arguable that, if the covenant amounts to a series of separate covenants to repair component parts of the demised property, the obligation will not extend to the replacement of the whole of one of those component parts. Accordingly, it is suggested that the draftsman should not attempt to enumerate all the parts of the demised property that the covenantor is called upon to keep in repair. The covenant should, whenever possible, be expressed simply as a covenant to 'keep the demised property in repair'. Such a covenant also has the advantage of preventing an argument whether the express inclusion of some parts of the demised property in the covenant is to be taken as impliedly excluding all other parts.

The scope of a repairing covenant is closely linked to the definition of the demised property in the parcels clause of the lease. If, for example, loadbearing walls are excepted from the demise, a tenant who covenants to keep the demised property in repair will not be obliged to repair those walls and would be guilty of a trespass if he attempted to do so. Similarly, the placing of a phrase in the parcels clause such as 'hereafter called the demised property' may affect liability to repair. If, for example, a right of way is granted to the tenant, and the grant of the right precedes that phrase, it is at least arguable that the way must be kept in repair under a covenant to keep the demised property in repair. Provision should be made for the repair of means of access and of services.

Particular problem areas in the context of repairing obligations include:

(1) windows, window frames, glass;
(2) floors, screeds, beams, columns;
(3) flat roofs, canopies;
(4) cladding panels.

These problems occur most frequently where a building is multi-let. In such cases it is vital to ensure that the dividing line between those parts of the building for which the landlord is responsible and those parts for which the tenant is responsible is clear. A phrase such as 'the interior of the demised property' is likely to lead to uncertainty about windows, doors etc (see *Reston v Hudson* [1990] 2 EGLR 51).

In addition it is helpful for the draftsman either to visit the building or at least to have a clear explanation of its method of construction. Too often a lease of a steel-framed building will refer to the main walls and timbers, although the court will interpret such phrases as encompassing steel girders, where appropriate (*Manchester Bonded Warehouse v Carr* (1880) 5 CPD 507).

(e) Physical deterioration

Before it can be said that work is work of repair, it must be shown that the building (or other subject matter of the covenant) is in a condition which is worse than that in which it was at some earlier time (*Quick v Taff-Ely BC* [1985] 3 All ER 321 at 328). Thus if the tenant covenants to keep the structure of the building in repair, it must be shown that the structure has deteriorated before the tenant's covenant begins to bite. So where the basement of a building became flooded, but no damage was done to the building itself, the tenant was held not liable to repair (*Post Office v Aquarius Properties* [1987] 1 All ER 1055). The tenant's repairing obligation is not therefore to be construed as a warranty that deficiencies in the original design or construction of the building will be rectified in any event. If, for example, a building is built with designed floor loadings of 120 lb per sq ft but achieves a loadbearing capacity of 70 lb per sq ft, the tenant cannot be compelled to strengthen the building. If, however, a deficiency in the original design or construction of the building causes the condition of the building to deteriorate, then the tenant may be liable if, as a matter of fact and degree, the necessary remedial work can fairly be called work of repair.

(f) Meaning of repair

Repair is restoration by renewal or replacement of subsidiary parts of a whole. Renewal, as distinguished from repair, is the reconstruction of the entirety, meaning by the entirety not necessarily the whole but substantially the whole of the subject matter under discussion (*Lurcott v Wakely* [1911] 1 KB 905). This is the classic definition of repair that will govern the construction of any repairing covenant. So a covenant to keep an industrial unit in repair will oblige the tenant to replace the roof where it can no longer be patched (*Elite Investment Ltd v TI Bainbridge Silencers Ltd* [1986] 2 EGLR 43). It appears to make no difference whether the covenant is a covenant to keep 'in repair', 'in good repair', 'in sufficient repair' or 'in tenantable repair' (*Calthorpe v McOscar* [1924] 1 KB 716 *per* Bankes and Scrutton LJJ). Whether the end product of work requiring to be done properly constitutes 'repair' is a question of degree in each case. The correct approach is to conclude on a fair interpretation of the precise terms of the lease in relation to the state of the property at the date of the lease whether the work can be called repair or not; and, in coming to that conclusion one must look at the work as a whole and not at individual parts of it (*Brew Brothers Ltd v Snax (Ross) Ltd* [1970] 1 QB 612). The work for which the tenant is liable will include the eradication of the cause of the inherent defect if that is what a sensible practical man would do, provided that the work does not amount to the rebuilding of the whole subject matter of the covenant (*Stent v Monmouth DC* [1987] 1 EGLR 59).

A variety of tests have been suggested to help in answering this question of fact and degree:

(1) whether the alterations go to the whole or substantially the whole of the structure or only to a subsidiary part;

(2) whether the effect of the alterations is to produce a building of a wholly different character to that which has been let;

(3) what is the cost of the work in relation to the previous value of the building and what is their effect on the value and lifespan of the building (*McDougall v Easington DC* [1989] 1 EGLR 93).

The 'fact and degree' approach will prevail no matter what the cause of the defect under consideration. Even if the work is necessitated by reason of an inherent defect in the design or construction of the demised property a covenant to repair will oblige the covenantor to eliminate that defect if it is not substantial (*Ravenseft Properties Ltd v Davstone (Holdings) Ltd* [1979] 1 All ER 929); but a covenant to repair will not oblige him to eliminate the defect if to do so would amount to the construction of property different in kind to that demised (*Pembery v Lamdin* [1940] 2 All ER 434; *Sotheby v Grundy* [1947] 2 All ER 761). In determining whether work is such as to amount to the construction of property different in kind to that which was demised, it is clearly necessary to compare one with the other. So in the case of an old building a covenant to repair does not require the replacement of wooden windows with aluminium double glazed windows (*Mullaney v Maybourne Grange (Croydon) Management Co Ltd* [1986] 1 EGLR 70). But in the case of a new building the relevant comparison is between the property contemplated by the parties at the date of the lease and the property as changed by the necessary works (*Smedley v Chumley and Hawke Ltd* (1981) 44 P&CR 50; *Crédit Suisse v Beegas Nominees* [1994] 4 All ER 803). In almost every case the building contemplated by the parties will be one that has been properly designed and constructed in the light of good practice at the date of construction. It follows that work necessary to correct faults in the design or construction of a new building will frequently fall within the scope of a covenant to repair. In the case of a new building, the tenant's adviser should seek to include in the repairing covenant an exclusion of liability for such work. It is not satisfactory simply to exempt the tenant from liability to eradicate 'inherent defects'. First, this expression has no clear meaning. Secondly, it may extend to defects which only become defects in the light of a change in standards (eg the presence of asbestos in workplaces). To exempt the tenant from liability in such a case is to make serious inroads into a full repairing liability. It is suggested, therefore, that the yardstick should be linked to a negligence or breach of contract test. If the landlord could have established liability against someone other than the tenant (eg the designer or constructor of the building) the tenant should not be held liable.

Example 7:1 Exemption of liability

> Provided that the tenant shall not be liable to remedy any defect in the design or construction of the demised property in respect of which the landlord or its predecessor in title is (or but for the operation of the Limitation Acts would be) entitled to claim damages from some person not a party to this lease

The tenant's adviser may also seek to tackle the problem of defective new buildings in a different way. The original design and construction team will owe a duty of care to the tenant as occupier of the building. But that duty is limited in two ways. First, it is limited to a duty to take reasonable care that the building is not a danger to health or safety. Defects in the building which fall short of causing a danger to health or safety are not covered by the duty of care. Secondly, loss is not recoverable if it is pure economic loss; ie the cost of putting right defects. In order to be recoverable the loss must consist of damage to property other than the defective building itself (*D & F Estates Ltd v Church Commissioners* [1988] 2 All ER 992). In the light of the restricted scope of the duty of care, the tenant's adviser should beware of accepting merely a 'duty of care deed' which acknowledges the duty. It must go further and amount to a contractual warranty that the building has been erected in a good and workmanlike manner in accordance with the specification; and that the building has been designed in accordance with proper professional standards. If the tenant is not in contact with the design and construction team (eg because the building has already been built before the tenant appears on the scene) the tenant's adviser may seek to obtain from the landlord an undertaking to pursue such remedies as he has against the design and construction team and to apply any damages recovered in remedying any defect discovered. Such an undertaking will inevitably be personal to the original landlord or developer, and will not bind the landlord's successors in title.

(g) Wider forms of covenant

It is, of course, possible as a matter of drafting to impose obligations on the tenant which go beyond mere repair. Thus in *Gooderham and Worts Ltd v Canadian Broadcasting Corporation* [1947] AC 66 the tenant covenanted to keep a radio broadcasting station 'modern and up-to-date'; and in *Norwich Union Life Insurance Society v British Railways Board* [1987] 2 EGLR 137 the tenant covenanted to keep a building in repair 'and when necessary to rebuild reconstruct or replace the same'. Such forms of covenant will take effect according to their terms, and will oblige the tenant to do more than merely keep the existing structure in repair. Similarly, in *Post Office v Aquarius Properties Ltd* [1987] 1 All ER 1055 Slade LJ indicated that it would be possible by clear words to impose upon a tenant a liability to eradicate inherent defects in a building before they had caused any damage to the building, but added that this was not an obligation which tenants under a commercial lease might readily be expected to undertake. In *Crédit Suisse v Beegas Nominees* [1994] 4 All ER 803 the landlord covenanted to maintain repair 'and otherwise keep in good and tenantable condition' certain parts of a building. It was held that a covenant to keep in good condition did not require proof of any deterioration in the subject matter of the covenant before the obligation came into play. Further, whether the subject matter of the covenant was in good and tenantable condition was to be judged not by reference to the actual state of the building at the date of the demise, but by reference to the requirements of a hypothetical reasonably minded tenant likely to take it. The same interpretation would, it is thought, apply to a tenant's covenant in the same form. Thus a covenant to keep in good condition (as opposed to a covenant to keep in repair) is potentially a far more onerous obligation.

If the draftsman contemplates extending the tenant's liability in one of these ways, he should carefully consider the impact which this would have upon the rent recoverable on review. In *Norwich Union Life Assurance Society v British Railways Board* above a combination of the length of the lease (150 years) and the rebuilding obligation resulted in a reduction in the rent of 27.5 per cent.

(h) Divided responsibility for repairs

In the case of a lease of part only of a building or of a unit in a shopping centre, it will not usually be practicable for one party to be responsible for all repairs. In such a case the tenant will usually be responsible for repairs to the internal non-structural parts of the demise, while the landlord undertakes the repair of the structure and common parts, recovering his costs of so doing through a service charge.

Until recently it could be confidently asserted that the law would not imply any repairing obligation by a landlord in a lease, even where the tenant undertook some obligations as respects the repair or maintenance of the property (*Sleafer v Lambeth BC* [1960] 1 QB 43; *Tennant Radiant Heat v Warrington Development Corporation* [1988] 1 EGLR 41). However, in *Barrett v Lounova (1982) Ltd* [1989] 1 All ER 351 the Court of Appeal held that a landlord was liable for structural repairs where it was necessary that the structure of a building be put in repair in order to enable the tenant to comply with her obligation to keep the interior of the property in repair. But it has been subsequently held that since there are cases in which neither landlord nor tenant has any responsibility for repairs (or for certain categories of repair), the court should not be astute to imply obligations (*Demetriou v Poolaction* [1991] 1 EGLR 100). Nevertheless the draftsman should make sure that the allocation of responsibility for repairs is fully covered by the lease, and that there are no gaps in that responsibility, particularly since it will not be presumed that the landlord will be entitled to recover all expenditure through the service charge.

Where repairs are to be carried out by a management company, there is no implied term to the effect that the landlord will undertake those obligations if the management company defaults (*Hafton Properties v Camp* [1994] 1 EGLR 67).

When defining the scope of the landlord's repairing obligation the expression 'structural repairs' should be avoided. It has been observed that 'structural repairs' mean 'repairs of or to a structure' (*Granada Theatres Ltd v Freehold Investment (Leytonstone) Ltd* [1958] 2 All ER 551 *per* Vaisey J). That definition divides all repairs between structural repairs and decorative repairs and may enlarge the obligation to carry out structural repairs beyond that intended by the draftsman. It is suggested that the draftsman should attempt to define with more clarity the parts of the property to be repaired by each party. Thus, for example, the landlord's repairing obligation might be 'to keep in repair the roof and loadbearing walls and main beams of the Building and the common parts of it'. Even this may not be adequate where the external walls of the building are not themselves loadbearing, but rest upon a loadbearing frame. In such a case the landlord's obligation should extend to external walls. If the obligation is to repair 'external walls of the demised property', the obligation will extend to all the walls enclosing the demised property, whether or not they are exposed to the air (*Pembery v Lamdin* [1940] 2 All ER 434). Thus, if the repair of external walls is excepted from the repairing obligations of a tenant of an office suite he will not be liable to repair a partition wall separating his suite from the corridor. It is suggested that if 'loadbearing walls' or external walls 'of the Building of which the demised property forms part' are excepted instead his obligation will extend to partition walls enclosing his suite.

The expression 'main walls' has been said to mean those walls which support the structure or have directly to do with its stability (*The Holiday Fellowship Ltd v Hereford* (unreported) *per* Harman J, approved on appeal [1959] 1 All ER 433).

The landlord's obligation is sometimes expressed as a covenant to keep in repair 'the structure and exterior of the Building of which the demised property forms part'. This is a less onerous obligation than a covenant to keep in repair 'the structure and exterior of the demised property'. In the latter case, but not the former, the obligation will extend to the repair of the outside of inner party walls (eg walls separating one part of the building from another) (cf *Campden Hill Towers Ltd v Gardner* [1977] 1 All ER 739 construing the expression 'structure and exterior of the dwelling house'). The 'exterior' of a building will include access ways and staircases (*Brown v Liverpool Corporation* [1969] 3 All ER 1345).

The repair of glass should always be considered, particularly where a substantial part of the demised property is enclosed by glass. Generally, windows will not be part of the 'main walls' of a building (*The Holiday Fellowship v Hereford* [1959] 1 All ER 433). Whether they are so is a question of fact and degree (*ibid*). Where, for example, property is enclosed by large plate glass windows, the windows will be part of the walls of the property and will not be included in an obligation to keep the interior of the property in repair (*Boswell v Crucible Steel Co* [1925] 1 KB 119). Thus, the tenant of an office suite will be liable to repair the windows if the building is constructed of brick with normal size windows, but not if it is constructed of steel and glass. Accordingly, the draftsman should take full instructions as to the construction of the property in question before drafting any repairing obligation. The draftsman should also consider defining precisely the limits of liability, particularly where the responsibility for repair is divided between landlord and tenant.

Example 7:2 Definition of structure

'the structure of the building' means:

(1) the roof and foundations of the building

(2) its loadbearing walls and columns (excluding plaster or other decorative finishes)

(3) its floor structures (including beams and joists but excluding floorboards floor screeds and floor finishes)

(4) all surfaces of the building exposed to the elements except surfaces made of glass and window frames

Example 7:3 Definition of interior of the demised property

'the interior of the demised property' includes:

(1) all non-loadbearing walls wholly within the demised property

(2) one half (severed vertically) of all non-loadbearing walls separating the demised property from any other part of the building

(3) all plaster or other decorative finish applied to any wall bounding the demised property and not falling within (1) or (2) above or applied to any column or loadbearing wall within the demised property

(4) the whole of all doors door frames windows and window frames bounding the demised property

(5) all ceilings bounding the demised property

(6) all floor finishes floorboards and floor screeds

(i) Fair wear and tear

The exception of fair wear and tear relieves a tenant from liability for repairs that are decorative and from remedying parts that wear out or come adrift in the course of reasonable use, but it does not exempt him from anything else. If further damage is likely to flow from the wear and tear he must do such repairs as necessary to stop that further damage (*Regis Property Co Ltd v Dudley* [1959] AC 370). In practice it is usually very difficult to determine what amounts to disrepair and what is covered by the exception. For that reason it is suggested that the landlord should resist the exception of fair wear and tear as it almost always leads to a dispute over terminal dilapidations. For the same reason, the parties should beware of a liability to repair qualified by reference to a schedule of condition. Such schedules are almost invariably too vague and generalised to be of any assistance at the end of the lease. If the repairing liability is to be qualified in this way the schedule should be in the nature of a full structural survey and should be accompanied by an agreed photographic record of the building.

(j) Fire damage

Although a tenant who covenants to repair property is not generally liable to rebuild the whole of the property he is liable to rebuild if it is destroyed by fire (*Matthey v Curling* [1922] 2 AC 180). Accordingly, where the landlord is bound to insure, the tenant's adviser should see that the repairing covenant exempts the tenant from liability to repair damage caused by a peril against which the landlord has insured. The landlord will usually wish to qualify this by restricting it to cases where the insurance has not been avoided or vitiated by the tenant.

The standard form of clause may not be entirely satisfactory to the landlord, particularly in the case of a total loss. The insurers may be entitled to limit the extent of the indemnity to the market value of the building if that is less than the reinstatement cost (*Leppard v Excess Insurance Co Ltd* [1979] 2 All ER 668). In the case of a partial loss the claim may be subject to average. Thus, the tenant may have been released from liability exempting him from having to remedy damage caused by an insured risk, yet the sum which the landlord recovers from his insurers may be insufficient to pay for the work. Accordingly, the draftsman should consider casting the clause in the form of an exemption from liability 'to the extent that the landlord recovers the cost of the necessary work from its insurers'. Such a form of words would deal both with the possibility that the insurance had become vitiated, and with the possibility that the measure of indemnity was insufficient to pay for the work. If the draftsman chooses this form of covenant, the tenant's adviser should be specially careful to see that the landlord is under an obligation to maintain adequate insurance cover. Thus if the landlord fails to insure, or underinsures, the tenant will have a remedy against him.

(k) Repair on notice

Where a landlord covenants to repair the demised property his obligation does not arise unless and until he had notice of a defect in the property, and he will not be in breach of his obligation thereafter if he carries out the necessary repairs with reasonable expedition (*O'Brien v Robinson* [1973] AC 912). This does not have to be expressly provided in the lease, but is implied by law. A landlord's obligation to effect repairs to the demised property carries with it an obligation to make good any consequential damage to decorations (*McGreal v Wake* (1984) 369 EG 1254). Where the landlord's obligation is to repair property which falls outside the demise, his obligation is not dependent on notice (*British Telecommunications v Sun Life Assurance Society* [1995] 4 All ER 44).

He is in breach of covenant as soon as the property in question falls into disrepair. The draftsman may wish to consider making the landlord's obligation to repair an obligation which is expressly dependent on notice being given of any defect.

Where a tenant covenants to repair it is common to impose on him an additional, but subsidiary, obligation to repair on notice. The draftsman should reserve to the landlord a power to enter the demised property to inspect the state of repair and a power to serve notice of disrepair. The tenant should covenant to repair on service of such a notice. The usual provision is 'to repair within three months' of service of a notice. The usual three-month period will often suffice for minor repairs, but major repairs may well take longer. In such a case the tenant may be at risk of forfeiture for breach of the covenant to repair on notice. It is suggested that a fairer obligation for both parties is for the tenant to covenant to begin the repairs within a shorter period (say forty-two days) and to proceed expeditiously to carry them out. In that way the tenant has sufficient time to arrange for contractors but he is not exposed to the risk of forfeiture if the repairs take a long time.

In all cases where the tenant covenants to repair on notice, the draftsman will usually seek to provide for the landlord to have the right to enter to carry out the necessary repairs if the tenant fails to comply with his obligation. In the absence of an express right to entry the landlord will not be entitled to carry out the work if the tenant defaults (*Regional Properties Ltd v City of London Real Property Co Ltd* (1980) 257 EG 64). Accordingly, such a right should be reserved. See further p 33 above. However, the reservation of such a right will impose upon the landlord a duty of care towards third parties (Defective Premises Act 1972, s 4(4)). The draftsman should therefore require the tenant to indemnify the landlord against such liability if the liability arises as a result of a defect the existence of which is a breach of the tenant's obligations. The cost expended by the landlord in exercising his right of entry should be expressed to be recoverable from the tenant as a debt. Until recently there had been a conflict of authority at first instance on the question whether a landlord's right to enter to carry out work which the tenant ought to have done, and then charge the tenant with the cost, fell within the Leasehold Property (Repairs) Act 1938 requiring the leave of the court to be obtained. The Court of Appeal has now decided that the landlord's remedy is a remedy in debt, not damages, with the consequence that it falls outside the scope of the Leasehold Property (Repairs) Act 1938 (*Jervis v Harris* [1996] 2 WLR 220). It would no doubt be helpful if the clause itself described the sum as a debt, but it is not considered essential to do so. Although the Court of Appeal did not say so in terms, it appears to follow that such a clause is also outside the statutory limitation on damages imposed by s 18 of the Landlord and Tenant Act 1927. Thus provided that he acts while the tenancy is still running, a landlord can ensure that the property is repaired at the expense of the tenant and, subject to the tenant's financial position, will recover his expenditure in full. Thus major pieces of legislative protection for tenants may be readily avoided. In those circumstances, although a clause giving the landlord the right to enter to carry out work at the tenant's expense has been a standard feature of leases for generations, the tenant's adviser should now consider whether to resist the inclusion of such a clause. If such a clause is to be included, the tenant's adviser should consider restricting the landlord's power to a power to remedy only those breaches which cause damage (or substantial damage) to the reversion.

(l) Supervision of works by landlord's surveyor

Where the landlord wishes to retain control over the execution of repairs the draftsman may provide that the tenant must repair to the satisfaction of the landlord's surveyor or that the repairs are to be carried out under the supervision of the landlord's surveyor. If the works are to be carried out to the satisfaction of the landlord's surveyor it appears that the appointment of a surveyor is a condition precedent to the tenant's liability under the covenant (*Combe v Greene* (1843) 11 M & W 480); and, further, that there will be no breach of covenant if the surveyor ought to have been satisfied (*Doe d Baker v Jones* (1848) 2 Car & Kir 743). On the other hand, if the works are to be carried out under the supervision of the landlord's surveyor the appointment of a surveyor does not appear to be a condition precedent to the tenant's liability (*Cannock v Jones* (1849) 3 Exch 233). It is suggested that the draftsman should provide for the tenant to repair to 'the reasonable satisfaction of the landlord or his surveyor'. It is conceived that this formula overcomes the difficulties of a failure to appoint a surveyor while at the same time preventing the landlord from being capriciously dissatisfied.

(m) Decorative repairs

A tenant who covenants to repair is liable to do such repapering and painting as would be necessary to satisfy a reasonably-minded tenant of the class likely to take the property (*Proudfoot v Hart* (1890) 25 QBD 42). However, there is doubt as to the scope of this obligation, particularly with regard to decoration during the term rather than at the end of it. Accordingly, the draftsman should make express provision for redecorating the demised property. Note, however, that in some circumstances a tenant may be relieved against liability to decorate (Law of Property Act 1925, s 147).

The most common fault in decorating covenants is that the nature of the property has not been considered. Thus, one finds covenants 'to paint with three coats of good oil paint' property that is constructed of brick, aluminium and plate glass. If the draftsman does not know what decorative process is necessary to keep the property in sound decorative condition he should not attempt to be specific. The tenant's obligation should be an obligation 'in a good and workmanlike manner and with appropriate materials of good quality to redecorate the demised property'. However, it is convenient to specify the number of coats of paint which should be applied where painting is appropriate, because this is often a point of dispute in dealing with a terminal schedule of dilapidations. In the case of a large office building the draftsman should consider whether the tenant should be required to undertake annual inspections of the exterior with a view to monitoring the performance of cladding panels, window frames, mastic joints and the like. In most cases the tenant is required to redecorate at fixed intervals. The requirement has the advantage for the tenant that he can plan his programme of redecoration well in advance, but it is doubtful how far such an obligation is really in the interest of either party. In so far as the tenant is concerned, an obligation to redecorate at fixed intervals may expose him to the risk of forfeiture for breach of the covenant at a time when the property is not in need of redecoration. Even if he is granted unconditional relief against forfeiture he may still become involved in tiresome litigation. Conversely, from the landlord's point of view the right to forfeit for breach of a covenant to redecorate in a specified year is easily waived. Once the year has passed the breach is complete. It is not a continuing breach of covenant and, accordingly, the receipt of rent in the following year will waive the right to forfeit once and for all (cf *Stephens v Junior Army and Navy Stores* [1914] 2 Ch 516: breach of covenant to build by a specified date waived by acceptance of rent after that date). It is usually a matter of practical indifference to the landlord when the tenant redecorates during the term. However, for the purposes of rent review, the building will be hypothetically more easily lettable if it has been recently redecorated. The draftsman should therefore consider linking the years in which the tenant is required to redecorate to the rent review dates. Since the rent review will be conducted on the assumption that the tenant has complied with his covenants, the property will be assumed to have been redecorated whatever the position in reality.

An obligation to decorate 'in the last year of the term' will not oblige the tenant to redecorate if his tenancy comes to a premature end by the service of a break-notice (*Dickinson v St Aubyn* [1944] KB 454) or, it is thought, forfeiture or surrender. It would be otherwise if the obligation was to decorate 'in the last year of the tenancy however determined and in the year preceding any surrender of it'.

It is suggested that many of the problems of the timing of periodical redecoration can be overcome if the tenant covenants to decorate 'as often as is reasonably necessary', or if the landlord wishes to retain greater control, 'as often as in the opinion of the landlord is reasonably necessary but not more often than once in every three years'.

Where the landlord covenants to redecorate and recovers the cost from the tenant by way of service charge, the draftsman should not impose a fixed timetable on him. If a fixed timetable is imposed and not complied with, the tenant may refuse to pay such part of the cost of the redecoration as is attributable to a rise in cost between the time when the redecoration ought to have been carried out and the time when it was in fact carried out. The landlord will be better protected if he covenants to redecorate 'as often as in his opinion is reasonably necessary'.

Example 7:4 Tenant's covenants to repair and decorate

(1) To keep the demised property in good repair

(2) To decorate the demised property in a good and workmanlike manner and with appropriate materials of good quality as often as in the opinion of the landlord is reasonably necessary but not more often than once in every three years and to decorate as aforesaid in the last year of the tenancy however determined and in the year preceding any surrender of it

(3) To permit the landlord and his agents at reasonable times and upon reasonable notice to enter the demised property and to inspect its condition and state of repair

(4) Within forty-two days after the service of a schedule of dilapidations to begin and to proceed expeditiously to comply with the same

(5) If the tenant shall not within forty-two days after the service of such schedule (or immediately in case of need) have begun or be proceeding expeditiously to comply with the same the landlord may

REPAIRS AND IMPROVEMENTS

(without prejudice to his right of re-entry) enter the demised property and execute such works as may be necessary to comply with the schedule and whose cost (including all professional fees and value added tax) shall be a debt payable by the tenant to the landlord on demand and in default shall be recoverable as rent in arrear

Example 7:5 Landlord's restricted power to enter to repair

If the tenant does not within forty-two days after the service of such schedule (or sooner in case of need) have begun or be proceeding expeditiously to comply with it the landlord may:
  (a) enter the demised property and
  (b) carry out works to remedy such of the defects specified in the schedule as have caused or are likely to cause substantial damage to or diminution in value of the landlord's reversion

and the cost of those works (including all professional fees and value added tax associated with them) shall be a debt payable by the tenant to the landlord on demand

Example 7:6 Tenant's covenant to repair and rebuild: insured risks excepted

(1) To keep the demised property in repair

(2) If necessary to rebuild the demised property in accordance with plans and specifications approved by the landlord (such approval not to be unreasonably withheld)

(3) To replace any landlord's fixtures or other plant and machinery which during the term become incapable of economic repair

(4) In the last year of the term to ensure that the electrical system in the demised property complies with the then current regulations of the Institute of Electrical Engineers

(5) The above obligations do not extend to damage by any insured risk save to the extent that the landlord is unable to recover the cost of any necessary works from its insurers

Example 7:7 Tenant's covenant to repair interior

To keep the interior of the demised property (including its windows window frames doors and door frames) in repair

Example 7:8 Tenant's covenant to decorate

(1) In every fifth year of the term and in its last year to decorate the inside of the demised property in a good and workmanlike manner and with appropriate materials of good quality

(2) In every third year of the term and in its last year to decorate the outside of the demised property in a good and workmanlike manner and with appropriate materials of good quality

(3) In the last year of the term the redecoration must be carried out with colours and materials approved by the landlord (such approval not to be unreasonably withheld)

(4) Where decoration involves the redecoration of previously painted surfaces they must be properly prepared and not less than two coats of paint must be applied

Example 7:9 Tenant's covenant to decorate linked to rent review dates

(1) In the six months preceding any rent review date under this lease and in its last year to decorate both the inside and the outside of the demised property in a good and workmanlike manner with materials of good quality

(2) In the last year of the term the redecoration must be carried out in colours approved by the landlord (such approval not to be unreasonably withheld)

(3) Where decoration involves the redecoration of previously painted surfaces they must be properly prepared and not less than two coats of paint must be applied

Example 7:10 Tenant's covenant to inspect

To cause a professional inspection of the demised property (both inside and out) to be carried out at least once a year for the purpose of identifying any defects in it

Example 7:11 Landlord's covenants to repair exterior and to decorate

(1) To keep in repair the roof and loadbearing walls (excluding the windows and doors therein) and main beams of the Building and the common parts of it

(2) To decorate in a good and workmanlike manner and with appropriate materials the exterior and common parts of the Building as often as in the opinion of the landlord is reasonably necessary

Example 7:12 Tenant's covenant to repair (fire damage excepted)

To keep the demised property in good repair (excepting damage caused by fire or any other peril against which the demised property is insured by the landlord under a policy which has not been vitiated by any act or omission of tenant or any person deriving title under him)

Example 7:13 Tenant's covenant to carry out work required by statute etc

To execute all works required by or by virtue of any Act of Parliament or regulation or directive of the European Union or any local or public authority to be done in or in respect of the demised property whether by the landlord or the tenant or any other person (however described)

2 ALTERATIONS AND IMPROVEMENTS

(a) Covenant against alterations

A covenant against 'alterations' is wider than a covenant against 'improvements'. Even minor operations may be caught by a covenant against alterations. On the whole the purpose of the covenant is to ensure that the tenant does not change the nature of the landlord's property or imperil its stability or safety. For that reason the word 'alteration' will usually be construed as meaning something which alters the form or construction of a building (*Bickmore v Dimmer* [1903] 1 Ch 158). Thus, a tenant will be entitled to erect a neon sign advertising his business (*Joseph v LCC* [1914] 111 LT 276). He will also be entitled to replace items of plant (eg air-conditioning equipment) by other items designed to fulfil the same function (*Hagee (London) v Co-operative Insurance Society* [1992] 1 EGLR 57). Where the letting is of a large office, the tenant's adviser should satisfy himself that the covenant permits the erection and removal of internal partitioning. Similarly, the tenant of a shop will require the right to alter the shop front. This may be done by limiting the covenant to alterations to the main structure or by inserting a proviso expressly permitting the work. Alternatively, the form of covenant recommended by the Law Commission may be used; namely, 'not to carry out any alterations or other works of which the actual or probable result is to destroy or alter the character of the property or any part of the property to the detriment of the interest of the landlord therein' (Law Com No 67, p 78).

If the landlord wishes to retain greater control, the draftsman should prohibit 'alterations to the demised property (including alterations to its appearance or lay-out)'. This form of covenant will prohibit such activities as letting a wall for billposting (*Heard v Stuart* (1907) 24 TLR 104). In the case of an actively managed shopping centre, the landlord may well wish to keep greater control over the appearance of the individual units, including their shop fronts and fascias. Often this is done by requiring any alterations to comply with a tenant's handbook which in turn contains detailed rules about materials, dimensions and other such matters.

In older buildings it may be appropriate for the lease to contain a covenant against cutting or maiming the main walls or timbers of the building. This form of covenant will prevent the tenant from attaching substantial fixtures to the building (*LCC v Hutter* [1925] Ch 626) or from notching the joists to receive ductwork (*Hagee (London) v Co-operative Insurance Society* [1992] 1 EGLR 57).

A covenant against alterations may be absolute (ie all alterations are prohibited) or qualified (ie alterations are prohibited except with the consent of the landlord). A common form of covenant is qualified as regards non-structural alterations and absolute as regards structural alterations. Where the covenant is qualified, the consent of the landlord may not be unreasonably withheld if the proposed alteration amounts to an improvement (Landlord and Tenant Act 1927, s 19(2)). If the proposed alteration does not amount to an improvement the landlord may arbitrarily withhold consent unless the lease itself provides that he may not. Whether an alteration amounts to an improvement must be judged from the point of view of the tenant (*Lambert v F W Woolworth & Co Ltd (No 2)* [1938] Ch 883). Surprisingly, 'an alteration may be an improvement although it produces damage or diminution in the value of the premises or does not add to the letting value of the holding so that the mere fact of damage or diminution in the value arising to the premises from their alteration will not of itself prevent the alteration from being an improvement' (*ibid, per* Slesser LJ). If the covenant against alterations is absolute the statutory proviso does not operate. It will, therefore, be in the landlord's interest to insist on an absolute covenant.

Where the lease contains an absolute covenant against alterations, or certain classes of alteration, the question arises whether the landlord has an 'absolute right' to refuse to allow the tenant to carry out alterations (or alterations of the prohibited class). This question is relevant because where the landlord has an 'absolute right' to refuse to allow a variation of the lease, and the lease is in fact varied neither a former tenant nor a guarantor will be liable to pay any amount in respect of the covenant to the extent that the amount is referable to the variation (Landlord and Tenant (Covenants) Act 1995, s 18). In deciding whether the landlord has an absolute right to refuse to allow a variation, regard must be had to the effect of any statute. Part I of the Landlord and Tenant Act 1927 will be of particular relevance in this respect. If the tenant could have obtained a certificate under that Act that the alteration was a proper improvement, then it is considered that the landlord would not have an absolute right to refuse to allow the variation.

(b) Statutory modification of covenants

A number of Acts of Parliament have modified the effect of covenants against alterations and improvements. The most important of them, and the most wide ranging, is the Landlord and Tenant Act 1927.

(i) Landlord and Tenant Act 1927, s 3

Whether a covenant against alterations is absolute or qualified, a tenant of business premises may apply to the court for authority to carry out improvements. The tenant must comply with the procedure laid down in s 3 of the Act, and the landlord is entitled to an opportunity of being heard if he objects.

Having heard all interested persons the court may certify that an improvement is a proper improvement if it is satisfied that the improvement:

(1) is of such a nature as to be calculated to add to the letting value of the holding at the termination of the tenancy; and

(2) is reasonable and suited to the character thereof (taking into account evidence that the improvement will not injure the amenity or convenience of the neighbourhood); and

(3) will not diminish the value of any other property belonging to the same landlord or to any superior landlord from whom he holds directly or indirectly (Landlord and Tenant Act 1927, s 3(1)).

If the court issues a certificate, or if the landlord does not object in time, the tenant is entitled to carry out the improvement notwithstanding any covenant in the lease (Landlord and Tenant Act 1927, s 3(4)). This means that the tenant can carry out the improvement even if there is an absolute covenant against alterations in the lease. Moreover, the tenant's right to carry out alterations despite an absolute covenant is not dependent on the giving of a certificate by the court. If the tenant gives notice to the landlord of his intention to make an improvement and the landlord does not object within three months, the tenant has the right to carry out the improvement. In addition, this right exists not only against the landlord but also against any superior landlord. In most cases the tenant will be entitled to compensation for the improvement on quitting.

(ii) Other Acts

Many other Acts of Parliament empower the court to modify obligations in leases if the effect of the obligation would be to prevent the tenant from carrying out works required by the Act in question. The most important of these in practice are the Fire Precautions Act 1971, the Health and Safety at Work etc Act 1974 and the Building Act 1984. Under the Telecommunications Code the court has extensive powers to override covenants in leases in order to enable telecommunications equipment to be installed (Telecommunications Act 1984, s 96). In addition, where the tenant is granted a waste management licence subject to conditions, and the conditions require him to carry out works or do things which he is not entitled to carry out or do, it is the duty of any person whose consent would be required to enable the conditions to be fulfilled to grant that consent (Environmental Protection Act 1990, s 35(4)). Similar provisions apply where a remediation notice has been served in respect of contaminated land (Environmental Protection Act 1990, s 78G). These provisions also require a person whose consent is required before any thing required by a remediation notice can be done to grant or join in granting such rights in relation to any of the relevant land or waters as will enable the appropriate person to comply with the requirements of the remediation notice. Thus they require the landlord to consent to variations in a lease which have the effect of prohibiting compliance with such conditions.

Another mechanism for overriding covenants against alterations is found in the Disability Discrimination Act 1995. This provides that where an employer or trade organisation is required to make alterations to premises in order to comply with a statutory duty under the Act, and is prohibited from doing so by a covenant, the covenant takes effect as if it provided for the occupier to be entitled to make the alteration with the written consent of the landlord, such consent not to be unreasonably withheld (Disability Discrimination Act 1995, s 16, s 27).

Some works required by statute are required to be carried out by the owner of the property in question, others by the occupier. For this purpose the owner is often defined as the person entitled to receive the rack rent of the property in question. This will usually be the landlord, unless the letting was initially made for a rent less than the rack rent, in which case the owner will be the tenant.

Many such Acts also empower the court to apportion any expenditure on improvements required by the Act in question between persons having an interest in the property in such proportions as is just and equitable. The Building Act 1984, s 102 also requires the court to consider the nature of the work and the benefit of the work to the different persons concerned. Thus, the common covenant by the tenant 'to execute all works required to be carried out by any Act of Parliament whether by the owner or occupier or any other person and to bear the cost of all such works' may be overridden by the court. Indeed it appears that the court has no jurisdiction to entertain an action on the covenant itself (*Horner v Franklin* [1905] 1 KB 479). Nevertheless, such a covenant is a material consideration in the apportionment of expenditure, and it will often persuade the court that the expenditure in question ought to have been in the contemplation of the tenant when he took the lease (*Monro v Burghclere* [1918] 1 KB 291). The draftsman should, therefore, insert such a covenant in the lease for the protection of the landlord. Although the landlord cannot bring an action on the covenant, it may be indirectly enforced through the apportionment mechanism. The tenant can be protected to some degree if the covenant is qualified by the insertion of some financial limit; for example, 'to bear the cost of all such works up to an amount equal to three times the rent payable under this lease at the commencement of such works'. Although the court can override such a financial limit, again it will be material in the apportionment of the expenditure (*Bedford v University College Medical School* (1974) CLY 2063 (county court)).

Where the landlord carries out work required by statute, he too is entitled to apply for an apportionment. Where he incurs costs in carrying out such work which he wishes to recover by way of service charge, it would seem that he cannot do so in the absence of an order from the court apportioning the expenditure.

Where the tenant has covenanted to comply with statutes, and carries out an improvement required by statute the effect on rent of the improvement will not be ignored in determining a new rent on a renewal under the Landlord and Tenant Act 1954 (and often on a rent review). Thus, the imposition on the tenant of an obligation to carry out works required by statute confers a double benefit on the landlord. This may, however, be redressed by the court in the exercise of its discretion to apportion expenditure. Thus the fact that the landlord will derive a rental benefit from the improvement, may be a reason for requiring him to contribute towards the capital cost of the improvement; while the fact that the improvement will be disregarded on review may be a reason for leaving the burden on the tenant.

(c) Initial improvements

At the beginning of the tenancy it is often intended that as part of the bargain between the parties the tenant will carry out improvements to the demised property, often in consideration of a rent-free period. Sometimes the tenant enters into a contractual undertaking to carry out the improvements in question. Whether this is in the interest of either party depends on the circumstances of the case, so the draftsman should not automatically impose on the tenant such an obligation.

The problem arises where the lease is less than fifty years for tax purposes. Where a lease of a duration not exceeding fifty years is granted on terms that the tenant is obliged to carry out any works on the demised property, the landlord is treated as having received a premium equal to the amount by which the value of his reversion immediately after the commencement of the lease exceeds the value it would have had at that time, if the obligation to carry out the work had not been imposed on the tenant (Income and Corporation Taxes Act 1988, s 34). Tax will be charged on a sliding scale, depending on the length of the lease: a reduction of two per cent of the notional premium is made for each full year of the term after the first year. What is taxed is not the cost of the works but the benefit accruing to the landlord as a result of the works. The benefit may accrue on a rent review or at the expiry of the term.

In addition, where the grant of a rent-free period is linked to an obligation by the tenant to carry out work, the rent foregone may be liable to VAT as being a supply by the tenant to the landlord of the rent foregone (*Ridgeons Bulk v Commissioners of Customs & Excise* [1994] STC 427 discussed in [1992] 37 EG 97).

Set against the charge to tax are two advantages to the landlord. First, the tenant is not entitled to claim compensation under Part I of the Landlord and Tenant Act 1927 in respect of improvements that he was obliged to make under a contract made for valuable consideration (1927 Act, s 2(1)(b)). Secondly, on a renewal of his lease under the Landlord and Tenant Act 1954 the tenant will have to pay a rent for the demised property as improved since the court will only disregard voluntary improvements in assessing the rent (1954 Act, s 34(2)). Further, as many rent review clauses follow the form of the Landlord and Tenant Act 1954, s 34, the tenant may pay a higher rent on an intermediate review if an obligation to improve is imposed.

It will usually be better for the tenant if he is not under an express covenant to carry out improvements since he will be entitled to claim compensation for them under the Landlord and Tenant Act 1927 and will not have to pay rent for the demised property as improved. Moreover, the absence of a covenant will minimise the risk of a charge to VAT arising. For the landlord, on the other hand, whether a covenant should be imposed will depend upon the weight of the respective financial burdens that he will have to bear. If an obligation to improve is imposed, the Revenue accept that the landlord will be able to avoid paying tax if, in addition to the covenant to improve, he also imposes on the tenant an obligation to reinstate at the expiry of the term if so required by the landlord (see Aldridge, *Letting Business Premises*, 7th edn (FT Law & Tax, 1996) p 54). The logic of this is hard to see, especially if in consequence of the improvements the landlord is entitled to exact a higher rent from his tenant on a rent review.

(d) Hidden obligations to improve

The tenant's adviser should be on his guard against hidden obligations to improve. Such an obligation usually arises in one of two ways.

First, a covenant to repair may require the covenantor to carry out improvements that are inherent in the particular repair. If, for example, a wall has to be rebuilt and the building regulations for the time being in force require it to be rebuilt with deeper footings the regulations must be complied with even if compliance involves a certain degree of improvement (*Lurcott v Wakely* [1911] 1 KB 905). Equally, if modern building techniques involve a certain degree of improvement such improvement will be included in the obligation to repair (*Ravenseft Properties Ltd v Davstone (Holdings) Ltd* [1979] 1 All ER 929). It appears that nothing can be done to avoid these obligations.

Secondly, a covenant to comply with Acts of Parliament may impose on the covenantor an obligation to carry out statutory improvements; for example, the installation of fire-resisting doors. If such a covenant is included in the lease, the tenant's adviser should check that the relevant statutes contain a power for the court to apportion expenditure required thereby between the landlord and the tenant. In some cases no such power exists (for example, works required to be carried out to hotels and boarding houses by the Fire Precautions Act 1971). In any event the tenant's adviser should press for the effect of such works to be disregarded in assessing the rent on a review.

Alternatively, the tenant's adviser may seek to limit the tenant's liability, either by reference to a financial limit or to a category of work. Examples are given below.

(e) Environmental matters

The control of pollution has become of great concern in recent years, particularly with respect to industrial processes. Greater enforcement powers have been conferred on the regulatory authorities (eg local authorities, the National Rivers Authority, HM Inspectorate of Pollution and, most recently, the Environment Agency). Enforcement powers may now require the carrying out of extensive work in order to prevent pollution or to deal with the effect of past pollution. These powers are contained in Part IIA of the Environmental Protection Act 1990 (inserted by the Environment Act 1995, s 57). In addition, conditions attached to licences (eg waste management licences) may require the carrying out of works even after waste disposal has ceased (Environmental Protection Act 1990, s 35(3)). A waste management licence is not required where the deposit of waste takes place on the premises on which it is produced, pending its disposal elsewhere, unless the presence of the waste is likely to give rise to an environmental hazard (Collection and Disposal of Waste Regulations 1988 (SI No 819) reg 9, Sched 6, para 14; Controlled Waste Regulations 1992 (SI No 588) reg 9). Thus no licence is required for waste placed outside a factory or workshop pending its removal.

The enforcement authorities may recover costs incurred in dealing with concentrations of noxious gas or liquids emanating from closed landfills from the owner of the land (Environmental Protection Act 1990, s 61) or works to prevent or remedy pollution of controlled waters (including groundwater) (Water Resources Act 1991).

But even in the absence of such powers, the landlord will wish to be protected against the effect of pollution and contamination of his property. In an extreme case the contamination of property with the waste products of an industrial process may result in the building having to be pulled down and the subsoil excavated and carted away. The traditional repairing obligation is not wholly adequate to deal with this problem, and in any case what is required may be alteration or even improvement. In cases of industrial property the covenant to comply with statutes should refer expressly to the Environmental Protection Act 1990 (which deals with contamination and pollution) and also to the Water Resources Act 1991 (which deals with discharge of effluent). The problems of leakage of potentially contaminative substances is not confined to industrial property. For example a dry cleaner will use chemicals which could cause problems of pollution if they escape into the aquifer. Similar problems might arise in the case of a warehouse storing chemicals or a DIY retail outlet selling paint and solvents. In addition, the draftsman should seek to impose on the tenant an obligation at the end of the term to yield up the demised property in a state which will enable

REPAIRS AND IMPROVEMENTS

it to be lawfully and immediately used for industrial purposes without expenditure on works. The tenant may resist such an obligation or at least qualify it so that it only applies where the unfitness arises out of the tenant's activities during the term. In some cases the conditions attached to a licence may not be capable of being performed at the expiry of the lease (eg methane gas may require to be burned off a landfill site for many years, or safety precautions may be required to be kept in place). In such a case the landlord should seek to require the tenant to provide security for the expenditure involved in compliance with such conditions.

Where the building has previously been used for industrial purposes, the incoming tenant may inherit a liability for pollution or contamination which arose during the time of a previous occupier. Ideally the tenant's adviser should secure a warranty from the landlord that at the date of the lease the property is fit for use for industrial purposes without expenditure on works. But most landlords will be unwilling to give such a warranty. In such a case the tenant's adviser should seek to exclude liability for dealing with such pollution or contamination from the tenant's covenants. He may also consider pressing for a tenant's break-clause exercisable in the event that statutory liability is imposed on the tenant over a stated amount (eg three times the annual rent).

Example 7:14 Tenant's covenant against alterations

(1) Not without the consent in writing of the landlord to make any alteration or addition to the demised property

(2) Upon each application for such consent to supply the landlord with drawings and specifications of each proposed alteration or addition for approval by him

(3) Not to carry out any works to which the landlord has consented save in accordance with drawings and specifications approved as aforesaid

(4) Before beginning any approved works to enter into such covenant with the landlord relating to the reinstatement of the demised property as the landlord may reasonably require

Example 7:15 Tenant's covenant against structural alterations; qualified covenant against non-structural alterations

(1) Not to make any structural alteration or addition to the demised property

(2) Not to unite the demised property with any other property

(3) Not without the landlord's written consent (such consent not to be unreasonably withheld) to carry out any non-structural alteration

(4) A non-structural alteration is one which:
(a) does not affect any loadbearing part of the demised property or consists of alterations to the electrical system or to service pipes or other conducting media or consists of the installation or removal of demountable partitioning; and
(b) is carried out in accordance with plans and specifications previously approved in writing by the landlord
(5) To carry out any approved non-structural alteration:
(a) in a good and workmanlike manner
(b) with materials of good quality and
(c) to the reasonable satisfaction of the landlord
(6) On demand to remove any alteration which:
(a) has not been approved in writing by the landlord or
(b) is required to be removed by any legislation or
(c) is required to be removed by the terms of any consent to the making of that alteration

and in any such case to make good all damage caused either by the alteration or by its removal or reinstatement

Example 7:16 Tenant's covenant relating to statutes

To comply with all present and future Acts of Parliament and subordinate legislation made thereunder relating to the demised property or the use of it and to execute at his own expense any work required to be carried out in the demised property whether such work is required to be carried out by the owner or the occupier or any other person

Example 7:17 Proviso limiting tenant's liability

Provided that this covenant shall not require the tenant to expend in any period of twelve months an amount greater than three times the amount of the annual rent then payable under this lease

Example 7:18 Alternative proviso limiting tenant's liability

Provided that this covenant shall not impose upon the tenant any liability to carry out work which is not fairly described as work of repair

Example 7:19 Tenant's covenant to carry out improvements

(1) To carry out in a good and workmanlike manner the works described in the plans and specifications approved by the landlord and attached hereto within [   ] months from the date of this lease or such further period as the landlord may allow in writing
(2) If so required by the landlord to reinstate the demised property to the state in which it now is on the expiry or sooner determination of this lease

Example 7:20 Tenant's covenant to yield up in a fit state

At the expiry or sooner determination of the term to yield up the demised property:
    (1) in repair and
    (2) free from contamination by substances potentially harmful to:
    (a) humans or
    (b) the environment or
    (c) the demised property and
    (3) in such a physical condition as will enable it to be used for industrial purposes without expenditure on works

Example 7:21 Covenant by tenant to give security for compliance with conditions

(1) In any case where:
- (a) the carrying on of any activity on the demised property is lawful by reason only of the grant of a permission licence or authorisation under environmental or planning legislation and
- (b) the permission licence or authorisation imposes conditions in connection with the carrying on of those activities (whether or not those conditions fall to be performed after the end of the term or after those activities have ceased) and
- (c) fulfilment of those conditions after the expiry or sooner determination of the term would fall to be undertaken by the landlord or a person (other than the tenant) deriving title under him

the tenant shall:
- (a) indemnify the landlord against any loss damage cost or expenditure incurred or suffered in connection with compliance with those conditions and
- (b) on demand (whether made before or after the expiry or sooner determination of the term) provide security in such form as the landlord may reasonably require for the estimated cost of complying with those conditions

(2)
- (a) 'Environmental legislation' means the Environmental Protection Act 1990 the Water Resources Act 1991 the Water Industry Act 1991 the Environment Act 1995 and any other legislation relating to the control of pollution or the protection of the environment
- (b) 'Planning legislation' means the Planning Acts 1990 and any other legislation relating to town and country planning or the control of development
- (c) 'Legislation' includes Acts of Parliament and regulations made under them and also regulations and directives of the European Union

8

Use of the Demised Property

1 Warranties as to Fitness for Use

Generally, there is no implied covenant or warranty by the landlord that the demised property is legally or physically fit for the use that the tenant proposes to make of it, even if the lease itself contains restrictive use covenants (*Hill v Harris* [1965] 2 QB 601). It is, therefore, incumbent on the tenant to ensure that his use of the property will be lawful both in terms of planning control and in terms of any restrictions imposed by a lease under which his landlord or any superior landlord holds, or any restrictive covenants that bind the land. An undertenant should call for his landlord's title to be produced in all but the most straightforward case, even if he is not strictly entitled to it (under the Law of Property Act 1925, s 44). Many landlords will co-operate with a tenant but a recalcitrant landlord should be asked for a warranty that the tenant's proposed use will be lawful. If all else fails, a tenant may still be able to sue his landlord for negligent misrepresentation (*Esso Petroleum Co Ltd v Mardon* [1976] QB 801: misrepresentation as to earning potential of petrol filling station); and it may be that the mere description of property (as, for example, 'offices') is of itself a representation that the property may lawfully be used as such during the term of the lease (*Laurence v Lexcourt Holdings Ltd* [1978] 2 All ER 810).

Express warranties by landlords that the property is fit for use are unknown in the current market. However, the problems of contamination and industrial pollution are likely to become of increasing importance in the future. In cases where the tenant is proposing to take a lease of property which has previously been used for industrial purposes, he should consider requiring the landlord to warrant either that the building is fit for use or that no work is required as at the date of the lease in order to deal with historic contamination or pollution.

2 Town and Country Planning Act 1990

The Town and Country Planning Act 1990 and the Orders made under it place statutory limits on the use that may be made of property and the operations that may be carried out on it. It is, nevertheless, common in leases for the tenant to covenant with the landlord to comply with the Town and Country Planning Act and not to apply for planning permission without the landlord's consent. Both of these covenants are important to the landlord and the draftsman should not lightly omit them. If the tenant commits a breach of planning control and the local planning authority decides to take enforcement proceedings, the enforcement notice will be served on the 'owner' of the land in question and any other person having an interest in that land (Town and Country Planning Act 1990, s 172(4), s 336(1)); that is, it will be served on the landlord. If the landlord falls within the statutory definition of 'owner' (ie the letting was originally at a rack rent (Town and Country Planning Act 1990, s 336(1); *Borthwick-Norton v Collier* [1950] 2 KB 594) he may be liable to prosecution if the notice is not complied with (Town and Country Planning Act 1990, s 179(1)). A covenant prohibiting a breach of planning control by the tenant adds the weapon of forfeiture to the landlord's armoury and may protect him against a prosecution.

The covenant prohibiting the tenant from applying for planning permission without the landlord's consent is equally important. If it is not included the tenant may lawfully change the use of the demised property, or carry out operations on it, although the landlord would have the opportunity of making representations to the local planning authority if he objected to the application. Such activity by the tenant may prove very detrimental to the landlord because a change of use by the tenant may result in the abandonment of an existing use, so that planning permission might be necessary to revert to that use.

In addition the landlord should have control over the entry into any agreement under s 106 of the Town and Country Planning Act 1990 and should prohibit the giving by the tenant of any unilateral undertaking under that section.

If the tenant applies for planning permission with the landlord's consent, he may be granted planning permission for a limited period (Town and Country Planning Act 1990, s 72(1)(b)). In such a case the permission will often be subject to a condition that the land to which it relates be reinstated at the expiry of the permission. In the absence of any specific provision in the lease, if the lease expired before the planning permission the tenant would be entitled to vacate, leaving the landlord to comply with the planning conditions. Accordingly, the draftsman should impose on the tenant an obligation to carry out any works required by planning permission before the expiry of the lease. In addition, the draftsman may consider requiring the tenant to give security for performance of this obligation and for such security to be provided before the planning permission is implemented. Security could be provided by the deposit of cash in a joint account or by the provision of a bond. The tenant's adviser should seek to limit an obligation to carry out works required by planning conditions to those required by permissions granted during the term.

Clearly, the tenant's obligations will be very different in the case of a lease under which the tenant is to carry out substantial improvements to the demised property. It would be inappropriate in such a lease for the tenant to covenant not to carry out development on the demised property, or even not to carry out material development thereon. Nevertheless, it is suggested that the draftsman should restrict the tenant's right to carry out development on the demised property as much as is consistent with the intention of the parties.

Some leases require the tenant not to make an application for an established use certificate without the landlord's consent. The reason behind the covenant was to prevent previous use rights from being lost and replaced with an established use. An established use was one which was immune from enforcement proceedings but was not lawful. Now, however, once the time for taking enforcement action has passed a use becomes lawful (Town and Country Planning Act 1990, s 191(2)) and an application for a certificate of lawfulness may be made (s 192). The danger of an anomalous position arising is therefore lessened. Nevertheless, the landlord may have a legitimate interest in ensuring that he keeps control over changes of use under the Planning Acts, since such changes may have repercussions beyond the term of the lease.

Example 8:1 Tenant's covenant relating to planning and development

(1) Not to commit any breach of planning control

(2) Not without the consent in writing of the landlord (such consent not to be unreasonably withheld):

(a) to apply for planning permission to carry out any development in or upon the demised property and in any event to supply to the landlord a copy of any application for planning permission together with such plans and other documents as the landlord may reasonably require and to supply to the landlord a copy of any planning permission granted to the tenant or

(b) to enter into any binding agreement with the local planning authority or to give any legally binding unilateral undertaking to such an authority

(3) To pay and satisfy any charge that may be imposed upon any breach by the tenant of planning control or otherwise under the Town and Country Planning Act 1990

(4) Unless the landlord shall otherwise direct to carry out before the expiry or sooner determination of this lease any works required to be carried out to or upon the demised property as a condition of any planning permission which may have been granted during the term of this lease irrespective of the date before which such works were thereby required to be carried out

(5) Expressions used in this clause shall be construed in accordance with the Town and Country Planning Act 1990

3 Absolute and Qualified Restrictions on Use

A restriction on the use of property may be absolute or subject to the proviso that the use may not be changed without the landlord's consent. In either case the landlord may withhold his consent arbitrarily (*Guardian Assurance Co Ltd v Gants Hill Holdings Ltd* (1983) 267 EG 678; *Pearl Assurance plc v Shaw* [1985] 1 EGLR 92). Accordingly, the tenant's adviser should insert a requirement that consent is not to be unreasonably withheld. If the restriction is not absolute the landlord is prohibited by statute from demanding a fine or premium as a condition of consent to a change of use (Landlord and Tenant Act 1927, s 19(3)). The fine or premium may not be disguised as increased rent or as the introduction of a landlord's break-clause (*Barclays Bank v Daejan Investments (Grove Hall)* [1995] 18 EG 117). However, the landlord will still be entitled to require the payment of expenses incurred in connection with consent to a change of use and a reasonable sum in respect of any damage to or diminution in the value of the demised property or any neighbouring property that belongs to him. If the change of use would involve structural alterations to the property the statute does not apply, and the landlord is free to demand a fine or premium (or increased rent) as a condition of consent to the change of use. A change of use 'involves' a structural alteration if the alteration is included in the proposed change of use even if it is not necessary to enable that change to take place (*Barclays Bank v Daejan Investments (Grove Hall)* above). In practice there are very few changes of use which do not involve some alterations. It then becomes a matter of debate whether or not they are structural. If the tenant wishes to protect himself against such a demand he must stipulate for an express provision that no fine or premium (or increased rent) will be demanded as a condition of consent to a change of use. It is, however, unlikely that a well-advised landlord would agree to such a provision.

Where the lease contains a covenant against changes of use without the landlord's consent, but does not state expressly that the landlord's consent is not to be unreasonably withheld, the question arises whether the landlord has an 'absolute right' to refuse to allow the change. The relevance of this is that if the landlord does have an absolute right to refuse to allow the change, but nevertheless allows it, a former tenant or guarantor will not be liable to pay any amount in respect of the covenant to the extent that the amount is referable to the variation (Landlord and Tenant (Covenants) Act 1995, s 18). In deciding whether the landlord has an absolute right to refuse to allow a variation, regard must be had to statutory provisions. Bearing in mind that, unless the change of use involves structural alterations, the landlord cannot charge a fine or premium as the price of consent, it is considered that he does not have an absolute right to refuse. Moreover, it is arguable that where the covenant contemplates that consent might be given, and it is in fact given, there is no variation of the lease at all (compare *Forte & Co v General Accident Life Assurance Co* [1986] 2 EGLR 115).

It will usually be in the interests of the landlord if the use of the demised property is capable of being changed with his consent because a greater rent will be payable on a rent review or under a new tenancy granted by the court (see *Plinth Property Investments Ltd v Mott, Hay & Anderson* (1978) 249 EG 1167, where the rent would have been fifty per cent higher if the use of the property had been capable of being changed). Nevertheless, the landlord may wish to impose limits on the extent to which the use can be changed in order to avoid the impact of the Town and Country Planning Act 1990 or for reasons of estate management. One problem, however, is that 'good estate management' is a phrase of no fixed meaning. In order to meet this difficulty the draftsman should consider framing a hybrid covenant which permits changes of use within absolute limits.

One possible compromise is for the clause to prohibit changes of use without the landlord's consent, but not to go on to provide that the landlord's consent may not be unreasonably withheld. This will preclude the landlord from charging a premium for consent to a change of use, but will not be as damaging on the rent review as an absolute covenant (*Forte & Co Ltd v General Accident Life Assurance Co Ltd* [1986] 2 EGLR 115).

Where the clause contemplates that the landlord may consent to a change of use, it is implicit that he will only do so at the request of the tenant (*C & A Pension Trustees Ltd v British Vita Investments Ltd* (1984) 272 EG 63). Thus the landlord will not be able unilaterally to widen the use covenant in order to increase the rent. However, for the purposes of rent review, the question will not usually be whether the landlord has actually permitted a wider use, but what prospects the hypothetical tenant would perceive of obtaining consent to a change (*Tea Trade Properties v CIN Properties* [1990] 1 EGLR 155).

Some landlords of shopping centres wish to maintain tight control over the permitted use of the trading units, but nevertheless to avoid any diminution in the rental income. The dual objective may be achieved by including in the rent review clause an assumption that the hypothetical lease contains a wider use clause than the actual lease. But since this requires the tenant to pay for a freedom which he has not got, the tenant should not accept an artificial assumption about the permitted use.

Example 8:2 Hybrid use covenant

> The demised property shall not be used otherwise than as a shop nor without the landlord's consent in writing (such consent not to be unreasonably withheld) otherwise than for the sale of [   ]

Example 8:3 Hybrid use covenant

> Not to use the demised property except as a shop for the sale of [   ] or for such other goods (not being goods which in the opinion of the landlord would be detrimental to the proper management of the centre) as the landlord may approve in writing

4 Negative and Positive Obligations

A tenant's use covenant is usually negative in form (ie 'not to use the demised property otherwise than as ...'). This form of covenant effectively prevents the tenant from carrying on the prohibited use. However, it does not impose on him a positive obligation to use the property for any particular use, or indeed at all. Thus, the landlord will have no remedy against the tenant if he allows the property to remain empty. In normal circumstances this will not concern the landlord, at all events if the tenant remains able to pay the rent; but there are cases in which the interest of the landlord may be seriously affected if the property is unused for business purposes.

First, a positive obligation to use the property for business purposes may help the landlord to prevent a business letting from turning into an assured tenancy. A tenancy cannot be an assured tenancy if it is one to which Part II of the Landlord and Tenant Act 1954 applies (Housing Act 1988, Sched 1, para 4). It has been held, however, that where a tenancy has once been a tenancy to which Part II of the 1954 Act applies, it does not cease to be such a tenancy even if the tenant gives up business occupation (*Esselte v Pearl Assurance* [1995] 37 EG 173). If this is correct, a positive covenant is of diminished importance from this point of view.

Secondly, in the case of a shopping centre, an empty unit may have a significant effect on the rental value of other units in the centre, as the traders are reliant on a high pedestrian flow. Thus the landlord may find himself penalised upon his rent review. Until recently it was the practice of the court in England to refuse an injunction to compel the tenant to carry on trading (*Braddon Towers Ltd v International Stores Ltd* [1987] 1 EGLR 209), although the position was different in Scotland where the equivalent of an injunction had been granted to compel a bank to trade (*Retail Parks Investments v Royal Bank of Scotland* (1995) *The Times*, 18 July). But the Court of Appeal has recently reconsidered this practice and has decided (by a majority) that an injunction will be granted in an appropriate case to compel a tenant to keep open (*Co-operative Insurance Society v Argyll Stores (Holdings)* [1996] 09 EG 128). The real possibility that an injunction may be granted may expose the tenant to a liability either to trade into insolvency or to suffer punishment for contempt of court. This makes a positive covenant extremely dangerous from the tenant's point of view. The landlord may find the danger reflected in the rent obtainable on review. But even if an injunction is unobtainable, a positive obligation will give the landlord a remedy in damages (*Costain Property Development Ltd v Finlay & Co Ltd* [1989] 1 EGLR 237; *Transworld Land Co v J Sainsbury* [1990] 2 EGLR 255). If required to enter into a positive covenant the tenant's adviser should ensure that no breach is caused if the unit is closed for repairs, refitting, stocktaking and the like. Where a positive use covenant is imposed on a retailer, it is often argued that this depresses the rent on rent review. In the case of a shopping centre, however, this should not unduly concern the landlord if the rental comparables will themselves come from the centre and are themselves let on similar terms. Moreover, it may fairly be said that in such a case all tenants benefit from the fact that their fellow traders can be compelled to keep open (see *Boots the Chemist v Pinkland* [1992] 28 EG 118).

USE OF THE DEMISED PROPERTY

Thirdly, in the case of industrial buildings, the landlord may be entitled to capital allowances on the cost of constructing the building. But capital allowances may be lost and a balancing charge may become payable if the building ceases to be used for a purpose qualifying for capital allowances (Capital Allowances Act 1990, s 4). Similar considerations apply to buildings in enterprise zones and to hotels (Capital Allowances Act 1990, s 6, s 7). However, temporary disuse will not bring these provisions into play (Capital Allowances Act 1990, s 15).

Fourthly, under the (now repealed) provisions relating to rating surcharge on unused commercial property, the person entitled to occupy the property became liable to pay a rating surcharge after the property had been unoccupied for more than six months (General Rate Act 1967, s 17A; suspended by the Rating Surcharge (Suspension) Order 1980 (SI No 2015)). Under those provisions, if the occupier failed to pay the surcharge, the rating authority was entitled to register a local land charge for the amount due. When registered, the charge bound not only the occupier's interest but also the landlord's reversion (*Westminster CC v Haymarket Publishing Ltd* [1980] 1 All ER 289). If a surcharge is ever brought back into force, a positive obligation will enable the landlord to forfeit the lease before any liability to pay the surcharge arises.

Where the parties have agreed on a positive use covenant, the obligation to trade must be clearly expressed. The court sometimes holds that what appears on the face of it to be a positive obligation is in fact no more than an 'emphatic negative' (*Tea Trade Properties v CIN Properties* [1990] 1 EGLR 155; *JT Sydenham v Enichem Elastomers* [1989] 1 EGLR 257; *Montross Associated Investments v Moussaieff* [1990] 2 EGLR 61). The draftsman should therefore use an expression such as 'to keep the demised property open for trading during normal business hours'.

The tenant must consider what his position is on Sunday trading. Sunday trading is now permitted (Sunday Trading Act 1994). A covenant made before 26 August 1994 which requires the tenant to keep open during normal business hours will not compel him to open on Sundays unless it refers specifically to Sundays. However, this does not apply to covenants entered into or varied after that date. Accordingly normal business hours may now include Sundays. If this is undesirable from the tenant's point of view, Sunday should be excepted from the positive covenant.

Example 8:4 Positive covenant: business use only

(1) To use and occupy the demised property for the purpose of the

tenant's business of the sale of [ ] or such other business as may be approved in writing by the landlord and not to use the demised property for any other purpose

(2) To keep the demised property open for business during normal business hours

Example 8:5 Tenant's proviso to keep open covenant

Provided that:
(1) this covenant shall not apply to Sundays
(2) the tenant is entitled, notwithstanding this covenant:
(a) to close the demised premises for reasonable annual holidays
(b) to cease to trade if and so long as the tenant requires to carry out repairs or alterations to the demised property which would be substantially more expensive or cause substantially more inconvenience if carried out while the demised property remained open for trading and is carrying out such repairs or alterations with all reasonable speed
(c) to cease to trade for not more than one month on the occasion of the assignment or subletting of the demised property (in either case to a person approved by the landlord)
(d) to cease to trade if unconditionally required to do so by any regulation or requirement of any competent authority and for as long as an unconditional prohibition on trading remains in force
(e) to cease to trade if and so long as physically prevented from trading by damage caused by an insured risk

Example 8:6 Positive covenant: mixed use

to use and occupy the demised property (as to the ground floor and basement) for the sole purpose of the tenant's business of [ ] or such other business as may be approved in writing by the landlord and not to permit any person to sleep or reside there and (as to the upper floors) solely as the residence of the tenant and his household or of a person employed by the tenant and required by the tenant to reside there for the better performance of his duties

5 Defining the Permitted Use

In defining the permitted use a great responsibility rests on the tenant's adviser because in most cases the tenant will know with more precision than the landlord what use is intended to be made of the property. The concern of the tenant's adviser is to ensure that the use covenant is sufficiently wide to enable the tenant to carry on his business (taking into account possible changes in the range of the business or the manner in which it is carried on) and to be able to dispose of the lease if necessary or, if the tenant is an investor rather than an occupying tenant, sufficiently wide to enable him to grant occupation leases to a wide class of potential occupiers. If the use covenant is too narrow the tenant's beneficial enjoyment of the property may be hampered, but on the other hand if it is too wide the tenant may be liable to pay a higher rent when the rent is reviewed. It is, as so often, a question of balance. The concern of the landlord will usually be to maximise the earning potential of the demised property while at the same time protecting himself against possible liability to others; and, if he is also interested in other property, protecting the earning potential of that other property. The use covenant should be drawn with those ends in mind.

The permitted use may be defined in various ways. First, it may be described by the name of the business which the tenant is to carry on (eg 'the business of a butcher' or 'solicitors' offices'). It will be a question of fact what is included in the permitted use, but it should be noted that the scope of the permitted use will be fixed by reference to the meaning of the description at the time of the demise (see eg *St Marylebone Property Co Ltd v Tesco Stores Ltd* [1988] 27 EG 72 although the point was reserved by Balcombe LJ in *Basildon Development Corporation v Mactro Ltd* [1986] 1 EGLR 137 at 139H). Thus, if the scope of the permitted business changes during the term of the lease it may be that the change will not be permitted under the lease. It is suggested that this difficulty may be overcome by framing the covenant to include a proviso that the permitted use shall extend to such trade or business as is from time to time usually carried on by persons on the named business. This would not however entitle the tenant to use the property for a business which had superseded the named business. Thus a covenant not to use the property otherwise than for the business of a blacksmith would not entitle the tenant to use the property as a motor repair workshop (*St Marylebone Property Co Ltd v Tesco Stores Ltd*).

Secondly, the use may be defined by reference to an existing statutory definition; for example, a definition in the Town and Country Planning (Use Classes) Order 1987 (SI No 764). The advantage of such definition is that a greater flexibility is given to the tenant while at the same time the landlord is able to prevent the development of the demised property. This form of definition is particularly useful where the landlord is not interested in other property and is not, therefore, concerned to prevent competition between his tenants. The draftsman should, however, make it clear whether the permitted use is to be restricted to the use class as defined by the Use Classes Order in force at the time of the demise (*Brewers Company v Viewplan* [1989] 2 EGLR 133) or whether it is capable of change if amendments are made to the order during the term.

Thirdly, the permitted use may be defined by enumerating the various activities to be carried on in the demised property. This form of definition is more suitable to lettings of shops than other business lettings, although it can be used for lettings of factories. The characteristic of this form of definition is that it regulates the use of the property with more certainty (eg 'the sale of raw meat poultry rabbits and game' rather than 'the business of a butcher'). If the landlord wishes to retain strict control over his tenant (as, for example, in a shopping development) this form of definition has much to recommend it. However, the tenant's adviser will in such a case need to take more detailed instructions as to the nature of the business the tenant proposes to carry on. If this form of definition is chosen it should be coupled with the ability to extend the permitted activities with the landlord's consent in order to accommodate unforeseen changes in the business. The draftsman adopting this form of clause should ensure that the landlord's rent will not be adversely affected on review.

Sometimes the permitted use is defined as 'the tenant's business of ...'. This form of definition will restrict the use of the property to the carrying on of a business by the tenant himself and will not permit it to be used for the carrying on of the same business if it is carried on by someone who is not the tenant (compare *Cramas Properties Ltd v Connaught Fur Trimmings Ltd* [1965] 2 All ER 382) unless the expression 'tenant' is itself widely defined. This form of definition may be unobjectionable in a short occupation lease where subletting is absolutely prohibited; but in another case its effect might be to destroy the value of the tenant's right to sublet since, because a subtenant is not a tenant, the consent of the landlord to a change of use would have to be obtained on any subletting.

From time to time the description of the permitted trade is prefaced with the epithet 'high class'. It has been suggested that this phrase is incapable of definition, but that it is possible to categorise an establishment as one which is not high class (*Rossi v Hestdrive Ltd* [1985] 1 EGLR 50 (provision of takeaway food not inconsistent with high class licensed restaurant)). However it has also been suggested that 'high class' means 'rather much better than average' or 'very much better than average' (*Patoner Ltd v Lowe* [1985] 2 EGLR 154 *per* Russell J at 156L); and that a 'high class' business is one which is respectable (*Ropemaker*

Properties v Noonhaven [1989] 2 EGLR 50). In view of the uncertainty, such phrases are probably best avoided.

6 Widening a Prohibition

A prohibition on a specified use of property can take one of four forms, which are listed below in ascending order of severity:
(1) 'not to use the demised property otherwise than as'
(2) 'not to use or permit the demised property to be used otherwise than as'
(3) 'not to use or permit or suffer the demised property to be used otherwise than as'
(4) 'the demised property shall not be used otherwise than as'.

Form (1) will effectively prohibit the tenant himself from using the demised property for the specified use, but it will not affect the activities of any subtenant or licensee of his. Form (2) extends the provision wider. The word 'permit' means one of two things: either to give leave for an act that could not be legally done without that leave; or, to abstain from taking reasonable steps to prevent the act where it is within a man's power to prevent it (*Berton v Alliance Economic Investment Co Ltd* [1922] 1 KB 742 *per* Atkin LJ). Form (3) goes wider still. The word 'suffer' is wider than the word 'permit' (*Barton v Reed* [1932] 1 Ch 362), although it is far from clear how much wider. Finally, form (4) is an absolute prohibition. A covenant that something shall not be done on demised property may be broken by an event over which the tenant has no control (*Prothero v Bell* (1906) 22 TLR 370).

7 Restrictions on Competition

Either the landlord or the tenant may wish to restrict the other's right to carry on, or to permit someone else to carry on, a competitive business. If so, it must be done expressly. In the absence of express provision the landlord will be entitled to let property next door to the demised property to a trade rival of the tenant even if the profitability of the tenant's business is thereby reduced (*Port v Griffith* [1938] 1 All ER 295). If the tenant has sufficient bargaining strength he may insist on the landlord entering into a covenant restricting his ability to deal with other property owned by him. Commonly, such a restriction takes the form of a covenant by the landlord 'not to let' adjoining property for the purposes of the tenant's business. Such a covenant will be narrowly construed.

'A covenant not to let other premises for the purpose of trade A does not prohibit a letting for trade B unless the carrying on of trade B can fairly be said to be, or to include, the carrying on of trade A, or, perhaps, a substantial part of it. In deciding this, what matters is the substance: it is not enough merely to establish that there is a minor degree of identity between the types of articles sold in the two trades' (*Rother v Colchester Corporation* [1969] 2 All ER 600 *per* Megarry J). Moreover, 'a covenant not to let premises for a particular purpose is not broken by the use of the premises for that purpose if the lessor has inserted in the lease a prohibition wide enough to prohibit the use. "Not to let" and "not to permit the use" are two different concepts' (*ibid*). The tenant will, therefore, be better protected if the restriction imposed on the landlord is in the form that adjoining property 'shall not be used' for the purpose of the specified business. In an extreme case an agreement by a landlord which restricted his erstwhile ability to let property as he pleased might be void unless registered under the Restrictive Trade Practices Act 1956 (see *Ravenseft Properties Ltd v Director-General of Fair Trading* [1977] 1 All ER 47).

Sometimes the landlord is willing to enter into a restriction on letting where the restriction only applies while the original tenant remains in occupation. Another variant is for the landlord to restrict initial lettings in a shopping centre. These types of restrictions protect the tenant while a shopping centre gets up and running, but leaves the landlord with flexibility in the longer term.

Where the landlord gives a covenant restrictive of the use of land, it is enforceable not only against an assignee, but also against any other person who is the owner or occupier of any demised premises to which the covenant relates, even though there is no express provision in the tenancy to that effect (Landlord and Tenant (Covenants) Act 1995, s 3(5)). It is not possible to contract out of this (s 25).

In defining a prohibited use it should be noted that a covenant prohibiting the carrying on of a specified business will not prohibit the carrying on of a business that overlaps with the specified business to a minor degree (*Lewis (A) & Co (Westminster) Ltd v Bell Property Trust Ltd* [1940] Ch 345). Moreover, it has been held that an obligation not to carry on a particular business is not an obligation not to carry on part of that business (*Stuart v Diplock* (1889) 43 ChD 343).

Example 8:7 Covenant by landlord

That no part of the Shopping Centre shall be used for the purposes of the business of a [   ] or for any other business which is likely substantially to compete with the business lawfully carried on in the demised property

Example 8:8 Covenant by tenant

That the demised property shall not be used for the purpose of the business of [   ] or for the sale by way of trade or business of any of the following articles namely

8 COVENANTS ANCILLARY TO USE

In addition to the principal use covenant it is likely that a number of ancillary covenants will be necessary.

(a) Illegal and immoral use

It seems that there is no implied obligation on the tenant not to use the demised property for an illegal purpose, and it has been held that there is no implied obligation against immoral use (*Burfort Financial Investments Ltd v Chotard* (1976) 239 EG 891: property in Soho used for prostitution). Accordingly, the draftsman should always include such a covenant in the lease. A covenant against immoral use will be construed as prohibiting the kind of conduct that the great majority of people in this country would condemn as being immoral (*London Scottish Properties Ltd v Mehmet* (1970) 214 EG 837). It should be noted that if the tenant is convicted of keeping a brothel the landlord may require him to assign the lease to a person approved by him, and in default thereof, within three months the court that convicted the tenant may make a summary order for possession (Sexual Offences Act 1956, s 35(2) and Sched 1).

(b) Licensing requirements

In many cases the carrying on of a business in property may not be lawfully done without a licence. An extensive list of such businesses will be found in Aldridge, *Letting Business Premises*, 7th edn (FT Law & Tax, 1996) pp 39–43. The loss of such a licence may be very serious. Accordingly, the tenant should be required to covenant to do all things necessary to maintain, and from time to time to renew, the licence and to comply with all requirements of the licensing authority. In addition, the draftsman should also consider whether the loss of the licence is a risk against which the tenant ought to be obliged to insure. Special considerations affect property licensed for the sale of intoxicating liquor. The tenant should be required to conduct the business in an orderly manner and to transfer the licence to any assignee and, on termination of the lease, to the landlord's nominee. He should also be required to comply with any undertakings given to the licensing justices, and with any conditions attached to the licence. Example 8:12 and Form 12 below contain covenants appropriate to licensed property.

Where the property is a public house which is to be a tied house there are additional factors which must be considered. First, the lease must comply with the Supply of Beer (Tied Estate) Order 1989 (SI No 2390). This states that where a lease of licensed premises is granted by a brewer holding more than 2,000 licensed premises (or a company within the same group) and the lease is a lease of a tied house:

(1) the lease cannot impose repairing obligations on the brewer or a group company; and
(2) the rent must be the market rent which would have been obtained on a letting by a landlord who was not a brewer or a member of a brewery group (arts 5, 6).

In practice, this means that the lease will impose full repairing obligations on the tenant. These provisions do not apply to licensed premises which are a notified tied house (ie notified to the Director-General of Fair Trading). Secondly, the products which are subject to the tie must be specifically stated and must be limited to beer, otherwise the tie will fall outside the Regulation (EEC) 1983/84 and may be void under Article 85 of the EC Treaty. Thirdly, the tie must confer 'special benefits' on the tenant otherwise it may be void under Article 85. A discount on normal selling prices of beer would be a special benefit for this purpose. In view of recital 13 to Commission Regulation 1984/83 it seems that the grant of the lease itself may be a special benefit.

(c) Nuisance and annoyance

It is common to find in leases a covenant against nuisance and annoyance. Such a covenant is of particular importance where the use of the property is otherwise relatively unrestricted. The word 'nuisance' is likely to be construed in its technical sense; that is, 'an inconvenience materially interfering with the ordinary comfort physically of human existence, not merely according to elegant or dainty modes and habits of living, but according to plain and sober and simple notions among the English people' (*Walter v Selfe* (1851) 4 De G & Sm 315) with the proviso that a nuisance in one area may not be a nuisance in another. However, 'annoyance' is a wider term than nuisance, and if you find a thing which reasonably troubles the mind and pleasure, not of a fanciful person or of a skilled person but of the ordinary sensible English inhabitant of a house ... that is an annoyance although it may not appear to amount to physical detriment to comfort' (*Tod-Heatly v Benham* (1888) 40 ChD 80). Although couched in the language of the nineteenth century, these definitions are still good law.

If the draftsman wishes to give the landlord a greater control over the activities carried out on the demised property the covenant may be a covenant against anything 'which in the opinion of the landlord' amounts to a nuisance or annoyance. Provided that the landlord directs his mind to the particular activity in question and forms his opinion honestly, he need not give the tenant an opportunity to be heard; nor, it seems, need his opinion be reasonable (*Zetland (Marquess) v Driver* [1939] Ch 1). It is suggested that a covenant of this kind, coupled with a wide permitted use, is less likely to have a detrimental effect on a rent review than a more restricted use and a covenant against nuisance and annoyance of the conventional kind. A covenant against nuisance and annoyance will usually prohibit acts that would be a nuisance or annoyance to owners and occupiers of 'adjoining' or 'adjacent' or 'neighbouring' property. It is a question of construction of the individual lease whether those words are limited to property in physical contact with the demised property. The modern tendency is to construe such words as not being limited to property in physical contact with the demised property (see *Norton v Deane (Charles) Productions Ltd* (1969) 214 EG 559 following *Cave v Horsell* [1912] 3 KB 533). However, the draftsman should take care to be consistent in his choice of expression because if one expression is found in one part of the lease and another expression in another part the two expressions will be taken to have different meanings (*White v Harrow* [1902] 86 LT 4: 'adjoining' restricted to property in physical contact because of the use elsewhere of the expression 'adjoining or neighbouring').

In addition to a covenant against nuisance and annoyance, a tenant often covenants not to carry on any 'offensive' or 'dangerous' trade or business on the demised property. It is suggested that in most cases the carrying on of such a trade or business would in any event be a breach of a covenant against nuisance or annoyance. If it would not be a breach of that covenant it is questionable whether it is reasonable to impose on the tenant an additional restriction, breach of which is unlikely to cause the landlord any damage. Covenants against the carrying on of offensive trades and businesses are discussed in Aldridge, *Letting Business Premises*, 7th edn (FT Law & Tax) pp 33–34.

The landlord does, however, have a legitimate interest in protecting both the property and himself from liability to deal with pollution or contamination engendered by the tenant's activities. The draftsman should therefore impose on the tenant an obligation to indemnify the landlord against any liability arising as a result of pollution or contamination caused or permitted by the tenant. In addition the tenant should have a contractual obligation to use the best practicable means to eliminate or minimise environmental pollution or the contamination of the building.

The draftsman should however be aware that if the landlord has extensive powers to prevent environmental pollution and fails to exercise them, he may himself be exposed to liability as a person who 'permitted' the pollution to take place. If the landlord has powers, it is important that he exercises them.

Example 8:9 Covenant ancillary to use: short form

That the demised property shall not be used:
(1) for any illegal or immoral purpose
(2) in such a way as in the opinion of the landlord causes or might cause nuisance or annoyance to the landlord or to the owners or occupiers of adjoining property

Example 8:10 Covenant ancillary to use: long form

Not:
(1) to use the demised property for any illegal or immoral purpose
(2) to store in or bring on to the demised property anything which is:
 (a) dangerous
 (b) offensive
 (c) explosive
 (d) radio-active or
 (e) easily inflammable (apart from petrol in the tanks of motor vehicles)
(3) to do anything in the demised property which would invalidate any policy of insurance taken out by the landlord or increase the rate of premium payable for it

USE OF THE DEMISED PROPERTY 229

(4) to do anything which causes nuisance or annoyance to neighbours or to the landlord

(5) to reside or sleep on the demised property

(6) to hold any political meeting or sale by auction on the demised property

(7) to use any machine on the demised property other than:
   (a) a normal office machine (including computers)
   (b) a machine necessary for carrying out repairs or authorised alterations

(8) to discharge into any pipe or drain any greasy oily or corrosive materials or anything likely to damage or block them or any substance likely to cause harm to humans living organisms or the environment if it escapes into any aquifer

(9) to permit or suffer anything prohibited by the preceding paragraphs of this subclause

Example 8:11 Covenant not to pollute

(1) To use the best practicable means to avoid or minimise pollution or contamination of the environment as a result of anything done or omitted to be done in the demised property during the term

(2) To indemnify the landlord against all costs and liabilities incurred by him in connection with carrying out work to prevent minimise or deal with the effects of pollution or contamination of the environment as a result of anything done or omitted to be done in the demised property during the term

(3)(a) the 'environment' means land, water and air
   (b) 'pollution' means the release into the environment of substances or articles capable of causing harm to humans or to any living organism supported by the environment or to any building or other structure
   (c) in interpreting 'best practicable means'
      (i) 'practicable' means reasonably practicable having regard among other things to local conditions and circumstances, to the current state of technical knowledge and to the financial implications
      (ii) the means to be employed include the design installation maintenance of plant and machinery and the design construction and maintenance of buildings
      (iii) the fact that the tenant has a limited interest in the demised property shall be disregarded

Example 8:12 Covenant relating to licence

To do all things necessary to maintain and from time to time renew the licence for [   ] and not to do or permit or suffer to be done anything which might prejudice the future grant or renewal of such licence (whether to the tenant or any future occupier of the demised property) and to comply with all requirements and recommendations of the licensing authority

9 Modification of Use Covenants

Usually a use covenant may only be modified or varied with the consent of the parties to the lease. However, where the lease was granted for a term of more than forty years and twenty-five years of the term have expired, the Lands Tribunal has power to discharge any restriction on use (Law of Property Act 1925, s 84). See Aldridge, *Letting Business Premises*, 7th edn (FT Law & Tax, 1996) p 36.

10 Renewal Leases

On the grant of a new tenancy under the Landlord and Tenant Act 1954 the restrictions on use will be such as are agreed by the landlord and the tenant or, in default of agreement, such as are determined by the court having regard to the terms of the old tenancy and to all relevant circumstances (Landlord and Tenant Act 1954, s 35). The terms of the new tenancy should be such as to enable the tenant to carry on his business as it is at the date of the renewal. They should not be cut down so as to prevent the tenant from carrying on an important part of it (*Gold v Brighton Corporation* [1956] 3 All ER 442). But the tenant's reluctance to accept a 'keep open' covenant was no justification for removing it from the lease (*Boots the Chemist v Pinkland* [1992] 28 EG 118). However, the court will not alter the restrictions on use merely to give a rental advantage to one or other party. Thus, where a tenant sought to introduce a restriction on use for the sole purpose of reducing the rent, the court refused to allow the change (*Aldwych Club Ltd v Copthall Property Co Ltd* (1962) 185 EG 219). Similarly, where the landlord sought to relax restrictions upon use for the purpose of increasing the rent, the court refused to allow the relaxation (*Clements (Charles) (London) Ltd v Rank City Wall Ltd* (1978) 246 EG 739).

9

Assignment and Subletting

In the absence of an express covenant to the contrary, a tenant is entitled to assign or underlet the demised property without the consent of his landlord. His right to do so may only be cut down by clear words, and a covenant against alienation will usually be construed strictly against the landlord (see *Sweet & Maxwell Ltd v Universal News Service Ltd* [1964] 2 QB 699 where Buckley J said: 'to underlet is an important incident of the normal property right which belongs to the tenant: it is one of the ways in which he can turn his property to good account and make it profitable to himself; and as a matter of construction I think a tenant should not be treated as deprived of that right except by clear words or circumstances which make it clear that the parties so intended').

The form of covenant now commonly found in a lease of commercial property is a covenant 'not to assign underlet or part with the possession of the demised property or any part thereof without the consent of the landlord (such consent not to be unreasonably withheld)'. Such a covenant is in reality three separate covenants that are not mutually exclusive (*Marks v Warren* [1979] 1 All ER 29). Each part of the covenant will be examined in turn.

1 Not to Assign

A covenant against assignment is not broken by anything short of a legal assignment (*Gentle v Faulkner* [1900] 2 QB 267). Thus, a tenant may, without breaking the covenant: underlet the demised property (*Sweet & Maxwell Ltd v Universal News Services Ltd* [1964] 2 QB 699); mortgage it (*Doe d Pitt v Hogg* (1824) 4 D & R KB 226); allow a potential assignee into possession pending completion of the assignment (*Horsey Estate Ltd v Steiger* [1899] 2 QB 79); declare a trust of the lease (*Gentle v Faulkner* above) or form a partnership that is to use the demised property for the purposes of the partnership business (*Singh (Gian) & Co v Nahar* [1965] 1 All ER 768) provided that no legal assignment takes place (*Langton v Henson* (1905) 92 LT 805). Most of these activities will be effectively prohibited by the other two parts of the covenant. It is, however, unusual to find in a lease a prohibition on declaring a trust of the lease except in the limited case of a declaration of trust for the tenant's creditors. This is sometimes made a condition of the lease, breach of which entitles the landlord to forfeit. More consideration should be given by draftsmen to specifically prohibiting all declarations of trust. The reason for this suggestion is that if the tenant declares a trust of the lease and the demised property is occupied by a beneficiary under the trust the tenant will continue to be entitled to the protection of Part II of the Landlord and Tenant Act 1954 (s 41), whereas if the occupier is a licensee of the tenant the protection will be lost. If the covenant prohibits holding the tenancy on trust, the tenant's adviser should ensure that an exception is made in the case of joint tenants each of whom has a beneficial interest in the tenancy, because they will automatically hold the tenancy on trust for sale. In addition, where the business to be carried on is operated under franchise, the franchisor may take the lease in its own name and declare a trust of it in favour of itself and the franchisee, thereby preserving security of tenure under the Landlord and Tenant Act 1954. For the tenant, therefore, the ability to hold the lease on trust may be a valuable right.

2 Not to Underlet

A covenant against underletting will not prevent the tenant from granting licences of the demised property; nor, it is submitted, will it prevent him from granting equitable leases of it. This may be of great importance to the landlord since a tenant under an equitable underlease will be entitled to the protection of Part II of the Landlord and Tenant Act 1954 (s 69(1)). However, the grant of equitable leases will effectively be prohibited by a covenant against parting with possession of the demised property. Since the decision of the House of Lords in *Street v Mountford* [1985] 2 All ER 289, it is now clear that, save in exceptional circumstances, a person having exclusive possession of property for a term at a rent, will be held to be a tenant. The status of possessory licensee has all but disappeared. Accordingly, many more transactions will now fall within the scope of a covenant against underletting. A covenant against underletting the demised property will probably effectively prevent the tenant from mortgaging his lease (*Sergeant v Nash Field & Co* [1903] 2 KB 304) because any mortgage of a leasehold interest must be effected either by way of sublease (Law of Property Act 1925, s 86(1)) or by way of legal charge, which takes effect as if a sublease had been created (Law of Property Act 1925, s 87(1)), although it was assumed but not decided in *Re Good's Lease* [1954] 1 All ER 275 that the grant of a mortgage by way of legal charge was not a breach. Accordingly, where there is likely to be any equity value in the lease (as where the tenant has paid a premium for it or where there is a long interval between rent reviews) the tenant's adviser should ensure that the tenant is entitled to charge the lease. This may be effected either by a proviso to the effect that the grant of a charge over the lease shall not be deemed to be a breach of covenant or by including in the lease a separate covenant dealing with the charging of the lease.

A covenant against underletting 'the demised property' will not prevent the tenant from underletting part only of the property (*Cook v Shoesmith* [1951] 1 KB 752) unless the underlettings in aggregate amount to an underletting of the whole (*Chatterton v Terrell* [1923] AC 578). If the draftsman intends to prevent underlettings of part of the demised property this must be clearly dealt with in the lease. Conversely, where the intention of the parties is that the tenant should be entitled to grant occupation leases of parts of the demised property, which in aggregate will amount to an underletting of the whole, the tenant's adviser should ensure that the tenant is not exposed to a forfeiture when the last part of the demised property is underlet. However, a covenant against underletting 'any part of the demised property' will prohibit an underletting of the whole (*Field v Barkworth* [1986] 1 EGLR 46; *Troop v Gibson* [1986] 1 EGLR 1).

A covenant against underletting will not prevent an undertenant from sub-underletting the demised property since the covenant will bind only the tenant and not an undertenant of his (*Mackusick v Carmichael* [1917] 2 KB 581). If the draftsman wishes to prevent sub-underletting it appears that he may do so only by providing that any underlease shall contain a covenant by the undertenant not to underlet without the consent of the superior landlord. The landlord will be able to take the benefit of the covenant even though he is not a party to the underlease, and the tenant will be under an implied obligation not to release the subtenant from the covenant (*Drive Yourself Hire Co (London) Ltd v Strutt* [1954] 1 QB 250 at 270 *per* Denning LJ). Some draftsmen prefer to make the implied obligation an express one.

3 Not to Part with Possession

A covenant not to part with possession of the demised property is wider than a covenant not to assign or underlet it. It may be broken by allowing a potential assignee into possession of the property pending completion (*Abrahams v MacFisheries Ltd* [1925] 2 KB 18) or by letting a wall for advertising (*Heard v Stuart* (1907) 24 TLR 104). However, 'a covenant which forbids a parting with possession is not broken by a lessee who in law retains the possession even though he allows another to use and occupy the premises. It may be that the covenant, on this construction, will be of little value to a lessor in many cases and will admit of easy evasion by a lessee who is competently advised but the words of the covenant must be strictly construed, since if the covenant is broken a forfeiture may result' (*Lam Kee Ying Sdn Bhd v Lam Shes Tong* [1975] AC 247). Thus the tenant will be entitled to grant licences of the property under which exclusive possession does not pass.

4 Wider Forms of Covenant

In an attempt to prevent the 'easy evasion' of a covenant against parting with possession of the demised property, draftsmen have included in leases a prohibition against 'sharing possession or occupation' of the demised property. Such a covenant will effectively prohibit anyone except the tenant from using the property. 'To part with possession is one thing; it is very much another to share possession, or to permit premises to be occupied by some other company without yielding up possession. In the case of associated companies carrying out industrial work in adjoining premises it might be necessary to conduct a precise analysis of which employees working in which premises were employed by which company before any answer could be made to the question whether there has been a parting with possession' (*VT Engineering v Richard Barland & Co Ltd* (1968) 19 P&CR 890 *per* Megarry J).

A covenant against sharing possession of the demised property should only reluctantly be accepted by the tenant. In most cases such a covenant goes beyond what is required for the protection of the landlord, while it imposes unwarranted restrictions on the tenant's ability to use the property. The problem is particularly acute in the case of a letting of a large shop, for in such a case it is becoming usual for the tenant to permit other traders to occupy portions of the shop on a licensed basis. Such occupiers seldom have exclusive possession of the portion of the property that they occupy. Nevertheless, the grant of a licence agreement would almost certainly be a breach of a covenant not to share possession. In a strict legal sense sharing possession is an unknown concept, but for the purposes of such a covenant it means 'sharing the use of the premises with somebody else' (*Tulapam Properties Ltd v De Almeida* (1981) 260 EG 919). It has been said that possession is shared where there is joint use of premises or a portion thereof irrespective of the fractions of time or space concerned (*Stapleton Enterprises of Man Ltd v Bramer Machine Shop Ltd* [1978] 1 WWR 29). Where the tenant is a member of a group of companies, the tenant's adviser should press for the right to share occupation with companies in the same group. However, if such a right is granted, the draftsman should ensure that the share capital of a company in occupation cannot be transferred without the landlord's consent, otherwise the right would be capable of being used to circumvent restrictions on alienation.

5 Absolute Prohibitions on Alienation

There is nothing to prevent a landlord from imposing on the tenant an absolute prohibition on alienation of the demised property. Such a prohibition is, however, unusual and should not be accepted by the tenant except in special circumstances. Nevertheless, it is not uncommon for the landlord to impose an absolute prohibition on alienation of part of the demised property. Such a prohibition enables him to prevent the fragmentation of his estate and may be amply justified on management grounds. In the case of a letting of a large building the draftsman should always consider the desirability of preventing the tenant from underletting small portions of the demised property. This is usually done by imposing an absolute prohibition on underletting or parting with possession of a part of demised property whose area is less than, say, one whole floor or a given number of square feet.

However, where the demised property consists of both business and residential property (eg a shop with residential accommodation over) an absolute prohibition on underletting part is highly desirable. If there is no such prohibition, and the tenant underlets the residential part, the residential subtenant may be entitled to the protection of the Housing Act 1988.

Even where the demised property consists entirely of business property (eg a large suite of offices) an absolute prohibition on underletting part may be of great advantage to the landlord. For example, if the tenant underlets a small part of the demised property to a business occupier and then vacates the remainder at the expiry date of his lease the occupying subtenant will be entitled under the Landlord and Tenant Act 1954 to hold over on the terms of his underlease. Thus, the landlord may find that the property is virtually unlettable, and in any event the terms on which the subtenant holds over may be wholly different from the terms of the original lease.

If the landlord imposes an absolute prohibition on alienation it will always be open to him to permit the tenant to deal with the demised property in a particular case. However, he will be entitled to refuse his consent to a proposed transaction without having to be reasonable in his refusal. The reason for this is that no statutory proviso to the effect that consent to an assignment or underletting may not be unreasonably withheld is read into an absolute prohibition on alienation (see, however, the contrary observations in *Property & Bloodstock Ltd v Emerton* [1968] Ch 94 *per* Dankwerts LJ). In addition an absolute covenant against alienation is not caught by the Landlord and Tenant Act 1988 which applies only to covenants against alienation without consent, where that consent cannot be unreasonably withheld (Landlord and Tenant Act 1988, s 1(1)). The advantages to the landlord of an absolute covenant are that he is able to regulate precisely who is to occupy the property and on what terms; and if the tenant wishes to leave the property he has the ability, if he chooses, to compel a surrender as the only practical way for the tenant to be rid of his obligations. The disadvantages are that the property is likely to be far less marketable with an absolute covenant against alienation; and even if a tenant is found, the effect of the restrictions on the rent achievable at rent review is likely to be significant.

However, some of the advantages of an absolute covenant may be preserved if the absolute covenant is confined to certain aspects of alienation. This technique is used more often in relation to prohibitions upon subletting rather than prohibitions on assignment. For example it will be desirable to prevent the tenant from granting a sublease of property which extends beyond the boundaries of the property comprised in the lease. If the tenant grants such a sublease, the landlord may be unable to determine it under the Landlord and Tenant Act 1954 (*Nevill Long & Co (Boards) Ltd v Firmenich & Co* (1983) 268 EG 572).

Equally an absolute prohibition may be combined with specified exceptions to the general prohibition. Many landlords for example insist upon an absolute covenant preventing the tenant from subletting except at a rack rent. If the tenant is prepared to accept such a clause, the tenant's adviser should try to provide for some machinery to determine disputes over value. In many cases the landlord seeks to impose a covenant which prohibits subletting at less than the rent payable under the lease, or in the case of a subletting of part, an apportioned part of it. The justification for this is that the landlord wishes his tenant to be in a position to pay the rent, and if the tenant has sublet the whole, and is therefore no longer trading in the property, his ability to pay the rent may be compromised. In addition in the eyes of many landlords a subletting at less than the passing rent establishes a bad precedent as to value and may have a detrimental effect on the capital investment of the investment. However, from the tenant's point of view such a clause is dangerous. In a falling market, it may effectively mean that the property cannot be sublet. Alternatively, the tenant may have to resort to subterfuges (eg the repayment of part of the rent or the grant of a long rent-free period or the payment of a large reverse premium) in order to maintain the rent. At the least his freedom to sublet is curtailed.

There may also be a prohibition on subletting except in units of a given size; or without including provision for rent review at dates which coincide with the review dates under the headlease. In addition there may be a limit to the number of permitted sublettings (eg in an office building not more than two per floor).

If the landlord wishes to retain tight control over sublettings of the demised property, a hybrid covenant of this kind may be the most acceptable compromise between the parties.

However, the tenant should be much less willing to accept fetters on his right to assign. An assignment is the primary means by which the tenant is able (in practical terms) to shed his liabilities under the lease and the tenant's adviser should ensure that this will be as easy as possible. It is probably acceptable for the tenant to agree to an absolute prohibition upon assignment except to a respectable and responsible assignee who has entered or is willing to enter into a direct covenant with the landlord to perform the tenant's obligations for the residue of the term. Further restrictions are likely to be required by landlords, following the introduction of the Landlord and Tenant (Covenants) Act 1995. These are considered below.

Even if an absolute covenant is imposed on the tenant, the landlord is not entitled to withhold consent if to do so would amount to racial or sexual discrimination (Sex Discrimination Act 1975, s 31; Race Relations Act 1976, s 24) or on the ground of disability (Disability Discrimination Act 1995, s 22).

6 SPECIFIED CIRCUMSTANCES IN WHICH THE LANDLORD MAY WITHHOLD CONSENT OR IMPOSE CONDITIONS

Where a covenant against assignment, underletting, charging or parting with possession is a qualified covenant, there is a statutory proviso to the effect that consent cannot be unreasonably withheld (Landlord and Tenant Act 1927, s 19(1)). The parties cannot contract out of this proviso, nor may they themselves determine what is reasonable. The question is objective: is it reasonable to withhold consent? That question will be decided without regard to the interpretation the parties have put on that expression (*Re Smith's Lease* [1951] 1 TLR 254).

However, in the case of a lease which is a new tenancy for the purpose of the Landlord and Tenant (Covenants) Act 1995 (other than a residential lease) there is a major exception to this rule. The parties may enter into an agreement specifying circumstances in which the landlord may withhold consent to an assignment or specify conditions which the landlord may impose on an assignment (Landlord and Tenant Act 1927, s 19(1A)). The following points should be noted:

(1) The agreement must be one which specifies the circumstances or conditions 'for the purposes of this subsection'. It is not clear whether the subsection must be expressly mentioned in the agreement, but it is clearly safer if it is.

(2) The agreement will only apply to assignments; it will not apply to underlettings, charges or parting with possession which will continue to be governed by s 19(1) in its unamended form.

(3) The agreement applies only to the giving or withholding of consent by the landlord; it will not apply to the consent of anyone else (eg a superior landlord or mortgagee).

Where the parties have entered into such an agreement then the landlord will not be regarded as unreasonably withholding consent to an assignment if he withholds it on the ground that any of the specified circumstances exist and they do in fact exist. It follows therefore that in most cases the specified circumstances must be ones which can be objectively verified. Equally, the landlord will not be regarded as giving consent subject to unreasonable conditions if he gives it subject to the specified conditions.

If the specified circumstances or conditions are framed by reference to any matter falling to be determined by the landlord or by any other person for the purposes of the agreement, s 19(1A) will not apply unless:

(a) that person's power to determine the matter is required to be exercised reasonably or
(b) the tenant is given an unrestricted right to have any such determination referred by a person independent of both landlord and tenant whose identity is ascertainable by reference to the agreement, in which case the agreement must provide for the determination to be conclusive

(Landlord and Tenant Act 1927, s 19(1C)). It is not clear whether the person referred to in paragraph (a) includes the landlord, or whether he is restricted to the other person previously referred to. If the latter, it would appear to follow that where the landlord is to determine a particular matter, then s 19(1A) will not apply even if he is required to act reasonably. But if he is required to act reasonably, it seems likely that the decision would be held to be reasonable under the unamended section without the need to rely on s 19(1A). The tenant's right to a review must be 'unrestricted'. This appears to mean that no time limit may be imposed within which the tenant must apply for a review.

These important amendments were designed to give landlords more certainty of control over assignments of new tenancies, where the tenant is released from liability on assignment.

The tenant may, however, be required to enter into an authorised guarantee agreement under which he guarantees the obligations of the immediate assignee (Landlord and Tenant (Covenants) Act 1995, s 16). The detailed requirements of an authorised guarantee agreement are considered in Chapter 11 below. However, it is important to note that a guarantee agreement will only be authorised if the tenant cannot assign without consent, and consent is given subject to a condition (lawfully imposed) that he is to enter into the guarantee agreement. It is considered that such a condition will be lawfully imposed in two cases only:

(1) where it is reasonable to impose the condition or
(2) where the lease specifies for the purpose of s 19(1A) that on any assignment the tenant is to enter into a guarantee agreement.

In order to achieve certainty, the draftsman should make it an express term of any alienation clause that on assignment consent may be given subject to the condition that the tenant enters into a guarantee agreement.

The amendments to the law now give landlords the opportunity to specify in advance their requirements for an assignee. In framing those requirements, the draftsman should take account of the changes to the contractual liability of the outgoing tenant. Since the outgoing tenant will be released from liability on assignment, the landlord should be able to withhold consent if rent or service charge is unpaid at the date of the assignment. The draftsman should also consider whether the landlord should be able to withhold consent if there are significant breaches of the tenant's obligations as respects repair and maintenance of the property. Since the tenant is released from liability on assignment, any guarantor for the tenant will also be released (Landlord and Tenant (Covenants) Act 1995, s 24(2)). The draftsman should therefore consider whether the landlord should be able to require a fresh guarantor for the assignee. It is not clear whether a guarantor of the tenant can be required to guarantee the obligations of the tenant under an authorised guarantee agreement, but it is considered that this would not be struck down by the anti-avoidance provisions. A condition requiring the guarantor to guarantee the tenant's obligations under an authorised guarantee agreement should, therefore, be included.

In evaluating the covenant strength of the assignee some landlords apply rules of thumb in looking at the assignee's pre-tax profits. The landlord now has the opportunity to make explicit in the lease the policy which he adopts.

Example 9:1 Absolute prohibition on alienation of part; qualified as to whole

(1) Not to assign underlet or part with or share possession or occupation of part only of the demised property

(2) Not without the landlord's consent in writing (such consent not to be unreasonably withheld) to assign underlet or part with or share possession or occupation of the demised property as a whole

(3) At his own expense to procure that any assignee of the demised property enters into a direct covenant with the landlord in such form as the landlord may reasonably require to pay the rent and perform the tenant's covenants herein

(4) Within one month after any transfer or devolution of the tenant's interest in the demised property or any part thereof to produce to the landlord's solicitors a copy of the instrument or other document under which it was made or which evidences the same and to pay a reasonable fee for its registration

Example 9:2 Absolute prohibition subject to exceptions

Not to assign underlet or part with the possession of part only of the demised property except where the proposed transaction consists of an underletting

(1) for a term of less than one year and

(2) at a rent equal to the rack rental value of the part in question at the date of the proposed transaction and

(3) to a person first approved by the landlord (such approval not to be unreasonably withheld)

Example 9:3 Absolute conditions for alienation

Not to assign underlet or part with possession or share occupation of the demised property or any part of it unless each of the following conditions is fulfilled:

(1) in the case of a proposed assignment the proposed assignee has before taking possession entered into a covenant with the landlord to perform and observe the tenant's covenants contained in this lease during the residue of the term

(2) in the case of a proposed underletting:
- (a) the proposed undertenant has before taking possession entered into a covenant with the landlord to perform and observe the tenant's covenants contained in this lease (except the covenant to pay rent) during the term created by the underlease so far as they affect the property to be underlet
- (b) the property to be underlet does not include any property or any right over any property which is not demised by this lease
- (c) the rent to be reserved by the underlease is the best rent reasonably obtainable for such underletting and the underlease provides for the upward revision of the rent payable thereunder at dates coincident with the dates upon which the rent is revised under this lease
- (d) the underlease is otherwise in a form approved by the landlord

(3) if the proposed assignee or undertenant is a limited company (other than a public limited company) two of its directors of satisfactory standing or a public limited company stand surety for the performance of its obligations to the landlord and enter into the standard form of surety covenant from time to time of the landlord

(4) the landlord has consented to the proposed transaction (such consent not to be unreasonably withheld)

(5) the transaction is completed by way of legal assignment or underlease within three months after the giving of consent

Example 9:4 Circumstances in which the landlord may withhold consent to assignment: objective criteria

The landlord may withhold consent to an assignment in any of the following circumstances which are specified for the purpose of section 19(1A) of the Landlord and Tenant Act 1927:
- (a) at the date of the application for consent to assign the rent is in arrear or any other sums payable by the tenant have not been paid
- (b) at the date of the application for consent to assign there are

[substantial] breaches of the tenant's obligations as respect the repair and maintenance of the demised property
(c) the proposed assignee has traded for less than three years immediately preceding the date of the application for consent to assign
(d) the proposed assignee has not demonstrated by production of audited accounts that in each of the three years immediately preceding the application for consent to assign it has made annual profits equal to at least three times the rent payable under this lease at that date
(e) the proposed assignee has no assets in England and Wales or no address for service in England and Wales

Example 9:5 Circumstances in which the landlord may withhold consent to an assignment: subjective criteria

(1) The landlord may withhold consent to an assignment in any of the following circumstances which are specified for the purpose of section 19(1A) of the Landlord and Tenant Act 1927:
(a) in the landlord's opinion the proposed assignee will be less able than the tenant to pay the rent and perform the tenant's obligations under this lease for the residue of the term
(b) in the landlord's opinion the use of the demised property proposed by the proposed assignee will reduce the capital value of the landlord's reversion
(c) in the landlord's opinion the substitution of the assignee for the tenant will reduce the capital value of the landlord's reversion
(d) in the landlord's opinion the use of the demised property proposed by the proposed assignee will be detrimental to the mix of uses current in the Centre at the date of the application to assign

(2) If the tenant is aggrieved by any opinion formed by the landlord for the purposes of subclause (1) above he may require it to be reviewed by an independent surveyor appointed (in default of agreement) by the President of the Royal Institution of Chartered Surveyors and the independent surveyor's determination on the review shall be conclusive

Example 9:6 Conditions which the landlord may impose on assignment

On any assignment the landlord may impose all or any of the following conditions which are specified for the purpose of section 19(1A) of the Landlord and Tenant Act 1927:
(a) a condition that the tenant enters into an authorised guarantee agreement in the form set out in the [   ] schedule
(b) a condition that any person who guarantees the obligations of the tenant under this lease enters into a guarantee of the ten-

ant's obligations under the authorised guarantee agreement
(c) a condition that the assignee will procure two persons of suitable standing to stand surety for the performance of his obligations under this lease
(d) a condition that the assignee deposits with the landlord an amount equal to one year's rent as security for the performance of his obligations
(e) a condition that before completion of the assignment the tenant makes good to the reasonable satisfaction of the landlord any breach of obligation of which the landlord has previously notified the tenant in writing

Example 9:7 Proviso permitting group company sharing

Provided that nothing in the preceding provisions of this subclause shall prevent the tenant from sharing occupation with another member of the same group of companies (as defined in section 42 of the Landlord and Tenant Act 1954 (as amended)) if and so long as that other member remains a member of that group and no relation of landlord and tenant subsists between the tenant and that other member

Example 9:8 Provisions regulating group company sharing

(1) For the purposes of this subclause:
(a) two bodies corporate are members of the same group if and only if one is for the time being a subsidiary of the other or both are for the time being subsidiaries of a third body corporate
(b) 'subsidiary' has the same meaning as in section 736 of the Companies Act 1985
(2) Where this lease is vested in [*name of original tenant*] or a body corporate to whom this lease has been lawfully assigned the tenant may by written notice to the landlord bring this subclause into operation until the next lawful assignment of this lease
(3) While this subclause is in operation:
(a) the tenant shall be entitled to share occupation of the demised property with another member of the same group and
(b) the tenant shall procure that that member does not cease to be a member of that group
(4) This subclause may be brought into operation once only during the tenure of any particular tenant

7 QUALIFIED COVENANTS AGAINST ALIENATION

Where a lease contains a covenant against assigning, underletting, charging or parting with the possession of the demised property or any part thereof without licence or consent, it is deemed to be subject to a proviso that licence or consent cannot be unreasonably withheld (Landlord and Tenant Act 1927, s 19(1)). The proviso does not, however, prevent the landlord from requiring payment of a reasonable sum in respect of legal or other expenses incurred in connection with the grant of licence or consent.

In relation to new tenancies for the purpose of the Landlord and Tenant (Covenants) Act 1995, the parties may now specify circumstances in which the landlord may withhold consent to an assignment and conditions which he may impose on assignment. This does not apply to consents to underletting or other forms of disposition, to which s 19(1) will continue to apply with full rigour. In such cases, the parties cannot restrict its operation by stipulating that this or that shall not be deemed to be unreasonable. The question is objective: is it reasonable to withhold consent? That question will be decided without regard to the interpretation the parties have put on that expression (*Re Smith's Lease* [1951] 1 TLR 254).

Many draftsmen seek to widen the ambit of the covenant by providing, for example, that on any assignment or underletting the tenant shall procure that the assignee or undertenant enters into a direct covenant with the landlord to pay the rent and observe the covenants in the lease. Since this is a free-standing obligation which is not dependent on consent, it is an effective obligation (*Vaux Group v Lilley* [1991] 1 EGLR 60), although if the lease were silent, the landlord probably could not impose such a liability as a condition of consent. Moreover, since the assignee or undertenant will be released from liability on assignment, such a covenant will cease to have effect at that time. In a case where the landlord sought to require a proposed undertenant to enter into a direct covenant with him to observe the terms of the headlease it was held that the landlord was acting unreasonably, although if the proposed transaction had been an assignment he might not have been (*Balfour v Kensington Gardens Mansions Ltd* (1932) 49 TLR 29). The landlord might have been protected if the lease had contained an absolute covenant against underletting except on the terms of the lease. On the other hand, it has been held reasonable for a landlord, who occupies part of a building and lets off another part to a tenant who seeks to underlet, to require the undertenant to enter into a direct covenant with him not to underlet further (*Re Spark's Lease* [1905] 1 Ch 456). If the draftsman wishes to impose terms on the tenant in relation to alienation of the demised property more extensive than the simple requirement that the landlord's consent be obtained the safer method of doing so is to frame the covenant as an absolute one. See Example 9:3 above. Even so, its effectiveness may yet be open to challenge. (For further examples of reasons for withholding consent see Aldridge, *Letting Business Premises*, 7th edn (FT Law & Tax, 1996) pp 70–72.)

Although the parties cannot restrict the operation of the proviso they may by agreement restrict the landlord's freedom to withhold his consent. Therefore, where the parties (probably by mistake) provided that the landlord's consent was 'not to be withheld in the case of a respectable and responsible person' it was held that once a respectable and responsible person had been produced the landlord could not withhold consent even on reasonable grounds (*Moat v Martin* [1950] 1 KB 175). The word 'respectable' points to the behaviour of the person, primarily in carrying on his business but probably also in the whole of his external relations (*Willmott v London Road Car Co Ltd* [1910] 2 Ch 525); while the word 'responsible' means able to pay the rent and perform the covenants and other obligations in the lease (*Re Greater London Properties Ltd's Leases* [1959] 1 All ER 728). Where the tenant is a company the tenant's adviser should seek to ensure that the lease permits the tenant to share occupation of the property with other members of the same group of companies without the need to obtain the landlord's consent.

Sometimes the statutory proviso is spelt out in the lease. The form of the proviso varies. It may be provided that the landlord may not withhold consent 'unreasonably' or 'wholly unreasonably' or 'without reasonable cause' or 'arbitrarily'. Whichever of these forms is chosen the effect is the same (*Mills v Cannon Brewery Co Ltd* [1920] 2 Ch 38).

It is well established that if the tenant's covenant not to assign etc without consent is merely qualified by a proviso that the consent of the landlord is not to be unreasonably withheld, there is no implied covenant by the landlord that he will not unreasonably withhold his consent. In the absence of an express covenant to that effect the tenant cannot maintain an action for damages against him for withholding it (*Ideal Film Renting Co Ltd v Neilson* [1921] 1 Ch 575). The position at common law was altered by the Landlord and Tenant Act 1988. Where a lease contains a qualified covenant against alienation, any person whose consent is necessary to a proposed transaction owes the tenant a duty within a reasonable time:

(1) to give consent except in a case where it is reasonable not to give consent; and
(2) to notify the tenant in writing of his decision; and
  (a) if the consent is conditional of the conditions;

> (b) if the consent is withheld of the reasons for withholding it

(Landlord and Tenant Act 1988, s 1(3)). In order to satisfy the duty, any condition imposed must be reasonable (s 1(4)). Section 1(5) of the Act provides:

> For the purpose of this Act it is reasonable for a person not to give consent to a proposed transaction only in a case where, if he withheld consent and the tenant completed the transaction, the tenant would be in breach of a covenant.

Although the drafting of this subsection is obscure, it is thought that it is not intended to change the law. Accordingly, if the completion of the proposed transaction without the landlord's consent would be a breach of the covenant against alienation, then the landlord will be justified in withholding consent under the Act. In order to appreciate the significance of this it is necessary to appreciate that at common law the effect of an unreasonable withholding of consent is to release the tenant from the covenant to obtain the landlord's consent (*Treloar v Bigge* (1874) LR 9 Exch 151), and consequently alienation in such circumstances would not be a breach of the covenant. Although the Act imposes the burden of proof on the landlord, so that it is for the landlord to show that his consent was reasonably withheld, it has not altered the rule that the landlord need not justify as matters of fact the matters on which he relies, if a reasonable person in his position could have reached the same conclusion as the landlord actually did (*Air India v Balabel* [1993] 2 EGLR 66).

The Act imposes a statutory duty rather than introducing an implied term into the lease. It follows, therefore, that the original landlord will not be liable for breach of the duty once he has parted with his interest in the property.

A claim that a person has broken the statutory duty is actionable in tort (s 4).

The Act does not expressly say whether parties may contract out of the duty, but it is most improbable that they can (cf *Johnson v Moreton* [1980] AC 37). However, it is possible that the landlord could require an indemnity from a third party (eg the surety) against his potential liability under the Act.

Example 9:9 Tenant's qualified covenants against alienation

> (1) The tenant must not assign underlet charge part with possession of or share possession or occupation of the demised property or

ASSIGNMENT AND SUBLETTING

part of it or hold this lease on trust except to the extent expressly permitted by this clause

(2) The tenant may assign the demised property as a whole if (and only if) each of the following conditions is fulfilled:
- (a) the intended assignee:
    - (i) is respectable and responsible and
    - (ii) enters into a covenant with the landlord to pay the rent and perform the tenant's covenants while he remains tenant
- (b) if the landlord reasonably requires two persons of satisfactory standing to stand surety for the performance by the intended assignee of his obligations
- (c) the tenant obtains the landlord's written consent (such consent not to be unreasonably withheld)
- (d) the assignment is completed and registered within one month after the giving of consent

(3) The tenant may underlet the demised property as a whole if (and only if) each of the following conditions is fulfilled:
- (a) the intended undertenant:
    - (i) is respectable and responsible
    - (ii) enters into a deed covenanting with the landlord to perform the tenant's obligations contained in the underlease
    - (iii) enters into a deed covenanting with the landlord to perform the tenant's covenants under this lease (except the covenant to pay rent) while he remains undertenant
- (b) the intended underlease:
    - (i) is granted without a premium and at a rent approved by the landlord (such approval not to be unreasonably withheld)
    - (ii) contains provisions approved by the landlord (such approval not to be unreasonably withheld) for rent review at the same times and on the same basis as in this lease
    - (iii) is so far as possible in the same form as this lease (except that all further subletting must be prohibited)
- (c) the tenant obtains the landlord's written consent (such consent not to be unreasonably withheld)
- (d) the underletting is completed and registered within one month after the giving of consent

(3) The tenant may underlet part only of the demised property if (but only if) each of the following conditions is fulfilled:
- (a) the intended undertenant:
    - (i) is respectable and responsible
    - (ii) enters into a deed covenanting with the landlord to perform the tenant's obligations contained in the underlease
- (b) the intended underlease:
    - (i) is granted without a premium and at a rent approved by the landlord (such approval not to be unreasonably withheld)

(ii) contains provisions approved by the landlord (such approval not to be unreasonably withheld) for rent review at the same times and on the same basis as in this lease

(iii) is so far as possible in the same form as this lease (except that all further subletting must be prohibited)

(c) the grant of the intended underlease will not result in the demised property being occupied in more than three different parts

(d) the property comprised in the intended underlease is either one whole floor of the demised property or a multiple of whole floors (but it may include rights to use car parking spaces and ancillary easements)

(e) the provisions of sections 24 to 28 of the Landlord and Tenant Act 1954 are excluded in relation to the intended underlease

(f) the tenant obtains the landlord's written consent (such consent not to be unreasonably withheld)

(g) the underletting is completed and registered within one month after the giving of consent

The drafting of the above form could be simplified if 'consent' and 'approved' were defined terms. See Example 1:1.

8 Building Leases

If the lease is for more than forty years and is a building lease (ie it is wholly or partially in consideration of the erection or the substantial improvement, addition or alteration of buildings) a further proviso is implied. If such a lease contains a qualified covenant against alienation no consent or licence is required if the transaction in question is effected more than seven years before the end of the term and written notice of the transaction is given to the landlord within six months (Landlord and Tenant Act 1927, s 19(2)). The proviso does not apply if the landlord is a government department, a local or public authority, or a statutory or public utility company; nor does it apply to mining leases. In addition, if the lease is a new tenancy for the purposes of the Landlord and Tenant (Covenants) Act 1995, and is not a residential lease, the proviso does not apply to assignments. This means that the landlord's consent to an assignment must be obtained, and that the landlord cannot withhold consent except:

(1) on reasonable grounds or

(2) in circumstances which have been specified in the lease.

But even in relation to a new tenancy the proviso will apply to underlettings.

Where a lease is both a building lease and a rent sharing lease, the draftsman may be faced with a difficulty in ensuring that the tenant is required to keep the property underlet at full market rents. However, s 19(2) of the 1927 Act does not apply to an absolute covenant even if it takes effect only on assignment (*Vaux Group v Lilley* [1991] 1 EGLR 60). Since s 19(2) does not apply to absolute covenants against alienation, the solution is to create a series of absolute conditions which must be satisfied before a subletting takes place, and for which no question of consent arises. Plainly, however, a tenant who carries out substantial building works is unlikely to accept highly onerous restrictions on his right to alienate the property; nor indeed should he.

Example 9:10 Restrictions on alienation in building lease

(1) not to underlet the whole or any part of the demised property:
(a) at a rent or rents less than the best rent reasonably obtainable for such underletting without a premium but taking into account any rent-free period granted to the undertenant
(b) without providing for the rent or rents thereby reserved to be increased at intervals of not more that the prescribed number of years to the rack rental value of the property comprised in the underlease at the date of the increase without fine
(2) 'the prescribed number of years' means:
(a) five years or
(b) such other number of years as the landlord may from time to time prescribe in writing; or
(c) if the tenant objects in writing within twenty-eight days (time being of the essence) such numbers of years as may be determined by an expert to be appointed by the President for the time being of the Royal Institution of Chartered Surveyors (acting as an expert) having regard to:
  (i) the terms of any existing tenancy of the property to be underlet and the rights (if any) of the undertenant thereof under the Landlord and Tenant Act 1954 as amended from time to time and any other Act of Parliament in respect of that property and
  (ii) market practice current at the time when any such underletting is to take place in relation to property of the same nature as the property to be underlet

9 Requirement to Surrender Before Assigning or Subletting

Draftsmen have attempted to avoid the effect of the implied proviso that consent to alienation is not to be unreasonably withheld by imposing on the tenant an obligation to offer to surrender his lease before asking for consent. Such an obligation is usually called an 'offer back clause'. It is not a usual term 'either in the technical or the colloquial sense, and it is a harsh term when applied to a business letting in which considerations of the sale of goodwill may arise' (*Cardshops Ltd v Davies* [1971] 2 All ER 721 *per* Widgery LJ). The tenant should, therefore, resist the inclusion of such a term.

After some doubt as to the effectiveness of such clauses (*Greene v Church Commissioners for England* [1974] Ch 467), it has now been established that if the tenant is obliged to offer to surrender before asking for consent to a proposed transaction, the landlord has an absolute discretion to accept or refuse the offer, and the statutory proviso that consent may not be unreasonably withheld never comes into play (*Bocardo SA v S & M Hotels Ltd* [1980] 1 WLR 17 approving *Adler v Upper Grosvenor Street Investment Ltd* [1957] 1 All ER 229 and *Creer v P & O Lines of Australia Pty Ltd* (1971) 125 CLR 84). The reason for this is that the offer to surrender is a condition precedent to the right to apply for consent to alienation. This is to be distinguished from the case in which the parties purport to provide for what is or is not a reasonable ground for refusing consent to a transaction once an application for consent has been made. In the latter case, the clause is invalid (*Re Smith's Lease* [1951] 1 All ER 346). This is, therefore, a case in which the form of the drafting is crucial.

An offer back clause will be upheld by the court, even in a lease which is protected by the Landlord and Tenant Act 1954 (*Allnatt London Properties Ltd v Newton* [1981] 2 All ER 290). Thus the tenant is required to make the offer to surrender as stipulated in the lease. However, if the landlord accepts the offer, an agreement to surrender will come into existence. If the tenancy is one to which Part II of the Landlord and Tenant Act 1954 applies at the date of the acceptance of the offer, the agreement to surrender will be void and hence unenforceable by either party (*Allnatt London Properties Ltd v Newton* [1984] 1 All ER 423). The operation of such a clause may therefore produce a deadlock, in which the tenant is unable to assign, but the landlord is unable to compel a surrender.

If at the date of the landlord's acceptance of the tenant's offer to surrender, the tenancy is not one to which Part II of the Act applies (eg the tenant has already moved out) the resulting agreement to surrender will be mutually enforceable.

If the tenancy is 'contracted out' of the 1954 Act, the clause will be fully enforceable. This is because an agreement to surrender a tenancy protected by the 1954 Act is only void because it has the effect of precluding the tenant from applying to the court for the grant of a new tenancy (Landlord and Tenant Act 1954, s 38(1): *Joseph v Joseph* [1967] Ch 78). If the tenant cannot make such an application anyway, the agreement to surrender cannot have that effect.

It seems that the operation of an offer back clause will not be affected by the Law of Property (Miscellaneous Provisions) Act 1989, s 2 (*Spiro v Glencrown* [1991] 2 WLR 931). Thus no special drafting precautions need to be taken in this respect.

Example 9:11 Requirement to offer to surrender

> Not to assign underlet or part with possession of the demised property or any part thereof unless each of the following conditions is fulfilled:
> (1) the tenant has offered in writing to surrender this lease to the landlord without consideration at the expiry date of four weeks from such offer
> (2) the landlord has not within two weeks of such offer accepted the same
> (3) not more than six months have elapsed since the last such offer and then not to assign underlet or part with possession of the demised property or any part thereof without the consent of the landlord (such consent not to be unreasonably withheld)

10 FINES AND PREMIUMS

Where the lease contains a covenant against alienation without licence or consent, the covenant is deemed to be subject to a proviso that no fine or sum of money in the nature of a fine shall be payable for or in respect of such licence or consent (Law of Property Act 1925, s 144). The proviso does not preclude the right to require payment of a reasonable sum in respect of legal or other expense incurred in relation to such licence or consent. More important, the proviso can be excluded by agreement. It may be desirable to exclude the proviso where the lease is a lease of property expected to be sublet on terms that require the subtenants to pay premiums to the tenant. In such a case, if the proviso is not excluded the landlord may find that if the headlease is determined his rental income declines sharply without any capital benefit having being received.

The proviso will prevent the landlord from asking for an increase in the rent as the price of his consent (*Jenkins v Price* [1907] 2 Ch 229) but it will not prevent him from requiring an assignee to enter into a direct covenant to pay the rent reserved by the lease (*Waite v Jennings* [1906] 2 KB 11). If the landlord does demand a fine and the tenant pays it, although not obliged to do so, he may not afterwards recover it from the landlord (*Comber v Fleet Electrics Ltd* [1955] 2 All ER 161).

Example 9:12 Simple exclusion of s 144

Section 144 of the Law of Property Act 1925 shall not apply to this lease

Example 9:13 Exclusion of s 144 where amount of permitted premium is defined

Notwithstanding anything in section 144 of the Law of Property Act 1925 the landlord shall be entitled to require as a condition of the grant of licence to assign or underlet the whole or any part of the demised property the payment by the tenant of an amount equal to one third of any fine or premium payable to the tenant by any proposed assignee or undertenant under the terms of the transaction for which the landlord's licence is sought

11 COSTS

The draftsman should always impose on the tenant an express obligation to pay the landlord's costs incurred in connection with an application for licence to assign or underlet even if the licence is not in the event granted. This obligation should extend to costs that the landlord reimburses to any superior landlord.

Example 9:14 Costs

To pay to the landlord on demand the amount of any costs or professional fees incurred by him in connection with any application for any licence required under the terms of this lease (including any costs or fees which are payable by the landlord to any superior landlord) whether or not such licence is in fact granted

Example 9:15 Costs: fuller version

To pay all costs and expenses incurred by the landlord including professional fees (or their equivalent in the case of solicitors or surveyors employed by the landlord) in connection with:
(1) the preparation or service of a schedule of dilapidations or a notice under section 146 of the Law of Property Act 1925

ASSIGNMENT AND SUBLETTING

(2) any application made by the tenant for any licence or consent under this lease (even if such licence or consent is not granted or the application is withdrawn)

(3) the preparation and engrossment of this lease and its counterpart (including stamp duty)

10

Statutory Protection

1 Part II of the Landlord and Tenant Act 1954

If Part II of the 1954 Act applies to a tenancy, three main consequences will follow:
- (1) the tenancy may not be determined except in accordance with the Act;
- (2) even if the tenancy is determined, the tenant will be entitled to apply to the court for the grant of a new tenancy;
- (3) if the court is unable to renew his tenancy, or if he makes no such application, he may in some circumstances be entitled to compensation on quitting.

Part II of the Landlord and Tenant Act 1954 applies 'to any tenancy where the property comprised in the tenancy is or includes premises which are occupied by the tenant and are so occupied for the purposes of a business carried on by him or for those and other purposes' (s 23(1)).

2 Tenancy

The Act applies only to tenancies. Thus if the occupier of business premises is a licensee, the Act will not apply. If the licence is a genuine licence it will be upheld by the court. 'One has first to find out what is the true nature of the transaction and then see how the Act operates on that state of affairs. One should not approach the problem with a tendency to attempt to find a tenancy because unless there is a tenancy the case will escape the effects of the statute' (*Shell-Mex and BP Ltd v Manchester Garages Ltd* [1971] 1 All ER 841 *per* Buckley LJ). In the absence of exceptional circumstances, a contractual arrangement giving exclusive possession to an occupier at a rent will be held to be a tenancy (*Street v Mountford* [1985] 2 All ER 289). Accordingly, if the parties wish to create a licence, the draftsman must take care that the licensee does not acquire exclusive possession. This may be achieved by including in the licence terms which are inconsistent with the grant of exclusive possession (provided that the terms are genuine). For example, a term requiring the occupier not to impede the exercise by the owner of the owner's rights of possession and control of the property was held to be fatal to a claim by the occupier to be a tenant (*Shell-Mex and BP Ltd v Manchester Garages Ltd* above). Similarly, exclusive possession may be negatived where the occupier does not have unlimited use of the property (*Manchester City Council v National Car Parks Ltd* (1981) 262 EG 1297) or where the owner is entitled to require the occupier to move to different premises (*Dresden Estates Ltd v Collinson* [1987] 1 EGLR 45). Thus the grant of front of house rights in a theatre was held to amount to a licence (*Clore v Theatrical Properties Ltd* [1936] 3 All ER 483). However, where two persons shared the use of a shop, each having a separate counter and using the area between the counters together, it was held that a tenancy had been created (*Piper v Muggleton* [1956] 2 QB 569). Had services been provided by the owner, it is suggested that the result would have been otherwise (cf *Ross Auto Wash Ltd v Herbert* (1978) 250 EG 971). Terms which point towards the grant of exclusive possession include:

(1) the reservation of limited rights of entry (*Facchini v Bryson* [1952] 1 TLR 1386);
(2) an express prohibition against subletting (*Facchini v Bryson* above);
(3) a covenant for quiet enjoyment (*Addiscombe Garden Estates Ltd v Crabbe* [1957] 1 QB 513);
(4) a proviso for re-entry on breach of obligation (*Addiscombe Garden Estates Ltd v Crabbe* above).

Some of the cases contain detailed analyses of whether terms are more consistent with the grant of a tenancy than a licence. Such analyses should be treated with the greatest caution in the light of the decision of the House of Lords in *Street v Mountford*.

In addition the Act does not apply to the following kinds of tenancy:

A tenancy at will A tenancy at will may be created by implication (eg where the tenant holds over or is let into possession pending negotiations for the grant of a lease) or by express agreement. In neither case will the Act apply (*Wheeler v Mercer* [1957] AC 416; *Hagee (London) Ltd v Ericson (AB) and Larson* [1976] QB 209).

A tenancy granted for a term of years certain not exceeding six months (s 43(3))   This exception will only apply in the case of new businesses. The exception will not apply if the tenant (together with any predecessor of his carrying on the same business) has been in occupation for a period exceeding twelve months (s 43(3)(b)). Note that occupation need not be as tenant. Thus, if the tenant is let into occupation as licensee pending completion of the lease that period of occupation will count towards the twelve months. Equally, if the landlord sells his own business to the tenant, the landlord's occupation may be aggregated with that of the tenant. Where a tenancy is granted for a term of six months to a person who begins a new business in the demised property it may be renewed once for a similar term before the Act applies; but the first tenancy must not contain any provision for renewing the term or for extending it beyond six months from its beginning, otherwise the Act will apply to it (s 43(3)(a)). Thus, even if the parties contemplate that the tenancy will in fact be renewed the lease itself should be silent on the point.

A tenancy granted for a term of years certain (of any length) approved by the court before it begins (s 38(4))   On the joint application of the persons who will be the landlord and the tenant the court may authorise an agreement excluding ss 24–28 of the Act. The tenancy in respect of which the application is made must be a term certain. Although the term may be for less than one year (*Re Land and Premises at Liss* [1971] Ch 986) and the terms of the tenancy may include a break-clause (*Scholl Mfg Co Ltd v Clifton (Slim-Line) Ltd* [1967] Ch 41), the court cannot authorise the exclusion of the Act in relation to a periodic tenancy (*Nicholas v Kinsey* [1994] 2 WLR 622). The court order must be obtained before the parties enter into the relation of landlord and tenant (*Essexcrest Ltd v Evenlex Ltd* [1988] 1 EGLR 69) but where parties agree upon a 'contracted out' tenancy it has been held that the agreement remains 'subject to contract' unless and until the court order is obtained (*Cardiothoracic Institute v Shrewdcrest Ltd* [1986] 1 WLR 368). If an order is obtained the Act will not apply to the tenancy even if the lease is never executed (*Tottenham Hotspur Football & Athletic Co Ltd v Princegrove Publishers Ltd* [1974] 1 All ER 17). The agreement must be contained in or endorsed on the tenancy agreement, unless the court specifies some other instrument.

Example 10:1 Exclusion of 1954 Act

   It is hereby agreed that pursuant to an order of [the county court] [the

High Court of Justice Chancery Division] made on [   ] sections 24 to 28 of the Landlord and Tenant Act 1954 shall not apply to this tenancy

3 Identity of the Tenant

(a) Service tenancy

The Act does not apply where the tenancy is granted because the tenant is the holder of an 'office appointment or employment' from the landlord, provided that the tenancy determines automatically (or may be determined by the landlord) on the tenant ceasing to hold the office appointment or employment in question or comes to an end at a time fixed by reference to the tenant ceasing to hold it (s 43(2)). Thus, the Act may be avoided if before the tenancy begins the tenant is given an 'appointment' by the landlord. It is thought that the appointment must not only be genuine (see *Teasdale v Walker* [1958] 3 All ER 307 and *Wang v Wei* (1975) 119 SJ 492, where 'management agreements' were held to be tenancies) but must also be related to the use the tenant is to make of the property. Thus, it is suggested that a mere agency to sell the landlord's products in the course of the tenant's business does not qualify (Woodfall, *Landlord and Tenant*, 28th edn (Sweet & Maxwell, 1978) para 22.035). The position may be different if the tenant is not permitted to sell anything except the landlord's products (ie the property is 'tied').

A service tenancy will only escape the Act if it is granted in writing and the written agreement states the purpose for which the tenancy is granted (s 43(2)).

Example 10:2 Statement of purpose of tenancy

> It is hereby declared that this tenancy is granted in consequence of the appointment of the tenant by the landlord as [   ] and in order to facilitate the duties of that appointment

(b) Non-occupying tenant

The Act only applies where the demised property is occupied by the tenant and is so occupied for the purposes of a business carried on by him (s 23(1)). Thus, the Act will not apply where the tenancy is granted to a person who does not occupy the demised property. Where, for example, a business is to be carried on by a limited company a tenancy granted to a director of the company will not attract the protection of the Act (*Pegler v Craven* [1952] 2 QB 693; *Tunstall v Steigmann* [1962] 2 QB 593) unless the tenancy is held on trust for the company (contrast *Palmer v Weaver* (1952) 159 EG 141 and *Beech v Bloomfield* (1953) CLY 1988, both county court cases). A similar situation arises where a tenancy is granted to a company engaged in franchising. The franchisor tenant will not be in occupation, while the franchisee occupier will not have security of tenure. If the tenancy is held on trust and the demised property is occupied by a beneficiary under the trust who has a right to occupy it by virtue of his beneficial interest (rather than by virtue of a commercial arrangement made between him and his trustee (*Frish v Barclays Bank Ltd* [1955] 2 QB 541)) the beneficiary's occupation will be sufficient to attract the protection of the Act (s 41). It may be that for all practical purposes the Act may be avoided if the tenancy contains an absolute covenant against holding the lease on trust. In those circumstances, if the tenant sets up a claim to hold the tenancy on trust for a business occupier he will simultaneously expose himself to the risk of forfeiture. The tenant would of course have the right to apply for relief against forfeiture.

If the tenancy is granted to a limited company and the demised property is occupied for business purposes by another company that is a member of the same group of companies the Act will apply to the tenancy (s 42; see Aldridge, *Letting Business Premises*, 7th edn (FT Law & Tax, 1996) p 88).

(c) Joint tenants

Where a tenancy is granted to joint tenants, all the joint tenants must be parties to any application to the court for the grant of a new tenancy (*Jacobs v Chaudhuri* [1968] 2 QB 470). Thus, it may be that the Act may be avoided if the tenancy is granted to two persons, one of whom will not occupy and who will not join in an application for renewal. Where joint tenants are the sole beneficial owners of the tenancy the court will not compel an unwilling tenant to join with the other in applying to the court (*Harris v Black* (1983) 266 EG 628). The position may be different where other beneficiaries are involved or where the unwilling joint tenant is a mere nominee (*Sykes v Land* (1984) 271 EG 1264; *Featherstone v Staples* (1984) 273 EG 193). However the decision in *Jacobs v Chaudhuri* above has been reversed in so far as it relates to partnership property (s 41A).

4 Nature of the Property

The Act applies only where the demised property includes 'premises which are occupied by the tenant'. Premises are not confined to buildings and may include open land (*Bracey v Read* [1963] Ch 88). However, a letting of fixtures and fittings is not within the Act (*Mirabeau v Scheckman* (1959) 174 EG 39). Nor is a lease of an easement, since an easement cannot be 'occupied' within the meaning of the Act (*Land Reclamation Co Ltd v Basildon District Council* [1979] 1 All ER 993). Thus, a 'desk hire' agreement would not be caught by the Act, nor would a lease of fishing rights (cf *Jones v Christy* (1963) 107 SJ 374).

5 Use of the Demised Property

The Act does not apply where the demised property is used for certain specified purposes.

(a) Use in breach of covenant

The Act does not apply where the tenant is carrying on a business in breach of a prohibition (however expressed) of use for business purposes (s 23(4)). The prohibition must be a general prohibition, and not a prohibition of use for a specified business or of use for any but the purposes of a specified business. Thus, if the lease contains a covenant 'not to use the demised property except for the purpose of a bakery' the Act will continue to apply if the use is changed to use as a butcher's shop. However, the prohibition may be a prohibition of use for trade in general or professional use in general. Thus, if the lease contains a covenant 'not to use the demised property otherwise than for professional purposes' or 'otherwise than as a dentist's surgery', it seems that the Act will not apply if the use is changed to use as the offices of a building society. If the use of the property has been changed in breach of covenant the Act will apply if the immediate landlord or his predecessor in title has consented to the breach, or the immediate landlord has acquiesced in it. Acquiescence is a passive failure to do anything in the face of knowledge of the breach, while consent involves something of a positive nature which amounts to an express affirmation of what is being done (*Bell v Franks (Alfred) and Bartlett Co Ltd* [1980] 1 All ER 356). Note that the prohibition must be one that is binding on the tenant. Thus, where a subtenant is let into possession in breach of a covenant against subletting, the subtenant will be entitled to the protection of the Act (*D'Silva v Lister House Development Ltd* [1971] Ch 17).

(b) Agricultural use

The Act does not apply to a tenancy of an agricultural holding or to a farm business tenancy (s 43(1)(a)); nor does it apply to a grazing and mowing licence for less than one year; nor to a tenancy approved by the Minister before it was entered into.

(c) Use for mining

The Act does not apply to a tenancy created by a mining lease (s 43(1)(b)). A mining lease means a lease for mining purposes (defined in the Landlord and Tenant Act 1927, s 25) and extends to a lease for the extraction of sand and gravel (*O'Callaghan v Elliot* [1966] 1 QB 601).

(d) Licensed premises

The former exclusion from the protection of the Act in relation to licensed premises was removed in stages by the Landlord and Tenant (Licensed Premises) Act 1990. All tenancies of licensed premises in existence on 11 July 1992 (whenever granted) and all tenancies of such premises granted since 11 July 1989, are capable of qualifying for protection if the ordinary criteria of occupation by the tenant for business purposes are satisfied.

6 Excluding the Right to Compensation

If the landlord opposes the renewal of a tenancy on any of the grounds set out in s 30(1)(e), (f) or (g) of the 1954 Act, and no other ground is made out, the tenant will be entitled to compensation on quitting. If the business has been carried on in the property for fourteen years the amount of the compensation will be the product of the appropriate multiplier and twice the rateable value of the holding; in all other cases it will equal the product of the appropriate multiplier and to the rateable value of the holdings (s 37). The right to compensation may be excluded by agreement where the business has been carried on in the property for less than five years preceding the date on which the tenant quits. Occupation by the tenant's predecessors may be aggregated for this purpose provided that the same business has been carried on throughout (s 38(2)). Once the business has been carried on for more than five years, the agreement becomes void.

At the beginning of a tenancy granted to a tenant who is to begin a new business in the property it will not be known whether an agreement excluding the right to compensation will be effective by the time that the tenant quits. Nevertheless, the draftsman should wherever possible seek to exclude that right. It may be worth doing so in a lease granted for a term exceeding five years just in case the tenant quits before the expiry of the term or there is a change both in the occupier and the business carried on.

Example 10:3 Exclusion of right to compensation

> The landlord and tenant hereby agree in so far as they are permitted to do so by section 38(3) of the Landlord and Tenant Act 1954 that the tenant shall not be entitled to compensation under section 37 of that Act on quitting the demised property or any part thereof

7 Property Where Subletting is Envisaged

Special problems arise where the tenant is expected to sublet the demised property (either in whole or in part). The first question is whether he is protected by the 1954 Act at all. If he sublets on a regular basis there is nothing to prevent the subletting itself from being a business for the purposes of the 1954 Act (*Bagettes Ltd v GP Estates Co Ltd* [1956] Ch 290). In most cases the problem will be to determine whether the tenant 'occupies' the demised property. Even if he retains possession of the common parts of the property, storage space and temporary voids, that will not be 'occupation' for the purposes of the 1954 Act. Equally, the mere fact that the tenant provides furniture for his subtenants will not entitle him to claim to occupy (*Narcissi v Wolfe* [1960] Ch 10). Where the tenant sublets parts of the property as part of his business, the subtenants will be entitled to the protection of the Act (if they are in occupation) and the tenant will not. The tenant cannot be said to occupy property in respect of which he has granted the right to exclusive possession to another (*Graysim Holdings v P & O Properties* [1994] 4 All ER 831).

If the 1954 Act does apply to the letting the second problem is to anticipate its effect both on the letting itself and on subtenancies. Even if the tenant does not occupy the whole of the demised property for the purposes of the 1954 Act, his tenancy of the whole will nevertheless continue until it is determined in accordance with the provision of the Act (s 24(1)). Once it has been determined, usually by notice served under s 25 of the Act, the tenant will only be entitled to renew his tenancy of the part that he actually occupies (s 32) unless the landlord requires him to take a new tenancy of the whole (s 32(2)).

If the tenant is not entitled to renew his tenancy of the whole of the demised property the subtenants may nevertheless be entitled to do so. Moreover, if the tenant does not occupy the demised property for the purposes of the Act the subtenancies will nevertheless continue provided that the subtenants are in occupation. *Prima facie* the terms on which the subtenancies continue are those agreed between the subtenants and the tenant, not the terms of the agreement between the tenant and the landlord. This may involve a radical change in the terms (see *Poster v Slough Estates Ltd* [1969] 1 Ch 495). It therefore becomes all the more important that the landlord be given the right to approve the terms of any proposed subletting.

8 Residential Accommodation

In some circumstances a tenancy of residential accommodation may be protected by the Act. Activities which are merely incidental to residential occupation do not amount to occupation 'for the purposes of' a business although they may properly be described as used for business. The businessman who takes work home in the evening which he does in a study set aside for that purpose may very well be said to be using the premises partly for carrying on business; but he is not occupying the premises for the purposes of a business. It is only if the business activity is part of the reason for, part of his aim and object in occupying the premises that the Act will apply (*Cheryl Investments Ltd v Saldanha* [1979] 1 All ER 5). Where the tenant takes a tenancy of residential accommodation for the purpose of providing house accommodation for his employees, the tenancy will not be protected by the Act unless the occupation of the employees is in furtherance of the business activities (*Chapman v Freeman* [1978] 3 All ER 878 as explained in *Linden v DHSS* [1986] 1 WLR 164). Thus where a flat let to a medical school was used to house students with a view to fostering a corporate spirit and thereby advance the educational process, the tenancy was protected by the Act (*Groveside Properties Ltd v Westminster Medical School* (1983) 267 EG 593), as was a house used by a health authority for housing employees of the National Health Service at a nearby hospital (*Linden v DHSS* above).

Property let for mixed use (ie partly for business purposes and partly for residential purposes) will not usually qualify for protection under the Rent Act 1977 (*Henry Smith's Charity Trustees v Wagle* [1989] 1 EGLR 124). The same approach would probably be adopted under the Housing Act 1988 in relation to assured tenancies.

11

The Liability of Sureties

The surety's obligation is to make good any default by the tenant. The draftsman's duty is, therefore, to ensure that the liability of the surety is co-extensive with that of the tenant so that the landlord does not find that the surety is unexpectedly released or discharged.

1 Co-extensiveness

In principle the surety's liability is co-extensive with the tenant's. Under a covenant of guarantee it is the duty of the surety to ensure that the tenant performs his covenants. If the tenant breaks any of his covenants, the breach automatically and instantly places the surety in breach of his own obligations (*Cerium Investments v Evans* (1990) 62 P&CR 203). In addition, the surety usually agrees to indemnify the landlord against losses suffered as a result of the tenant's breach of obligation. This is not a guarantee but an indemnity, and is usually dependent on both a breach and a demand by the landlord for compensation.

Where the tenant is released from liability by the Landlord and Tenant (Covenants) Act 1995, the surety will also be released from liability to the same extent (Landlord and Tenant (Covenants) Act 1995, s 24(2)). In certain circumstances the tenant may be required to enter into an authorised guarantee agreement guaranteeing his immediate assignee's liabilities under the lease. The surety's obligation should require the surety to guarantee the tenant's liabilities under an authorised guarantee agreement as well as his liabilities under the lease.

2 Termination of the Tenancy

Prima facie the surety's obligations will come to an end on the date on which the contractual term is expressed to expire. Thus, if the tenant holds over as a continuation tenant under the Landlord and Tenant Act 1954, s 24, the surety will not be liable during the continuation period unless the lease provides to the contrary (*Junction Estates Ltd v Cope* (1974) 27 P&CR 482; *Plesser (A) & Co Ltd v Davis* (1983) 267 EG 1039). Curiously, although a surety is not liable during a period in which the tenant holds over lawfully, he will be liable to pay damages if the tenant holds over unlawfully as a trespasser (*Associated Dairies Ltd v Pierce* (1982) 265 EG 127). But the surety will not be obliged to enter into a guarantee of the tenant's obligations under a renewed lease, and the absence of a surety is not a ground for objecting to a renewal (*Barclays Bank Ltd v Ascott* [1961] 1 All ER 782). However, the provision of a surety is a term of the new tenancy that the court could order under the Landlord and Tenant Act 1954, s 35 (*Cairnplace Ltd v CBL (Property Investment) Co Ltd* [1984] 1 All ER 315). Further, there appears to be nothing to prevent the landlord from taking a covenant from the surety to guarantee a renewed lease (compare *Hollies Stores Ltd v Timmis* [1921] 2 Ch 202, where an option to renew a lease failed because one of the guarantors of the original lease had died).

Example 11:1 Basic covenant by surety

In consideration of the grant of this lease to the tenant having been made at his request the surety hereby covenants with the landlord that the tenant will punctually pay the rent and will observe and perform all the tenant's covenants in this lease both during the term hereby expressed to be granted and during any continuation or renewal thereof and will comply with any obligations imposed on him under an authorised guarantee agreement and that in case of any default by the tenant in the payment of the rent or the observance or performance of his covenants as aforesaid the surety will make good to the landlord all loss damage costs and expenses arising out of such default and suffered or incurred by the landlord

3 Discharge of the Surety

The surety will be discharged from liability under his guarantee if the landlord acts to his prejudice since the landlord must act with the utmost good faith towards him. This rule may be modified or excluded by the express terms of the guarantee. Thus, it has become usual for the basic obligation to be qualified by a proviso that any time given to the tenant or any neglect or forbearance on the part of the landlord to enforce the covenants shall not discharge the surety. From the landlord's point of view it may be that the usual form of proviso does not go far enough. For example, if the tenant is in breach of covenant but tenders the rent the landlord will almost invariably refuse to accept it in order not to waive the breach. It is doubtful whether a refusal by the landlord to accept rent tendered falls within the expression 'neglect or forbearance'. Accordingly, it may be that the surety would be discharged once rent has been tendered by the tenant and refused. It has, however, been suggested that the landlord is not obliged to accept a tender of rent from a third party where the acceptance would prejudice him (*Richards v De Freitas* (1974) 29 P&CR 1); but the tenant is not a third party, so this rule may not extend to the refusal of a tender by the tenant. It is suggested that the draftsman should make express provision for this eventuality.

The surety will be similarly discharged if the tenant surrenders part of the demised property, even if the rent is reduced (*Holme v Brunskill* (1877) 3 QBD 495), because his rights of subrogation are thereby prejudiced. There seems to be nothing in principle to prevent the draftsman from providing that in the event of a surrender of part of the demised property the surety's liability should continue in respect of the remainder. In all cases the draftsman should consider doing so.

Where the lease provides that the surety is not to be discharged if the landlord 'gives time' to the tenant, the surety will not be discharged even if the landlord contractually binds himself not to sue for the rent or agrees to authorise an alteration made in breach of covenant (*Selous Street Properties Ltd v Oronel Fabrics Ltd* (1984) 270 EG 643).

Another method of dealing with the possibility of inadvertently discharging the surety is to provide that as between the landlord and the surety he is to be treated as a principal debtor. In addition the surety may be asked to confer irrevocable authority upon the tenant for the time being to bind him with reference to the subject matter of the lease. A provision to this effect is likely to defeat most defences based upon alleged variations to the lease. The words of the provision must be clear, as the court construes contracts of suretyship strictly in favour of the surety. Thus where the contract provided that the surety should not be released in certain circumstances, it was held that the clause did not cover new terms introduced by a licence to assign (*West Horndon Industrial Park v Phoenix Timber Group* [1995] 1 EGLR 77; *Howard de Walden Estates v Pasta Place* [1995] 1 EGLR 79).

However, where the principal debtor has ceased to be tenant as a result of an assignment, and the surety remains liable on his guarantee, he is not liable to pay any amount in respect of a tenant covenant of the

THE LIABILITY OF SURETIES

tenancy to the extent that the amount is referable to any relevant variation of the tenant covenants of the tenancy effected after the assignment (Landlord and Tenant (Covenants) Act 1995, s 18(2)). A relevant variation is one which the landlord has an absolute right to refuse, or would have had such a right but for a previous variation which was effected after the assignment (s 18(4)). The effect of this provision is that although the draftsman may provide for the surety to be bound by variations effected while the principal debtor remains tenant, he cannot provide for the surety to be bound by variations made after an assignment by the principal debtor. Indeed it appears to be the case that a surety will not be bound by a variation effected after an assignment by a principal debtor even if he expressly consents to the variation. The practical answer for landlords is to refuse to agree to variations of the tenancy unless the surety enters into a fresh guarantee. However the section does not say that the surety is discharged by a relevant variation, and it seems probable that although the surety's liability cannot be increased by such a variation, the draftsman can provide that his original liability will continue despite such a variation.

Example 11:2 Proviso limiting discharge of surety

Provided that:
(1) no neglect or forbearance of the landlord in enforcing the payment of the rent or the observance or performance of the tenant's covenants nor any refusal by the landlord to accept rent tendered by or on behalf of the tenant during a period in which the landlord is entitled or would after service of a notice under section 146 of the Law of Property Act 1925 be entitled to re-enter the demised property nor any time given by the landlord to the tenant shall discharge the surety either in whole or in part or in any way affect his liability under this covenant

(2) in any event that the tenant surrenders part of the demised property the liability of the surety shall continue in respect of the part of the demised property not so surrendered after making any necessary apportionments under section 140 of the Law of Property Act 1925

Example 11:3 Surety deemed to be principal debtor

Provided that as between the landlord and the surety the surety shall be deemed to be a principal debtor and accordingly the landlord shall be at liberty to forbear or refuse to accept payment of the rent hereby reserved or enforce performance or observance of the tenant's covenants or to give time to the tenant or to vary the terms of this lease without discharging the surety wholly or partly or in any way diminishing his liability under this covenant

Example 11:4 Surety to be bound by variations

The surety agrees:
(a) to be bound by any variation of this lease made in good faith by the landlord and the tenant at any time before an assignment of this lease by the tenant
(b) that any variation of this lease after such an assignment will not discharge his liability under this guarantee

4 Disclaimer

If the tenant for the time being becomes insolvent his trustee in bankruptcy (or in the case of a company the liquidator) may disclaim the lease (Insolvency Act 1986, ss 178–182 (companies); ss 315–321 (individuals)).

Before the Insolvency Act 1986 came into force, the liquidator of a company was required to obtain the leave of the court before disclaiming. He is no longer obliged to do so, and consequently the landlord now has no opportunity to oppose disclaimer.

Disclaimer of a lease will not discharge a surety (*Hindcastle v Barbara Attenborough Associates* [1996] 1 All ER 737). However, the surety's obligations will come to an end if the landlord retakes possession. It follows that in order to retain his rights against a surety the landlord must leave the property empty. If he wishes to avoid this undesirable result, the draftsman should include a covenant on the part of the surety to take a lease of the demised property if the existing lease is disclaimed. Some clauses place a time limit on a request by the landlord to the surety. If a time limit is imposed, it should run not from the date of the disclaimer, but from the date on which the landlord receives notice of it.

Although the surety enters into such a covenant as a principal (since *ex hypothesi* his liability as surety will have come to an end before the time for performance arrives), nevertheless he remains collaterally liable. Thus, if the surety is discharged from liability under the covenant imposing his primary liability upon him, he will also be discharged from his obligation to take a lease on disclaimer (*Selous Street Properties Ltd v Oronel Fabrics Ltd* (1984) 270 EG 643, 743 at 747). However, the disclaimer itself does not discharge the surety from his obligation to take a new lease (*Re Yarmarine* [1992] BCLC 276). The covenant runs with the land, and consequently a successor in title to the original landlord may enforce it (*Coronation Street Industrial Properties v Ingall* [1989] 1 WLR 304).

Example 11:5 Covenant by surety to take a lease on disclaimer

If:
- (a) a liquidator or trustee in bankruptcy disclaims this lease so that it comes to an end or
- (b) the tenant (being a company) is dissolved or struck off the Register of Companies or
- (c) this lease vests in the Crown as *bona vacantia* and is disclaimed by the Crown

then at the written request of the landlord (made not more than three months after notice of the event in question has been given to him or the event has otherwise come to his knowledge) the surety will take from the landlord a new lease of the demised property:
- (i) for a term equal to the residue of the term unexpired at the date of the event in question
- (ii) at the rent then payable under the terms of this lease
- (iii) otherwise on the terms of this lease

and will pay the landlord's costs of the grant of the new lease

5 PROTECTING THE SURETY

In recent years more thought has been given to the position of the surety and to ways of protecting him against unlimited liability. Where a surety is required upon the grant of a lease the selected person is usually closely connected with the tenant (eg a director or parent company of a limited company, or a relative of an individual tenant). For as long as the original tenant holds the lease the surety is likely to be aware of the tenant's financial strength; indeed he may directly control it. However, once an assignment takes place the surety will lose direct contact and is likely to become aware of his liability only when he is faced with meeting a demand from the landlord. Accordingly, in the first instance the surety should seek to limit his liability to the tenure of the original tenant.

If the landlord will not agree, the surety should seek to limit his retrospective liability. For this purpose Example 3:1 may be suitably adapted. If such a limitation is introduced into the lease, the landlord will be under pressure to enforce his remedies in good time, and the surety will be to a large extent protected against the width of a proviso enabling the landlord to refrain from enforcing obligations.

Since the surety will be liable to pay not only the rent initially agreed, but also any increased rent which becomes payable on review, he should seek to secure a right to participate in the determination of the reviewed rent. It seems that this may be done by requiring rent review notices to be served on 'the parties' rather than on 'the tenant' (*Cressey v Jacobs*

(1977) unreported, Case no 17 in Bernstein and Reynolds, *Handbook of Rent Review* (Sweet & Maxwell, 1981)). A surer way would be to require the surety to be a party to any rent review memorandum. From the landlord's point of view this would have the added advantage of preventing any later argument that the review had been irregularly conducted.

Finally, since the role of the surety is essentially passive, he may find it advantageous to convert his role into an active one. Thus, consideration should be given to enabling the surety to require the tenant to assign the lease to him if he is called upon under the guarantee. Although the surety will not escape liability, he will at least have the opportunity of finding a solvent assignee. Such an option would amount to an estate contract and must be protected by registration. The surety should stipulate, where possible, for a provision exempting the transaction from the requirement of obtaining the landlord's consent. The need to obtain consent may be time consuming, and the tenant, who is being compelled to assign, may be reluctant to expend energy in obtaining it. It is not unreasonable to expect the landlord to waive the requirement of consent, since he will have initially approved the surety as a person of financial responsibility. These questions are more fully discussed in Reynolds and Fogel, *Commercial Lettings: Liability of Original Tenant and of Successive Sureties After Assignment(s)*, Blundell Memorial Lecture, 22 May 1984.

Since the Landlord and Tenant (Covenants) Act 1995 a surety who pays in full an amount which he has been required to pay is entitled to the grant of an overriding lease. The overriding lease will be on the same terms as the lease itself (subject to any agreed modifications) and will be for the residue of the term of the lease plus three days (Landlord and Tenant (Covenants) Act 1995, s 19). This may be sufficient for a surety to dispense with a contractual right to call for an assignment, although the grant of an overriding lease will still leave the defaulting tenant in possession of the property.

Example 11:6 Surety's right to require assignment

(1) At any time after the surety has been lawfully required by the landlord to discharge any liability of the tenant and has discharged that liability either wholly or partly he shall be entitled to serve notice on the tenant under this clause

(2) Within fourteen days after service of such notice on the tenant he shall deliver up vacant possession of the demised property and shall execute and deliver to the surety an assignment of this lease and

the surety shall accept it
(3) The landlord's consent to any such assignment is not required

6 Authorised Guarantee Agreements

Under the Landlord and Tenant (Covenants) Act 1995 a tenant is released from liability on an assignment of his lease (unless the assignment is an excluded assignment). However, the landlord may require him to guarantee the obligations of his immediate assignee. This can only be done by an authorised guarantee agreement. An agreement is an authorised guarantee agreement if:

(1) under it the tenant guarantees performance of the tenant covenants of the tenancy to any extent by the assignee;
(2) it is entered into in the following circumstances:
   (a) by virtue of a covenant against assignment (whether absolute or qualified) the assignment cannot be effected without the consent of the landlord or some other person;
   (b) consent is given subject to a condition (lawfully imposed) that the tenant is to enter into an agreement guaranteeing the performance of covenants by the assignee; and
   (c) the agreement is entered into by the tenant in pursuance of that condition;
(3) its provisions conform with ss 16(4) and 16(5) of the Act (Landlord and Tenant (Covenants) Act 1995, s 16).

The formal conditions are that the agreement must not:
(1) impose on the tenant any requirement to guarantee in any way the performance of the relevant covenant by any person other than the assignee; and
(2) impose on the tenant any liability, restriction or other requirement (of whatever nature) in relation to any time after the assignee is released from liability by virtue of the 1995 Act.

However, an authorised guarantee agreement may:
(1) impose on the tenant any liability as sole or principal debtor in respect of any obligation owed by the assignee under the relevant covenant;
(2) impose on the tenant liabilities as guarantor in respect of the assignee's performance of that covenant which are no more onerous that those to which he would be subject in the event

of his being liable as sole or principal debtor in respect of any obligation owed by the assignee under that covenant;
(3) require the tenant, in the event of the tenancy assigned by him being disclaimed, to enter into a new tenancy of the premises comprised in the assignment:
   (a) whose term expires not later than the term of the tenancy assigned by the tenant, and
   (b) whose tenant covenants are no more onerous than those of the tenancy;
(4) make provision incidental or supplementary to any provision made by virtue of (1) to (3).

(Landlord and Tenant (Covenants) Act 1995, s 16(5)).

Example 11:7 Authorised guarantee agreement

AN AGREEMENT made the [   ] of [   ] between [   ] ('the Tenant') (1) and [   ] ('the Landlord') (2)

RECITES THAT

(1) the Tenant is the tenant of [   ] under a lease dated [   ]

(2) the Tenant has applied to the Landlord for consent to assign the lease to [   ] ('the Assignee')

(3) the Landlord has granted consent subject to the condition that the Tenant enters into this agreement

(4) the condition was lawfully imposed

(5) the Tenant enters into this agreement in pursuance of that condition

AND NOW WITNESSES

1. In consideration of the grant of consent by the Landlord to the assignment of the lease to the Assignee the Tenant covenants with the Landlord that:
   (a) from completion of the assignment until he is released from liability by the Landlord and Tenant (Covenants) Act 1995 the Assignee will punctually pay the rent reserved by the Lease and will perform all the tenant covenants contained in it
   (b) in case of any default by the Assignee the Tenant will indemnify the Landlord against all loss damage costs and expenses suffered or incurred by the Landlord

2. As between the Landlord and the Tenant the Tenant shall be treated as a principal debtor and accordingly:
   (a) the Tenant's liability under clause 1 is not dependent on any demand being made by the Landlord
   (b) the Tenant's liability will not be discharged by any forbearance or indulgence by the landlord or by the giving of time to

the Assignee or by any refusal on the part of the Landlord to accept rent from the Assignee
(c) the Tenant's liability will not be discharged by any variation of the terms of the Lease made after the Lease has been assigned to the Assignee

3.(1) In the event of the Lease being disclaimed the Landlord shall be entitled to require the Tenant to enter into a new tenancy of the property comprised in the assignment:
(a) for a term equivalent to the term of the Lease unexpired at the date of the disclaimer
(b) on the same terms as the terms of the Lease at that date
(2) The Landlord requires the Tenant to enter into a new tenancy by giving written notice to that effect not later than three months after the disclaimer has come to his notice
(3) The Tenant shall complete the new lease within ten working days after receipt of written notice under subclause (2)

7 Change of Landlord

It has now been authoritatively determined that a covenant by a surety that the tenant will perform his obligations runs with the land, and subsequently may be enforced by a successor in title to the original landlord (*P & A Swift Investments v Combined English Stores Group plc* [1988] 2 All ER 885). Accordingly, the problems which had previously been thought to exist no longer apply. All that is necessary is for the lease to state clearly that 'the landlord' includes successors in title.

8 Renewal Leases

On a renewal, the court has no power to order the grant of a new tenancy to be conditional on the provision of a surety, since this could be to introduce a new non-statutory ground of opposition into the Act (*Barclays Bank Ltd v Ascott* [1961] 1 All ER 782). However, the court may order the new tenancy to contain a term which requires the tenant to procure a person to stand surety for him within a fixed period (*Cairnplace Ltd v CBL (Property Investment) Ltd* [1984] 1 All ER 315). Where the liability of the tenant is guaranteed under the current tenancy, it will usually be fair and reasonable to order the provision of sureties in the new tenancy (*Cairnplace Ltd v CBL (Property Investments) Ltd* above). Breach of the obligation would entitle the landlord to forfeit the new tenancy, and it is unlikely that the tenant would obtain relief against forfeiture unless the sureties were provided. However, failure to provide sureties within a fixed period would amount to a once and for all breach, and consequently would be capable of inadvertent waiver. The draftsman should therefore provide for the period to be capable of extension by the landlord.

Example 11:8 Requirement to provide sureties

(1) Within twenty-eight days of the grant of this lease (or such longer period as the landlord may from time to time prescribe by notice given to the tenant) the tenant shall procure that two persons approved by the landlord shall stand surety for the performance of the tenant's obligations under this lease

(2) The landlord's approval shall not be unreasonably withheld

(3) The obligations to be assumed by the sureties shall be contained in a deed and shall take such form as the landlord shall reasonably require

Example 11:9 Alternative form of surety covenant including obligation to take lease on disclaimer

(1) The surety covenants with the landlord:
 (a) that the tenant will pay the rents promptly and perform all his other obligations under this lease
 (b) to make good to the landlord all losses occasioned by any breach of paragraph (a) above
 (c) if this lease is disclaimed in circumstances in which the disclaimer brings it to an end to take a new lease of the demised property for the residue of the term as at the day preceding the disclaimer on the same terms as this lease
(2) The surety's liability will not be discharged or diminished by:
 (a) any neglect or forbearance by the landlord in enforcing payment of rent or performance of the tenant's obligations
 (b) any refusal by the landlord to accept rent following a breach of covenant by the tenant
 (c) any time given to the tenant
 (d) any variation of this lease or any consent given under it (and the surety's liabilities will extend to the lease as varied so far as permitted by the Landlord and Tenant (Covenants) Act 1995)
 (e) any surrender of part of the demised property (except that the surety's liability will be limited to the part not surrendered)

Form 1

Standard Form of Lease for Letting of Shop in Parade

[**General note**: In this form all the variable parts of the lease are collected, so far as possible, at the front, thereby reducing the possibility of mistakes. The lease contains a 'keep open covenant' subject to exceptions.]

Column 1	*Column 2*
Landlord	
Tenant	
Surety	
Property	
Commencement Date	
Term	
Initial Rent	
Review Date	
Permitted Use	

THIS LEASE which is made on the [   ] of 19[   ] between the Landlord (1) and the Tenant (2) and the Surety (3)
WITNESSES as follows:

1.(1) In this Lease the following expressions have the following meanings:
    (a)   expressions in Column 1 of the preceding table have the meanings assigned to them by Column 2 thereof
    (b)   the Landlord and Tenant include the persons deriving title under them respectively
    (c)   the Parade means [   ]
    (d)   [*Definition of rate of interest, 'the Prescribed Rate'—see Example 5:34*]
  (2) Where the Tenant or the Surety is more than one person their covenants shall be joint and several

(3) Any reference to an Act of Parliament includes a reference to that Act as amended or replaced from time to time and to subordinate legislation or byelaw made thereunder

2. In consideration of the rents and covenants on the part of the Tenancy contained below the Landlord DEMISES the Property to the Tenant TOGETHER with the rights set out in Part I of the First Schedule but EXCEPTING AND RESERVING the rights set out in Part II of that Schedule TO HOLD the Property to the Tenant from the Commencement Date for the Term YIELDING AND PAYING therefor the Initial Rent (exclusive of value added tax) (subject to review as set out in the Second Schedule) by equal quarterly payments in advance on the usual quarter days the first payment (or a duly apportioned part of it) to be made on the date hereof

3. The Tenant hereby covenants with the Landlord as follows:

(1) (a) to pay the rent promptly without any set-off or deduction whatsoever

(b) to pay interest on all arrears of rent and other moneys due under the Lease at the Prescribed Rate

(2) to pay on demand such sums as the Landlord may expend from time to time in insuring the Property or as the case may be a proportion calculated by reference to the proportion which the area of the Property bears to the area of all the buildings comprised in the Parade of the sums expended by the Landlord in insuring the Parade

(3) to pay all rates and outgoings payable in respect of the Property or its ownership or occupation (except such as are payable on a disposal of the Landlord's interest in the Property and Schedule A income tax charged on the Landlord)

(4) (a) to execute all works required in pursuance of any Act of Parliament or required by any local or public authority to be done in respect of the Property whether by the Tenant the Landlord or any other person (however described)

(b) without prejudice to the generality of the preceding paragraph to comply in all respects with the Offices Shops and Railway Premises Act 1963 the Fire Precautions Act 1971 and the Health and Safety at Work etc Act 1974

(5) [*To repair and decorate—see Example 7:4, substituting 'the property' for 'the demised property'*]

(6) [*Not to alter without consent—see Example 7:14 substituting 'the property' for 'the demised property'*]

(7)(a) not to use or permit or suffer to be used the Property for any purpose other than the Permitted Use and to keep the Property open for business during normal business hours PROVIDED THAT it shall not be a breach of this clause if during a period of twenty-four months the Property is not open for business for a period not exceeding three months by reason of:

(i) the carrying out of works (whether of repair or not) to the Property or

(ii) the tenant having ceased to trade in the Property with a view to disposing of it either by way of assignment or sublease

(b) not to carry on any offensive or noisy trade or business nor to hold any sale by auction in the Property nor to permit any person to sleep or reside therein nor to do anything therein which in the opinion of the Landlord causes or might cause nuisance or annoyance to the Landlord or any ten-

STANDARD LEASE FOR LETTING SHOP IN PARADE 277

ant of his

(8) [*Planning covenant—see Example 8:1, substituting 'the property' for 'the demised property'*]

(9) [*Not to cause increase in premium etc—see Example 6:8, substituting 'the property' for 'the demised property'*]

(10) not to exhibit any signboard advertisement placard or name-plate on or in the Property except:
    (a)   as part of a normal window display or
    (b)   with the previous approval in writing of the Landlord

(11) [*Covenant against assignment etc—see Examples 9:1 and 9:5, substituting 'the property' for 'demised property'*]

(12) not to permit any easement to be acquired or encroachment made against or upon the Property and promptly to give notice to the Landlord of any attempt to make or acquire the same and to take such steps (whether by legal proceedings or otherwise) to prevent the same from being acquired or made as the Landlord may reasonably require

(13) not to stop up darken or obstruct any window or other aperture in the Property

(14) to pay all costs charges and expenses (including any professional fees) incurred by the Landlord in and about the preparation or service of a schedule of dilapidations or a notice under section 146 or 147 of the Law of Property Act 1925 (even if forfeiture is avoided otherwise than by relief granted by the court)

(15) to pay the Landlord's solicitors costs and disbursements and surveyor's fees and annual stamp duty in connection with:
    (a)   the preparation and grant of this lease
    (b)   any application by the Tenant for any licence or consent under this lease (whether or not such licence or consent is actually granted)

4. The Landlord hereby covenants with the Tenant as follows:

(1) that the Tenant paying the rent and performing and observing his covenants shall peaceably and quietly hold and enjoy the Property for the Term without any interruption by the Landlord or any person claiming under or in trust for him

(2) [*Covenant to insure and reinstate—see Example 6:2, substituting 'the property' for 'the demised property,' and adding the following subparagraph: '(5) for the avoidance of doubt it is hereby declared that the Landlord need not maintain a separate policy of insurance in respect of the Property only but may insure the Parade as a whole'*]

5. PROVIDED ALWAYS and it is hereby agreed as follows:

(1) if the rent or any part thereof shall be unpaid for twenty-one days after becoming payable (whether formally demanded or not) or if there shall be a breach of any of the Tenant's covenants or if the Tenant or the Surety (being a company) shall enter into compulsory or voluntary liquidation (otherwise than for the purposes of reconstruction or amalgamation) or (not being a company) shall become bankrupt or have a receiving order made against him or call a meeting of or enter into any composition with his creditors or suffer any distress or execution to be levied on the Property then and in each such case the Landlord shall be entitled (in addition to any other right) to re-enter upon the Property and thereupon this lease shall absolutely determine

(2) [*Proviso for abatement of rent—see Example 6:6, substituting 'the property' for 'the demised property'*]

(3) [*Tenant's break-clause on total loss—see Example 6:7*]

(4) section 196 of the Law of Property Act 1925 shall apply to all notices or schedules required or permitted to be served hereunder

6. In consideration of the demise contained above and made at the Surety's request (as he hereby acknowledges) the Surety hereby covenants with the Landlord as follows:

(1) [*Basic covenant—see Example 11:1*]

(2) [*To take a lease on disclaimer—see Example 11:5, substituting 'the property' for 'the demised property'*]

THE FIRST SCHEDULE

Part I: Rights included in the demise

1. The right in common with the Landlord and all others having the like right to pass and repass (but not to park) with or without vehicles at all times and for all purposes connected with the Permitted Use but not otherwise over the service road at the rear of the Property but this right is conditional on the Tenant paying a fair proportion (to be conclusively determined by the Landlord's surveyor) of the cost of repairing and maintaining the same

2. The right in common with the Landlord and all others having the like right to the free passage of water soil gas and electricity through the pipes conduits sewers and wires serving the Parade but this right is conditional on the Tenant paying a fair proportion (to be conclusively determined by the Landlord's surveyor) of the cost of repairing and maintaining the same

3. The right for the Tenant and the Tenant's customers to pass and repass on foot only at all times and for all purposes connected with the Permitted Use but not otherwise over the common parts of the Parade

4. The right to the support and shelter of any part of the Parade in physical contact with the Property

Part II: Exceptions and reservations

1. Rights corresponding to those granted to the Tenant in Part I of this Schedule

2. The right to enter the Property in case of emergency to carry out any works thereon making good all physical damage caused by such entry

3. Such other rights of entry upon the Property as are necessary for the proper performance of his covenants by the Landlord making good all physical damage caused by such entry

4. Section 62 of the Law of Property Act 1925 shall not apply to this lease

THE SECOND SCHEDULE

[*Rent review—see Example 5:37, substituting 'the property' for 'the demised property,' and deleting the definition of 'Review Date'*]

Form 2

Lease of Shop in Shopping Centre

[**General note**: This form is suitable where the landlord is to provide services to the shopping centre. Since the landlord may wish to exercise his option to charge VAT on the rent, the VAT has itself been reserved as rent. The landlord recovers a service charge. The service charge deals with major expenditure by allowing the landlord to build up a reserve fund.]

Column 1	Column 2
Landlord	
Tenant	
Demised Property	the property known as Unit [　　] in the Centre which is described further in Part I of the First Schedule and identified by red edging on the Plan
Term	[　　] years beginning on [　　] and ending on
Basic Rent	£[　　] per annum
Review Date	the [　　] of [　　] and every fifth anniversary of that date
Permitted Use	use as a retail shop for the sale of [　　] or such other goods as the Landlord shall from time to time approve (such approval not to be unreasonably withheld)
Service Charge Proportion	[　　] per cent

THIS LEASE which is made the [　　] of 19[　　] between the Landlord (1) and the Tenant (2)

WITNESSES as follows:

INTERPRETATION

1. In this Lease
    1.1 the following definitions apply:
        1.1.1 expressions in Column 1 of the Particulars have the meanings opposite them in Column 2
        1.1.2 the Plan means the attached plan
        1.1.3 the Landlord's Surveyor means the surveyor from time to time appointed by the Landlord for the purposes of this lease (who may be employed by the Landlord or an associated company of the Landlord)
        1.1.4 the President means the President for the time being of the Royal Institution of Chartered Surveyors or a person acting on his behalf
        1.1.5 [*Definition of interest rate 'the Prescribed Rate'—see Example 5:34*]
        1.1.6 the Centre means the shopping centre known as [   ] and edged blue on the Plan
        1.1.7 [*Definition of the interior of the Demised Property—see Example 7:3 substituting 'the Centre' for 'the building' and adding '(7) the shop front and fascia'*]
        1.1.8 the Common Parts means the service roads and loading bays coloured brown on the Plan
        1.1.9 the Public Parts means the malls stairs escalators lift car parks and other parts of the Centre not comprised in a demise to which the public has access during business hours
        1.1.10 the Retained Parts means those parts of the Centre whose possession is retained by the Landlord including storerooms restrooms and offices for managerial staff within the Centre
        1.1.11 the Structure means:
            1.1.11.1 the roof and foundations of the Centre
            1.1.11.2 its loadbearing walls and columns (excluding plaster or other decorative finishes)
            1.1.11.3 its floor structures including structures supporting malls and walkways (but excluding floor screeds and floor finishes outside the Public Parts or the Retained Parts)
            1.1.11.4 stairs escalators and lifts within the Public Parts
            1.1.11.5 all surfaces of the Centre exposed to the elements
        1.1.12 the Plant means all mechanical electrical heating air-conditioning and ventilating apparatus and all sprinkler systems within the Centre which have been provided by the Landlord and all wires pipes conduits sewers and flues which serve more than one unit
    1.2 the Landlord and the Tenant include their respective successors in title
    1.3 covenants given by or implied on more than one person are joint and several
    1.4 any reference to an Act of Parliament includes a reference to that Act as amended or replaced from time to time and to any subordinate legislation or byelaws made under it.
    1.5 the paragraph headings shall not affect the interpretation of this lease

DEMISE

2. In consideration of the rent and the tenant's covenants the Landlord demises the Demised Property to the Tenant for the Term together with the rights specified in Part II of the First Schedule and Reserving the rights specified in Part III of that Schedule yielding and paying:

2.1 the Basic Rent (exclusive of value added tax) (subject to review in accordance with the Second Schedule) payable (if so required by direct debit) by equal quarterly instalments in advance on the usual quarter days

2.2 an amount equal to the gross premium (before deduction of discount or commission) paid by the Landlord from time to time in insuring the Demised Property (or if the Landlord chooses the Service Charge Proportion of the amount equal to the gross premium paid by the Landlord from time to time in insuring the Centre) in either case payable on demand

2.3 the Service Charge calculated in accordance with the Third Schedule and payable as there set out

2.4 where value added tax is payable on the rent (whether as a result of an election by the Landlord or otherwise) the amount of that value added tax

together with interest at the Prescribed Rate from the due date for payment until payment in full

TENANT'S COVENANTS

3. The Tenant covenants with the Landlord:

To pay rent

3.1 to pay the rent promptly and without deduction or set-off

To pay outgoings

3.2 to pay all rates taxes charges and outgoings of any kind which are now or may during the term become payable in respect of the Demised Property or its ownership or occupation (except such as are payable on a disposal of any interest in reversion to this lease and income or corporation tax charged on the Landlord)

Services

3.3 to pay all charges (including statutory charges and equipment rental) for gas electricity oil and telecommunication used in the Demised Property during the term and to comply with all requirements and recommendations of the appropriate statutory undertaker or public corporation

Statutory works

3.4.1 to execute all works required by or by virtue of any Act of Parliament or by any local or public authority to be done in or in respect of the Demised Property whether by the Landlord or the Tenant or any other person (however described)

3.4.2 without prejudice to paragraph 3.4.1 above to comply in all respects with the Offices Shops and Railway Premises Act 1963 the Fire Precautions Act 1971 and the Health and Safety at Work etc Act 1974

Repair and decoration

3.5 [*Covenants to repair and decorate—see Example 7:4 substituting 'the interior of the demised property' for 'the demised property'*]

Alterations
3.6 [*Covenant restricting alterations—see Example 7:15*]

Planning and Development
3.7 [*Covenant restricting development—see Example 8:1*]

Notices
    3.8.1 upon receipt by the Tenant of any notice proposal or order likely to affect the Demised Property forthwith to supply a copy of it to the Landlord

    3.8.2 if any such notice proposal or order comes to the attention of the Tenant (without having been received by him) forthwith to supply the Landlord the best particulars of it which the Tenant is able to give

Use
    3.9.1 not to use the Demised Property otherwise than for the Permitted Use

    3.9.2 not to use the Demised Property:
        3.9.2.1 for any illegal or immoral purpose
        3.9.2.2 for any offensive or dangerous trade or business
        3.9.2.3 in such a way as in the opinion of the Landlord's Surveyor is likely to cause nuisance or annoyance to neighbours

    3.9.3 [*Covenant not to avoid insurance—see Example 6:8*]

    3.9.4 not to accumulate any refuse or trade empties in or outside the Demised Property

    3.9.5 not to display or offer for sale any goods outside the Demised Property

    3.9.6 not to permit or suffer any obstruction of the Public Parts and not to load or unload goods in or convey goods through the Public Parts

Roads and parking
    3.10.1 not to obstruct any service road
    3.10.2 not to park on any service road
    3.10.3 to comply with any scheme of traffic management from time to time promulgated by the Landlord

Advertisements
3.11 not to exhibit any advertisement signboard name-plate or inscription upon any part of the Demised Property except:
    3.11.1 as part of a normal window display or
    3.11.2 on the fascia to the shop front or
    3.11.3 with the previous written consent of the Landlord (such consent not to be unreasonably withheld)

Plate glass insurance
3.12 to insure all plate glass in the Demised Property to its full reinstatement value in a reputable insurance office and to produce to the Landlord on demand the receipt for the last premium payable

Alienation
3.13 [*Covenant restricting alienation—see Examples 9:1, 9:4 and 9:5*]

Registration
3.14 to give notice to the Landlord within one month after the creation transfer or devolution of any interest in the Demised Property and to produce to the Landlord a

copy (duly stamped) of any instrument effecting or evidencing it and to pay a reasonable registration fee

Costs of notices and consents

3.15 to pay all costs and expenses incurred by the Landlord (including professional fees) in connection with

    3.15.1   the preparation or service of a notice under section 146 of the Law of Property Act 1925 or a schedule of dilapidations

    3.15.2   any application made by the Tenant for any licence or consent under this Lease (even if such licence or consent is not granted or the application is withdrawn)

To yield up

3.16 at the expiry or sooner determination of the term to give vacant possession of the Demised Property in conformity with the covenants contained in this clause (especially those relating to repair and decoration)

Tenant's fixtures

3.17 on quitting to remove such tenant's fixtures as the Landlord may require

Not to permit breaches

3.18 not to permit or suffer the doing of anything expressly prohibited by this clause

LANDLORD'S COVENANTS

4. The Landlord covenants with the Tenant:

Quiet enjoyment

4.1 that on condition that the Tenant pays the rent and performs and observes his covenants he shall have quiet enjoyment of the Demised Property as against the Landlord and persons lawfully claiming in trust for it

To insure

4.2 [*Covenant to insure—see Example 6:5 substituting 'the Centre' for 'the building'*]

To provide services

4.3 to try his best to provide the services and to carry out the works listed in the Third Schedule

ADDITIONAL PROVISIONS

Forfeiture

5.1 the Landlord shall be entitled to re-enter the Demised Property or any part of it in the name of the whole in any of the following cases:

    5.1.1   the rent or any part of it is in arrear for fourteen days after becoming due (whether formally demanded or not)

    5.1.2   the Tenant fails to comply with any of his covenants

    5.1.3   the Tenant or a surety for the Tenant has a receiving order made against him or is adjudged bankrupt

    5.1.4   a receiver is appointed of all or any of the Tenant's assets

> 5.1.5 the Tenant or a surety for the Tenant (being a company) goes into liquidation (otherwise than for amalgamation or reconstruction) or ceases to exist

and upon such re-entry this lease shall absolutely determine but without prejudice to any accrued cause of action

Rent suspension

5.2 [*Proviso for rent suspension—see Example 6:6 omitting the concluding words after 'President'*]

Interest

> 5.3.1 if any sum payable by the Tenant is not paid in full on the due date for payment it shall bear interest at the Prescribed Rate from that date until payment in full
>
> 5.3.2 an instalment of rent is due on the date fixed for payment under Clause 1 above even if the amount of the instalment is not then ascertained

Standard of work

5.4 any work carried out by the Tenant (whether of repair or not) shall be carried out to the reasonable satisfaction of the Landlord's Surveyor

Service of notices

5.5 any notice or other document required or permitted to be served under the terms of this lease may be served in accordance with section 196 of the Law of Property Act 1925

EXECUTED AS A DEED etc

THE FIRST SCHEDULE

Part I

DESCRIPTION OF THE DEMISED PROPERTY

1. The Demised Property includes
    1.1 all landlord's fixtures and fittings in or upon the Demised Property
    1.2 all additions to the Demised Property

2. The Demised Property excludes the Structure and the Plant

Part II

THE TENANT'S RIGHTS

1. A right for the Tenant and all persons authorised by the Tenant (in common with the Landlord and all others entitled to the like right)
    1.1 of way with or without vehicles over the Common Parts
    1.2 of way on foot only over the Public Parts
    1.3 to use the loading bay hatched brown on the Plan for the sole purpose of loading and unloading vehicles
    1.4 to use the Plant serving the Demised Property
    1.5 to the free passage and running of water soil gas electricity and other services through and along the pipes drains wires cables and other conductors which are now or may within the Term be within the Centre and serve the Demised Property

LEASE OF SHOP IN SHOPPING CENTRE

2. The right of shelter protection and support from all parts of the Centre in physical contact with the Demised Property

Part III

THE LANDLORD'S RIGHTS

1. Rights over the Demised Property corresponding to those set out in paragraph 1 of Part I of this Schedule

2. The right for the Landlord and all persons authorised by it at reasonable times and on reasonable written notice (but in emergency at any time and without notice) to enter the Demised Property for any or all of the following purposes:
    2.1 carrying out work (whether of repair or not) to the Structure or the Plant
    2.2 inspecting the Demised Property
    2.3 showing the Demised Property to any person with a view to that person acquiring an interest in it
    2.4 measuring the Demised Property
    2.5 carrying out work (whether of repair or not) for which the Landlord or the Tenant is liable under the terms of this lease

3. The right to build on alter or deal with the Centre and every part of it (including the right to erect scaffolding or hoardings) even though the amenity of the Demised Property or access to it or the flow of light or air to it may be diminished or obstructed

THE SECOND SCHEDULE

Rent review

1. The Basic Rent payable from any Review Date shall be the higher of:
    1.1 the Basic Rent contractually payable immediately before that Review Date (disregarding the operation of clause 5.2) and
    1.2 the Market Rent of the Demised Property on the Review Date in question
2. [*Disputes procedure—see Example 5:13*]
3. [*Definition of market rent—see Example 5:23*]

THE THIRD SCHEDULE

Service charge

1. In this Schedule the following definitions apply:
    1.1 Financial Year means a period of twelve months ending on [   ] in each year or such other period as the Landlord may specify
    1.2 the Service Costs means the total sum computed in accordance with paragraph 3 below
    1.3 the Service Charge means the Service Charge Proportion of the Service Costs
    1.4 the Expert means the Landlord's Surveyor or professionally qualified accountant (who may also be employed by the Landlord or an associated company of the Landlord)

2. The Service Costs in respect of any Financial Year shall be calculated not later than the beginning of the Financial Year in question

3.1 The Service Costs are:
- 3.1.1 the expenditure estimated by the Expert as likely to be incurred by the Landlord in the Financial Year in question in connection with the Services and
- 3.1.2 the Major Expenditure Contribution less any amount standing in the Reserve referred to in paragraph 7 below to be applied towards Major Expenditure to be incurred by the Landlord in that Financial Year

3.2 Major Expenditure is expenditure on one or more of the Services which in the opinion of the Expert:
- 3.2.1 is likely to be substantial and
- 3.2.2 is likely to be incurred once only during the term or at intervals of more than one year or is likely to be incurred after the expiry of the term

3.3 the Major Expenditure Contribution is the sum determined by the Expert as being an appropriate annual contribution towards that Major Expenditure to be held by the Landlord as a Reserve

4. The Service Charge shall be paid by the Tenant in equal quarterly instalments in advance on the usual quarter days

5.1 As soon as practicable after the end of the Financial Year in question the Expert shall determine and certify the amount by which the estimate referred to in paragraph 3.1.1 above exceeds or falls short of the actual expenditure incurred by the Landlord in connection with the Services in that Financial Year

5.2 The Expert shall also certify those items of expenditure which are Major Expenditure and the amount (if any) applied from the Reserve in or towards payment of them

5.3 The Tenant shall be supplied with a copy of the certificates

6. Within fourteen days after the receipt by the Tenant of the certificates the Tenant shall pay to the Landlord the Service Charge Proportion of the deficiency or as the case may be the Landlord shall give credit to the Tenant for the Service Charge Proportion of the excess

7. [*Trust of major expenditure contribution—see Example 6:11*]

8. Nothing in this lease shall confer upon the Tenant the right to challenge the Service Costs

9. The Services are:
9.1 the repair maintenance and renewal of the Common Parts
9.2 the repair maintenance cleaning lighting heating ventilation cooling and decoration of the Public Parts and the Retained Parts
9.3 the inspection servicing repair maintenance and renewal of the Plant
9.4 the repair maintenance and renewal of the Structure
9.5 the provision of security to the Centre and the management of traffic in it
9.6 the maintenance of public liability insurance to such sum as the Landlord considers adequate and the insurance of the Plant
9.7 the provision of ornamental features displays and decorations in the Public Parts
9.8 the employment of such staff (including managerial staff surveyors and accountants) as the Landlord considers desirable to facilitate the provision of the serv-

ices (including uniforms national insurance contributions pensions bonuses gratuities and perquisites)

9.9 the supply of materials and equipment necessary for the provision of the services

9.10 if the Landlord thinks fit expenditure on advertising the Centre including promotion displays and exhibitions

9.11 any outgoings payable by the Landlord in respect of the Retained Parts (including a sum equal to the fair letting value of any office accommodation in the Centre used by the Landlord's employees in managing the Centre)

9.12 compliance with all statutory obligations affecting the Centre

9.13 any other service or expenditure relating to the Centre requested by a majority in number of the tenants

10. [*Provision entitling landlord to replace plant—see Example 6:12*]

Form 3

Underlease of Motor Showroom

[**General Note**: A shop used for the sale of motor cars is outside the general provisions of the Town and Country Planning (Use Classes) Order 1987 (SI No 764), Class AI. Planning permission is therefore necessary before a shop can be turned into a shop for the sale of motor vehicles. Note also the restrictions imposed on the storage of petrol by the Petroleum (Consolidation) Act 1928 which are reflected in the user covenants in this form.]

BY THIS UNDERLEASE which is made on the [ ] of 19[ ] between [ ] of [ ] ('the Landlord') (1) [ ] of [ ] ('the Tenant') (2) and [ ] of [ ] ('the Surety') (3)
The Landlord in consideration of the rents and covenants on the part of the Tenant contained below DEMISES ALL THAT [ ] ('the Demised Property') TOGETHER WITH the following rights (to the exclusion of all others) but EXCEPTING AND RESERVING TO HOLD the Demised Property to the Tenant for a term of [ ] years beginning on [ ] YIELDING ANY PAYING THEREFOR the annual rent of £[ ] payable by equal quarterly instalments in advance on the usual quarter days and subject to review in accordance with the Schedule

1. The Tenant hereby covenants with the Landlord as follows:
    (1) to pay the rent promptly without any deduction or set-off whatsoever
    (2) to pay all rates taxes and outgoings payable in respect of the Demised Property or the ownership or occupation of it (subject to any statutory provision expressly to the contrary)
    (3) [*To insure and reinstate—see Example 6:1*]
    (4) [*To repair and decorate—see Example 7:4*]
    (5) [*Not to alter without consent—see Example 7:15*]
    (6) [*Planning covenant—see Example 8:1*]
    (7) (a) the Demised Property shall not be used otherwise than as a shop nor without the Landlord's consent in writing (such consent not to be reasonably withheld) otherwise than for the sale of motor cars
        (b) not to have or store on the Demised Property any petrol or other inflammable substance of a like nature save for such quantity of petrol (not exceeding two gallons per vehicle or sixty gallons in total whichever is the less) as may be from time to time in the petrol tanks of vehicles await-

UNDERLEASE OF MOTOR SHOWROOM

ing sale or collection
- (c) not to carry out any repairs to or work on any motor vehicle
- (d) not to display or store more than [   ] vehicles on the forecourt of the Demised Property at any one time
- (e) *[Covenant ancillary to use—see Example 8:10]*
- (f) that the demised property shall not be used for any sale by auction

(8) not without the Landlord's consent in writing (such consent not to be unreasonably withheld) to exhibit any signboard advertisement placard or name-plate on the Demised Property

- (9) (a) not to obstruct any window light or other aperture of the Demised Property
- (b) not to permit any encroachment into the Demised Property nor to permit any easement to be acquired over it
- (c) forthwith to notify any activity known to the tenant which might be or result in encroachment or the acquisition of a right or easement

(10) *[Not to stop up windows—see Form 1, clause 3(13)]*

(11) *[To pay costs of notices—see Example 9:14]*

(12) to observe and comply with the covenants which the Landlord is liable to observe and comply with under the headlease of the Demised Property (except the covenant to pay rent) in so far as they relate to the Demised Property

(13) *[Covenant against alienation—see Examples 9:1, 9:4 and 9:5]*

2. The Landlord hereby covenants with the Tenant as follows:

(1) punctually to pay the rent reserved by and to indemnify the Tenant against breach by the Landlord of covenants in the headlease under which the Landlord holds the Demised Property

(2) on condition that the Tenant performs his obligations he shall have quite enjoyment of the Demised Property as against the landlord and those lawfully claiming under him

3. PROVIDED ALWAYS and it is hereby agreed as follows:

(1) *[Proviso for re-entry—see Form 1, clause 5(1)]*

(2) *[Proviso for abatement of rent—see Example 6:6]*

(3) any notice or schedule required or permitted to be served under the provisions of this underlease shall be validly served if served in accordance with the provisions of section 23 of the Landlord and Tenant Act 1927

(4) the expressions 'the Landlord' and 'the Tenant' include their respective successors in title

4. In consideration of the demise contained above and made at the Surety's request (as he hereby acknowledges) the Surety hereby covenants with the Landlord as follows:

(1) *[Basic covenant—see Example 11.1]*

(2) *[To take a lease on disclaimer—see Example 11.5]*

(3) *[Proviso limiting discharge of surety—see Example 11.2]*

EXECUTED AS A DEED etc

Form 4

Lease of Secondary Shop with Upper Part

[**General note**: This form is designed to be as simple as possible. It is a non-institutional form written in plain English, suitable for secondary property.]

THIS LEASE is made the [ ] of [ ] 19[ ] Between [ ] of [ ] ('the Landlord') and [ ] of [ ] ('the Tenant') (2) And WITNESSES that:

1. In consideration of the rent and the Tenant's covenants the Landlord LEASES to the Tenant the property known as [ ] (the Property) identified by red edging on the attached plan for a term of [ ] years beginning on [ ] at an annual rent of £[ ] (exclusive of value added tax) (subject to increase but not decrease every five years) payable by equal quarterly instalments in advance on the usual quarter days

2. The Tenant covenants with the Landlord:

    (1) to pay the rent promptly without any deduction or set off

    (2) to pay all rates taxes and other outgoings payable in respect of the Property

    (3) to reimburse the Landlord on demand the amount of the insurance premium payable by the Landlord for insuring the Property

    (4) to keep the Property in repair

    (5) to decorate the Property (both inside and outside) every five years in a good and workmanlike manner with appropriate materials

    (6) promptly to comply with any schedule of dilapidations served by the landlord

    (7) if the Tenant does not comply with subclause (6) above then the Landlord may do so and may enter the Property and carry out works for that purpose and the cost of those works will be a debt payable by the Tenant to the Landlord on demand

    (8) not without the Landlord's written consent to alter or add to the Property or its external appearance

    (9) (a)   not to commit any breach of planning control
        (b)   not to carry out any development in the Property
        (c)   expressions used in this subclause have the same meaning as in the Town and Country Planning Act 1990

    (10)(a)   not to part with possession of the Property or any part of it except by an assignment of this lease
        (b)   not without the Landlord's written consent to assign this lease

(c) to notify the Landlord within fourteen days of any assignment
(11)(a) not to use the Property except as a shop on the ground floor and as a residence on the upper floors
(b) not to use the Property for any illegal or immoral purpose or in such a way as to cause nuisance to neighbours

(12) to pay the Landlord's costs in connection with any application for consent under this lease (whether or not the consent is granted) and of any notice of breach of obligation served on the Tenant

(13) at the expiry or sooner termination of the tenancy to give up vacant possession of the Property and to remove all tenant's fixtures

3. The Landlord covenants with the Tenant:
(1) that the Tenant shall have quiet enjoyment of the Property as against the Landlord and anyone lawfully claiming under him
(2) to keep the Property insured in a sum equal to its full reinstatement value against damage by fire and other risks selected by him and to expend moneys payable under the policy in reinstating the damage which gave rise to the payment

4. It is also agreed that:
(1) the Landlord may repossess the Property and forfeit this lease if:
(a) the rent is in arrear for fourteen days (whether formally demanded or not) or
(b) the Tenant fails to comply with his obligations or
(c) the Tenant becomes insolvent

(2) arrears of rent and other moneys carry interest at the rate of two per cent over [   ] Bank plc base rate from the due date for payment until payment in full

(3) notices may be served in accordance with section 196 of the Law of Property Act 1925

5. (1) with effect from every fifth anniversary of the beginning of the tenancy the rent shall be increased to the Market Rent as at that anniversary

(2) if the parties have not agreed the Market Rent three months after the relevant anniversary it shall be fixed by an independent expert appointed (in default of agreement) by the President of the Royal Institution of Chartered Surveyors

(3) the Market Rent is the rent which the Property would fetch if let in the open market by a willing landlord to a willing tenant on the terms of this lease for the unexpired residue of the term disregarding the Tenant's occupation and goodwill and improvements carried out by him

EXECUTED AS A DEED etc

Form 5

Quarterly Tenancy of Lockable Stall in a Market or Store

[**General note**: A periodic tenancy cannot be contracted out of the Landlord and Tenant Act 1954.]

AN AGREEMENT MADE the [ ] of [ ] 19[ ] between [ ] of [ ] ('the Landlord') (1) and [ ] of [ ] ('the Tenant') (2) WHEREBY IT IS AGREED as follows:

1. The Landlord lets and the Tenant takes the property ('the Demised Property') known as Stall No [ ] at [ ] for a term from the date hereof until [*insert the next quarter day*] and thereafter from quarter to quarter until determined as provided below

2. The rent shall be £[ ] *per* quarter (exclusive of value added tax) payable in advance on the usual quarter days the first payment or an apportioned part of it to be made on the signing hereof

3. The Tenant agrees with the Landlord as follows:
    (1) to pay the rent as aforesaid without any deduction or set-off whatsoever
    (2) to keep the Demised Property in good repair
    (3) not to alter the Demised Property or change its external appearance
    (4) not to use the Demised Property for any illegal or immoral purpose nor for any purpose other than the sale of [ ]
    (5) not to cause or permit any nuisance or annoyance to the Landlord or to any stallholder
    (6) not to permit the accumulation of any rubbish in or about the Demised Property
    (7) not to bring or do on the Demised Property anything which may invalidate or increase the premium payable for any policy of insurance of the Demised Property maintained by the Landlord
    (8) not to hold any sale by auction in or about the demised property
    (9) not to assign underlet or part with or share possession of the demised property or any part thereof
    (10) to pay £[ ] as a contribution towards the cost of preparing this agreement

4. The Landlord agrees with the Tenant as follows:

(1) to pay the general and water rates payable in respect of the Demised Property

(2) to permit the Tenant and his staff to use the sanitary facilities provided for stallholders and to keep the same clean and in good order and properly equipped

(3) to permit the Tenant and his staff to have access to the Demised Property at all reasonable times

(4) to try his best to keep the market open for trading on at least six days per week (excluding public holidays)

(5) that the Tenant paying the rent and complying with the terms of this agreement shall have quiet enjoyment of the Demised Property for the duration of this tenancy without any interruption by the Landlord or any person lawfully claiming under or in trust for him

5. This tenancy may be determined by either party giving to the other not less than one quarter's notice in writing expiring on one of the usual quarter days (and in the case of a notice given to the Tenant it may be left for him on the Demised Property)

6. The Landlord reserves to himself:

(1) the right to enter the Demised Property for the purpose of inspecting it and of carrying out any works therein which the Tenant ought to have carried out but has failed to carry out

(2) the right to deal with any adjoining property belonging to him in such way as he thinks fit without making any compensation to the Tenant

7. It is hereby agreed that the Landlord may re-enter the Demised Property (in which case this tenancy shall immediately determine) in any of the following cases:

(1) the rent is in arrear for more than fourteen days after becoming due (whether formally demanded or not)

(2) the Tenant is in breach of any of his obligations under this agreement

(3) the Tenant ceases to occupy the Demised Property

(4) the Tenant has a receiving order made against him or is adjudicated bankrupt or execution is levied against him on the Demised Property or any goods in it

Signed etc

Form 6

Underlease of Office Accommodation above a Shop

[**General note**: This form is intended for use where the property is not a large office building, and where no services are provided, but the tenant contributes towards repair and maintenance.]

THIS UNDERLEASE which is made the [ ] of [ ] 19[ ] between [ ] of [ ] ('the Landlord') and [ ] of [ ] ('the Tenant') WITNESSES that

1. Interpretation

    1.1 In this Underlease the following definitions apply:

        1.1.1 the Property means the Property described in Part I of the Schedule

        1.1.2 the Building means the building of which the Property forms part and known as [ ]

        1.1.3 the Headlease means a lease of the Building made the [ ] of [ ] between [ ] (1) and [ ] the Landlord (2)

        1.1.4 the Head Landlord means the person from time to time entitled to the reversion immediately expectant upon the determination of the Headlease

        1.1.5 [*Definition of the rate of interest, 'the Prescribed Rate'—see Example 4:34*]

        1.1.6 consent means the written consent of the Landlord and the Head Landlord

    1.2 the Landlord and the Tenant include their respective successors in title

    1.3 where two joint or more persons are the Tenant their obligations are joint and several

    1.4 expressions used in this Underlease which are used in the Town and Country Planning Act 1990 (as amended) have the same meaning as in that Act

2. Demise

The Landlord demises the Property to the Tenant together with the rights set out in Part II of the Schedule but reserving the rights set out in Part III of that Schedule and

UNDERLEASE: OFFICE ABOVE SHOP

subject to all rights vested in the Head Landlord by virtue of the Headlease to hold to the Tenant for a term beginning on and ending on yielding and paying the following rents:

2.1 until the [   ] of [   ] the annual rent of £[   ] (exclusive of value added tax)

2.2 from the [   ] of [   ] the higher of the rent specified in clause 2.1 above and the Market Rent on that date ('a review date')

2.3 from the [   ] of [   ] the higher of the rent payable under clause 2.2 above and the Market Rent on that date ('a review date') in each case payable by equal quarterly instalments in advance on the usual quarter days

2.4 if value added tax is payable on the rent (whether because of an election by the landlord or not) the amount of the value added tax

3. Tenant's covenants
The Tenant covenants with the Landlord:

3.1 to pay the rent (if so required by banker's standing order) promptly and without deduction or set-off

    3.2.1 to pay the general and water rates payable for the Property or (if the Property is not separately assessed for rating) a fair proportion of the general and water rates payable for the Building

    3.2.2 to pay all taxes assessments and outgoings payable for or in respect of the Property

3.3 [*To keep the interior in repair—see Example 7:7*]

    3.4.1 to decorate the interior of the Property with appropriate materials of good quality and in a good workmanlike manner every five years and in the last year of the tenancy (however terminated)

    3.4.2 where any part of the Property is to be painted at least two coats of paint shall be applied and in the last year of the tenancy the colours shall be approved by the Head Landlord

    3.5.1 within twenty-eight days after the service of a schedule of dilapidations to begin and to proceed quickly to comply with it

    3.5.2 if the Tenant does not comply with clause 3.5.1 above then the Landlord or Head Landlord may do so and may enter the Property and carry out works for that purpose and their cost will be recoverable from the Tenant as a debt payable on demand together with interest at the Prescribed Rate from the date of demand

    3.6.1 to pay the Landlord on demand [   ] per cent of the expenditure incurred from time to time by the Landlord in keeping the structure and exterior of the Building in repair

    3.6.2 the amount of the Landlord's expenditure shall be certified from time to time by the Landlord's surveyor (acting as an expert) whose certificate shall be conclusive of all matters of fact which it purports to certify

    3.6.3 to reimburse the Landlord a fair proportion of any sums payable by the Landlord to the Head Landlord pursuant to the terms of the Headlease

3.7 not without consent to alter or add to the Property

    3.8.1 not to commit any breach of planning control

    3.8.2 not without consent to apply for planning permission

    3.9.1 not to use the Property except as offices

3.9.2 not to use the Property in such a way as in the opinion of the Landlord:
    3.9.2.1 would be in contravention of the terms of the Headlease
    3.9.2.2 is likely to cause nuisance or annoyance to neighbours
    3.9.2.3 might avoid or make more expensive any policy of insurance maintained by the Landlord or the Head Landlord in respect of the Building

3.10.1 not to display or erect any sign or advertisement without (a) consent and (b) obtaining any necessary approval from the local planning authority

3.10.2 to remove any such sign or advertisement at the end of the tenancy

3.11.1 not to assign underlet or part with possession of part only of the Property nor to underlet the Property as a whole

3.11.2 not without consent to assign the Property as a whole

3.12.1 to supply the Landlord within one month of its date a copy of any instrument effecting or evidencing the disposition or creation of any interest in the Property and to pay a reasonable registration fee

3.12.2 promptly to notify the Landlord of any change in the Tenant's address or registered office

3.13 [*Costs of consent—see Example 9:15*]

3.14 to permit the Landlord and the Head Landlord and all persons authorised by either of them to enter the Property at all reasonable times and (except in emergency) on reasonable notice for any of the following purposes:
    3.14.1 inspecting the Property
    3.14.2 carrying out any works (whether of repair or not) to the Building

3.15 during the last six months of the tenancy to permit the Landlord to maintain a letting board on the Property

3.16 at the end of the tenancy to give vacant possession of the Property and to remove all tenant's fixtures

3.17 not to permit or suffer anything which would be a breach of the Headlease or which is expressly prohibited by this clause

4. Landlord's covenants

The Landlord covenants with the Tenant:

4.1 that if the Tenant pays the rent and complies with his obligations he shall have quiet enjoyment of the Property during the tenancy as against the Landlord and all persons claiming under or in trust for it

4.2 to keep the structure and exterior of the Building in repair

4.3 to indemnify the Tenant against any breach by the Landlord of its obligations under the Headlease

5. Provisos

Provided always and it is agreed:

5.1 the landlord shall be entitled to re-enter the Property (or any part of it in the name of the whole) in any of the following cases:
    5.1.1 the rent or any part of it is in arrear for more than twenty-one days (whether formally demanded or not)
    5.1.2 the tenant breaks any of his obligations
    5.1.3 the tenant becomes insolvent or goes into liquidation otherwise than for

the purpose of amalgamation or reconstruction
and upon such re-entry the lease shall terminate but without prejudice to accrued causes of action

5.2 [*Proviso for abatement of rent—see Example 6:6*]

5.3 [*Service of notices—see Form 2, clause 5.5*]

6. Rent Reviews

6.1 [*Definition of market rent—see Example 5:27*]

6.2 [*Disputes procedure—see Example 5:15 adding 'of the Royal Institution of Chartered Surveyors' after 'President'*]

EXECUTED AS A DEED etc

THE SCHEDULE

Part I

ALL THAT property on the first and second floors of the Building excluding:
>the roof and roof timbers of the Building
>the external surfaces of exterior walls

Part II

1. The right to use the staircase from the ground floor to the first floor on foot only for obtaining access to and egress from the Property
2. The right to the free passage of water gas electricity and soil through any wire pipe or conduit in the Building and serving the Property

Part III

3. All rights reserved to the Head Landlord by the Headlease
4. The right to use the Building in any manner in which the Landlord thinks fit without making any compensation to the Tenant

Form 7

Lease of Office Block: Rent Geared to Sublettings

[**General note**: This form is designed for a lease taken primarily for investment purposes. If the tenant erected the building, and the lease is for more than forty years, s 19(1)(b) of the Landlord and Tenant Act 1927 will apply to any qualified covenant against alienation (other than assignment). In the case of assignment, parties can specify circumstances in which the landlord may withhold consent, and conditions which he may impose in a licence to assign. The tenant should delete clauses 4(1)(c) and 4(1)(d) which may make the lease unmortgageable.]

THIS LEASE which is made the [ ] of [ ] 19[ ] between [ ] of [ ] ('the Landlord') (1) and [ ] of [ ] ('the Tenant') (2) WITNESSES as follows:

1. In consideration of the sum of £[ ] (receipt of which the Landlord acknowledges) and of the rents and covenants contained below the Landlord DEMISES to the Tenant ALL THAT [ ] ('Demised Property') BUT RESERVING to the Landlord the right to build on develop deal with and use any adjoining property owned by the Landlord (whether at the date hereof or in the future) in such manner as he thinks fit even though the amenity of the Demised Property or the access of light or air thereto may be lessened thereby and without making any compensation to the Tenant TO HOLD to the Tenant for a term of [ ] years beginning on [ ] YIELDING AND PAYING (exclusive of value added tax) [*see Example 5:7*]

2. The Tenant covenants with the Landlord as follows:
    (1) to pay the rent as aforesaid without any deduction or set-off whatsoever
    (2) to pay all existing and future rates taxes assessments and outgoings payable in respect of the Demised Property or the ownership or occupation thereof (except such as are charged on a disposition of any interest in reversion to this lease)
    (3) [*To insure and reinstate—see Example 6:1*]
    (4) [*To repair and decorate—see Example 7:4*]
    (5) [*To comply with statutes—see Example 7:13*]
    (6) (a)　not to make any external additions to the Demised Property
    　　(b)　not without the Landlord's consent in writing to make any alteration to

LEASE OF OFFICE BLOCK: SUBLETTING

the structure of the Demised Property and not to make any such alteration save in accordance with drawings and specifications first approved by the Landlord

(7) [*Planning covenant—see Example 8:1*]

(8) that the Demised Property shall not be used for any purpose other than as offices

(9) [*Not to cause nuisance etc—see Example 8:10*]

(10)(a) not to assign part only of the Demised Property
  (b) not to assign underlet or part with possession of the Demised Property as a whole without the Landlord's consent in writing (such consent not to be unreasonably withheld in the case of a respectable and responsible person)
  (c) not to underlet or otherwise part with or share the possession of part only of the Demised Property:
    (i) being less than one whole floor of the demised property (excluding lift shafts staircases and common parts)
    (ii) for a term exceeding five years without the Landlord's consent in writing (such consent not to be unreasonably withheld in the case of a respectable and responsible person)
  (d) not to mortgage or charge this lease without the Landlord's consent in writing (such consent not to be unreasonably withheld)
  (e) within one month after any assignment underletting mortgage or charge of the whole or any part of the Demised Property or any transfer or devolution of the Tenant's title thereto to produce and register with the Landlord any document by which the same was effected or which evidences the same and to pay the Landlord a reasonable fee for such registration
  (f) subject to the preceding provisions of this subclause to try his best to keep the Demised Property fully let at rack rents and to maximise the income derived from it

(11) to supply the Landlord with a copy of any order notice direction permission or consent issued by any local or public authority in relation to the Demised Property within seven days of the receipt thereof by the Tenant

(12) to take all reasonable steps to prevent encroachment on the Demised Property and to notify the Landlord forthwith of any such encroachment or any adverse claim to the Demised Property or any notice or proceeding known to him (whether addressed to or taken against him or not) which may affect the Landlord's interest in the Demised Property

(13) not to stop up darken or obstruct any window or other aperture in the Demised Property

(14) [*To pay costs—see Example 9:15*]

3. The Landlord covenants with the Tenant that if the Tenant pays the rent and observes and performs his covenants he shall peaceably hold and enjoy the Demised Property for the term of this lease without any interruption by the Landlord or any person lawfully claiming under or in trust for him

4. PROVIDED ALWAYS and it is agreed as follows:
  (1) the Landlord shall be entitled to re-enter the Demised Property or any part thereof in the name of the whole upon the happening of any one or more of the follow-

ing events:

- (a) the rent or any part of it is in arrear for twenty-one days or more (whether formally demanded or not)
- (b) the Tenant fails to comply with any of his covenants
- (c) the Tenant makes any composition with his creditors or execution against the Tenant is levied on the Demised Property
- (d) the Tenant enters into liquidation (otherwise than for the purposes of amalgamation or reconstruction) or is adjudicated bankrupt or a receiving order is made against him and upon such re-entry this lease shall absolutely determine but without prejudice to any accrued cause of action

(2) any notice or schedule required or permitted to be served under this lease may be served in accordance with section 196 of the Law of Property Act 1925

(3) the expressions 'the Landlord' and 'the Tenant' include their respective successors in title and any reference to any Act of Parliament includes a reference to that Act as amended or replaced from time to time and to any subordinate legislation made thereunder

EXECUTED AS A DEED etc

SCHEDULE

[Detailed provisions for calculation of rent—see Example 5:7]

Form 8

Lease of Suite of Offices

[**General note**: This form is suitable where the Landlord is to provide services.]

THIS LEASE which is made the [   ] of [   ] 19[ ] between [   ] of [   ] ('the Landlord') (1) [   ] of [   ] ('the Tenant') (2) and [   ] of [   ] ('the Surety') (3)
WITNESSES as follows:

1. (1) In this lease the following expressions have the following meanings:
    (a) 'the Landlord' and 'the Tenant' include their respective successors in title
    (b) 'the Building' means [   ]
    (c) ['the structure of the building'—see Example 7:2]
    (d) 'the exterior of the Building' means all surfaces of the Building exposed to the elements except surfaces made of glass
    (e) ['the interior of the demised property'—see Example 7:3]
    (f) ['the prescribed rate'—see Example 5:35]
    (2) any reference to any Act of Parliament includes a reference to that Act as amended or replaced from time to time and to any subordinate legislation made thereunder

2. In consideration of the rents and covenants on the part of the Tenant contained below the Landlord DEMISES to the Tenant ALL THAT suite of rooms on the [   ] floor of the Building ('the Demised Property') TOGETHER WITH the following rights (to the exclusion of all others):
    (1) [*Right of access—see Example 2:9*]
    (2) [*Right to use lifts—see Example 2:10*]
    (3) [*Right to display advertisement—see Example 2:14*]
    (4) [*Right to use sanitary facilities—see Example 2:15*]
    (5) the right to use the existing and future drains sewers and gas electricity and telephone and other wires and pipes serving the Demised Property and which pass through the Building
    (6) all rights of shelter protection and support now enjoyed by the Demised Property
    (7) such rights of entry upon the Building as are necessary for the proper performance of the Tenant's covenants and for the purpose of escape in case of fire or other

emergency
BUT EXCEPTING AND RESERVING to the Landlord [*see Example 2:16*]
TO HOLD to the Tenant for a term of [   ] years from [   ] YIELDING AND PAYING therefor (exclusive of value added tax) first the annual rent of £[   ] (subject to review as provided in the First Schedule) payable by equal quarterly payments in advance on the usual quarter days the first payment (or a duly apportioned part of it) to be paid on the date hereof and secondly by way of service charge the annual sum calculated in accordance with the Second Schedule and payable as therein provided

3. The Tenant covenants with the Landlord as follows:

(1) to pay the rent and service charge as aforesaid without any deduction or set-off whatsoever together with interest at the prescribed rate on all arrears from the due date for payment until payment in full

(2) to pay the general and water rates payable in respect of the Demised Property and all charges for gas electricity and telecommunications (including any standing charges) used or consumed in the Demised Property

(3) to clean the windows at least once a month

(4) [*To repair and decorate—see Examples 7:6 and 7:7 substituting 'the interior of the demised property' for 'the Demised Property'*]

(5) [*Not to alter—see Example 7:15*]

(6) [*Planning covenant—see Example 8:1*]

(7) [*Not to vitiate insurance—see Example 6:8*]

(8) not to use the Demised Property for any purpose other than as offices

(9) [*Not to assign etc without consent—see Examples 9:1, 9:4 and 9:5*]

(10) [*Not to cause nuisance etc—see Example 8:10*]

(11) not to overload the floors ceilings or walls of the Demised Property (the permitted loadings being [   ])

(12) not to display any sign or advertisement in the Demised Property except as expressly provided above

(13) not to stop up darken or obstruct any window or other aperture in the Demised Property

(14) not to deposit any refuse save in such place as may be designated by the Landlord

(15) to comply with any written regulations about the use of the Building which may be made by the Landlord from time to time

(16) to pay all costs charges and expenses (including any professional fees) incurred by the Landlord in and about the preparation or service of a notice under section 149 or 147 of the Law of Property Act 1925 (even if forfeiture is avoided otherwise than by relief granted by the court)

(17) to pay the Landlord's solicitors' costs and disbursements and surveyors' fees and any stamp duty in connection with:

    (a)   the preparation and grant of this lease

    (b)   any application by the Tenant for any licence or consent under this lease (whether or not such licence or consent is actually granted)

4. The Landlord covenants with the Tenant as follows:

(1) [*To insure and reinstate—see Example 6:5*]

(2) to keep in repair the structure of the Building and the exterior of the Building and to decorate the exterior of the Building in a good and workmanlike manner at

regular intervals

(3) to keep the lifts in the Building in good working order and to replace them as and when necessary

(4) to keep the common parts of the Building in repair properly lit and cleaned and to decorate them in a good and workmanlike manner at regular intervals

(5) to provide and maintain in adequate supply of hot water to the washbasins and sinks in the Building and to the heating system in the Demised Property

(6) that the Tenant paying the rent and service charge and performing and observing his covenants the Tenant shall peaceably and quietly hold and enjoy the Demised Property for the term hereby granted without any interruption by the Landlord or any person claiming under or in trust for him

5. PROVIDED ALWAYS that:

(1) if the rent or service charge is in arrear for more than fourteen days after becoming due (whether formally demanded or not) or if the Tenant is in breach of any of his covenants or if the Tenant or the Surety (being a company) shall enter into compulsory or voluntary liquidation (other than for the purpose of amalgamation or reconstruction) or (not being a company) shall have a receiving order made against him or call a meeting of or enter into any composition with his creditors or be adjudicated bankrupt or suffer any distress or execution to be levied on the Demised Property then and in each such case the Landlord shall be entitled (in addition to any other right) to re-enter upon the Demised Property or any part thereof in the name of the whole and thereupon this lease shall absolutely determine

(2) [*Proviso for abatement of rent—see Example 6:6*]

(3) any notice or other document required or permitted to be served under this lease may be served in accordance with section 196 of the Law of Property Act 1925

6. (1) [*Basic covenant—see Example 11:1*]

(2) [*To take a lease on disclaimer—see Example 11:5*]

(3) [*Proviso limiting discharge of surety—see Example 11:2*]

EXECUTED AS A DEED etc

THE FIRST SCHEDULE

[*Provision for rent review—see Example 5:37*]

THE SECOND SCHEDULE

[*Provision for service charge—see Example 6:10, adapting as necessary*]

Form 9

Lease of Industrial Property on Industrial Estate

[**General note**: This form includes a limited form of service charge for the upkeep of common parts of the estate and the cost of insurance.]

THIS LEASE which is made the [   ] of [   ] 19[ ] between [   ] of [   ] ('the Landlord' which expression includes his successors in title) (1) and [   ] of [   ] ('the Tenant' which expression includes his successors in title) (2)
WITNESSES as follows:

1. In consideration of the rents and covenants contained below the Landlord DEMISES to the Tenant ALL THAT [   ] ('the Demised Property') TOGETHER WITH the following rights (to the exclusion of all others):

    (1) [*Right of way over estate roads—see Example 2:8*]

    (2) the right in common with the Landlord and all others having the like right to park not more than [   ] private motor cars and motor cycles in the area designated 'Car Park' on the attached plan

    (3) the right to the free passage of water soil gas and electricity through the pipes drains and wires now serving the Demised Property

    (4) the right to maintain a signboard of a size and form approved by the Landlord in a position along the perimeter of the estate of which the Demised Property forms part ('the Estate') such position to be designated by the Landlord

BUT EXCEPTING AND RESERVING to the Landlord

    (1) the right to the free passage of water soil gas and electricity through the pipes drains and wires passing through the Demised Property (whether at the date hereof or in the future)

    (2) the right at reasonable times and (except in emergency) on reasonable notice to enter the Demised Property for the purposes of inspecting the condition and state or repair thereof carrying out any works (whether of repair or otherwise) for which the Landlord or the Tenant is liable under this lease or carrying out any works (whether of repair or otherwise) to any property adjoining the Demised Property or to any party structure pipe drain or wire or other thing used by the Tenant in common with others

LEASE OF INDUSTRIAL PROPERTY

but making good any physical damage caused by such entry
TO HOLD to the Tenant for a term of [   ] years beginning on [   ]
YIELDING AND PAYING therefor (exclusive of value added tax) the annual rent of £[   ] (subject to revision in accordance with the Schedule) payable by equal quarterly instalments in advance on the usual quarter days the first payment to be made on [   ] and also by way of additional rent payable on demand a service charge calculated in accordance with clause 2(3) of this lease

2. The Tenant covenants with the Landlord as follows:

(1) to pay the rent as aforesaid without any deduction or set-off whatsoever

(2) to pay all rates taxes and outgoings payable in respect of the demised property or the occupation thereof

(3) to pay on demand an amount equal to [   ] per cent of the costs incurred by the Landlord in and about:

- (a) the repair maintenance and replacement from time to time of all roads parking areas and loading bays on the Estate and any pipe drain wire or other thing not used exclusively by a single tenant on the Estate
- (b) the repair maintenance and replacement from time to time of the fence enclosing the Estate
- (c) the insurance of the Estate
- (d) the lighting of any common part of the Estate
- (e) the cultivation of any planted or grassed part of the Estate

the said amount to be certified in writing by the Landlord's surveyor for the time being

(4) [*To repair and decorate—see Example 7:6*]

(5) [*Not to alter—see Example 7:15*]

(6) [*To comply with statutes—see Example 7:16*]

(7) at least once in every six months to cause the sprinkler system and other fire-fighting equipment to be inspected by a competent person and to keep the same in efficient working order at all times and not to permit any fire door to be locked

(8) [*Not to cause increase in insurance premiums—see Example 6:8*]

(9) not to use or permit or suffer to be used the Demised Property for any purpose other than one falling within class B1 or B2 or B8 of the Town and Country Planning (Use Classes) Order 1987

- (10)(a) not to permit or suffer any person to park any vehicle on any road in the Estate
- (b) not to permit or suffer any accumulation of refuse or trade empties in or about the Demised Property
- (c) not to affix any machinery to the roof or walls of the Demised Property without the Landlord's consent in writing
- (d) that the Demised Property shall not be used for any illegal or immoral purpose or in such a way as in the opinion of the Landlord causes or might cause nuisance or annoyance to the owners or occupiers or any neighbouring property

(11) [*Covenant against alienation—see Examples 9:1, 9:4 and 9:5*]

(12) [*To pay costs—see Example 9:15*]

(13) during the last six months of the term to permit the Landlord to affix to a conspicuous part of the Demised Property a notice advertising the same for reletting and to permit all persons authorised by the Landlord to inspect the same

(14) to comply with any written regulations made by the Landlord from time to

time in connection with the use of the common parts of the Estate

(15) [*Covenant to yield up in a fit state—see Example 7:20*]

3. The Landlord covenants with the Tenant as follows:

(1) that the Tenant paying the rent and performing and observing his covenants the Tenant shall peaceably hold and enjoy the Demised Property during the term without any interruption by the Landlord or any person lawfully claiming under or in trust for him

(2) [*To insure and reinstate—see Example 6:2*]

(3) to take reasonable care to keep in repair all roads parking areas and loading bays on the Estate and the fence enclosing the Estate

(4) to take reasonable care to ensure that the common parts of the Estate are adequately lit during the hours of darkness

(5) to keep any planted or grassed part of the Estate properly cultivated

4. PROVIDED ALWAYS and it is hereby agreed as follows:

(1) if the rent or service charge is in arrear for more than fourteen days after becoming due (whether formally demanded or not) or if the Tenant is in breach of any of his covenants or if the Tenant enters into liquidation (otherwise than for the purposes of amalgamation or reconstruction) or a receiving order is made against him or he is adjudicated bankrupt then the Landlord shall be entitled to re-enter the Demised Property or any part thereof in the name of the whole and thereupon this lease shall absolutely determine but without prejudice to any accrued cause of action

(2) [*Proviso for abatement of rent—see Example 6:6*]

(3) any notice or other document required or permitted to be served hereunder may be served in accordance with section 196 of the Law of Property Act 1925 (as amended by the Recorded Delivery Service Act 1962)

(4) arrears of rent and other moneys due under this lease shall bear interest at the rate of two per cent above the base lending rate from time to time of [   ] Bank plc ('the Prescribed Rate')

EXECUTED AS A DEED etc

THE SCHEDULE

1. In this Schedule:

(1) 'the Review Date' means the [   ] of [   ] and every fifth anniversary of that date

(2) 'the President' means the President for the time being of the Incorporated Society of Valuers and Auctioneers

2. With effect from each Review Date the rent payable by the Tenant shall be the higher of:

(1) the rent contractually payable immediately before that date and

(2) the Market Rent on that date

3. [*Definition of market rent—see Example 5:22*]

4. [*Disputes procedure—see Example 5:13*]

5. [*Payment on account—see Example 5:36*]

Form 10

Underlease of Part of Building Let as Clothing Factory

THIS UNDERLEASE which is made the [ ] of [ ]19[ ] between [ ] of [ ] ('the Landlord' which expression includes his successors in title) (1) and [ ] of [ ] ('the Tenant' which expression includes his successors in title) (2) and [ ] of [ ] ('the Surety') (3) WITNESSES as follows

1. In consideration of the rent and the covenants contained below the Landlord DEMISES to the Tenant ALL THAT property comprising ('Demised Property') and being part of the building at [ ] ('the Building') TOGETHER WITH the following rights (to the exclusion of all others):

(1) [*Right of access—see Example 2:9*]

(2) [*Right to display advertisement—see Example 2:13*]

(3) [*Right to use sanitary facilities—see Example 2:15*]

(4) the right to use the existing and future drains sewers and gas electricity telephone and other wires and pipes serving the Demised Property and which pass through the Building

(5) such rights of entry upon the Building as are necessary for the proper performance of the Tenant's covenants and for the purpose of escape in case of fire or other emergency

BUT EXCEPTING AND RESERVING to the Landlord and the Superior Landlord [*see Example 2:16*] TO HOLD to the Tenant for a term of [ ] years beginning on [ ] YIELDING AND PAYING THEREFOR the annual sum of £[ ] (exclusive of valued added tax) payable by equal quarterly payments in advance on the usual quarter days

2. The Tenant covenants with the Landlord as follows:

(1) to pay the rent promptly without any deduction or set-off whatsoever

(2) to pay all rates taxes assessments and outgoings of any nature payable in respect of the Demised Property or the ownership or occupation thereof and to pay a fair proportion of such of them as are payable in respect of the Building as a whole

(3) to pay a fair proportion of the cost of repairing and maintaining all party structures sewers drains means of access or escape in case of fire wires and pipes the use of

which is common to the Demised Property and other property

(4) to pay a fair proportion (having regard to the area of the Demised Property and the use of the Demised Property and other parts of the Building) of the cost to the Landlord of insuring the Building in accordance with his covenant in that behalf

(5) to repair and keep in repair the interior of the Demised Property and all windows and doors enclosing the same (except damage caused by fire or any other peril against which the Demised Property is insured by the Landlord under a policy which has not been vitiated by any act or omission of the Tenant or any person deriving title under him)

(6) [*To comply with statutes—see Example 7:16*]

(7) not to make any alteration or addition to the Demised Property save such as are required in order to comply with the last preceding subclause

(8) that the Demised Property shall not be used:
- (a) for any purpose in respect of which a licence is required under the Rag Flock and Other Filling Materials Act 1951
- (b) for any illegal or immoral purpose
- (c) in such a way as to cause nuisance or annoyance to any other occupier of the Building or to the Landlord or the Superior Landlord
- (d) with the Landlord's consent in writing (such consent not to be unreasonably withheld) for any purpose other than the manufacture of clothing and as ancillary offices

(9) [*Planning covenant—see Example 8:1*]

(10) at any time when any person is working in the Building to keep closed but not locked all fire doors in the demised property and not to permit or suffer any obstruction of any means of escape in case of fire

(11) [*Not to vitiate insurance—see Example 6:8*]

(12) [*Covenant against alienation—see Examples 9:1, 9:4 and 9:5*]

(13) at least once each day to sweep up all waste material and to place the same in such place as may be designated from time to time by the Landlord

(14) not to overload the floors walls or ceilings of the Demised Property

(15) not to stop or obstruct any window or other aperture in the Demised Property

(16) to pay all costs charges and expenses incurred by the Landlord (including any professional fees stamp duty and any sum payable by him to the Superior Landlord) in connection with:
- (a) the preparation and grant of this underlease
- (b) any application by the Tenant for any licence or consent hereunder (whether or not such licence or consent is actually granted)
- (c) the preparation or service of a schedule of dilapidations or a notice under section 146 of the Law of Property Act 1925 (even if forfeiture is avoided otherwise than relief granted by the court)

(17) during the last six months of the term (unless the Tenant shall have made an application to the court for a new tenancy of the Demised Property) to permit the Landlord to affix and maintain on the Demised Property a notice for the reletting of the same

3. The Landlord covenants with the Tenant as follows:

(1) [*To insure and reinstate—see Example 6:2 substituting 'the building' for 'the demised property'*]

(2) [*To repair exterior and to decorate—see Example 7:11*]

(3) to keep clean and in good order the sanitary facilities in the Building

(4) that the Tenant paying the rent and performing and observing his covenants he shall peaceably and quietly hold and enjoy the Demised Property for the term hereby granted without any interruption by the Landlord or any person claiming under or in trust for him

4. PROVIDED ALWAYS and it is hereby agreed as follows:

(1) if the rent is in arrear for twenty-one days after becoming due (whether formally demanded or not) or if the Tenant is in breach of any of his covenants or if the Tenant or the Surety calls a meeting of his creditors or has a receiving order made against him or is adjudicated bankrupt or (being a company) goes into liquidation otherwise than for the purpose of amalgamation or reconstruction or if any execution or distress is levied on the Demised Property then and in each such case the Landlord shall be entitled (in addition to any other right) to re-enter the Demised Property or any part of it in the name of the whole and thereupon this demise shall absolutely determine

(2) [*Proviso for abatement of rent—see Example 6:6*]

(3) where the consent of the Landlord is required for anything under this underlease the consent of the Superior Landlord is also required

(4) any dispute as to any proportion payable by the Tenant under clauses 2(2) 2(3) or 2(4) hereof shall be determined by the Landlord's surveyor for the time being acting as an expert

(5) any notice or schedule required or permitted to be served hereunder may be served in accordance with section 196 of the Law of Property Act 1925

(6) any reference to any Act of Parliament includes a reference to that Act as amended or replaced from time to time and to any subordinate legislation made thereunder

5. In consideration of the demise contained above and made at the Surety's request (as he hereby acknowledges) the Surety covenants with the Landlord as follows:

(1) [*Basic covenant—see Example 11:1*]

(2) [*To take a lease on disclaimer—see Example 11:4*]

(3) [*Proviso limiting discharge of surety—see Example 11:2*]

EXECUTED AS A DEED etc

Form 11

Tenancy Agreement of Start Up Workshop

[**General note**: This form is designed for property to be used by small businesses; and it is therefore drawn in plain English]

BY THIS TENANCY AGREEMENT [   ] THE LANDLORD [   ] of [   ] LETS TO [   ] THE TENANT THE PROPERTY known as [   ] from [   ] to [   ] on the following terms

1. Rent

(1) Your rent is £[   ] per month (exclusive of value added tax)

(2) Your rent is due monthly in advance on the first day of each month

(3) You may pay your rent in cash or by cheque

(4) If you pay your rent in cash you must bring it to the office of the landlord's managing agents at [   ] during normal office hours. If you pay your rent by cheque you may sent it by post to that address

(5) Rent arrears are not allowed and may lead to the landlord terminating your tenancy

(6) Your rent is exclusive of general and water rates and does not include charges for electricity or gas or value added tax

(7) The landlord may increase the rent by giving you two months' written notice

2. Repairs and maintenance

(1) The landlord is responsible for repairs to the structure (including the roof walls and floor) of the property

(2) You are responsible for the general cleanliness of the property and for doing ordinary running repairs which would normally be done by a householder

(3) The landlord may ask to enter the property in order to inspect it; to read or empty meters; to do repairs or other work or for other reasonable purposes. You must not refuse if it is a reasonable time of day, but you can insist on twenty-four hours' written notice

(4) If a repair is needed to the property you must report it to the landlord as soon as possible. You should not instruct a builder yourself unless you have the landlord's permission to do so

(5) At the end of the tenancy you will have to pay for the redecoration of the property to a reasonable standard

(6) If any damage is caused to the property by you or your visitors you will be responsible for the cost of putting it right

(7) You must not make any alteration to the property even if you think the alteration would be an improvement

3. Your general responsibilities

(1) You must pay the rent on time

(2) You must pay the general and water rates and any other outgoings (including gas and electricity)

(3) You must occupy the property personally

(4) You must use the property only for the business of [   ]

(5) You must not assign this tenancy without the landlord's permission (not to be unreasonably refused)

(6) You must not sublet the property or any part of it or share the use of it with anyone else

(7) You must not do anything which causes a nuisance or annoyance to neighbours

(8) You must comply with planning control

(9) At the end of the tenancy you must vacate the property and take with you all your belongings including machinery and equipment installed by you

4. The landlord's general responsibilities

If you comply with your obligations the landlord will make sure that you are allowed to occupy the property until the tenancy ends (but the landlord cannot be responsible for persons over whom he has no control)

5. Termination of the tenancy

(1) Either you or the landlord may terminate the tenancy by four weeks' written notice if the property burns down or is otherwise unfit for use

(2) The landlord may also terminate the tenancy without notice if the rent is two weeks in arrear (even if he has not formally demanded it) or if you do not comply with your obligations. If the landlord does terminate the tenancy this may lead to a court order making you vacate the property

6. Deposit

On signing this agreement you must pay the landlord a deposit equal to one month's rent. The landlord will keep the deposit until the end of the tenancy. At the end of the tenancy the landlord will take out of the deposit any compensation to which he may be entitled on account of any breach by you of your obligations as tenant. Any balance of the deposit remaining will then be returned to you. You may not use the deposit to pay the last month's rent

Signed etc

Form 12

Lease of Hotel: Rent Based on Turnover

[**General note**: Capital expenditure incurred on the construction of certain hotels may qualify for capital allowances under the Capital Allowances Act 1990. The hotels that qualify are those defined in s 19 of the Capital Allowances Act 1990. Since the definition depends in part on the use of the hotel in question and the nature of the service provided for guests, this form has been drawn so as to ensure that the hotel does not cease to be a qualifying hotel. In some areas a hotel proprietor may need to be registered with the local authority (see, for example, the Greater London Council (General Powers) Act 1984, s 17). A general power to compel registration of hotels exists under the Development of Tourism Act 1969, but to date the power has not been exercised.]

THIS LEASE which is made the [ ] of [ ] 19[ ] between [ ] of [ ] ('the Landlord') (1) and [ ] of [ ] ('the Tenant') (2) WITNESSES as follows:

1. In this lease:

(1) the expressions 'the Landlord' and 'the Tenant' include their respective successors in title

(2) any reference to any Act of Parliament includes a reference to that Act as amended or replaced from time to time and to any subordinate legislation made thereunder

2. In consideration of the rents and covenants on the part of the Tenant contained below the Landlord DEMISES to the Tenant ALL THAT building known as the [ ] Hotel together with the gardens and grounds belonging to it ('the Demised Property') more precisely delineated and edged in red on the attached plan TOGETHER WITH the exclusive right to take fish from so much of the River [ ] as flows through the Demised Property BUT RESERVING to the Landlord the right to build on develop deal with and use any adjoining property owned by him (whether at the date hereof or in the future) in such manner as he thinks fit even though the amenity of the Demised Property or the access of light or air thereto may be lessened thereby and without making compensation to the Tenant TO HOLD to the Tenant for a term of [ ] years beginning on [ ] YIELDING AND PAYING therefor (exclusive of value added tax) by equal quarterly payments in advance on the usual quarter days:

(1) the annual sum of £[   ] ('the basic rent') and
(2) such sum as is calculated in accordance with the Schedule hereto ('the turnover rent')

3. The Tenant covenants with the Landlord as follows:
   (1) to pay the rents as aforesaid without any deduction or set-off whatsoever
   (2) to pay all rates taxes and outgoings payable in respect of the Demised Property or the ownership or occupation of it (subject to any statutory direction to the contrary)
   (3) [*To insure and reinstate—see Example 6:1*]
   (4) to execute all works required in pursuance of any Act of Parliament or required by any competent local or public authority to be done in the respect of the Demised Property whether by the Tenant or the Landlord or any other person (however described)
   (5) that at all times there shall be a valid and subsisting fire certificate in respect of the Demised Property
   (6) [*To repair and decorate—see Example 7:4*]
   (7) (a) not without the consent in writing of the Landlord nor (where such consent is required by any Act of Parliament) without the consent of the licensing justices to make any alteration or addition to the Demised Property
       (b) upon each application to the Landlord or such consent to supply him with drawings and specifications of each proposed alteration or addition
       (c) not to carry out any work save in accordance with drawings and specifications approved as aforesaid and in accordance with any directions which may be given by the licensing justices
       (d) before beginning any approved works to enter into such covenant with the Landlords relating to the reinstatement of the Demised Property as the Landlord may reasonably require
   (8) (a) not to use the Demised Property for any purpose other than as a high class hotel
       (b) to keep the Demised Property open for business for at least four months during the months of April May June July August September and October in each year
       (c) during the time when the Demised Property is open for business to offer sleeping accommodation consisting wholly or mainly of bedrooms available to the public generally
       (d) not to permit any person to occupy a bedroom for more than one month save for staff employed in the Demised Property
       (e) to provide for guests services including the provision of breakfast and an evening meal the making of beds and the cleaning of rooms
   (9) (a) that nothing shall be done or omitted to be done on the Demised Property whereby any justices' licence may be forfeit suspended or otherwise imperilled
       (b) to do all things necessary to maintain and from time to time renew any such licence and not to do or permit or suffer to be done anything which might prejudice the future grant or renewal of such licence (whether to the Tenant or any future occupier of the Demised Property) and to comply with all requirements and recommendations of the licensing justices
   (10) to cultivate and maintain the gardens and grounds forming part of the Demised

Property and to keep them properly planted with healthy plants

(11) that no person shall fish in such part of the River [   ] as flows through the Demised Property during any close season

(12) [*Planning consent—see Example 8:1*]

(13) [*Covenants ancillary to use—see Example 8:9*]

(14)(a) not to assign part only of the Demised Property nor to underlet the whole or any part thereof

(b) not to assign the Demised Property as a whole without the Landlord's previous consent in writing (such consent not to be unreasonably withheld)

(c) not to part with or share possession of the Demised Property or any part thereof save that the Tenant shall be entitled with the Landlord's previous consent in writing (such consent not to be unreasonably withheld) to grant a licence to a respectable and responsible person for the occupation of a part of the hotel building not exceeding [   ] square feet in area for the sale of newspapers periodicals tobacco confectionery and other like goods

(d) at his own expense to procure that any assignee of the Demised Property enters into a direct covenant with the Landlord in such form as the Landlord may reasonably require to pay the rent and perform the tenant's covenants herein

(e) within one month after any assignment or devolution of the Tenant's interest in the Demised Property or any part thereof to produce to the Landlord's solicitors a copy of the instrument or other document whereunder the same was made or which evidences the same and to pay a reasonable fee for the registration thereof

(15) not to permit any easement to be acquired or encroachment made against or upon the Demised Property and promptly to give notice to the Landlord of any attempt to acquire or make the same and to take such steps (whether by way of legal proceedings or otherwise) to prevent the same from being acquired or made as the Landlord may reasonably require

(16) to pay all costs charges and expenses (including any professional fees) incurred by the Landlord in and about the preparation or service of a notice under section 146 or 147 of the Law of Property Act 1925 (even if forfeiture is avoided otherwise than by relief granted by the court)

(17) to pay the costs incurred by the Landlord (including any professional fees) and any stamp duty in connection with:

(a) the preparation and grant of the lease

(b) any application by the Tenant for any licence or consent under this lease (whether or not such licence or consent is actually granted)

4. The Landlord covenants with the Tenant that the Tenant paying the rents and performing and observing his covenants shall peaceably and quietly hold and enjoy the Demised Property for the term hereby granted without any interruption by the Landlord or any person lawfully claiming under or in trust for him

5. PROVIDED ALWAYS and it is hereby agreed as follows:

(1) if the rents or any part thereof shall be unpaid for twenty-one days after becoming payable (whether formally demanded or not) or if there shall be a breach of any of the Tenant's covenants or if the Tenant (being a company) shall enter into compulsory

LEASE OF HOTEL: RENT BASED ON TURNOVER

or voluntary liquidation otherwise than for the purposes of reconstruction or amalgamation or (not being a company) shall have a receiving order made against him or call a meeting of his creditors or be adjudicated bankrupt or if any distress or execution shall be levied on the Demised Property then and in each such case the Landlord shall be entitled (in addition to any other right) to re-enter upon the Demised Property or any part thereof in the name of the whole and thereupon this lease shall absolutely determine

(2) [*Proviso for abatement of rent—see Example 6:6, substituting 'the basic rent' for 'the rent'*]

(3) section 196 of the Law of Property Act 1925 shall apply to all notices or schedules required or permitted to be served hereunder

EXECUTED AS A DEED etc

THE SCHEDULE

1. In this Schedule the following expressions have the following meanings:
    (1) 'gross turnover' means the aggregate of all sums:
        (a) received by the Tenant in return for the provision of accommodation services goods facilities food and drink at the Demised Property or received by the Tenant in the course of carrying on any trade or business in or from the Demised Property and
        (b) payable to the Tenant by any person (other than an over-night guest) in consideration of the use or occupation of any part of the Demised Property
    (2) 'a rental year' means a period of twelve months beginning on [   ] in each year
    (3) 'net turnover' means the gross turnover less:
        (a) any sum actually paid by the Tenant to HM Commissioners of Customs and Excise by way of value added tax or other tax payable on the supply of goods and services
        (b) any sum received by the Tenant which is exclusively attributable to any revenue or excise duty imposed on intoxicating liquor or tobacco and
        (c) any sum refunded by the Tenant to his guests or customers in respect of defective or unsatisfactory goods or services
    (4) 'qualified accountant' means a member of the Institute of Chartered Accountants in England and Wales

2. The turnover rent for a rental year shall be:
    (1) [   ] per cent of the net turnover for the year immediately preceding that rental year exceeding £[   ] but less than £[   ] and
    (2) [   ] per cent of the net turnover for the year immediately preceding that rental year exceeding £[   ] but less than £[   ]

3. Within one month after beginning of each rental year (time being of the essence) the Tenant shall deliver to the Landlord a certificate signed by a qualified accountant giving particulars of the Tenant's gross turnover and net turnover for the year immediately preceding that rental year

4. The Tenant shall upon reasonable notice permit the Landlord or his agent to inspect and take copies of the Tenant's books of account or any other document or record which in the opinion of the Landlord or such agent is relevant to the determination of the turnover rent and shall bear the costs of such inspection if there shall be any material discrepancy between the information supplied by the Tenant under paragraph 3 above and the results of such inspection

5. The turnover rent shall be determined by an expert to be appointed by the President for the time being of the Institute of Chartered Accountants in England and Wales

(1) if the Tenant fails to supply a certificate in accordance with paragraph 3 above (in which case the Landlord's costs of the determination and the expert's fee shall be borne by the Tenant) or

(2) if there shall be any dispute between the parties as to the calculation of the turnover rent (in which case the costs of the determination and the expert's fee shall be borne as the expert directs)

6. Until the determination of the turnover rent of any rental year the Tenant shall continue to pay rent at the rate payable immediately before the beginning of the rental year in question and upon such determination there shall be due as arrears of rent or as the case may be refunded to the Tenant the difference (if any) between the rent paid by the Tenant for that year and the rent which ought to have been paid by him for that year plus (if the turnover rent is determined by an expert) such amount of interest as may be directed by the expert

7. If the turnover rent for any rental falls below £[   ] the Landlord may by notice in writing served on the Tenant not more than one month after the determination of the turnover rent for that rental year (time not being of the essence) require that there be substituted for the basic rent and the turnover rent for that rental year the amount for which the Demised Property might reasonably be expected to be let in the open market at the beginning of the rental year in question for a term equal to the then unexpired residue of this lease and on the same terms as this lease (save as to rent but on the assumption that the rent may be revised upwards only every five years) there being disregarded the matters set out in section 34 of the Landlord and Tenant Act 1954 (as amended) and the effect on rent of works carried out by the Tenant in pursuance of any requirement of the fire authority or the licensing justices and in default of agreement the said amount shall be determined by an independent surveyor (acting as expert not as arbitrator) to be appointed by the President for the time being of the Royal Institution of Chartered Surveyors and whose fee shall be borne as he directs

Form 13

Lease of Licensed Squash Club

[**General note**: Because of the difficulty of finding comparable properties for the purposes of rent review, a rent based on turnover has been adopted. An alternative method of rent fixing would have been to tie the rent to a notional building—see Example 5:18]

THIS LEASE which is made the [   ] day of [   ] 19[   ] BETWEEN [   ] of [   ] ('the Landlord') (1) and [   ] of [   ] ('the Tenant') (2) WITNESSES that

1. (1) In this Lease the following definitions apply:
    (a) 'the Demised Property' means the property described in the First Schedule
    (b) 'the Landlord' and 'the Tenant' include their respective successors in title
    (c) 'the Justices' means the licensing justices for the licensing district in which the Demised Property is situated
    (d) 'Liquor' means ale beer porter and other malt liquors and all cider perry wines spirits liqueurs and alcoholic cordials and British wines
    (e) [*Definition of rate of interest, 'the Prescribed Rate'—see Example 5:34*]
   (2) where the Tenant is more than one person the Tenant's covenants are joint and several
   (3) any references to any Act of Parliament includes a reference to that Act as amended or replaced from time to time and to any subordinate legislation made under it

2. In consideration of the rent and the Tenant's covenants the Landlord DEMISES the Demised Property to the Tenant for a term of [   ] years beginning on [   ] and ending on [   ] YIELDING AND PAYING (exclusive of value added tax) for the first year of the term of rent of one peppercorn and thereafter a rent determined in accordance with the Second Schedule to be paid by equal quarterly instalments in advance on the usual quarter days

3. The Tenant covenants with the Landlord:
    (1) to pay the rent punctually and without deduction or set-off

(2) to pay interest at the Prescribed Rate on all arrears of rent and other moneys due under this lease from the due date for payment until payment in full

(3) to pay all rates taxes charges duties assessments and outgoings of whatsoever nature which are now or may during the term become payable in respect of the Demised Property or its ownership or occupation (except such as are payable on a disposal of the landlord's reversion)

(4) [*To insure and reinstate—see Example 6:1*]

(5) [*To comply with statutes—see Example 7:16*]

(6) that there shall at all times during the term be a valid and subsisting fire certificate for the Demised Property

(7) [*To repair and decorate—see Example 7:4*]

(8) (a) not without the previous written consent of the Landlord (such consent not to be unreasonably withheld) and of the Justices (where such consent is required by virtue of any Act or Parliament) to make any addition or alteration to the Demised Property

    (b) upon each application to the Landlord for such consent to supply it with drawings and specifications of each proposed addition or alteration

    (c) not to carry out any works save in accordance with drawings and specifications approved as aforesaid and in accordance with any directions or conditions which may have been given or imposed by the Justices

(9) not without the previous written consent of the Landlord (such consent not to be unreasonably withheld) to display any sign or advertisement on the exterior of the Demised Property

(10) [*Planning covenant—see Example 8:1*]

(11)(a) as soon as may be to apply for the grant to an individual approved by the Landlord (such approval not to be unreasonably withheld) of a justices' licence for the sale of Liquor in the Demised Property and for such purpose to give all necessary notices

    (b) not without the previous written consent of the Landlord to apply for the insertion of any conditions in the justices' licence

    (c) to apply for and try his best to obtain the renewal of the justices' licence as and when it becomes renewable

    (d) not without the previous written consent of the Landlord to surrender or try to surrender the justices' licence or allow it to lapse or become forfeit or to take any steps to procure its transfer to any other premises

    (e) that nothing shall be done or omitted to be done on the Demised Property whereby any justices' licence may be forfeit suspended or otherwise imperilled

(12)(a) not without the previous written consent of the Landlord to have any gaming machine or machine for amusement with prizes in the Demised Property

    (b) in the case of any such machine permitted by the Landlord to be in the Demised Property:
        (i) not to install it until all necessary licences and permits have been obtained and the appropriate duty (if any) paid
        (ii) to display all licences and permits as required by law and to produce them to HM Customs and Excise as and when required

(13)(a) [*Covenants ancillary to use—see Example 8:10*]

LEASE OF LICENSED SQUASH CLUB

- (b) that no more than one hundred persons shall simultaneously be in the Demised Property
- (c) not without the previous written consent of the Landlord (such consent not to be unreasonably withheld) to use the Demised Property or permit it to be used otherwise than as a private members' club for playing of squash rackets and the provision of ancillary facilities including light meals and refreshments and a bar for the sale of Liquor
- (d) notwithstanding paragraph (c) above the Tenant shall be entitled to hold not more than twice a month exhibition matches of squash rackets attended by members of the public

(14) [*Covenant restrictive of alienation—see Examples 9:1, 9:4 and 9:5*]

(15) to supply the Landlord with a copy of any order notice direction permission or consent issued by any local or public authority or by the Justices in relation to the Demised Property within seven days of its receipt by the Tenant

(16) [*To pay costs—see Example 9:14*]

(17) to keep full and accurate books of account recording all the Tenant's receipts and expenses in connection with the business carried on in the Demised Property

(18) at the expiry or sooner termination of the term to give vacant possession of the Demised Property and to remove such tenant's fixtures as the Landlord directs in writing

4. The Landlord covenants with the Tenant that on condition that the Tenant pays the rent and complies with his covenants he shall have quiet enjoyment of the Demised Property as against the Landlord and those claiming under or in trust for it

5. It is agreed and declared that:
   (1) the Landlord may forfeit this lease in any of the following cases
   - (a) the rent or any part of it is more than fourteen days in arrear (whether formally demanded or not)
   - (b) the Tenant is in breach of any of his obligations under this lease
   - (c) the Tenant is adjudicated bankrupt or (if a company) is wound up by order of the court

   (2) [*Proviso for abatement of rent—see Example 6:6*]

   (3) section 196 of the Law of Property Act 1925 applies to any notice or schedule required or permitted to be served under this lease

EXECUTED AS A DEED etc

THE FIRST SCHEDULE

[*Description of the demised property*]

THE SECOND SCHEDULE

1. In this Schedule:
   (1) 'Accountable Recipts' means the aggregate of all sums received by the Tenant (or any associated company of the Tenant) by way of:
   - (a) membership subscriptions

(b) court fees (including any separate charge made for the provision of electricity changing facilities hot water and hire of equipment)
(c) payment for sales of meals refreshments and Liquor
(d) entrance fees for attendance at exhibition matches
(e) sale of sports equipment
(f) any other income received by the Tenant in the ordinary course of carrying on business in the Demised Property less any sum actually paid by the Tenant by way of value added tax excise duty or tobacco duty

(2) 'the Rent Fraction' means the fraction of which the numerator is £[   ] and the denominator is the Accountable Receipts during the first year of the term

(3) 'Qualified Accountant' means a member of the Institute of Chartered Accountants in England and Wales

(4) 'Review Date' means the sixth anniversary of the beginning of the term and every fifth anniversary thereafter

(5) 'Review Period' means the period between one Review Date and the next and between the last Review Date and the expiry date of the term

2. The rent for the second to fifth years (inclusive) of the term shall be £[   ] per annum

3. The rent for each Review Period shall be an annual sum equal to the product of the Accountable Receipts for the year immediately preceding the beginning of the Review Period in question and the Rent Fraction

4. Within one month after the beginning of each Review Period (time being of the essence) the Tenant shall deliver to the Landlord a certificate signed by a Qualified Accountant giving full particulars of the Accountable Receipts for the year immediately preceding the beginning of the Review Period in question

5. The Tenant shall upon reasonable notice permit the Landlord or his agent to inspect and take copies of the Tenant's books of account or any other document or record which in the opinion of the Landlord or such agent is relevant to the determination of the Accountable Receipts and shall bear the costs of such inspection if it reveals any material inaccuracy in the information supplied by the Tenant under paragraph 4 above

6. The Accountable Receipts shall be determined by an independent Qualified Accountant (acting as an expert) to be appointed in default of agreement by the President for the time being of the Institute of Chartered Accountants in England and Wales:
   (1) if the Tenant fails to deliver a certificate in accordance with paragraph 4 above (in which case the costs of the determination shall be borne by the Tenant) or
   (2) if there is any dispute about the calculation of the Accountable Receipts (in which case the costs of the determination shall be borne as the independent accountant may direct)

7. If the membership subscription or the court fees are materially less than the average membership subscription or court fees charges by other similar members' clubs in the counties of [   ] then in the calculation of the Accountable Receipts the Tenant shall be deemed to have received such amounts as would have been received if the membership subscription and/or the court fees had been equal to such average (but on the assumption that there would have been no fewer members or court bookings)

8. Until the determination of the annual rent for any Review Period the Tenant shall

continue to pay rent at the rate payable immediately before the beginning of the Review Period in question and upon such determination there shall be due as arrears of rent (or as the case may be refunded to the Tenant) the difference (if any) between the rent paid by the Tenant for the period and the rent which ought to have been paid together with interest at the Prescribed Rate calculated from the date when each instalment of rent fell due

Form 14

Agreement for Lease of Land to be Used as Car Park Pending Redevelopment

[**General note**: It would be advisable for the provisions of the Landlord and Tenant Act 1954, ss 24–28, to be excluded from the agreement. It includes a redevelopment break-clause.]

AN AGREEMENT made the [   ] day of [   ] 19[ ] between [   ] of [   ] ('the Landlord') of the one part and [   ] of [   ] ('the Tenant') of the other part
WHEREBY IT IS AGREED as follows:

1. The Landlord agrees to let and the Tenant agrees to take ALL THAT [   ] ('the Demised Property') for a term of [   ] years beginning on [   ] determinable as provided below YIELDING AND PAYING therefor (exclusive of value added tax) the annual sum of £[   ] payable by equal quarterly payments in advance on the usual quarter days

2. The Tenant agrees with the Landlord as follows:

 (1) to pay the said rent as aforesaid without any set-off or deduction whatsoever

 (2) to pay all rates taxes and other outgoings (except such as are charged on a disposal of the Landlord's reversion) payable in respect of the Demised Property or the ownership or occupation thereof

 (3) to erect as soon as may be and thereafter keep in repair a close boarded fence along the boundaries of the Demised Property

 (4) to keep the Demised Property properly drained and in good order and condition and free from rubbish

 (5) not to use the Demised Property for any purpose other than as a car park for motor cars and motor cycles only

 (6) to provide attendants to supervise parking in the Demised Property at all times

 (7) not to assign underlet charge or part with the possession of the Demised Property or any part thereof without the prior written consent of the Landlord (such consent

CAR PARK USE PENDING REDEVELOPMENT

not to be unreasonably withheld) provided that it shall not be a breach of this covenant if the Tenant grants to another the right to park not more than ten vehicles in a specified part of the Demised Property for a period of not exceeding one year at a time

(8) to keep the Landlord indemnified against any claim loss or damage whatsoever in respect of any loss or damage to any person using the Demised Property

(9) not to carry out any development on the Demised Property other than the use thereof as a car park as aforesaid nor to apply for planning permission to carry out any such development

(10) not to use the Demised Property for any illegal or immoral purpose nor for any purpose which causes or might cause a nuisance or annoyance to the Landlord or to neighbouring occupiers

(11) to permit the Landlord at any time during the term to erect and maintain a notice or advertisement for letting or selling any interest in the Demised Property

(12) to permit the Landlord and all persons authorised by him at reasonable times and on reasonable notice to enter the Demised Property for the purposes of inspecting surveying or repairing the same or for storing any plant machinery or materials in connection with the development of any adjoining property belonging to the Landlord

(13) to supply to the Landlord a copy of any notice order direction consent or permission relating to the Demised Property within four days of the receipt thereof by the Tenant

(14) not to bring or do anything upon the Demised Property which may invalidate or increase the premium payable for any policy of insurance of the Demised Property maintained by the Landlord

(15) to take all reasonable steps to prevent any encroachment on the Demised Property or the acquisition of any easement thereover and promptly to notify the Landlord of any attempt or claim to make or acquire the same

3. The Landlord agrees with the Tenant that the Tenant paying the said rent and performing and observing his agreements the Tenant shall peaceably hold and enjoy the Demised Property for the term hereby granted without any interruption by the Landlord or any person claiming under or in trust for him

4. Provided always that if the rent or any part thereof shall be in arrear for days after becoming payable (whether formally demanded or not) or if the Tenant shall commit any breach of agreement or shall be adjudicated bankrupt or (being a company) enter into liquidation then and in each case the Landlord shall be entitled to re-enter the Demised Property or any part thereof in the name of the whole and thereupon this agreement shall forthwith determine but without prejudice to any accrued right of action vested in the Landlord

5. [*Landlord's break-clause—see Example 4:4*]

Signed etc

Form 15

Renewal of Lease by Reference to Expired Lease

[**General note**: The covenants in a lease are construed by the reference to the date of the demise. Accordingly, when granting a lease by way of renewal it will be in the interest of the landlord if some obligations (particularly those relating to repair) are construed by reference to the date of the original demise, rather than to the date of the renewal. This form provides for all obligations to be construed as if entered into at the date of the original demise. The operation of s 62 of the Law of Property Act 1925 is excluded, in order to avoid informal licences being upgraded into legal easements.]

THIS LEASE which is made the [ ] of [ ] 19[ ] between [ ] of [ ] ('the Landlord') (1) [ ] of [ ] ('the Tenant') (2) and [ ] of [ ] ('the Surety') (3)
SUPPLEMENTAL TO a lease made the [ ] of [ ] between the Landlord (1) the Tenant (2) and the Surety (3) ('the Original Lease')
WITNESSES as follows:

1. In consideration of the rent and the covenants contained below the Landlord DEMISES to the Tenant ALL THAT property ('the Demised Property') which was demised to the Tenant by the Original Lease TOGETHER WITH the rights granted to the Tenant by the Original Lease and subject to the exceptions and reservations therein containing TO HOLD to the Tenant for a term of [ ] years beginning on [ ] YIELDING AND PAYING (exclusive of value added tax) by equal quarterly payments in advance on the usual quarter days the annual rent of £[ ]

2. The Tenant covenants with the Landlord to observe and perform all the covenants and conditions on his part contained in the Original Lease

3. The Landlord covenants with the Tenant to observe and perform all the covenants and conditions on his part contained in the Original Lease

4. PROVIDED ALWAYS and it is agreed as follows:
    (1) if the rent or any part of it is in arrear for twenty-one days after becoming payable or there is any breach of any of the Tenant's covenants or if the Tenant is adjudicated bankrupt or (being a company) goes into liquidation otherwise than for the

purpose of amalgamation or reconstruction then in any such event the Landlord may re-enter the Demised Property or any part of it in the name of the whole and thereupon this lease shall absolutely determine

(2) the covenants given by the Landlord and the Tenant shall be construed as if they had been given at the date of the Original Lease

5. In consideration of the demise contained above which was made at the request of the Surety (as he acknowledges) the Surety covenants with the Landlord as follows:

    (1) [*Basic obligation—see Example 11:1*]

    (2) [*To take a lease on disclaimer—see Example 11:5*]

    (3) [*Proviso limiting discharge of surety—see Example 11:2*]

6. Section 62 of the Law of Property Act 1925 shall not apply to this lease

EXECUTED AS A DEED etc

Form 16

Licence to Share Professional Offices

[**General note**: This form is reproduced from *Lease or Licence* (Longman, 1991) by the author.]

BY THIS LICENCE which is made the [ ] day of [ ] 19[ ] of [ ] ('the Licensor') grants to [ ] of [ ] ('the Licensee') licence to share with the Licensor the use of the Licensor's offices at [ ] ('the Offices') from until determined in accordance with the provisions of this licence

1. The Licensee shall pay the Licensor £[ ] a month on the first day of each month (the first payment to be made on signing)

2. The Licensee shall be entitled:
   (1) to carry on business as in such part of the Offices (consisting of not less than one private office and [ ] square feet of other space) as the Licensor shall from time to time direct
   (2) to use (in common with the Licensor) the sanitary facilities in the Offices
   (3) to install a telephone line (and all necessary telephone receivers) for his own exclusive use
   (4) to install his own office furniture and equipment in the Offices

3. The Licensee shall not:
   (1) impede or interfere with the Licensor's rights of possession and control of the Offices
   (2) use the Offices for any purpose other than for the business mentioned in clause 2(1) above
   (3) be entitled to a key to the Offices
   (4) do anything which may avoid or increase the premium payable for any policy of insurance maintained by the Licensor or to which he is liable to contribute
   (5) alter the Offices or their internal layout
   (6) interfere with the conduct of the Licensor's business as a [ ]
   (7) solicit or attempt to solicit any client of the Licensor
   (8) read or make copies of any books (other than published works of reference)

papers or documents addressed to or in the possession or custody of the Licensor

(9) permit or suffer the doing of anything prohibited by this clause

4. The Licensor shall:

(1) try his best to give the Licensee and his staff and clients access to the Offices during normal office hours

(2) pay the general and water rates payable for the Offices and the rent payable to the Licensor's landlord

(3) keep the sanitary facilities in working order and properly cleaned and equipped

(4) keep the Offices adequately heated and lit during normal office hours

(5) indemnify the Licensee against any breach by the Licensor of any of the terms upon which the Licensor holds the Offices

5. The Licensor shall not:

(1) interfere with the conduct of the Licensees' business

(2) solicit or attempt to solicit any client of the Licensee

(3) read or make copies of any books (other than published works of reference) papers or documents addressed to or in the possession or custody of the Licensee

(4) permit or suffer the doing of anything prohibited by this clause

6. Either party may terminate this agreement by three months' written notice and the Licensor may also terminate it by two weeks' written notice if the Licensee commits a serious breach of his obligations

Signed etc

Index

Access—
  lifts, 28–9
  roads, rights over, 24–6
  stairs and passages, 26–8
Adjoining property—
  right to develop, 35
Advertisements—
  restrictions on, 31
  right to exhibit, 30–1
Agricultural use—
  statutory protection, exclusion of provisions, 260
Airspace—
  parcels clause excluding, 21
  rights to, 19–20
Alienation—
  absolute conditions for, 241
  absolute prohibition on, 235–7
    exceptions, subject to, 240–1
    part, as to, 240
  building lease, of, 248–9
  conditions, imposing, 238–40
  consent, withholding, 238–40
  costs, payment of, 252–3
  covenant against, construction of, 231
  covenant not to part with possession, 234
  fines, 251–2
  premiums, 251–2
  qualified covenants—
    consent, not unreasonably withholding, 243–6
    form of, 246–8
    statutory proviso, 244–5
  requirement to surrender before, 249–51
  sharing possession—
    covenant against, 234–5
    group company, by, 243
Alterations—
  authority to carry out, 203

Alterations—*contd*
  covenant against—
    absolute or qualified, 202
    main walls or timbers, cutting or maiming, 202
    scope of, 201
    statute, works required by, 204–5
    statutory modification of, 203–5
    tenant's, 209–10
  landlord's refusal to allow, 202
  meaning, 201
  previous lease, under, 40
  statute, required by, 204–5
  tenant's handbook, complying with, 201
Annoyance—
  covenant against, 226–8
Appurtenances—
  general words, implied, 24
  incorporeal hereditaments, 23
  land, not including, 23
  matters included in, 23
Arbitrator—
  rent review, for, 104–7
Assignment—
  absolute conditions for, 241
  absolute prohibition on—
    exceptions, subject to, 240–1
    part, as to, 240
  assignee, covenants by, 244
  authorised guarantee agreements, 43, 271–3
  building lease, of, 248–9
  conditions, imposing, 238–40, 242–3
  consent, not unreasonably withholding, 236–7
    statutory provisions, 244
  consent, withholding, 238–42
  costs, payment of, 252–3
  covenant against, 231–2
  fines, 251–2

Assignment—*contd*
  guarantee agreement on, 239
  premiums, 251–2
  release of covenants on, 42–3
  requirement to surrender before, 249–51
  right of, 231
  surety, protection of, 269–71
Authorised guarantee agreements—
  effect of, 43, 272
  example of, 272–3
  formal conditions, 271
  meaning, 271

Boilers—
  insurance of, 163
Boundaries—
  airspace, 19–20
  external walls, 18
  fences, 20
  hedges and ditches, 17
  horizontal divisions, 18
  parcels clause with details of, 21
  plan, shown on, 17
  projections, 19
  roads, 17
  underground, 19
  windows, 20
Break-clause—
  drafting, 56
  effect of, 60–1
  examples of, 61–2
  exercise of—
    circumstances of, 59–60
    conditions, 60
    manner of, 57–8
    notice in writing, by, 57–8
    time of, 56–7
  part of property, relating to, 59
  renewal lease, in, 69
  total loss, on, 162
Building lease—
  alienation of, 248–9

Car parking—
  composite rights, 30
  private motor vehicles, for, 30
  rights to, 29–30
  specified spaces, designation of, 29
Common parts—
  access rights, 26–8
  repair, cleaning and maintenance of, 27
Compensation—
  opposition of renewal, on, 260–1
Construction of lease. See Interpretation of leases
Contract—
  lease as, 1
Covenants—
  anti-avoidance, 46

Covenants—*contd*
  assignment, release on, 42–3
  authorised guarantee agreements, 43
  curtilage, relating to, 24
  fixed charges, for, 44–5
  joint and several liability, 43
  land, running with, 42
  landlord's liability, limitation on, 42
  liability of tenant for, 49
  new tenancy, for, 41
  overriding leases, 43–4
  personal, 42
  running of, 41–2
  statutory provisions, new, 41
  variation of lease, effect of, 44
Curtilage—
  covenants, 24
  general words, implied, 24
  meaning, 23–4

Demise—
  extent of, 38–9
Development—
  adjoining property, right as to, 35
Disclaimer of lease—
  covenant by surety to take lease on, 269, 274
  effect of, 268
  power of, 268
Ditch—
  boundary, as, 17

Easements—
  curtilage, over, 24
  implication of, 6
  non-existing rights, over, 36
  sanitary facilities, to use, 33
Exceptions—
  construction of, 33
  examples of, 36
  meaning, 33

Fair wear and tear—
  concept of, 193
Fence—
  boundary, as, 20
Fixed charges—
  former tenants and guarantors, liability of, 44–5
  meaning, 45
Fixed term tenancy—
  characteristic of, 51
  commencement of, 54
  fifty years, for, 54
  five years, for, 52–3
  forty years, for, 54
  fourteen years, for, 53
  one year, for, 52
  security of tenure, contracting out of, 51

INDEX

Fixed term tenancy—*contd*
  seven years, for, 53
  six months, for, 52
  sixty years, for, 54
  thirty-five years, for, 54
  three years, for, 52
  twenty-one years, for, 53
Fixtures—
  annexation to land, effect of, 37
  demise, treated as, 37
  tenant's—
    covenants, 38
    removal of, 37–8

Goodwill—
  rent review, disregard for, 123

Heating—
  cost, recovery of, 171
Hedge—
  boundary, as, 17

Implied terms—
  demise, 5–6
  easements, 6
  express terms, negatived by, 7
  interpretation of, 5–7
  reluctance of court to find, 6
  statute, by, 7
Improvements—
  alterations. See Alterations
  authority to carry out, 203
  compensation for, 206
  environmental matters, 207–9, 211
  fit state, tenant's covenant to yield up in, 211
  hidden obligations, 207
  increase of insurance due to, 151
  initial, 205–7
  rent review, disregard for—
    carrying out, 127
    clause for, 128
    consideration for grant of lease, as, 124
    demised property, to, 125
    exclusion of, 134–5
    fitting out costs, 127
    improver, identification of, 125–6
    meaning, 124–5
    obligation to landlord, under, 125–6
    previous lease, under, 128
    renewal lease, 148
  statute, required by, 204–5
  statutory, 207
  tenant's covenant, 210
  tenant's liability, provisos limiting, 210
Income tax—
  deduction from rent, 73
Insurance—
  abatement of rent, proviso for, 160–2

Insurance—*contd*
  boilers, of, 163
  company, approval of, 152
  covenant for, 149
  cover, amount of, 152–3
  improvements, increase due to, 151
  landlord's covenants, 158–60
  lifts, of, 163
  loss of rent, including, 153
  moneys, application of, 153–4
  person effecting—
    existing obligations, 149
    lease, provisions of, 150–1
    property, nature of, 150
  plate glass, of, 163
  production of policy, right to require, 150–1
  proviso for protection of landlord, 158
  public liability, 163
  reinstatement of property—
    application of moneys on, 153–4
    common parts, of, 156–7
    covenant for, 154
    landlord's obligation, qualification of, 155
    meaning, 156
    shortfall of money for, 155
    tenant's repairing covenants, 156
    timetable for, 156
  risks, 151–2
  subrogation, 157
  tenant's covenant, 157
  use, and, 162
Interpretation of leases—
  clear words, requirement of, 4
  commercial contract, as, 1
  commercial solutions, 12
  contra preferentum rule, 5
  date for applying rules, 11
  definitions clause, 13
  eiusdem generis rule, 8
  express terms, implied terms negatived by, 7
  expressio unius est exclusio alterius, principle of, 7
  grantor, construction against, 5
  implied terms, 5–7
  inconsistency, resolving, 4
  intention of parties—
    ascertainment of, 1–2
    construction of, 1
    oral evidence of, 2
    relevant matters, 2
    words of lease, ascertained from, 2
  making lease work, importance of, 12
  matters deliberately not mentioned, 7
  ordinary and technical words, 3
  own wrong, party not to take advantage of, 8–9

Interpretation of leases—*contd*
  practicalities, 12–13
  prima facie assumptions, 10
  statutory rules, 10–11
  uncertainty, 9
  void terms, 9
  whole, construction as, 3–4

Joint tenants—
  renewal of tenancy, 258

Lease—
  interpretation. See Interpretation of leases
Legal costs—
  recovery of, 174
Licence—
  examples of, 255
  genuine arrangement for, 254–5
Licensed premises—
  statutory protection, exclusion of provisions, 260
Lifts—
  insurance of, 163
  repair and maintenance, 28
  right to use, 28–9

Management fees—
  recovery of, 169–70
Mining lease—
  statutory protection, exclusion of provisions, 260

Nameplates—
  right to exhibit, 30–1
Nuisance—
  covenant against, 226–8

Option to renew—
  conditions precedent, 64–5
  contracted out tenancy, of, 62
  drafting, 63
  examples of, 67–8
  exercise of—
    manner of, 63–4
    time of, 63
  new lease, terms of, 65–6
  practical value of, 62
  registration, 66–7
  renewal lease, in, 70
  rent under, 65–6
Overriding lease—
  claim of, 43–4
  statement contained in, 44

Parcels clause
  airspace, excluding, 21
  boundaries, with details of, 21
  office suite, of, 20
  open land, of, 21

Party structures—
  common law, regulation by, 22
  declaration as to, 23
  Inner London, in, 22
  landlord and tenant, questions between, 21–2
  responsibility for, 22
Passages—
  access rights, 26–8
Perpetuity—
  rules against, application of, 36
  specified period of, 37
Planning—
  established use certificate, tenant applying for, 214
  permission, tenant applying for, 213
  tenant's covenant, 214–15
Plans—
  accuracy of, 16
  boundaries, showing, 17
  construction, objective approach to, 17
  forms of, 16–17
  ordnance map, based on, 16
  use of, 15–16
  verbal description, relation to, 15–16
Plant and machinery—
  cost, recovery of, 172, 183
Plate glass—
  insurance of, 163
Pollution—
  control of, 207–9
  fitness for use, warranties as to, 212
  use covenants, 228–9
Projections—
  demised property, as part of, 19
Promotional expenses—
  recovery of, 174

Renewal lease—
  alterations carried out under previous lease, reinstatement of, 40
  ancillary rights, 39
  break-clauses, 69
  covenants, law on, 41
  duration of tenancy, 68
  extent of demise, 38–9
  liberties, privileges, etc, including, 39–40
  option to renew, 70
  part of holding, of, 39
  rent review, 147–8
  service charges, 179–80
  surety on, 273–4
  use, restrictions on, 230
Rent—
  abatement, proviso for, 160–2
  collection, cost of, 169
  covenant to pay, 73
  deductions from, 73
  head rent, geared to, 92–3

Rent—*contd*
  holding over period, in, 49
  income tax, deduction of, 73
  index-linked—
    abandonment of index, 76
    base figure, up-dating, 75
    basis of calculation, change in, 75
    choice of index, 75
    disadvantages of, 74
    drafting clause, 74–5
    mathematically correct, index to be, 76
    official index, link to, 74
    upwards only from initial rent, clause for, 77
  initial, fixing, 71
  liability of tenant to pay, 50
  loss, insurance of, 153
  option to renew, under, 65–6
  rent-free period—
    expiry, 137
    fitting out, for, 136
    improvements during, 206
    inducement, as, 137
    new lettings, for, 136
    valuation formula with, 138
  reservation by reference to commodity, 76
  review. See Rent review; Rent review clause
  service charge reserved as, 164–5
  stamp duty, assessment for purposes of, 71
  statutory control, 132
  subrents, geared to—
    clause for, 89–90
    concept of, 83
    deductions, 84–5
    headtenant, occupation by, 87
    improvements, 87–8
    obligations, tenant entering into, 88
    premiums, 85–6
    receipts, 83–4
    side by side scheme, 83, 90–2
    voids, 86
  term, falling due during, 56
  turnover, linked to—
    apportionment, 78
    basic rent, reservation of, 78
    clause for, 80–1
    commercial lettings, in, 77
    credit transactions, 78
    definition of turnover, 78
    disadvantages of, 77
    inspection of books, power of, 79
    licence or subtenancy, grant of, 79–80
    profit, element of, 77–8
    recession, in, 78
    theatre or cinema, for, 82–3
    trading, property ceasing to be used for, 79
  unascertainable, 71

Rent—*contd*
  VAT, potential impact of, 71–2
Rent review—
  clause. See Rent review clause
  counter-notices, 102–3
  disregards—
    goodwill, 123
    improvements, 124–8
    statutory, 130
    tenant's occupation, 123
    unusual terms of lease, 128–30
  fitness for use, 113–14
  initiation of, 101
  interim provisions, 142–3
  new rent—
    agreeing, 103
    expert or arbitrator, appointment of, 104–7
    independent determination of, 103–8
    independent surveyor, appointment of, 105
    interest on, 142–4
    procedure for fixing, 107
    reasonable, 110
    retrospective operation of, 142–3
    valuation formula. See Rent review clause
  notice, service of, 101
  payment on account pending, 144
  planning permission, provision for, 131
  profits valuation, 140–1
  property to be valued, 112–13
  renewal lease, 147–8
  rent-free period—
    expiry, 137
    fitting out, for, 136
    inducement, as, 137
    new lettings, for, 136
    valuation formula with, 138
  review notice, form of, 101
  review of review periods, 141–2
  review to market rent, upwards only, 144–7
  sublease, 147
  tenancy, duration of, 115–17
  terms of letting—
    alienation, 118–19
    assumed compliance with, 121
    geared rents, 122
    personal rights, 122
    reality, presumption in favour of, 118
    statement of, 117–18
    use, restrictions on, 119–21
  time limits—
    contra-indications to, 97–9
    delay, effect of, 97
    express words as to, 96–7
    last step in procedure, for, 97
    other clauses, interrelationship with, 99–100

Rent review—*contd*
  time limits—*contd*
    presumption, 95–6
    rebuttal of presumption, 96–100
    time of the essence, tenant's power to make, 101
  vacant possession, assumption of, 131–2
  VAT, effect of, 138–9
Rent review clause—
  clear words in, 4
  discount from headline rent, justification of, 138
  dispute resolution, choice of methods, 108
  disregard of, 130
  either party to initiate procedure, 109
  interest, provision for—
    new rent, pending determination of, 142
    overdue payments, on, 143
    rate of, definition, 143–4
  machinery, 108
  market rent, periodic review to, 93
  modern ground rent, review to, 135–6
  payment on account pending review, 144
  physical condition of property, assumptions as to, 115
  provisions in, 94
  purpose of, 93–4
  reliance on other awards, permitting, 109
  renewal lease, in, 147–8
  review dates, choice of, 94–5
  review to market rent, upwards only, 144–7
  revision, means of, 74
  sublease, in, 147
  time, stipulations as to, 7, 10
  underlease, disputes procedure for inclusion in, 109
  valuation date, 95
  valuation formula—
    access for fitting out, assumption of, 138
    alternative, 133–4
    basic definition, 110–12
    best rent, ascertainment of, 111
    disregards, 123–30
    fitness for use, 113–14
    hypothetical letting in open market, for, 111
    importance of, 109
    occupational lease, for, 133
    planning permission, provision for, 131
    profits valuation, 140–1
    property to be valued, 112–13
    rent-free period, 136–8
    review clause, disregard of, 134–5
    short form, 134
    tenancy, duration of, 115–17
    tenant's improvements, no disregard of, 134–5

Rent review clause—*contd*
  valuation formula—*contd*
    terms of letting, 117–22
    vacant possession, assumption of, 131–2
    VAT, 138–9
    willing landlord and willing tenant, provision for, 112
    valuation of notional building, requiring, 114–15
Repair—
  concept of, 184
  cost, recovery of, 172–3
  covenant. See Repairing covenant
  decorative, 196–8
  divided responsibility for, 190–2
  exemption of liability, 189
  fair wear and tear, 193
  fire damage, 193–4
  glass, of, 192
  inherent defect, of, 187–8
  interior of demised property, definition of, 193
  landlord entering to effect, 195–6, 199
  management company, carried out by, 191
  meaning, 187–9
  notice, on, 194–6
  obligations—
    landlord, implied for, 191
    mere repair, going beyond, 190
    problem areas, 186
  responsibility, allocation of, 184
  standard of, time for determining, 11–12
  structural, 191
  structure, definition, 192–3
  supervision of works, 196
Repairing covenant—
  age and nature of property, 185
  divided responsibilities, 190–2
  framework, 184
  interpretation, 185
  landlord's, 200
  physical deterioration, showing, 186–7
  putting property in repair, requiring, 185
  reinstatement, provision for, 156
  repair, meaning, 187–9
  repair on notice, obligation of, 194–6
  scope of, 186
  structure and exterior of building, relating to, 192
  subject matter of, 185–6
  tenant's, 198–201
  wider forms of, 190
Reservations—
  adjoining property, right to develop, 35
  construction of, 33
  entry, right of, 34
  examples of, 36
  meaning, 33

INDEX

Reservations—*contd*
  reciprocal rights, 35–6
  services, right to use, 35
Right of entry—
  landlord, of, 33–4
  repairs, to effect, 195–6, 199
  reservation of, 34
Roads—
  access rights, 24–6
  ancillary rights over, 25
  boundary, as, 17
  mode of use, definition of, 25
  obstruction, prevention of, 25
  rights of way clauses, 26

Sanitary facilities—
  demise, included in, 32
  easement to use, 33
  number of conveniences required, 32
  pipes and drains, keeping in repair, 32
  right to use, 32
Service charge—
  apportionment—
    anticipated use, according to, 176
    fair or proper, 177
    floor area, by, 175–6
    methods of, 175
    unlet parts, provision for, 176
  capital value of reversion, effect on, 164
  certification of, 178–9
  consideration for grant of lease, as, 165
  covenant to pay, 164
  demand, payable on, 165
  landlord's obligation to provide services, 166–7
  payment—
    advance, in, 165, 181–3
    fixed sum, of, 166
    maintenance company, to, 168
    method of, 164–6
  purpose of, 163
  recoverable items—
    construction of lease, 168–9
    heating, 171
    legal costs, 174
    management fees, 169–70
    plant and machinery, 172, 183
    promotional expenses, 174
    rent collection, 169
    repairs, 172–3
    staff and staff accommodation, 170–1
    sweeping up provision, 174–5
  renewal leases, terms of, 179–80
  rent, reserved as, 164–5
  reserve funds, 177–8, 181–3
  sinking funds, 177–8
  tenant's covenant to pay, 180–1
  trust funds of, 168

Service tenancy—
  statutory protection, exclusion from, 257
Services—
  pipes, definition of, 36
  reservation of right to use, 35
Signs—
  right to exhibit, 30–1
Staff—
  cost, recovery of, 170–1
Stairs—
  access rights, 26–8
Stamp duty—
  rent, assessing for purposes of, 71
Statutory protection—
  exclusion of provisions, 256
  joint tenants, of, 258
  nature of property, 259
  non-occupying tenant, exclusion of, 257–8
  residential accommodation, for, 262–3
  right to compensation, exclusion of, 260–1
  service tenancy, exclusion of, 257
  statutory provision, 254
  subletting envisaged, where, 261–2
  tenancy—
    at will, 255
    requirement of, 254–7
    term of years certain, for, 256
  tenant, identity of, 257–9
  use of property—
    agricultural, 260
    breach of covenant, in, 259–60
    licensed premises, 260
    mining, 260
Sublease—
  rent review, 147
Subletting. See also Underletting
  control of, 237
  protection of head lease, 261–2
  rack rent, at, 236–7
Sureties—
  assignment, protection on, 269–71
  authorised guarantee agreements, 271–3
  basic covenant by, 265
  change of landlord, effect of, 273
  discharge of—
    inadvertent, 266
    landlord acting to prejudice of, 265
    proviso limiting, 267
    surrender of part of property, on, 266
  disclaimer of lease, effect of, 268–9, 274
  liability of—
    co-extensive, 264
    principal debtor ceasing to be tenant, on, 266–7
    release from, 264
    variation of covenants, effect of, 267–8
  principal debtor, deemed to be, 267
  protection of, 269–71
  renewal lease, on, 273–4

Sureties—*contd*
  termination of tenancy, ending of
    obligations on, 264–5

Telecommunications—
  rights relating to, 33
Tenancy at will—
  features of, 50
  grant of, 50–1
  statutory protection, exclusion from, 255
Tenancy—
  fixed term. See Fixed term tenancy
  statutory protection—
    requirement for, 254–7
    tenancy at will, exclusion of, 255
    term of years certain, for, 256
Term of lease—
  break-clauses. See break-clause
  certain, 51–4. See also Fixed term tenancy
  certainty of, 9
  commencement of, 54–6
  commercial considerations, 47
  earlier than date of execution, running
    from, 55
  expiry, right to terminate before, 47–8
  landlord's lease, duration of, 48–9
  norm for, 47
  particular date, running from, 55
  payments of rent during, 56
  redevelopment, plans for, 48
  renewal lease, 68
  tenancy at will, 50–1
  whole number of years, expressed as, 55

Underletting—
  absolute conditions for, 241
  absolute prohibition on, 235–7
    exceptions, subject to, 240–1
    part, as to, 240
  conditions, imposing, 238–40
  consent—
    not unreasonably withholding, 236
    withholding, 238–40
  costs, payment of, 252–3
  covenant against, 232–3
  fines, 251–2
  part of property, of, 233
  premiums, 251–2
  rack rent, at, 236–7
  requirement to surrender before, 249–51
  right of- 231
  undertenant, covenants by, 244
Use—
  absolute and qualified restrictions on,
    215–17
  ancillary covenants—
    illegal and immoral use, against, 225
    licensing requirements, 225–6, 229
    long form, 228–9

Use—*contd*
  ancillary covenants—*contd*
    nuisance and annoyance, covenant
      against, 226–8
    pollution, concerning, 228–9
    short form, 228
  business, obligation of, 21820
  change, consent for, 215–17
  competition, restrictions on, 223–5
  established use certificate, tenant applying
    for, 214
  fitness for, warranties as to, 212
  hybrid use covenant, 217
  illegal and immoral, 225
  industrial, obligation of, 219
  insurance, relation to, 162
  keep open covenant, proviso to, 220
  licensing requirements, 225–6, 229
  mixed, positive covenant, 220
  modification of covenants, 230
  negative and positive obligations, 217–20
  obligation to trade, 219
  permitted, defining—
    activities, with reference to, 222
    existing statutory definition, with
      reference to, 221
    high class, meaning, 222
    means of, 221
    name of business, by, 221
    scope of, 221
    tenant's adviser, responsibility of, 220
    tenant's business, as, 222
  planning legislation, limits under, 213–15
  prohibition, widening, 223
  renewal lease, restrictions in, 230
  restrictions on, 119–21
  statutory protection. See Statutory
    protection
  unoccupied property, rating surcharge on,
    219

Value added tax—
  clause preventing landlord from charging,
    72
  exemption, clause preventing landlord
    from waiving, 73
  general principle of, 72
  rent—
    potential impact on, 71–2
    reserved as, 72
  rent review, effect on, 138–9
Variation of lease—
  covenants, effect on, 44

Wall—
  external, as boundary, 18
Windows—
  demise, inclusion in, 20
  repair of, 192